NEW PLAYWRIGHTS
The Best Plays of 2003

SMITH AND KRAUS PUBLISHERS
Contemporary Playwrights / Full-Length Play Anthologies

Humana Festival: 20 One-Act Plays 1976–1996
Humana Festival 1993: The Complete Plays
Humana Festival 1994: The Complete Plays
Humana Festival 1995: The Complete Plays
Humana Festival 1996: The Complete Plays
Humana Festival 1997: The Complete Plays
Humana Festival 1998: The Complete Plays
Humana Festival 1999: The Complete Plays
Humana Festival 2000: The Complete Plays
Humana Festival 2001: The Complete Plays
Humana Festival 2002: The Complete Plays
Humana Festival 2003: The Complete Plays

New Playwrights: The Best Plays of 1998
New Playwrights: The Best Plays of 1999
New Playwrights: The Best Plays of 2000
New Playwrights: The Best Plays of 2001
New Playwrights: The Best Plays of 2002

Women Playwrights: The Best Plays of 1992
Women Playwrights: The Best Plays of 1993
Women Playwrights: The Best Plays of 1994
Women Playwrights: The Best Plays of 1995
Women Playwrights: The Best Plays of 1996
Women Playwrights: The Best Plays of 1997
Women Playwrights: The Best Plays of 1998
Women Playwrights: The Best Plays of 1999
Women Playwrights: The Best Plays of 2000
Women Playwrights: The Best Plays of 2001
Women Playwrights: The Best Plays of 2002
Women Playwrights: The Best Plays of 2003

If you require prepublication information about forthcoming Smith and Kraus books, you may receive our semiannual catalogue, free of charge, by sending your name and address to *Smith and Kraus Catalogue, PO Box 127, Lyme, NH 03768*. Or call us at (888) 282-2881, fax (603) 643-1831. www.SmithKraus.com.

NEW PLAYWRIGHTS

The Best Plays
of 2003

CONTEMPORARY PLAYWRIGHTS
SERIES

SK
A Smith and Kraus Book

A Smith and Kraus Book
Published by Smith and Kraus, Inc.
177 Lyme Road, Hanover, NH 03755
www.SmithKraus.com

© 2005 by Smith and Kraus, Inc.
All rights reserved
Manufactured in the United States of America
Cover and text design by Julia Gignoux, Freedom Hill Design, Reading, Vermont

First Edition: March 2005
10 9 8 7 6 5 4 3 2 1

The Library of Congress Cataloging-In-Publication Data

New Playwrights: the best plays of 2003. —1st ed.
p. cm. — (Contemporary playwrights series)

ISBN 1-57525-386-0
1. American drama—20th century. I. Series.
PS634.N416 2000
812'.5408—dc21   00-029707

CONTENTS

FOREWORD

After going to the theater approximately 200 times during the 2002–2003 season, and reading maybe 500 plays in manuscript, here are my choices for the "best" plays I could come up with during the above time period. I put "best" in quotations marks because, let's be honest, any selection process of this sort is more or less subjective — which means *I* think these plays are worthy of Smith and Kraus' exemplary New Playwrights series.

For one thing, all seven authors whose work you will find here not only wrote their fine plays, but show great promise for writing more. None is what you might call an A-list playwright — but all show great promise of becoming one. They may work in very disparate styles, but all have demonstrated the ability to tell a compelling story, in a theatrical way.

Hunt Holman's work has been popping up regularly at small theaters in New York. I saw *Spanish Girl* in a workshop series produced by Off-Broadway's Second Stage, and I was most impressed with Mr. Holman's ability to create compelling, college-age characters and to take their concerns seriously, treating them with much wit and good humor.

Tim Dowlin's *Corner Wars* was also produced in a small New York theater, though by a company from Philadelphia. Like *Spanish Girl*, it is about young people; here, teenaged drug dealers on a Philly street corner. Mr. Dowlin has beautifully captured the world of these characters and made us care about them, rather than dismiss them as a bunch of thugs.

The Sweepers, by John C. Picardi, is a drama about Italian-American women keeping the home fires burning while the men are off at war, during the Second World War. It was produced Off-Broadway by Urban Stages, whose Artistic Director, Frances Hill, has contributed the Introduction to this anthology. Urban Stages produced another play in Mr. Picardi's cycle of plays about Italian American life, *Seven Rabbits on a Pole*, during the 2003–2004 season. It was even more highly acclaimed than the well-reviewed *The Sweepers*.

Javon Johnson's *Homebound* has been produced in regional theaters but has not, as of this writing, been done in New York. Like *Corner Wars*, it's about teenage criminals — in this case, four young men incarcerated in a juvenile detention facility. Like Mr. Dowlin, Mr. Johnson treats his characters with wit and compassion.

Smashing by Brooke Berman focuses on a teenaged girl who learns, to her chagrin, that a very successful, very visible novelist, once a protégé of her novelist father, has published a thinly-veiled roman à clef about the torrid affair he had with her before he became famous.

Debbie Lamedman's *phat girls* is also about a teenager. Its subject is eating disorders and self-esteem issues among teenaged girls, and it handles this subject in a very inventive, theatrical way.

While all the plays in this book have humorous moments, mostly they are what we tend to call serious plays. David Epstein's *Midnight*, on the other hand, is an out-and-out, unabashed, honest-to-goodness *comedy*, reminiscent of show-biz comedies from yesteryear, such as *The Butter and Egg Man* or *Light Up the Sky*. I think Mr. Epstein is a comic talent to watch, and I hope you'll find *Midnight* as funny as I do.

Well, that's it. I hope you like all these plays.

D.L. Lepidus

INTRODUCTION

Twenty years ago as a writer of several plays, I asked myself a few questions. "Who helps playwrights?" "Who seeks out the unknown brilliant writer who has a fascinating tale to tell?" "Who develops the new play and brings it to the stage in a noncritical environment?" "Who encourages the playwright who embodies the soul of the theater?" "Where would the theater be if there were no writers to address the confusions of the world and try to put some order to our chaos?" "Who helps the playwright develop the skill to make us laugh at ourselves and see our follies?" "What would all those actors do if they could not find a talented playwright?"

There are several theaters across the country that desperately try and reach out to the talented writers who surface in their piles of scripts. However, I realize there are not enough theaters and facilities for good playwrights, especially when I see the piles of manuscripts that stack up on the floor of my office in New York. I look at the stacks every day with great passion as I touch the play on top and realize all the work, the love, the dedication, the concentration, the research it took to produce the play that I am holding in my hand. I feel the energy of the writer who is waiting to hear that we would like to consider his or her script for a New York production. With great interest I read the writer's biography and many times I am amazed at the level of education, life experience, and breadth of writing experience. In my stacks are writers of every age from children to senior citizens, from every profession, and from every ethnic background. That is what I love about these scripts — each one is a surprise, each one is a lesson in a different subject, and each one has a story to tell.

I love writers. I understand their agony when they are writing a play, since no one said playwriting is easy. It is very hard to keep an audience interested AT ALL TIMES in what the writer wants to say through the characters the writer has created. Theater cannot be boring or it is DREADFUL. So that is a great challenge to the writer, who must have many talents to stimulate an audience and create an emotional response to the words in the script. The writer must have a keen imagination, a sense of humor, a writing style, a good understanding of the language, and most important have a desire to communicate through words and actions.

How do I choose a play from this large stack? It breaks my heart as I realize we can only hold readings and workshops of eighteen plays and produce three, which is a big problem for these hopeful writers. Like many decisions, an emotional reaction to a play often allows me to make the choice. When I read John Picardi's *The Sweepers,* it said to me that the play had legs and through my tears at the end of the play, I decided to put it in the pile to be read in our reading series.

I applaud Smith and Kraus for helping playwrights by publishing volumes dedicated to new plays. These books allow readers and theaters to be aware of new thoughts, new conclusions, and new characters. In this book you will have the thrill of discovering these new stories and new friends.

D. L Lepidus' dedication to theater, plays, and playwrights is beyond anyone's I have ever known. Many thanks, D. L., for all your work tracking down the most exciting, entertaining, and provocative plays of the 2003 season. I know you readers will love these plays and the writers as much as I do.

Frances Hill
Founder and Artistic Director
of Urban Stages — New York City

SMASHING

By Brooke Berman

I think I've unconsciously chosen people who are emotionally crippled, who need mothering . . . I'm really good at it, and it mirrors something in me that needs mothering.

MADONNA, *Truth or Dare*

I wanted to make people happy, I wanted to be famous, I wanted everybody to love me, I wanted to be a star. I worked really hard and my dream came true.

MADONNA, *Truth or Dare*

PLAYWRIGHT'S BIOGRAPHY

Brooke Berman's work has been read, workshopped, and produced across the United States and in London. Productions include The Play Company, Steppenwolfe Theatre Company in Chicago, The Second Stage, and the Humana Festival. Brooke's short play *Dancing with a Devil* was co-winner of the Heideman Award at Actors Theatre of Louisville in 1999 and nominated for an American Theater Critics Best New Play award that year. Readings and workshops: The National Theatre, London, The Royal Court Theatre in London, The O'Neill Playwrights Conference, MCC Theater, The Culture Project, Williamstown Theater Festival, ASK Theater Projects, Rattlestick, The Hourglass Group, The Womens Project, the Denver Center Theater Company, Soho Rep, HERE, and the Juilliard School, Brooke's play *Defusion* was included as part of Christine Jones' "Theater for One" project at New York Theatre Workshop and has been included in an anthology of new American one-act plays. Awards and Fellowships: Berilla Kerr Foundation grant (2002), Helen Merrill Award (2000), two Francesca Primus awards (1998, 2000), Lila Acheson Wallace American Playwrights Fellowship at the Juilliard School, two Lecomte du Nouy awards (in both 1998 and 1999), an Independent Artist Challenge grant, and a recent commissioning grant from the National Foundation for Jewish Culture. Brooke is a graduate of The Juilliard School

Originally a performer, Brooke wrote and performed autobiographical monologues for over ten years, most recently at The Culture Project. She trained with Anne Bogart and has studied playwriting with Marsha Norman, Christopher Durang, Jon Robin Baitz, and Maria Irene Fornes. Brooke is a resident playwright of New Dramatists, a member of the Dramatists Guild, PEN, and the MCC Playwrights Coalition. She is, proudly, the Playwright Mentor to the MCC Youth Company.

ORIGINAL PRODUCTION

Smashing was originally produced for the stage in New York City by the Play Company in October of 2003, directed by Trip Cullman and featuring the following actors:

ABBY	Katharine Powell
CLEA	Merritt Weaver
JASON	David Barlow
NICKY	Lucas Papaelias
JAMES	Joseph Siravo
Set Design	Erik Flatmo

```
Costume Design . . . . . . . . . . . . . . . . . . . . . . . . . . . .Michael Krass
Lighting Design . . . . . . . . . . . . . . . . . . . . . . . . . . . .Paul Whitaker
Sound Design  . . . . . . . . . . . . . . . . . . . . . . . . . . . . .Scott Myers
Stage Manager . . . . . . . . . . . . . . . . . . . . . . . . . . . .Janice Brandine
```

Smashing was developed at the Eugene O'Neill National Playwrights Conference, directed by Michael John Garcès, featuring Monica Koskey, Vanessa
Aspillaga, Ebon Moss-Bachrach, Dallas Roberts, and Reid Birney. The play
was subsequently developed by the Play Company in their New Work/New
World Lab Series in New York, directed by Michael John Garcès and featuring Mary Catherine Garrison, Elizabeth Bunch, Peter Sarsgaard, Michael Wig-
gins, and Larry Pine.

PRODUCTION NOTE

This play takes place in three very distinct levels and time frames. The first is
the present reality. The second is the fiction world of the book. The third is
the past. These areas should be clearly indicated in the design or lighting of
the play, so that it is clear when and where we move. Also, Jason should have
some sort of podium or "reading" area when he reads from or narrates his book.

Everyone speaks their text very well and very accurately. Use the language
as a driving force. The play should move very quickly with no break between
scenes. Everything happens on top of itself. It is a rhythmic, hypertext influenced structure. Characters speak directly to the audience, narrating themselves, and acting as the "link" on a Web site. The text of Jason's book may
be wound through or looped in a sound-scape.

All of this is intentionally theatrical. The characters love to perform, and
the act of "telling" is a major part of the story itself. In a very active and lit-
eral sense, the telling *is* the story. These characters, writers all, use language
as a weapon, an instrument to manipulate in order to get attention and sus-
tenance. Embrace the act of "telling."

*Special thanks to Linsay Firman, Michael John Garcès, Dallas Roberts, Monica
Koskey, Rising Phoenix Rep, Morgan Jenness, Kate Loewald, Jack Temchin, James
Houghton, Stephen Willems, Trip Cullman,and Penney Leyshon.*

CHARACTERS

ABBY MEADOW: Beautiful and precocious college student, 21. Grew up in New York City. Carries herself with an air of privilege. Direct and to the point. Exudes confidence.

JAMESESON ADDIE: Is Abby's alter ego, the girl in Jason's novel

JASON STARK: Twenty-nine, hot-shot young writer. From Iowa, living in London. He writes about not being able to feel. In grad school, he worked for Abby's dad, James, whom he may attempt to emulate. Not traditionally handsome, his novel is his masculine prowess. A misfit in Iowa (and in grad school), success becomes him. Gatsby-esque in his reinvention. He embraces celebrity.

JAMES MEADOW: Born James Medowski. Changed his name in the sixties. Abby's dad. World-famous, award-winning novelist and essayist. His work crosses the lines of both critical and popular acclaim. Every one knows his work, either from reading it in college or seeing the big screen movie adaptations. One of the voices of his generation. His wife died young.

CLEA: Abby's best friend, also a precocious college student. However, where Abby is absinthe, Clea might be the bubbles on top of pink champagne. Fiercely loyal, intelligent, and imaginative, feels things deeply. Working her way through college in New York City. Idolizes Madonna and Abby.

NICKY: The boy Clea befriends in the youth hostel. An energetic complement to Clea. Funky. Collects guitar picks, paints his own wall murals.

PRECOCIOUS YOUNG GIRL: Turns up at the end.

SETTING

The action takes place in the present-day New York and London; it also takes place in the past (New York, five years earlier), as well as the fantasy world of Jason's novel.

Smashing

ACT I

OVERTURE

The stage is bare. Enter Jason Stark, an average-looking, perhaps tall and skinny, writer. He reads from his novel:

JASON: Book Number One. Jameson Addie. The Girl.
(Lights up on Abby Meadow. A beautiful thin girl in her very early twenties. A student. She is rational, gutsy, and self-possessed.)

ABBY: Every day you can wake up new. There's nothing permanent about the self. "Reality" either.
(Add Clea, Abby's best friend, slightly rougher around the edges, marches to a different drummer. Also twenty-one. Obsessed with two things — Madonna and Abby.)

CLEA: Says my best friend Abby —

JASON: Says the Buddha through the mouth of Jameson Addie.

ABBY: It's always shifting.

CLEA: At least, this is the position put forth by numerous schools of thought, mostly coming from the teachings of the Buddha. Abby says:

ABBY: Impermanence is key.
Nothing's fixed — except your projections in the moment, which is eternally now.
(Lights up on James Meadow, a charismatic novelist and Abby's dad.)

JAMES: It's called *Eternally Now*. Which is a comment on one of my earlier novellas, *Now, Eternal*. The new piece uses a character from *The Eden Trilogy* and takes him into the far reaches of Bhutan; it's the last Buddhist kingdom in the Himalayas . . . You see, I should probably mention that my daughter went to India this past year and I started to think about, see kids are just great for bringing up ideas because they're basically search engines.

ABBY: So every day you can wake up new.

CLEA: It's summer now.

ABBY: Without attachment or projection.

CLEA: She's back at her dad's brownstone, sleeping late. I work in Admissions. And in the evenings, we meet.

ABBY: No past, no future, nothing holding you to who you were a day ago, an hour ago —

JASON: She will always be sixteen. She will always be The Girl.

ABBY: Except —

JASON: Beautiful. Smashing . . .

CLEA: And here is the exception.

JASON: " . . . With a mean streak. A talent for hurting, for hitting, for driving a stake. At least that is how I remember her, this vicious Jameson Addie. I remember her wet. Dripping. Sixteen and mean.

Out for blood. Out for my blood. And I remember liking it. "

ABBY: The exception is if you fucked some guy when you were sixteen and he wrote a book about it and this book is roughly everywhere. I mean, if some asshole you slept with when you were like basically still in high school writes a best-selling book all about your pussy and what a bitch you are and reveals things to the world, aren't you kind of forced into being someone you got through being a long time ago?

If a tree falls in the forest —

CLEA: And it's reviewed by the *New York Times*, by the *New York Review of Books*, by *People Magazine* even —

ABBY: If actresses you don't like at all are considering doing the movie, well, you're just stuck with this projection, aren't you?

JASON IS A HERO, TO HIMSELF

Jason Stark talks about himself like he's a superhero.

JASON: In the fabulous cities of the New World, the Young Writer Jason Stark reads from his fabulous new book. *Cherry Pie @ the Hungarian.* The young writer Jason Stark, the celebrated young — OK, so I'm twenty-nine but I still get grants for "emerging" — writer is on his American book tour, giving readings, attending cocktail parties, answering "questions" about his second book because he has a three-book deal — only he's preoccupied. Thinking only of her. Wondering if he will run into Her, The Girl. He sees the ghost of her sixteen-ness everywhere, on every subway, at every bookstore and every cafe. But she misses her entrance. She (deliberately? He thinks, deliberately due to the revealing nature of his scandalous debut) refuses to be seen. And he returns to London — that's right, London — the city where he makes his Young Writer Home — ready for Books Number Two and Three. But what are Books Number Two and Three going to be about? Norman Mailer says that writer's block is a failure of the ego. Yeah, well my fucking ego is fucking failing. I kind of said it with Book Number One. Love turned sour. Fucked up fucking with sixteen-year-old muse/tornado/Lolita-girl —

(Abby cuts him off before he can say her name.)

ABBY: Abby. Abby Meadow. Once it was Medowski but my dad, the famous novelist James Meadow, changed it when he was a hippie and my mom, whose name was originally Daphne, changed hers to Dandelion or something that sounded like that in French, she was French, well she died when I was a little girl, yeah, it's OK, I mean I'm fine about that, but anyway, I'm sixteen and kinda running wild, alone in the house when you come, this guy working for my dad. Who's just not around much that Spring and Summer. But you, Jason, are around. Doing whatever it is you are being paid to do. Which is not, I gather, to crush out on the daughter of your boss.

You read me poems.

JASON: e.e. cummings.

"inane, the poetic carcass of a girl"

ABBY: And we have sex —

JASON: Mad passionate sex —

ABBY: — all over my dad's black leather writer's chair while he's in Prague. My dad says Prague's his favorite city. And we fuck on his chair. A lot. And then I break your heart, which just really can't be helped, and you go away.

JASON: Until now.

SHE TOUCHES THINGS AND THEY MOVE

CLEA: Madonna Marathon. Three whole days of nonstop Madonna on your favorite music video network. One must stay in for events like this. One must ferret out the people one knows with television sets and cable. To absorb all the imagery surrounding Her. The most famous woman in the world. Self-made, self-invented, and totally self-serving. Unapologetic. Fierce. A goddess. She touches things and they move. She shifts and the culture shifts with her. She gets everything right, even when she's wrong. Clearly, she is my hero. I mean, she would be if I believed in that kind of thing, which I don't because Abby says they break your heart, but if I did, she'd be it. She helps me persevere in the face of great odds. And a girl alone in college in New York City with an insufficient Pell Grant and an overdeveloped inner life does face these odds. Rather a lot. But She walked this path before me. Alone in the City without resources. Getting into the groove. Deeper and deeper. Into the groove.

(*Scene. The girls watch VH-1.*)

ABBY: She's all about herself.

CLEA: So?

ABBY: So, that's ego.

CLEA: So? (*Beat.*) I mean, don't you think that's a bold statement? She's not self-effacing. Or self-punishing. And her drive is like, you know, we should support drive. And blonde ambition.

ABBY: Sure. But for good causes. Her cause is just, herself —

CLEA: Not true. She does a lot for AIDS groups and — she totally raises money for AIDS groups. And besides, some people have to get themselves out of a bad place and into a better one before they can be like, a statement for larger forces.

ABBY: Maybe.

CLEA: I took this religion class last semester where they said that the sacraments were conceived on this totally patriarchal model and that for women it's a different thing altogether. I mean, like, for us, anger and drive and ambition, all that stuff female characters always get totally punished for? those might be our sacraments.

ABBY: What class was this?

CLEA: Women and Religion.

ABBY: I see.

CLEA: It was a good class.

ABBY: I'm sure.

ABBY: Hey, do you want this stuff? (*Points to a bag of clothes.*) Just isn't me anymore. Maybe you'll find something.

CLEA: (*Holds something up.*) Would you be completely offended and freaked out if I made a mini-skirt out of this?

ABBY AT SIXTEEN

JASON: Jack Kerouac says the girls in Iowa City are the prettiest in the whole damn country. But what does he know about it? He was passing through in a hot rod car with Dean Moriarty. He never had to live there. No, no. Jack was Jack and I was Jason, someone else entirely, and I couldn't wait to get to New York. The girls in New York, especially the ones who grew up there, are my favorite in all the world. Abby at sixteen. My favorite in all the world.

(She becomes Abby at sixteen. There is a shift indicating we are now in the past, or possibly the novel.)

JASON: Short for Abigail?

ABBY: I wish. I had weird parents.

JASON: Absalom, Absalom?

ABBY: Not Faulkner. You didn't really think . . .

JASON: I was joking.

(She twirls a little, flirting. She, everything about her, already mesmerizes him.)

ABBY: So you wanna know what it is?

JASON: Sure.

ABBY: Absinthe.

JASON: Really?

ABBY: That's what's on the birth certificate. Ask my dad.

JASON: Wow. Mine's just Jason. Like, I don't know. I think I was named after someone on a soap opera.

ABBY: My dad's a freak.

JASON: Your dad is my hero.

ABBY: That's stupid.

JASON: Why is it stupid?

ABBY: It just is.

JASON: His books changed my life.

ABBY: Which ones?

JASON: *The Eden Trilogy.*

ABBY: Yeah. They're pretty good. Still though. I don't think you should have a hero. Heroes are dangerous.

JASON: Why's that?

ABBY: They break your heart. They just do.

JASON: How old are you?

ABBY: Sixteen.

JASON: Wow.

(Abby smiles. They share a moment. Danger, Will Robinson.)

CLEA: Abby and I have been friends since the first day of school. Her house is AMAZING. Life is good when you get invited to the brownstone. They have these dinners all the time with writers and artists, and you never know what poet you'll meet or who will tell you embarrassing things about their love lives and rehab experiences, and what things were like in "the Factory days." They talk about "movements" in literature and culture. This is very different than where I come from. I listen. I take it all in. I absorb. I don't say a word. If I talk, they'll notice me, and they may ask me to leave. And I can't leave. I have too much at stake. A whole life. Waiting and at stake.

(This is broken as *Jason, returning* to *the present, picks up his novel and reads* —)

JASON: Her name was Addie, though on the birth certificate it said "Jameson." But this was no Jamie, no Jan, she was Addie short for Jameson, because she liked it and she had always been allowed to do as she liked. She was named after her father's favorite drink, a drink he liked when he was young, an expatriate hippie, but he was old when I met him, when I met them both, and she was just Addie. For addiction, addled with guilt, address the problem. A dirty little girl with a truck driver's mouth and the face of a saint. A poor little rich girl. The daughter of a literary legend —

JAMES IS A FAMOUS WRITER

JAMES: *(As if lecturing* to a *class.) The Eden Trilogy. Eternally Now. Daphne/Delphine,* that one's about my wife who died very young. *Genius in the Heartland. A River in the Sun. Grass in the Blade.* That's my personal favorite, though I didn't care much for the movie adaptation. I mean, I just didn't understand some of the casting. But, you know, the movies. They seem to take great pleasure in getting things wrong. *(To Jason:)* I was wondering if you could do me a favor.

JASON: Sure.

JAMES: Good. I'll pay you extra if you can hang out with my daughter, keep an eye on her.

JASON: Like babysit?

JAMES: Just keep her busy. She's fairly self-sufficient. But I travel quite frequently, and it would help me out a lot if you'd be willing to "like babysit," as you call it, while I'm away. Just keep an eye on her. She's a great kid. Smart. Doesn't eat much. Knows all those writers you like. A good editor, too. You can show her what you're working on. Take her to a movie here and there. On me. I'd appreciate it.

JASON: Sure. I don't mind at all.

(The scene switches almost immediately as *Jason turns* to *Abby, and* —)

ABBY AT SIXTEEN, CARPE DIEM AND ALL THAT

JASON: Your dad said to keep you busy. Want to go to a movie?

ABBY: Do you want to kiss me?

JASON: — *(Maybe stammering.)*

ABBY: You do, don't you? I know. You've been looking at me like that all week
and it's making me sort of impatient. So, I think you should just do it.
Carpe Diem, and all that. *(She waits.)* Well?

(He makes no move to kiss her.)

ABBY: Come on. Just fucking kiss me.

JASON: Not when you put it like that.

ABBY: Fine.

(She kisses him. He kisses her back. It's good.)

THE THINGS YOU ARE MISSING

CLEA: When Abby was in India, I took notes. So we'd be on the same page
when she got back. *(She opens a notebook or journal.)* The Things You Are
Missing (this starts out lame, but gets better)

(Clea looks at her notes, then begins.)

— Coffee prices increase at University Food Market.

— Kissed Nietzsche Surfer Guy (finally) in front of Avery library. Not
memorable. Followed by Hungarian Pastry. Also not memorable. Really
wish I could call you. You'd say this is not a sign of things to come, and
frankly, I hope you are right.

— OK, this is interesting. Went to Times Square to see *The Next Best
Thing* and — well, it's disappointing but she looks great. Only she's talking like a Brit. Do you think is a conscious appropriation for some meta-
purpose we don't yet understand? You'd say no, but I might disagree.

— Nietzsche Surfer Guy has defected to the Dark Side. He's dating Bar-
bie Girl. It's a mess. Again, *really* wish I could call you.

— Oh. Started writing my first short story. Or novella. It might be a
novella. It's about this girl Louise. Louise has a best friend, Veronica, who's
the center, the absolute center of everything —

Anyway. I never read the list to Abby.

JASON: I call. I'm drunk. It's late. But who can sleep when you're on the verge of fame but have nothing to say in Books number two and three? And you need to talk to the inane carcass of a girl you wrote about and loved and loved and got hurt by and wrote about. *(He picks up the phone —)*
>Is it you, Pretty Girl? Inane Carcass?
(Abby answers the phone. Stage goes split screen.)

ABBY: Jason?

JASON: Have you seen it?

ABBY: Seen what?

JASON: The book. Have you seen the book?

ABBY: Uh-uh. What book?

JASON: What book? My book?

ABBY: You have a book?

JASON: You don't know about my book?

ABBY: No. Where are you? Are you in New York? I thought you were, like, weren't you living somewhere else?

JASON: My book got published. It's huge. There was a piece in the — I'm in London.

ABBY: What are you doing in London?

JASON: Didn't you get the letter?

ABBY: No. You wrote me a letter? What did you say?

JASON: I can't believe you didn't get the letter.

ABBY: Well. I didn't. I was in India, traveling and stuff. Did you send it to my dad's? Cause he's been away too. Or school? Traveling was amazing, it was just amazing, I saw all these —

JASON: You were supposed to get my letter.

ABBY: Yeah, well I didn't. I was traveling. In India. Wait, can you hold on? That's call waiting —

JASON: Abby, I am calling you from London. England. I cannot just hold on —

ABBY: OK, hold on. *(She clicks flash.)* Yeah?

CLEA: Hey. What's wrong?

ABBY: Oh, God, just come over.

CLEA: Why? What's up?

ABBY: Remember that guy I told you about who I slept with when I was in high school while my dad was in Prague?

CLEA: Yeah?

ABBY: Well, I'm on the phone with him, so just come over.

(Overlapping, they speak "just come over" at about the same time.)

CLEA: OK, I'll just come over. I'm at the deli. You want anything?

ABBY: No. Yeah. Diet Coke.

CLEA: No, bad for you. Aspartame. It actually creates this insulin release effect
    in the body which then subsequently makes you crave —

ABBY: Fine. I gotta get back to this weird guy. He's weird.

CLEA: Weird how?

ABBY: Obsessive.

CLEA: Dangerous?

ABBY: No. Just obsessive. OK, I gotta get back to him. Just come over.

CLEA: *(Aside.)* things like this happen to her all the time.

ABBY: *(Clicks back to Jason —)*
    I'm back —

JASON: So I have to write another one.

ABBY: So write another one. What did you say in this letter?

JASON: You don't understand. They want me to write another book.

ABBY: Yeah. You said.

JASON: Well, I can't just do that.

ABBY: Why not?

JASON: I don't know.

ABBY: Why are you calling me?

JASON: You really haven't read the book? You didn't even notice it? It's huge.
    There are movie rights — I have a three-book contract —

ABBY: I told you. I was in India. Do you want to hear about India? India was —

JASON: Chloe Sevigny wants to play . . . the girl.

ABBY: What's the girl like?

JASON: It's getting good reviews.

ABBY: What do you want from this conversation? I mean, it's not like we're in
    touch —

JASON: I just want to talk to you.

ABBY: Well, you're talking to me.

JASON: I just, I can't, I mean, it's great, and I'm really lucky, it's just that now
    with this contract and — you know they want me to write — and I just —

ABBY: Oh. You have writer's block. Deal with it. My God. Writers are so self-
    indulgent.
    *(The following occur simultaneously — overlapping to the public school line,
    then overlapping again until Abby breaks it.)*

JASON: *(Sparring, liking it.)*	ABBY: WHY ARE YOU
Don't —	CALLING ME, JASON?

JASON: I mean, you just —
   that's like reductive,
   just because,
JASON: *You're* yelling at *me!*

JASON: Yeah whatever with your
   "poor people in India" you
   were just this white tourist
   anyway and it's not like the
   poor people in India give
   one rat's ass about —
JASON: Look who's calling who
   over-privileged. *I went to public
   schools you know.* Just don't call
   it "writer's block" like it's this
   totally pat ordinary *thing* —
   (Abby breaking the simultaneity.)

ABBY: I don't really want
   to talk to you. Or have
   you yell at me, OK?
ABBY: I mean, there are
   poor people, I have seen
   people in India —
ABBY: I mean, you are just
   this totally over-privileged,
   I mean, freaking out because
   you have a book contract —

ABBY: WHATEVER.

ABBY: You called me. Why did you call me? Right before you picked up the
   phone to dial, you probably had a thought about something. What do
   you think it was? Try to remember —
JASON: Well, I didn't go and call it "writer's block." That's so dismissive.
ABBY: I'm hanging up.
JASON: No. Don't go. Nothing is happening in my life besides being a writer.
   Not even writing, just being a "writer." And, I'm sure that, I'm having
   these — I can't write, I think about you all the time. And I need to see
   you. OK? I need to see you.
ABBY: You want to see me?
JASON: Need. Not want. Need.
ABBY: Oh.
JASON: I just think that it would help me right now. I think I'd write again.
   There. OK? There. I just need to see you, Abby.
ABBY: Well. You're in London.
JASON: Come here.
ABBY: I can't —
JASON: You're my good luck charm.
ABBY: That's dumb.
JASON: It's not. Why is it dumb?
ABBY: It just is.

JASON: You're my muse. Is that dumb?

ABBY: You haven't seen me in — a long time. Years.

JASON: Yes. That is the point. That is the whole point exactly.

ABBY: Yeah. That *is* the point.

JASON: I have a picture of you in my mind. Do you think about me? Ever?

ABBY: No. I'm sorry. But, no. I never think about you.

JASON: You're lying.

ABBY: Maybe. OK, so maybe I think about you. So? Maybe every now and then. But not a lot. I mean, I do not think about you a lot.

JASON: You recognized my voice.

ABBY: You called me "inane carcass."

JASON: So? Come here. Please? I want to see you. I want to touch you. I'm a novelist. Don't you want to see me be a novelist?

ABBY: I grew up with novelists. I don't need to see another one.

JASON: *(Direct, not pathetic.)* I'll beg. Want me to beg?

ABBY: No.

JASON: Where are you right now?

ABBY: In my apartment, Jerkoff, where do you think I am? You called me.

JASON: I know. But . . . Tell me where you are. So I can see it. Describe it to me. The room, what you look like . . .

ABBY: Jason, I'm not having phone sex with you. Go fuck yourself.

JASON: Come here.

ABBY: I'll think about it. OK? I will think about it once I've read your stupid, pathetic little book. Where can I get it?

JASON: Anywhere. You can get it most anywhere. There was a piece in the — It's huge.

(Somewhere during this sequence Clea enters, silently, carrying her bag from the store. She tries to interest Abby in water or some non-aspartame-laden soft drink, Abby shakes her head no, Clea listens, silently to rest of conversation. Abby and Clea might gesture to one another in appropriate moments.)

ABBY: Great. Are you happy? You should be really happy.

JASON: I'm still in love with you.

ABBY: No you're not.

JASON: I am, though. You're the only thing that makes me want to write.

ABBY: Thing?

JASON: Look. OK, I'm older than you —

ABBY: Not that older —

JASON: And at my age, my friends have had relationships that were good and then went bad. And, they're ready, this makes them ready for the one that works. And I think, it's you. OK? The good one. I think it's you. For me. You're old enough now. It wouldn't be weird. Your dad's out of it. What if we had, or even tried . . . ? What if it's You?

ABBY: Jason. It's not me. It wasn't me then. And it isn't me now. Go find someone in England. There are plenty of girls in England.

JASON: I want you.

ABBY: You don't want me.

JASON: Don't tell me what I want. I do. I want you.

ABBY: I say this with great compassion. Go fuck someone in England and write about them. It's what my dad does when he can't think of what to write.

JASON: Yeah?

(He considers this. It is a worthwhile option . . . Abby hangs up. Abby and Clea share a moment.)

ABBY: Obsession is a perfume, not a way of life.

CLEA: Too bad he's not dangerous.

ABBY: No, not dangerous. Just obsessive.

CLEA: Obsessive?

ABBY: Yes. And there's a book

A BOOK ABOUT BEING NUMB

JASON: — about pain. It is a book about pain. About being numb and then waking to pain. You are numb, then you are shocked into awareness and once you're aware, you are aware of pain. You were perhaps in pain all along but you were numb so you didn't feel it. Anything. You didn't feel anything. This is what the book is about. And the catalyst for all of this is The Girl. The Girl is really important because she is the Thing that shocks the Guy into awareness.

A DANGEROUS HOBBY

CLEA: We make heroes. We can't help it. We kill our heroes. We make words about them. I'm only just starting, and let me tell you, it's a dangerous hobby.

ON FANCY STATIONERY FROM LONDON

JAMES: *(Reading a letter:)*

Dear James,

No doubt you have seen my best-selling debut *Cherry Pie @ The Hungarian* which in my mind, if not in print, I dedicate to you and all you taught me. You are my literary hero, and although it has been said that heroes are dangerous and break one's heart, I am writing to you in hopes that you will read my book and possibly review it for a special feature on writers and their protégés . . .

READING SAID BOOK

James holds a copy of Jason's book. The cover is obscured, perhaps it is a "review copy" with generic covering — in any case, not yet the picture of Abby.

JAMES: Have you seen this book?
ABBY: No.
JAMES: Do you know what it's about?
ABBY: No. What's it about?
JAMES: I think it's about you.
ABBY: Me how?
JAMES: You naked.
ABBY: Really? How strange.
JAMES: I'm going to pretend it's fiction.
ABBY: Yes. I'd do that.

ABBY MEETS ADDIE

Abby buys the book. She stands at a bookstore. There is an enormous display poster of a young girl with mousy blonde hair and fishnet stockings. She is a cross between Lolita, Eloise at the Plaza, and an Egon Schiele drawing, hair tousled, black stockings or knee highs, skirt around her ankles. This is the cover of Jason's book. The girl looks exactly like Abby.

Quite possibly, Abby becomes the poster image — i.e., she morphs into the version of herself that appears on the cover of this book. It is a specific physical pose, ripe with innuendo — and this is how Abby becomes Jameson Addie. She holds this pose long enough for us to feel the impact of this fictional character —

Then, she becomes herself again.

ABBY: Oh. Fuck. It's about me.

ABBY, CLEA, THE BOOK

ABBY: I can't read it alone.
CLEA: Of course.
ABBY: Stay.
CLEA: Of course.
ABBY: Oh.
CLEA: What?
ABBY: He didn't.
CLEA: What!?
ABBY: That motherfucker —
CLEA: What!?
ABBY: He wrote about me.
CLEA: You knew that.
ABBY: I didn't know how.
CLEA: How?
(And the book goes:)
JASON: . . . tormenting me, making me ache . . . selfish, self impressed . . . her literary references covering her fear of fellatio, I never got to see her empty selfish meaningless face suck my cock . . . give me head, you selfish selfish selfish bitch . . . "
(Abby looks up from book, horrified. Both girls turn back to the text reading more. It is a bad dream.)
JASON: . . . her mom died leaving her alone in an empty house full of books . . . with an egomaniacal father who worshiped her and left her alone to rot, ignored her, adored her . . . set me up to fuck her because he couldn't do it himself. No wonder she was such an easy lay, wide open, she was wide open, waiting. She had been prepared for it . . ."
ABBY: A lot. He wrote about me a lot.
(And once more:)
JASON: At least if she'd sucked my cock, I'd have something to remember her by. The image of . . ."
(The girls discard the book entirely.)
CLEA: Wow. He's mad.

ABBY: Clearly.

CLEA: You dumped him, right? He's mad that you dumped him and not the other way around.

ABBY: It wasn't like that. Like how he says. I can never go out.

CLEA: It's a revenge novel.

ABBY: Ever again.

CLEA: People will think he made it up.

ABBY: Her name is Addie. Her dad's a writer. Author of *Three Books of the Apple*. Her mom is dead. She fucks this guy in her dad's black leather chair. Her hair is the color of bones. I mean, it's me.

(Addie the Poster for the Book hovers nearby. She grins evilly.)

ABBY: Clearly it's me.

JAMES ON WHINY PROSE

JAMES: I should mention here that I wrote about my first love. Years ago. Her name was Isobel, and we both worked at the Public Library in Brooklyn when I was young and saving money for Columbia. (The school, not the country.) I wrote about her, every detail of our tragic affair, something about fucking her near the stack containing Hemingway's *The Sun Also Rises,* but I have not published this piece of work. The prose whines. You can tell when the prose itself does this, whines. So, the Isobel stories remain unpublished in a drawer.

ALL GEOGRAPHY

ABBY: Look. It was all geography — he was in my house. And I liked him enough. Enough to lose my virginity, enough to spend, I don't know, maybe five months, six, fucking his brains out behind my dad's back.

CLEA: I see.

ABBY: He was . . . I didn't know anyone from Iowa. It was exotic.

CLEA: I'm from Michigan. It's not very far away from, well, I guess it is from Iowa because there is Illinois, you see, not to mention Wisconsin, and —

ABBY: *(Bringing her back from the digression.)* I was really young. And he loved me. I mean, I didn't think about it too much, but, of course he loved me, I was me, and he was like this older guy, twenty-four, skinny, a grad student, kinda strung out or something. Shy. It wasn't like in that book:

WHAT IT WAS REALLY LIKE:
JASON AND ABBY FIVE YEARS EARLIER

ABBY: You're shy.

JASON: Is that bad?

ABBY: It is if you want to kiss girls. We like you to make the moves.

JASON: How do you know so much?

ABBY: You can't kiss and talk at the same time. Pick one.
   (They kiss.)

JASON: Here. I'm giving you this.
   (Hands her a book.)

ABBY: Oh, I know him. He and my dad were at St. Mary's on that teaching thing — I think we even have this book —

JASON: Yeah. Your dad. Knows everyone. Whatever. I bought this for you because it's my favorite. (Right now. Right now it's my favorite.) So, say thank you, OK? Comprende? Learn to take a gift. Say fucking thank you.

ABBY: Thank you.
   (They share a moment.)

JASON: "the stalks are very prickly, a penalty
   they earn for knowing the black art
   of blackberry-making . . . "
   — Galway Kinnell
   See, that's you. The prickly part. Anyway, forget it. You already have it or something.

ABBY: No. I mean, I haven't read it. I just, know him.

JASON: You should read it.

ABBY: I will.

JASON: You don't know everything.

ABBY: I know.

JASON: You might be pretty and you might be bold, but you don't know everything.

A COUPLE OF NICE TIMES

CLEA: You were with him how long?

ABBY: A couple months. Five or six.

CLEA: And then you broke up with him.

ABBY: I wanted to date someone else. The Spanish guy. In Spain. Jason sort of freaked out when my dad and I came back from Spain. He stopped work-ing for us. He went away.

CLEA: Completely?

ABBY: Well. Every now and then he'd send some weird inappropriate letter. I didn't answer them. Mostly.

CLEA: Hmmm . . .

ABBY: There were a couple of nice times. Like one night I went up to his place, way the fuck uptown. We just, like, made dinner. But it was so nice. Just making dinner. And then we went up to the roof and he told me about being sixteen. How he took this trip to the Grand Canyon with his older brother and they smeared mud all over their faces. He called me a wise child.

CLEA: Wise child?

ABBY: Salinger.

CLEA: Oh. He should have written about that.

ABBY: Instead, there is this —

CLEA: Work of problematic angst featuring you.

JAMESON ADDIE
Abby appears as in Jason's book — A deadly dirty little girl.

ABBY: In the book, in Jason's book, my name is Jameson Addie. I'm a New York City girl, and Jason, whose name is Wolf (HIS NAME IS WOLF! !??), fucks me again and again on my dad's black leather chair. This really happened in real life, it's where I lost it, you know, but in the book it seems to hap-pen again and again and again and in the book, there is this event, totally blown out of proportion where I won't give him a blow job. One night. Once. O-N-C-E.

Wolf says, You're a good girl, and when he says it, I feel like cream, sweet cream, buttermilk, and Iowa pie. Cherry pie. From Iowa.

Wolf can't feel anything. He says it a lot. So I hurt him. To make him feel.

Anyway. I'm just using Wolf 'til I get into Harvard. My dad went there. My dad teaches there too. Have you read my dad's new book? My dad is the best writer in the whole world. Wolf is an idiot. He'll never be my dad. But he'll make my dad a hero. And then everyone will break everyone's heart. It all just can't be helped.

PLANS BEGIN TO FORM. IMPULSIVE PLANS.

ABBY: I'm going there.

    (Suddenly in scene with James:)

JAMES: Where?

ABBY: London.

JAMES: Why would you possibly want to do that?

ABBY: To tell him off.

JAMES: Darling, can't you call instead?

ABBY: I think I should go.

JAMES: This would be a bad idea.

ABBY: We need to talk.

JAMES: And so you're going to cross the ocean?

ABBY: Yes. We need to talk face-to-face. He wrote about me. He wrote mean, untrue things.

JAMES: Darling Daughter —

ABBY: He called and begged me to go there. And I think it's the best way to work things out with the most compassion and equanimity.

    (James might snort here.)

JAMES: Writers say a lot of things. I wouldn't take any of it seriously. I have said a great many things to a great many women —

ABBY: He's not you.

JAMES: That's evident. I have talent.

ABBY: I'm going.

JAMES: You're paying for it on your own.

ABBY: I have savings. I have frequent flyer miles.

JAMES: Good.

ABBY: Good.

    (Clea draws her back.)

CLEA: I'm coming with you.

ABBY: Really? You'd really come?

CLEA: Of course. You shouldn't be alone when you kill him. When you rip his heart out.

ABBY: His heart, and then his hands. I will rip them out of the wrist sockets. He will never write again.

CLEA: This is so Titus.

ABBY: Fuck Titus.

CLEA: Oh, no. Voice-activated software.

ABBY: What about it?

CLEA: Well, I'm just saying, there is voice-activated software. So he can still —

ABBY: Who's side are you on?

CLEA: Yours.

ABBY: I will rip Jason's hands off with my teeth and tear out his vocal cords and poison his imagination, his mind, his craft. I will poison him against writing. Murderous Everything.

CLEA: We can get cheap tickets on the Web.

ABBY: I have frequent flyer miles. And we'll stay with him. After we inflict injury and get revenge. I mean, I'm sure we could stay with him.

CLEA: Interesting paradox. But I'm sure you know what you're doing.

ABBY: Fuck the eternal now. This is war.

CLEA: We're going to London.

SCRAMBLING

CLEA: We scramble. I cash in my paycheck from the work study job and I am able to get this really cheap ticket on the Web. I am able to get a passport in a one-day emergency rush. I've never had one before. Abby already has a passport, but she goes with me to the passport office, just because this is what friends do. I go to London to help her inflict torture and she goes to the passport office to save me from frustration with bureaucratic waiting. She is my best friend who I adore more than anyone in the world even more than my idol the superstar celebrity pregnant icon, who is also in London. And two days later, we are on a plane to the United Kingdom. London, England. Heathrow Airport. Virgin Atlantic. Reading Jason's book. Again.
(Girls on plane; Jason's lines may be real [i.e., staged with the actor physically in the scene] or he may be sound only.)

JASON: . . . a dirty little blonde, an unfeeling bone-colored bitch, her fingers twirling her hair in a diner on Sixth Avenue, while I ate shit and drank coffee . . .

ABBY: He's so dramatic.

CLEA: I'm kind of getting sick of hearing what a dirty little blonde you were. Does he have to keep saying it over and over again?

ABBY: It's repetition.

CLEA: Yeah.

ABBY: No, I mean, he's doing it on purpose. It's a technique. He's a Gertrude Stein person.

CLEA: Well, it bugs (me).

JASON: " . . . you fade me out, turn to ice, stop wanting me, how can you stop wanting me when I could just stay with my legs wrapped around yours for hours and hours? but you withdraw, change your mind and tell your friends, and I see you all together, giggling like you know something you don't — and I want to fuck them to get you back, but it doesn't even matter, because I win. Don't you get it? I have the final word."

CLEA: Why is he holding on to this thing with you?

ABBY: Writers hold on to things.

CLEA: I don't.

ABBY: You're not a writer.

CLEA: But if I were . . . I'm just saying, this book disturbs me.

ABBY: Art is disturbing.

CLEA: I don't think it's art. Do you think it's art?

ABBY: Don't try to make me feel better. Watch the cheerleader movie.
  (*She goes back* to *the book. Clea doesn't watch the movie.*)

ARRIVAL

ABBY: *(As if in* a *guidebook.)* Declare yourself a tourist.

CLEA: Just to be here is beautiful. Thrilling and strange.

ABBY: Exchange your dollars for pounds.

CLEA: I am shocked to find our American money doesn't go very far. It's roughly half of what it'd be worth at home.

ABBY: Become accustomed to feeling like an American. Less than refined.

CLEA: Shit. It's expensive here. I'm glad we'll be staying with Jason. That's all I can say.
  (*The following is more like a normal "scene" than the preceding guidebook lines; Abby drops her guidebook tone.*)

ABBY: The exchange rate sucks. But, it'll be fine. Jason'll take us out, pay for us. I'm his muse. He owes us.

CLEA: Good. 'Cause I'm gonna be broke by lunch tomorrow.

ABBY: Too bad you have to eat. That's what makes it expensive. All that eating.

CLEA: Normal people eat.

ABBY: I'm just saying it's expensive.

CLEA: Are you gonna call him?

ABBY: Oh. Right. You need a telephone card in Britain. Maybe we should just show up.

CLEA: What time did you say we were coming?

ABBY: Let's just show up.

CLEA: Do you know how to, where he lives?

ABBY: Sure. We can take the Tube.

CLEA: This is going to be fantastic. Smashing.

SOUND

Cue in which the disparate elements come together in an overlapped fusion sound-scape — Madonna music, British Punk, Indian raga, text from Jason's book are sampled and mixed. The expectation of London and all that the girls believe this trip will hold.

The girls "arrive." Lights down.

END OF ACT I

ACT II

Sound Cue as the act begins: "You've reached the prerecorded Jason Stark. I'm away 'til the 4th, leave a message, or if it's urgent, you can call my agent . . ." "Have you read my book? Have you read my book about Abby Meadow? My book, my book, my book, my book. . . dirty little blonde my book. . . ." ending with "I'm totally unreachable." Lights up. The girls and their backpacks.

CLEA: He didn't know we were coming?

ABBY: Well.

CLEA: Well, what?

ABBY: I mean, I know he lives here. He called me. He asked me to come.

CLEA: And did you tell him you were?

ABBY: Well.

CLEA: Well, what?

ABBY: I thought we could surprise him. In all the scrambling and whatever, I just —

CLEA: You didn't tell him.

ABBY: Well.

CLEA: You've got to stop saying that.

ABBY: OK, look. He'll be back soon. We'll go to a hostel. We'll leave messages. And in the meantime, we will get our bearings. We will see London and get acclimated here. Do you have, can I look at . . . the *Lonely Planet* guide?

(Clea has a copy of Lonely Planet London, *which Abby takes.)*

CLEA: It is a lonely planet isn't it? It shouldn't be. But sometimes it is.

ABBY: Don't be dramatic. I'm glad you brought this.

CLEA: I was hoping it'd say something about where Madonna's living, because after we cut Jason's balls off, I might need something to do. I hope getting acclimated doesn't cost much.

ABBY: OK. Something close.

CLEA: And cheap.

ABBY: Easy.

THE PALACE HOTEL, A NICE LITTLE PLACE

NICKY: Welcome to the Palace Hotel. A nice little place in Bayswater. It's not much, but it's ours. Girls on this side. Blokes on the other. It's twenty pounds a night, please pay in advance for the night you'll be staying. There's tea in the tea room, and it's free, though you should bring your own mug, messages are over here, there's e-mail on two computers, one pound for twenty minutes, and you have to sign the guest register. Please sign the guest register. Where are you from?

CLEA: New York.

NICKY: Very good. I want to go to New York.

ABBY: Of course you do.

NICKY: I'm a musician.

ABBY: Of course you are.

CLEA: Excuse her, she's very tired. I'm Clea. Do you know where Madonna lives?

ABBY: Oh, God.

NICKY: We call her Madge, over here. She's pregnant you know.

CLEA: I know. I know everything about her. Except her address in London. Do you know where she does yoga?

ABBY: Can we go to our room?

NICKY: Sure. Upstairs on the left. The key's in the door. You're sharing with a couple of Swedish girls. They're very nice. And you pay each morning for that night. Did I already say that?

(*The girls nod.*)

NICKY: Right. Do you know yet, the tenure of your —

ABBY: A few days. *(To Clea.)* You coming?

CLEA: Sure. *(To Nicky, in a dramatic whisper.)* Do you think later we could conference on The Whereabouts?

ABBY: Come on.

NICKY: Good night.

(*Nicky is already slightly mesmerized by funny little Clea.*)

CLEA CAN'T SLEEP

Clea sits at the lobby desk where Nicky works. She can't sleep.

CLEA: She makes it OK for a girl to be ambitious. To want. She takes things we think of as "bad" — ambition, sex, Catholicism — and reinvents them so that —

NICKY: Look. She's got no talent. I'm a musician. I don't mean to knock your idol or anything but, I'm a musician. And her —

CLEA: NO TALENT? How can you say no talent!? I'm going to pretend you didn't say that. What about postmodernism and appropriation? Gender iconography in the late twentieth century? She didn't just do yoga. She did Kabbalah. She did burning crosses. She vogued.

NICKY: She did vogue.

CLEA: Yes. And she did *Evita*. The Argentines freaked, but controversy feeds her whole deal.

NICKY: OK, but, Evita, besides being the wife of a very disturbing dictator —

CLEA: *(Cutting him off, maybe even earlier?)* The tabloids say, Madonna: Has She Gone Too Far?

But I say, is there such a thing? Is there such a thing when you are Madonna and the world is your oyster because you never let anyone tell you who to be or what to do or what your limitations are? No. No. There is no such thing. Get into the groove. Open your heart. Express your-self, don't repress yourself. Music makes the people come together. The Bourgeoisie and the Rebel.

NICKY: Does she really say "bourgeoisie"?

CLEA: Yes. We have a lot in common. Her and me, not you and me though maybe you and me have a lot in common too, I don't know yet, but her and me, she and I, we have a bond. We're both from Detroit. And that's not all. The list goes on and on.

NICKY: Detroit. That's Motown?

CLEA: Exactly.

NICKY: The Def Jam of another era.

CLEA: Loads of very creative people come from Detroit. Like Madonna and Diana Ross and me. And cars are made there. So you see. We are deeply connected by our Root Geography. And, OK this sounds fantastic but it's true — we were tigers in another life and she scratched my eyes out. It's OK though.

NICKY: Did you say you can't sleep?

CLEA: Yes.

(Beat.)

NICKY: It's common. Your first night somewhere new.

CLEA: You think?

NICKY: Oh yes. Very common.

CLEA: This is my first time out of the country.

NICKY: I see.

CLEA: Except Canada. From Detroit, you can just drive into Canada.

NICKY: Well, then it's very common. To not sleep.

CLEA: Thank you.

NICKY: I'm here all night. Watching the desk. So you can talk to me.

CLEA: Night shift?

NICKY: Right.

CLEA: I understand. I work in Admissions.

NICKY: Right. Well, so you can stay, if you want.

CLEA: Thanks.

NICKY: Not at all.

   (Beat.)

NICKY: Will you see the sights while you're in London? There are great sights.

CLEA: We're kind of here on business.

NICKY: I see.

CLEA: Yes. There may not be time for sights.

NICKY: What kind of business?

CLEA: Well, waiting for Her to give birth. But also, see, I'm actually her illegitimate secret daughter from the early days in Detroit and I need to let her know that I exist, which I plan to do when I find her in downward facing dog at the yoga center. Or at her house, when I slip a note with my half of the secret locket, the one my adopted mom gave me when I turned eighteen, to her doorman.

   No, I'm totally lying. Really, really what happened is: *(In one big gulp.)* Jason Stark, he's this writer Abby lost her virginity with when she was sixteen, he wrote a book about her and called her in the middle of the night to let her know that the book has come out and it's like, essentially all about how much she sucked as a person, but how he wants her anyway, and he needs her to be with him because he's losing his mind or something, and I'm here because I am her best friend. But Abby was retarded and didn't tell Jason we were coming so we got here and he was, I don't even know where he is, but I don't have any money, I mean, I have like ten pounds or something for the whole weekend, after paying for this place. So, he has to show up soon so I can eat. Abby doesn't eat, but I like need to.

NICKY: I have food. If you run out of money. I have just, you know, you can come to me. I'm staff. I will feed you.

CLEA: That's very nice.

NICKY: Oh. Don't mention it. I'm staff.

CLEA: I wish I were more like her.

NICKY: Madonna? Or your friend?

CLEA: Both. They're very fierce. You know, both their moms died when they were little. Why can't one of my stupid parents be dead? I mean, I don't really want them to be dead, but it's so much more romantic than work-ing for Chrysler, you know? How about you? Are your parents dead?

NICKY: No. They're quite alive. On British soil.

CLEA: See what I mean? Do you collect things?

NICKY: I do.

CLEA: I thought so. What do you collect?

NICKY: Guitar strings. Picks. Music magazines. Gabardine shirts. You?

CLEA: Bracelets. And gloves, not the keep-warm kind, but the old lady lace kind.

NICKY: Candy wrappers.

CLEA: Sure.

NICKY: It's a weird one.

CLEA: No, I get it.

NICKY: I just like the way they look.

CLEA: I know. I went through a gum wrapper phase myself. The colors . . .

NICKY: Right.

CLEA: I love the colors.

NICKY: The green ones.

CLEA: Right.

CLEA WORRIES, ABBY FRETS

CLEA: Why aren't there any vegetarians in England?

ABBY: There's a lot of butter.

CLEA: What do I eat here?

ABBY: Scones. And a lot of butter. If you can take butter.

CLEA: I need vegetables.

ABBY: Can't help ya. This is England. Scones and lots of butter.

CLEA: Someone at the hostel last night called America "the Evil Empire." She was wearing Nike's.

ABBY: The Brits used to own India. Everyone's been the Evil Empire some time or other.

CLEA: She wasn't British. I think she was German or something.

ABBY: Exactly.

CLEA: I had insomnia.

ABBY: I thought you were so tired . . .

CLEA: I was. But in the room with the Swedish girls, I had insomnia. I stayed up talking to —

ABBY: We'll go to Jason's house. It'll all work out. He just . . .

CLEA: Isn't here.

ABBY: Right.

CLEA: Maybe we need a plan. I'm going to run out of money.

ABBY: We'll hear from him.

CLEA: We have to. 'Cause I'm gonna run out of money.

ABBY: Look. He worships me.

CLEA: Well, that's good. 'Cause I'm gonna run out of money.

HARD AT WORK

JASON: The young writer Jason Stark smokes too many cigarettes and drinks whiskey. He is hot on the trail of his new book. He has gone away, left the City impulsively. Locked himself in a small hotel room in a small town with a bottle of whiskey and the desire to write. And occasionally girls he brings home from the local pub. The waitresses there are something to behold.

A new book. A new heroine. Her name is Roxanne. No, her name is Nicolette. No, it's Roxanne. And she's smashing. Positively smashing. Young and slightly naughty. Roxanne, Roxanne, I want to be your man. Oh. No. *(He hurls something across the room. Then he tries again.)*

Her name is Gabby. Short for Gabrielle. She's mute. Born that way. She gives . . . Ax . . . the hero . . . no, maybe his name is . . . Rex . . . she gives him a blow job in the opening scene, and he thinks this is like the best thing ever because he's never gotten a blow job before from a girl who can't talk. It's pretty wild. A turn-on. It lasts for HOURS. And her dad, he's this famous . . . painter. Like Picasso. And he paints his mute daughter a lot. Until she runs away with Rex/Ax and they live in a . . . well, it's like a shack cause he's really poor and they're like, like the road warriors in *Road Warrior*, it's futuristic, and . . .

Well. At least we know there is Gabby and Rex.

And Rox. Roxanne. Roxanne, who I have to call. She gets really mad if I keep her waiting. Roxanne, little slut waitress with electric hair, messy and flying about her face. I love it.

A REAL WRITER

JAMES: I wrote a story about Abby once. It was soon after her mother died. Abby asked where her mother had gone, and I wrote to answer. There was another story, incidental, and a scene in the *Eden Trilogy* that came the day my best friend noticed that my daughter had breasts. Which was awful, if you ask me. Just awful. And I guess one might say that Constance, the sister of the narrator in *Grass in the Blade* sounds something like Abby. I might have used some of her syntax, although probably without noticing it much. But the point is, a Real Writer will transmute the source material. Not so much disguise it as let it all digest and settle in the unconscious, so that later, you see there is a marriage between the real and the imagined. It all pours out in an undistinguishable reshaped new form. Of course, the problem is that everything in the writer's domain is up for grabs. It becomes material. Who is to say what and who are drawn from . . . what and whom.

GREEN PARK WITH SWANS THE SIZE OF BUICKS
Clea and Nicky list items they collect (shoelaces, doll parts . . .) as Abby enters holding Time Out London.

ABBY: I found him.
CLEA: Guy Ritchie?
ABBY: Jason.
CLEA: Oh. Jason. Right. Where's he?
ABBY: Giving a reading the day after tomorrow. Some bookstore. West End. We're going to be there.
CLEA: *(Referring to Nicky.)* All of us?
ABBY: *(Getting it.)* I guess.
CLEA: You are still killing him, aren't you?
ABBY: Of course.
CLEA: Because we did not come all this way for any lesser action.
ABBY: Trust me. I'll poison him against writing. Which is the same as killing. It's more deadly than killing.
CLEA: So long as we take revenge. Or avenge. Are we avenging or revenging?
ABBY: We're revenging.
CLEA: Because I am worried that the focus is shifting from "killing" to "shocking."

ABBY: I think you should fake a seizure.

CLEA: Excuse me?

ABBY: At the reading. I'll be sitting next to you, and then, when they have to stop the reading and carry you off, he'll see me, and I'll stand. But, first, you convulse.

CLEA: Can't we confront him directly?

NICKY: They do say that direct methods —

ABBY: I just think convulsions will be interesting.

CLEA: Well. Sure. But I'm kind of a Direct Girl myself. I don't know if I can be convincing convulsing.

NICKY: Uh, hate to interrupt, but uh, I rather agree with — *(Motioning toward Clea.)*

ABBY: I'm sorry. Who are you again?

CLEA: Remember? He's Nicky. From the hostel —

NICKY: Well, not really from the hostel. Originally North London. At the Palace about two years. The Hotel, not the . . . well, not the actual "palace." And I'm a musician, classical violin ten years, then I began to experiment with emergent forms, abstract and then street-influenced, I listened to quite a bit of strange French pop music, but then New York started calling, as they say, since, well, there's really a fusion there of street and also —

ABBY: OK. I get it. I thought you were just some guy who worked at the hostel.

CLEA: Nicky is a stellar being.

ABBY: Great. Because I thought he was just some guy who worked at the hostel.

CLEA: Excuse her. She's very tired.

ABBY: OK. So long as I know who —

CLEA: What about Madonna's House? Can we —? The Swedish girls said —

ABBY: I doubt the Swedish girls would know.

CLEA: She said, "I'm having a love affair with England." I want to have a love affair with England.

NICKY: Right.

ABBY: Please stop talking about her. We have to focus on Jason right now.

CLEA: Abby is in a very bad mood.

ABBY: Abby is in a fine mood. Clea has some strange attachment to celebrity street maps.

CLEA: They're called Star Maps.

Look. I am financially challenged and single minded. There is one thing

I want to do in this country, just one. I don't like butter. I just want this one thing. Can't we just do this one thing that I want to do!?

ABBY: There will be plenty of time later for Madonna sightings. Right now, we have to have priorities. Which means you have to convulse.

CLEA: I'm here to have a love affair with England.

NICKY: I could show you Princess Diana's House.

ABBY AND CLEA: Oh, no, not Princess Diana's House.

CLEA: We're sorry she's dead, but we don't want to go there. But what about, I mean, you know who I mean. With Child and Empire?

NICKY: The Queen?

ABBY: Clea. This is called stalking, and famous people don't like it. She is not some icon for your consumption, she's a person. Probably not even very nice.

NICKY: I'm sure the house is fairly hidden and —

ABBY: You need a role model. And I don't think she's the right one.

CLEA: You've just never had anything like this. A person you believed in —

ABBY: When I was in India, I met people with gurus.

CLEA: Sure.

NICKY: My aunt, she follows that woman with the peacock feather —

ABBY: But Madonna is not an enlightened being.

CLEA: How do you know?

NICKY: I do sort of doubt she's enlightened. That takes a lot of work, doesn't it? I mean, her mixes are all right, but enlightened conjures up images of —

ABBY: She's a pop star. Not even rock.

CLEA: So? Nobody said "That Joan of Arc, she isn't a saint, just a soldier. Not even a soldier. Just a girl with a . . ." what did they have then? Spears? Lancets? What did they have?

NICKY: I think they had swords.

CLEA: Right.

ABBY: They did so say that! Anyway, it doesn't matter.

CLEA: It did to them.

ABBY: What I'm getting at is —

CLEA: I know what you're getting at.

ABBY: It's just like Jason. Don't you see that?

NICKY: Jason's the one with the "dirty little girl" book?

CLEA: No. It's not like that at all.

ABBY: Fine.

CLEA: It's not.

ABBY: Sure.

CLEA: I didn't fuck her and write a book about it.

NICKY: Oh, right. Jason is the bloke with the —

ABBY: It's The Waiting Period. I'm going to go completely crazy if I have to wait much longer. I'm not good at waiting. Why wasn't he here?

CLEA: You didn't call first.

ABBY: Why is there this waiting period?

CLEA: You didn't call.

ABBY: No. It's not that. We're just waiting. That's all we do. And we can't spend money because somebody is financially challenged.

NICKY: Lots of things are free.

CLEA: It's the eternal now.

(Abby scowls.)

NICKY: *(Breaking up the fight.)* OK. Time to see sights. We will go to the museums. The Tate's free, and I'll pay the Tube fare. Come on. Both of you.

ABBY: No.

CLEA: Yes.

CLEA: Well?

NICKY: I'll wait over there. By the big swans.

ABBY: You go. I have stuff to do.

CLEA: Come with us. Please?

ABBY: I'll find you later.

CLEA: Are you sure?

ABBY: Sure.

CLEA: I — *(As if to say I'm sorry/I love you . . .)*

ABBY: Really. It's fine.

(Clea leaves. Abby takes out Jason's book. Begins to read again. Strikes the pose of Jameson Addie.)

OUTSIDE THE TATE MODERN, WHICH IS FREE
Nicky is attempting to draw Clea who keeps inadvertently moving.

CLEA: She's different. I mean, this is not the strong-willed exuberant fuck-you Abby of our youth. Mine and hers, not mine and yours.

NICKY: She's upset.

CLEA: Abby?

NICKY: Under pressure. Hold still.

CLEA: Abby doesn't get upset. She doesn't eat, remember?

NICKY: Hold —

CLEA: I know, still. I've never been drawn before. And I think that was our first fight. Mine and hers, not mine and yours.

NICKY: Yes, I know. Keep your head still.

CLEA: Sorry.

NICKY: It takes twenty drawings to know a face.

CLEA: It's thrilling. To be drawn. Does that mean we have nineteen more?

NICKY: You've got to stop moving, Cle.

CLEA: I know. Sorry. Do you think it's me? Or do you think she's different too?

NICKY: This is where you really have got to stop moving altogether.

CLEA: It's terrible having to sit still. I might not be able to stand nineteen more.

NICKY: Come on. Just . . . breathe.

(Clea breathes.)

NICKY: Without moving. Breathe without moving.

(She tries to do this.)

CLEA: Can I draw you back?

NICKY: In a minute.

CLEA: Nobody told me this would be work.

(Beat.)

NICKY: There. I'm done. We can switch.

(They switch roles. He hands her the pad and pencils.)

CLEA: Ah. Much better.

(She moves now, delighting in doing so. She positions him for her drawing. Moving all the time.)

NICKY: Do you draw?

CLEA: I do now.

SO AT HOME

JASON: No, I'm not British. I'm sensitive to sound. I'm an artist. I absorb. In the States, I was always an outsider. But here I feel I belong. So, I can't help it, Roxanne, if I speak this way. I feel at home here. Your people are mine. Your sounds and inflections. I've never felt so at home.

AN EASY TARGET

ABBY: She wasn't a dirty little girl. She was smart and lonely. And you're right, Jason. An easy target. Just waiting to be found.

A BOY IN A POST FEELING AGE

JASON: We are in a post feeling age. Nobody in the *New York Times Sunday Magazine* or book review can feel. Indie film doesn't feel. *The Face* doesn't feel. *Interview* never felt. It has all been taken from us. Where do you think our feelings have gone, Roxanne? Do you know? Do you care? Do you want to hear about my book?

LIKE A LITTLE PRAYER

CLEA: In this moment, I feel we need to acknowledge that Jason Stark is wrong. It is not an unfeeling age, not an age of dead vacant people. It's just not. Because I'm here, and I feel and I want and I'm good. And Abby's here. And Nicky's here. And I could just not know this person, Nicky, and come to England and here he is, just waiting for me to show up and rock his world. Who could have known? I mean, who could have known?

WHERE THE GODDESS LIVES, WAITING

NICKY: I found out where she lives.

CLEA: I love you.

NICKY: The general area. Yeah?

CLEA: For finding her house. The general area.

NICKY: Oh. Right. Well. We'll go there. Tonight.

CLEA: You're going to take me?

NICKY: Can't have you getting lost on your pilgrimage. Pilgrims usually have a guide.

CLEA: She's going to have her baby soon. And her new CD will be released. The cycle of creation goes around and around.
(Nicky impulsively kisses Clea.)

NICKY: I've been wanting to do that all weekend. Is it OK?

(She nods. Speechless and delighted.)

CLEA: Can I do it back?

(He nods. She kisses him back. It's fabulous.)

CHAPTER 86. LAST PARAGRAPH, CHERRY PIE . . .

JASON: Once upon a time, there was an ugly ducking. A misfit boy who traveled to New York City where, by virtue of his talent, drive, and hunger, and one devastating love affair, he became a handsome prince. I want you to see me like this, Jameson. Jameson Addie. Inane carcass, lethal intoxicant, girl. I want you to see me handsome. And a prince. Because I still hate everything in the world except the way I felt with you.

HATING EVERYTHING: ABBY AND JASON, FIVE YEARS AGO

ABBY: That's pretty strong.

JASON: I guess.

ABBY: Why do you hate everything?

JASON: Don't you?

ABBY: I don't know. I don't think I hate everything. No.

JASON: What do you not hate?

ABBY: Being alive. I don't hate being alive. My friends. My dad. Travel. Poetry. The way the stars look at night, especially when you're out of the City. Lots of things. There are lots of things I do not hate.

JASON: I wish I were like you. You're a very wise child.

ABBY: I'm not a child.

JASON: It was a literary reference. Salinger.

ABBY: Fucking writers.

JASON: What?

ABBY: Nothing. I just hate fucking writers and their fucking literary fucking references.

JASON: I want to stay like this, with you, forever.

ABBY: No, you don't. You'll have stuff you want to do.

JASON: No. Nothing.

ABBY: Um, how about graduate and get your MFA? Write a book. You'll want to do that. And even on a very basic level, you'll want to get up from here so you can do basic things. Like shave or whatever.

JASON: No. I'll grow a beard. A long one. I'll stop eating. I can write a book from here, from the roof in the middle of this one night with you.

ABBY: Well, I'm going to want to do stuff. I don't want to stay here forever.

JASON: Sure you do. You want to stay with me. Forever. Who else will adore you like this?

ABBY: Someone will.

JASON: No. Never. No one will ever love you like me. And I will love you forever. Just like this.

MEANWHILE . . .

Abby prepares for the reading.

CLEA: You look great.

ABBY: I look old.

CLEA: You can't look old. We're twenty-one.

ABBY: I look fat.

CLEA: You can't look fat. You don't eat.

ABBY: He liked me when I was sixteen and going to Spence. Now I'm aging and fat.

CLEA: You're not aging and you're not fat. I like it here.

ABBY: It's OK.

CLEA: Have you ever been drawn?

ABBY: Sure.

CLEA: He got that thing I do with my mouth.

ABBY: What are you talking about?

(Clea does the thing.)

ABBY: Oh, that.

CLEA: I get why she likes it here.

ABBY: She likes it because she's in love. People do all kind of things out of the mythology of romantic love.

CLEA: Yes. They do.

ABBY: Do I look OK?

CLEA: You look beautiful.

ABBY: I see.

CLEA: You'll kick ass. You'll kick his ass, but also, you'll kick ass.

ABBY: Right. I will kick ass.

THE READING

Enter Jason. Steps up to a podium, about to start his reading, takes a sip from a glass of water. Abby and Clea are unseen. Jason experiences all sorts of technical difficulties, the mike is weird, something in the air feels . . . wrong. He finds himself unusually tongue-tied as The Young Writer Jason Stark and the skinny kid from Iowa tango in his mind.

JASON: Hello. I'm Jason Stark.

(Nicky/Clea attempt to hijack.)

JASON: Thank you. This is my first novel . . . It's set in . . . .

(NICKY/CLEA: I'm not in a post-feeling age. My feelings are fine. NICKY: Mine are all right.)

(Abby hushes them more aggressively.)

JASON: well, see there was a girl . . . sixteen, smashing, and mean . . . see, first there was this Smiths song, it was before her time . . . but when I said . . . sixteen, smashing, and . . . I was referring to the cadence of . . .

(Nicky/Clea attempt to make more noise. Abby hushes them.)

JASON: and then, blackberries, well I liked that poem and the power of making language, the black art of making well, fruit of course . . .

(Jason sees Abby, or thinks he does, out of the very corners of his eye — or mind's eye, or memory — he isn't even sure. She still affects him that way — a mixture of dread and desire, attraction and fear — it's hot. But also freaky.)

JASON: she seduced me, I did not seduce her . . . she started it, she kissed me first, told me I was stupid, oh, she was mean . . . she was mean . . . she kissed me first but would never give me a blow job . . . and I'm sure she had done it before, this guy she was with before me, he was like . . . she was beautiful, my god, she was beautiful, and self-assured . . . I wish I could be her, only I couldn't be her, that would be weird, but she was my ideal, perfect, and —

(He realizes that yes indeed, she really is there, right where he thinks she is.)

JASON: Here. She is here. Why is she here?

(She stands. They face one another.)

ABBY: Hi, Jason.

(Blackout.)

(ANOTHER) SURPRISE!

Lights up.

ABBY: This is Clea. And her friend.

NICKY: Nicky. Pleased to —

CLEA: We hate your book.

JASON: Thanks.

ABBY: Clea has to go now.

CLEA: I'm on a pilgrimage.

JASON: Really?

ABBY: So, bye.

(Clea leaves while silently gesturing secret things to Abby about killing Jason but having mercy while she does this. Abby and Jason are now alone.)

ABBY: She's protective.

JASON: What are you doing here?

ABBY: I came to see you. You begged, remember?

JASON: Yeah, but I didn't think you'd really come.

ABBY: Yeah. *(Beat.)* So buy me a drink.

JASON: I can't believe you're here.

ABBY: You begged.

JASON: But you really came. It's so rash.

ABBY: Yeah.

JASON: Indeed.

ABBY: You said you needed me to write.

JASON: You said to go fuck someone else.

ABBY: You said I was your muse.

JASON: Well. You were. You were my muse.

ABBY: So I'm here.

JASON: But I did it.

ABBY: You did what?

JASON: What you said.

ABBY: What did I say?

JASON: I fucked someone else.

ABBY: Oh.

JASON: And wrote about it. The writing's not that great, actually, but it gave me hope.

ABBY: I see.

JASON: Can I take you to dinner or something?

ABBY: Dinner? Can you take me to dinner? You can fucking pay my bills for

the last three days is what you can do. Fuck! Fucking self-centered, nar-
cissistic, writers who cannibalize other people for their —

JASON: Do you think you're just mad at your father?

ABBY: OK, that's really it. YOU CALLED ME. I AM YOUR MUSE. DO YOU
NOT REMEMBER THIS PART? YOU CALLED ME.

JASON: Come on. Let me take you to dinner.

ABBY: Dinner is the least you can take me to. Asshole.

NEVER FORGET WHO YOU ARE

CLEA: You're a ray of light. A superstar. A lucky star. You get up again, over
and over. Don't let them tell you you're nothing. They'll try. Over and
over. They will tell you to be small. And you will say, No. They will tell
you to go away. And you will not go away. They will tell you to stop, and
you will say "Don't tell me to stop." You can be loud, vulgar, and overly
publicized. But you're here. And so am I.

AT THE HOUSE OF HER HOLINESS
Nicky and Clea outside Madonna's house. They are quiet.

NICKY: This is it. It's through that fence over there. It's hard to see.

CLEA: I can't believe you found it.

NICKY: Oh. It was nothing. Well, I mean I had to do research and bribe that
girl from, but it was —

CLEA: *(Reverent.)* We should be quiet.

NICKY: You think?

CLEA: Sure.
    (Beat. They are quiet. They wait. Reverently. They kiss.)

CLEA: Do you think we'll know each other?

NICKY: Us? Or you and Madonna?

CLEA: Us.

NICKY: Yes. I think we will know each other.

CLEA: Do you think we can be new?

NICKY: New how?

CLEA: New in all ways. In every moment. Want to go?

NICKY: No. This is important to you.

CLEA: I think Abby's right.

NICKY: No, it's important to you. Let's wait.

> (Beat.)

CLEA: You're nice.

NICKY: Oh. No. It's fine.

CLEA: Do you want to go?

NICKY: I told you, I really don't mind.

CLEA: I know. It's just . . . Do you know what I mean?

NICKY: Well . . .

CLEA: She's still my hero.

NICKY: Of course.

CLEA: It's just right now I'd rather be with you.

NICKY: Then . . .

CLEA: Let's go.

DRUNK ON CHARDONNAY AND LOVE

JASON: You're amazing.

ABBY: I thought you were with someone else.

JASON: I was. But, I was lying to myself. Roxanne was nothing.

ABBY: Roxanne? Was that her name?

JASON: It's amazing. You. You're still amazing.

ABBY: You were right. I do think about you.

JASON: You were right too.

ABBY: What was I right about? Fucking Roxanne?

JASON: You were right about everything.

ABBY: Here we are in London. And here we are. You wrote that disgusting book.

JASON: It isn't disgusting.

ABBY: It is. Do you know what you did to me?

JASON: I lay a garland of roses at your feet.

ABBY: Fuck that. You made me an oversexed, mean-spirited freak, a dirty little girl, what the Hell is a dirty little girl anyway? I mean, it's fucked up how you just —

JASON: It's not fucked up. I immortalized you, I said no one would ever love you like me, and I was right. Let's go back to my place.

ABBY: OK.

EVERYONE AT EVERYONE ELSE'S PLACE

Nicky takes Clea to his room at the hostel. Somewhat awkwardly at first, they kiss. This blossoms into a fabulous (and slightly awkward) make-out session. Meanwhile, on the other side of the city, Abby and Jason violently bust through the door, hit the walls and sink to the floor making love.

Blackout on both couples.

LOST TO US ALL

Clea waits for Abby, bags at her feet.

CLEA: In the early hours of the morning Madonna gave birth to a boy. It was a C-Section. She was rushed to the hospital, and if I had stayed in my hiding place all night, I might have seen her as she emerged from the house and into the waiting automobile which whisked her into the dawn. However, I was busy. With Nicky. And now it's time. Our flight leaves in a few hours. There's just Abby. Who isn't here. Apparently there were two empty beds in the room with the Swedish Girls.

(Abby appears, coat on, no suitcase.)

CLEA: Where have you been!?

ABBY: I was with Jason.

CLEA: Jason!? Whoa. That's — OK, story on plane. We have to get to the airport. If you're not there a whole hour and a half in advance, they do not let you on the plane. I was informed about this last night —

ABBY: I'm staying.

CLEA: No. You're coming home with me. Come on.

ABBY: No. I'm staying with Jason. He doesn't know yet. It's a surprise.

CLEA: You can't. Jason's horrible.

ABBY: He's fragile.

CLEA: He's horrible.

ABBY: Not inside.

CLEA: Abby. You cannot stay here. What about the Buddha? What about college?

ABBY: Jason and I love each other.

CLEA: You and Jason do not love each other. Go get your suitcase.

ABBY: You're jealous. It's totally understandable, Cle. You don't have anyone of your own, and it's time to outgrow your movie star fixations, but you haven't found an acceptable substitute —

CLEA: That's wrong.

ABBY: You need to have a lot of sex.

CLEA: How do you know I'm not having a lot of sex?

ABBY: Are you having sex?

CLEA: Maybe.

ABBY: Who are you . . . ? Oh, Front Desk? You two hooked up?

CLEA: No time for this. Get your stuff. Now.

ABBY: Listen I know this is hard for you to understand, but I can't go anywhere right now. Jason needs me. He's like my dad.

CLEA: You hate your dad.

ABBY: I don't hate my dad.

CLEA: Yes, you do. Everyone knows you hate your dad.

ABBY: Who is everyone?

CLEA: Everyone that we know together knows that you hate your dad. This is very available knowledge.

ABBY: My dad —

CLEA: Is totally oblivious to you. Your whole dad thing is deeply riddled with problems and you can't stay with this person who reminds you of him.

ABBY: Maybe you should go to the airport.

CLEA: You are just not staying in fucking London where you can't even be a vegetarian for God's Sake. Even Madonna is going home.

ABBY: OK, first of all Madonna's staying too. Second this is not your problem. Go home. We'll stay in touch if you stop saying things that you know nothing about.

CLEA: So basically you just want to give up your education and your life in New York to be written about? Is that it?

ABBY: You don't get it.

CLEA: Why? Because I'm not pretty enough to be written about?

ABBY: It's not just that.

CLEA: Of course it's not. I was joking.

ABBY: Sorry.

CLEA: Don't be.

ABBY: It has to happen this way.

CLEA: But —

ABBY: I know it's right, I just know.

CLEA: Look. You are abandoning everything that we talked about, everything that I thought you —

ABBY: No, that's just you. I'm abandoning you.

CLEA: No.

ABBY: Bye, Clea. Go home without me. Keep in touch. Visit.

(Nicky enters or appears, ready to escort Clean to the airport. Clea, however, is still engaged in this moment with Abby.)

NICKY: Clea, we really should go.

CLEA: This is what you wanted? This? You just wanted — this — !? I guess I didn't realize —

ABBY: What?

CLEA: That you wanted this. *(She turns to Nicky.)* I'm ready.

ABBY: Well, you could say good-bye.

CLEA: *(But she can't. To Nicky:)* Let's go.

(They leave. Abby stays.)

STAYING

JASON: What about school?

ABBY: Don't you want me to?

JASON: It's not about what I want.

ABBY: So?

JASON: You need to finish school.

ABBY: I don't need to do anything. I choose to stay here with you.

JASON: You can't do that.

ABBY: You need me to write.

JASON: No, I don't.

ABBY: You said you did.

JASON: I was deluded. I'm glad you came though.

ABBY: You motherfucker.

JASON: Abby. It's not like it was. We're not the same. I'm going to be thirty in a few months.

ABBY: So!?

JASON: I needed HER. *(Pointing to the poster.)* You're not her.

ABBY: Of course I'm her. I am her. She's me.

JASON: No. She's my creation.

ABBY: You said —

JASON: I know. But I was wrong.

ABBY: I'm me. You wrote about me.

JASON: It's different.

ABBY: I'm her. The girl in your book. Look —

(She tries to be the girl in her book — She takes the pose of the girl on the

poster. This takes a while. Maybe it is awkward for her. She falls out of the picture.)

JASON: You're not her, Abby. She is a work of fiction. You are a work of . . . life.

ABBY: I'm her, I'm her, I'm her, I'm her.

JASON: No. You're not.

(He leaves. Lights down on everyone.)

SMASHING

JAMES: which brings us to *Smashing*. My most recent piece of fiction, in which a neophyte first-time lucky stiff of a mediocre writer publishes a book about the daughter of his idol, an aging rock star. The daughter declares her love for the young novelist and he rejects her, as young novelists are apt to do, and she comes home. To her father. While the young novelist takes up with assorted unnamed girls whom he later discards. And the daughter, she returns to her father in order to sort out the threads and threats of their past and weave together a future that is eternally now and eternally kaleidoscopic. I was somewhat influenced by something minor that happened to my own daughter, Abby. Who lives in London.

ABBY: Dear Daddy. . .

Jason is hard at work on his second book. Still. He's had some troubles. That really sucked about *Cherry Pie* and how they cast that girl and had to make up all that new dialogue, but he's not taking it too hard, or the reviews either, he's just trying to get through a draft of the new one. It is not called *Roxanne, Roxanne* anymore. I convinced him to change it. I don't know if we'll make it home for Christmas. Things have been . . . we fight a lot. And I still don't know about finishing school. I just don't know.

. . . ON AN AIRLINE CALLED VIRGIN
Clea reads from her own writing

CLEA: At the end of the summer that She would call "pivotal," Louise found herself crossing the ocean on an airline called Virgin. Once this would be an appropriate play on words, but clearly not anymore. Louise thought, "I have lost my best friend, and gained an ocean. And new friends who offer to feed me, only it doesn't matter because I am already fed. And it is all just starting. Everything. Now."

EPILOGUE

Lights up on a new young girl-woman. She is fresh and very pretty, a student.

GIRL: Dear Mr. Stark,

I have just finished reading your wonderful book, and I am writing to you care of your agent, to tell you how deeply and profoundly it moved me. I too feel that I have gone to sleep and your book shocks me awake by taking me to the very depth of the pain of love. I am a college student, although I have seen and felt things that are older than my years. And I am in love with your book. It reminded me of events in my own life, and I just wanted you to know how much I relate to Addie, the girl in your book who is mean to the hero and breaks his heart. I understand this girl. I would love to meet you, Mr. Stark, if you are ever in Kansas City. Missouri, not Kansas. I would like to meet you. And talk about your book.

END OF PLAY

CORNER WARS

By Tim Dowlin

I would like to dedicate this play, first and foremost, to all the fallen soldiers, casualties of the corner wars. To all my real-life influences still living and struggling in North Philadelphia. To the organization and leadership that helped put everything in perspective, and always believed in me. To all true Philly graffiti writers: I hope this play will allow our story to live on. Most importantly I hope this play will highlight an epidemic — which every day across the country is a matter of life and death — and feed the fire of change that is more necessary than ever. The war on drugs in America is a war on the poor, and in every street there is evidence that we are being annihilated. This play is a mirror of what my eyes and ears have seen and heard. Take it for what it is, no more, no less. Last but not least, I would like to thank my amazing friends, my loving mother, my inspirational father, and my wonderful sister. I love you all, always.

BIOGRAPHY

Tim Dowlin is a Philadelphia native who studied theater with Mel Williams at the High School for Creative and Performing Arts. He has been pursuing acting, writing, and directing for over six years in New York City. Dowlin's literary debut, *Corner Wars* has been awarded *Newsday's* George Oppenheimer award. Dowlin is also a veteran member of Theatre for a New Generation, and the Kensington Welfare Rights Union. He has been seen in TFANGs off-Broadway productions of *Zoo Story* and *Indian Wants the Bronx,* and he can be seen in upcoming independent films such as *Bomb the System* and *Winter Solstice.* Dowlin is also looking forward to starring in the TFANG production of *Julius Caesar* and is eager to meet every challenge ahead.

ORIGINAL PRODUCTION

Corner Wars was produced at 47th Street Theatre in New York by Theater for a New Generation, January 12, 2003. It was directed by Mel Williams with the following cast:

KAREEM	David Shaw
BRODY	Cornell McIntosh
JANE	Kyra Knox
SMOKEY	Warren Merrick III
RAUL	Ramon Aponte
JAY	Eric Carter
CHRIS	Joel Holiday
DEX	Omar Evans
NATASHIA	Erika Myers
MARISOL	Carolina Rios
JAH	Christopher Williams
MS. ROBERTS	Susie Amato
TROY	Ray Thomas
DET. CIRILLI	Mike Sharp
DET. GRABANSKI	Joyce Storey
BUCKSHOT	Rick Cao
NEW KIDS ON THE CORNER	Shamel Owens, Andre King, Rahim Wilson

CHARACTERS

KAREEM: Tall, wiry; hurt from neglect, African American

BRODY: Calm, introspective; hides his hurts, African American

JANE: Anybody's sister; a victim; a mark; African American

SMOKEY: A "could have been"; smart; an addict; African American or Latino

RAUL: He made it out; a police office; Latino

JAY: Obvious leader; older brother to Kareem; confident, African American

CHRIS: Acts hard but soft; sensitive; sharp; African American or Latino

DEX: Smart; artistic; caught up; African American or Latino

NATASHIA: A survivor; a rap artist; African American

MARISOL: Neighborhood girl; trying to make it, very attractive, Latina

JAH: Larger than life; big not fat; a leader; African American

MS. ROBERTS: Social worker; committed; Caucasian

TROY: Ex-con; older brother to Brody; wise and experienced, African American

DET. CIRILLI: Career cop; racist but thinks he is a realist; knows his beat; Caucasian

DET. GRABANSKI: Female; fair-minded by the book; can be tough as nails, Caucasian

BUCKSHOT: Drug dealer; smooth dresser; Asian or Latino

KIDS ON CORNER: Average-looking, 10-12 years old

SETTING

A dead-end street in a rundown urban area. This is the corner where drugs are sold. Stage right is abandoned house where drugs are stored. Downstage left, an old unworkable fire hydrant. The entire play takes place in this space.

TIME

Today

Corner Wars

ACT I

SCENE ONE

Early morning. The streets are deserted . . . two guys are keeping each other awake.

KAREEM: Spell *electronic.*

BRODY: *Electronic.* E-L-E-C-T-R-O-N-I-C. *Electronic.*

KAREEM: Aight, cool. Now spell . . . *promise.*

BRODY: *Promise.* P-r-o-m-i . . . c . . . e. *Promice?*

KAREEM: Naw, man. Almost. It's a *s,* not a *c.* Aight, now spell *nutrition.*

BRODY: Aw, c'mon, I spelled that yesterday. I ain't spelling that again.

KAREEM: Spell *transport.*

BRODY: *Transport.* T-r-a-n-s-p-o-r-t. *Transport.* right?

(Enter Customer, gives money, gets crack. Exits.)

KAREEM: Spell *objective.*

BRODY: *Objective.* O-b-j-e-c-t-i-v-e. *Objective.*

KAREEM: That's right. You ready for a hard one?

BRODY: Whatever.

KAREEM: *Righteousness.*

BRODY: *(Laughs.)* Naw, I ain't spelling that. I can't spell that.

KAREEM: What? You better try.

BRODY: Naw, man. Not right now.

KAREEM: Aight, well, you better learn it for tomorrow.

(Enter, Smokey gives money to Kareem, he holds the crack and keeps it from him.)

KAREEM: I bet Smokey can spell that shit. Smokey spell *righteousness.*

SMOKEY: Aww come on guys don't mess with me, just give me my shit and let me get out of here.

KAREEM: Nope. You ain't getting shit till you spell it. I know you can, now just spell *righteousness.*

SMOKEY: Fine. *Righteousness,* R-I-G-H-T-E-O-U-S-N-E-S-S.

KAREEM: Damn, Brody, a crackhead can spell better than you. Here you go Smokey.

(Kareem gives Smokey his crack, Smokey exits.)

BRODY: How does Smokey know that shit?

KAREEM: Smokey's a smart motherfucka you didn't know? He used to teach school.

BRODY: Word, naw I didn't know, what happened?

KAREEM: Yo can you spell *addiction*.

BRODY: You funny man.

KAREEM: It's not funny at all Man spell that shit.

BRODY: OK, damn, *addiction.* A-D-I-C-K-T-I-O-N. *Adicktion?*

KAREEM: Naw Man you way off and you think: Shit's funny.

BRODY: I didn't say shit is funny I said you're funny, cuz you are funny.

KAREEM: Now I'm not even gonna tell you how to spell that jawn you gonna have to look it up.

(Enter Cop Raul Rodriguez. Pause.)

RAUL: Yo Brody, c'mere.

BRODY: Aww shit. Hold up. *(Gets rid of bundle.)* Whassup?

RAUL: Just c'mere a sec.

(Brody comes over.)

RAUL: I hear your brother's out.

BRODY: Oh yeah? You heard that?

RAUL: How long he been out?

BRODY: Yo he just got out. He don't even want people to know yet.

RAUL: Does he know you work here?

BRODY: Fuck are you talking about?

RAUL: Don't play that shit. Does your brother know you hustlin'?

(Brody doesn't answer. He looks away.)

RAUL: Brody you're smarter than this, why you doing this?

BRODY: Doing what? Man you know exactly why, man. There ain't shit else.

RAUL: Aren't you in school?

BRODY: Yeah I'm in school. That shit ain't free. I pay my own tuition.

KAREEM: Yo BRODY!

RAUL: He's busy right now.

KAREEM: *Perbona me las mamasita!*

RAUL: *Carrajo que carrajo dejiites?*

KAREEM: *Puta!*

(Raul is pissed about the last insult in Spanish, he grips up Kareem and pushes him against the wall.)

KAREEM: Yo chill damn!! What the fuck I do?

RAUL: Shut the fuck up, asshole.

KAREEM: You're harassing me and I'm the asshole?

RAUL: Shut the fuck up. Before I run your ass in.

KAREEM: Why so I can be back out before your shift is over.

RAUL: NOT FOR THIS!

(Runs up in Kareem's pockets, takes weed, and steps on it.)

BRODY: Hey Raul what's this all about why you fucking with us?

RAUL: Y'all think I don't know what's up? Y'all been sellin' weed here for years but I didn't fuck with y'all, did I? This is my hood, and I know y'all been selling crack!

BRODY: Aww that's not true.

RAUL: Bullshit. I see fiends coming round here all the time so don't bullshit me aight. *(Pause.)* I'm tellin' you, y'all ain't pushin' that poison round here. Not in my district.

KAREEM: Are you serious? This is like the fuckin' crack district, practically every other corner is a drug spot. You could lock up my whole squad and you know it don't mean shit. Them fiends is still gonna get high.

BRODY: Yeah Raul, why you trippin', this is the biggest drug neighborhood on the East Coast. And I thought you was cool wit' us?

RAUL: I've known y'all a long time. and that's why I don't want nothing bad to happen to y'all. It's not my problem you don't care about your future, but for now this is still my community, and I still care, I still give a fuck. Ya got me?

KAREEM: Oh, please! You're so high and mighty. What the fuck do you do around here?

BRODY: Fuck you know about my future!!?

KAREEM: Don't gimme that community bullshit. We do more for this community than you we built the damn playground wit' our own money. All you do is lock up the people that you supposed to be protecting. Three hots and a cot, that's your little charity?

RAUL: Three hots and a cot is what I offer to criminals, look I don't even have time to argue with you. Brody you tell your brother that I'm looking for him, aight.

(Pause. Raul gets call on his radio. Raul exits.)

KAREEM: I'm getting real tired of that muthafucka. He always fucks with somebody.

BRODY: He think all because him and my brother grew up together that he can come around here and fuck with me.

KAREEM: Well fuck that, I'm not you. He ain't gonna be fuckin' with me like that.

BRODY: Yo, forget that Puta!!

(Kareem and Brody laugh. Kareem gets up to stretch and look around the corner. He's a little antsy. He sits back down. Enter Customer, who cops then leaves.)

KAREEM: Yo, I ain't know your brother was out?

BRODY: He's laying low. So don't tell nobody he's out yet. He just want to spend a few days in the crib with the fam, after two years not seeing your kid grow. Ya nah' mean. He'll come out around here when he's ready.

KAREEM: Does my brother know he's out?

BRODY: I don't even know, but here comes your brother right now.

(Enter Kareem's brother, Jay.)

JAY: G'morning fellas. What's the deal?

KAREEM: S'been slow. We ain't even finish the bundle.

JAY: Damn, really?

(Jay goes around the back, behind the corner. Exchanges bundle with Kareem through a small window. Chris walks up, clearly just woke up. Dawn is just breaking. Brief greetings. Jay comes back around.)

JAY: *(To Chris.)* Where's Dex at?

CHRIS: I dunno.

JAY: Can one of y'all stay till he gets here?

(Kareem and Brody look at each other.)

BRODY: Naw man, I gotta go to this thing . . . I gotta go to my GED class . . .

KAREEM: Aight, it's cool. I can stay.

JAY: *(To Brody.)* Hey, remember I'm gonna need your help in the kitchen later.

BRODY: Yeah, you wanna come scoop me up after this class?

JAY: Yeah what time you get out?

(Jay and Brody leave together. Kareem begins to roll a blunt. Chris is eating a TastyCake crumbcake and drinking a fruit beverage. A few moments go by.)

KAREEM: What's up with you?

CHRIS: Nothin' Man just chillin'.

(The blunt is ready.)

KAREEM: You wanna burn this?

CHRIS: Naw I'm straight.

(Kareem puts the blunt away. Dex shows up on a bike, out of breath. Stashes the bike and a small bag of spray paint.)

DEX: Sorry, y'all, my bad. I know I'm late.

KAREEM: It's cool, man. I'm outta here.

(Kareem pulls blunt out, gives them both a pound, exits stage right.)

CHRIS: You're lucky it's been slow. Jay said you might lose this shift if you late again.

DEX: I know, man. I'm a talk to him.

CHRIS: What did you do?

DEX: I just did this big ass straight letter on one of the EL roofs they buffed — yo that shit looks proper! I used four colors. Almost got caught too. I couldn't get my bike out from behind the fence, this dog was barkin' at me it was crazy all types of cops with flashlights and shit. I had to dip to the back of Manny's bar, switch my shirt, clean the paint from my hands, then go back around to get my bike, then take the long route here. I'm lucky nobody stole my bike the way I left it halfway stuck between the fence and the wall. I'm surprised the cops didn't take the bike. That shit looked banging though.

CHRIS: What do you mean the long route?

DEX: Well I couldn't go straight down the ave they're looking for me so I had to zigzag the long way, you knew zigzag that's how I bomb catch a big tag then zigzag big tag then zigzag.

CHRIS: Oh I get it zigzag like a big fag who always be late.

DEX: Owww shut up with your reject Twinkies for breakfast your mom still shop at the TastyCake outlet?

CHRIS: Ay boy, don't start talking 'bout moms now, I don't think you really want that, cuz your mom, well it's just too much shit I could say about her, your mom — she crazy. Ha ha.

DEX: Well I could say a lot more than just Twinkies about your mom too.

(Enter Jane, a customer.)

JANE: Let me get two.

DEX: Aight. Hold up. *(Jane gives Dex $3.)* What's this?

JANE: I'm sorry. Can you help me out this one time.

DEX: Naw. Go get two dollars.

JANE: Aww come on, Dex. Just this one time. Please. Please.

DEX: All right. Just this one time. But don't come back short again. *(Hands Jane two.)* Shouldn't be smoking that shit anyway.

JANE: Thanks Dex. Thank you. Thank you.

(Transition: Customers coming up, music. Song playing over, lights come up with daylight. Shifts change, business comes in, shifts change again. Music fades out and lights go back to normal.)

SCENE TWO

Five P.M. Jay, Jah, Dex, and Chris all working. Natashia walks up.

CHRIS: Hey girl, how you doing?

NATASHIA: Fine. What's up with you Chris?

CHRIS: Oh, you know, chillin' like a villain, same shit.

NATASHIA: Word, that's what's up, lemme get two nicks.
   (Gives Chris ten dollars.)

CHRIS: Yeah I got you — hold up.
   (Chris gives Natashia two five-dollar crack rocks.)

NATASHIA: What the fuck is this shit Chris! I don't smoke no fuckin' crack! Do I look like a fuckin' crackhead to you? I just want two bags of weed, damn.

CHRIS: Oh, my bad, damn. Don't get pissed, that's just what I got, I didn't know what you wanted. YO DEX! DEX — give shorty two nicks.
   (Chris gives the ten dollars to Dex.)

DEX: Hey what's up sexy, here you go.
   (Natashia takes the weed from Dex and puts it away.)

CHRIS: So what you been up to? I heard you've been recording at a real studio, what's the deal with that?

NATASHIA: Yeah, I linked up with these people that used to do management for EVE before she blew up. I spit a couple of bars off the top, and they was feeling me. They offered to let me record a demo for free. It's not 100 percent official yet so I don't want to jinx anything by talking about it.

CHRIS: Well it sounds good, you can never be to sure about those industry people, they always tryin' to get over.

NATASHIA: Trust me, Chris, I'm playing it smart.

CHRIS: I believe you. I don't mean to discourage you, I just meant be careful that's all.

NATASHIA: Well thanks for the warning, but it's under control.

CHRIS: If you when you make a tape you should let me say some shit on it.

NATASHIA: *(Laughs.)* What the hell you gonna say on my tape?

CHRIS: What? I can rap too girl you didn't know?

NATASHIA: Oh really, rap what, Saran Wrap?

CHRIS: Naw, it's cool, I ain't gonna steal your spotlight. Just lemme get some shout outs on some of gangsta shit, hold it down for north side.

NATASHIA: Yeah well, we'll see.

CHRIS: I'm just messin' with ya, do whatever you want with your tape. I'm sure it'll be banging and I can't wait to hear it.

NATASHIA: All my shit is banging! I should make you wait and cop it in the stores.

CHRIS: I thought you were the one tryin' not to jinx it by talking about it.

(Enter Customer, buys crack from Chris, exits.)

NATASHIA: Yeah, you're right. So how's your mom doing?

CHRIS: *(Sighs.)* She just got laid off. And now she's working two jobs, one of 'em is all the way out in King of Prussia, it takes her hours just to commute back and forth so I don't never see her no more. When she is home she asleep, then she gets right up and goes.

NATASHIA: Damn, that's fucked up. My dad just got laid off too. He ain't even find nothing new yet. Shit's rough right now.

CHRIS: Yeah, for real.

NATASHIA: Well I'm actually on my way to the studio right now so I gotta go.

CHRIS: Aight, well, it was nice talking to ya.

NATASHIA: Aight, I'll see you around.

CHRIS: Hey, hold up a sec.

(Enter Customer, buys crack from Chris, Natashia waits impatiently. Enter Marisol.)

MARISOL: Yo Tash, what's up

NATASHIA: Hey Marisol.

(Exit Customer.)

CHRIS: I like talking to you.

NATASHIA: Well that's nice, but I still have to go.

CHRIS: Aight go ahead, good luck with your demo.

NATASHIA: Peace Chris.

MARISOL: Yo did you get the weed already?

NATASHIA: Yeah I got it. Stupid Chris gave me crack first, but I got it.

MARISOL: Oh aight, I'll pay you back.

NATASHIA: It's cool. Did you pick up the blunts?

MARISOL: Yeah I got 'em.

(Jay has had his eye on Marisol, he decides to approach her.)

JAY: Hey Marisol, how you doin'?

MARISOL: Hey what's up Jay, I'm good, and yourself?

JAY: Yeah I'm good, just chillin', holdin' it down.

NATASHIA: Hey girl what's up? You coming or what?

MARISOL: Yeah I'm comin'.

(She gives Jay a look, Jay gives her a smile, she looks back at Natashia.)

MARISOL: You know what, gimme a minute, is it cool if I just meet you there? I won't be long.

NATASHIA: Aight whatever, you know where right? It's the fifth floor.

MARISOL: OK, I got it. Thanks Tash.

(Natashia exits.)

JAY: Where y'all going? The studio?

MARISOL: Yeah I'm so excited for her, I think she's gonna make it happen with this, it's the opportunity that she always needed. She just wanted to show off the spot to me, and she wanted some company and moral support.

JAY: Word. That's hot. So what about you though? What have you been up to?

MARISOL: Just working really, not much time for anything else.

JAY: Where you work now?

MARISOL: I work at the hospital.

JAY: Oh, shit! That's right, what do you do over there now?

MARISOL: I'm an X-ray technician, I do the MRIs.

JAY: Damn! You're like the illest! You must be getting paper for that shit!

MARISOL: Yeah it's alright. I mean it pays the bills and all. Usually.

JAY: I hear that. Whatever it takes right. Hey, don't you have a lil seed?

MARISOL: Yeah I do, my little boy, he's now eighteen months old. He's so cute, too.

JAY: Damn, a year and a half already, time just flies don't it.

MARISOL: Yeah it's crazy, right.

JAY: So you got a man in your life?

MARISOL: No. No time for that.

JAY: Aww, you don't mean that, I bet you could make time, if it was the right guy?

MARISOL: I don't know.

JAY: Well, I'm mad busy myself. But if I find some time I'd like to spend it with you. What's up? Can we chill out together sometime?

MARISOL: I'll think about it.

JAY: Aight, that's not a no. So can I get your phone number?

MARISOL: I think it would be best if you gave me yours.

JAY: Aight, that works. Um, uh, hold up YO DEX, lemme get a pen. I know you got one.

(Dex brings him a pen without hesitation.)

JAY: Aight here you go, I hope you use it.

MARISOL: Aight cool. We'll see. I gotta go meet Tash, she's waiting for me.

JAY: Yeah I know, aight then, peace.

MARISOL: Bye, Jay.

(Marisol exits.)

DEX: What's up Jay is that your girl?

JAY: I don't think so, not yet anyway.

CHRIS: Why she going to the studio too? She don't rap.

JAY: Naw, she don't rhyme, she just going to hang out.

DEX: Yo, ya'll think that Tash can rap.

JAH: She aight but she ain't nicer than me.

CHRIS: Then why is she the one with demo then?

JAH: It don't matter if she got a demo, she ain't nicer then me.

JAY: Whateva man.

JAH: See y'all don't know nothing bout rap. The first rule to rap is sell crack then rap. Biggie, sell crack then rap. Jay-Z sell crack then rap. Scarface sell crack then rap. Myself sell crack then rap.

CHRIS: Fuck it, then if you so nice then spit something, nothing written but off the top.

JAH: Whateva, man, all I need is a beat. Yo somebody give me a beat.

SOMEBODY: Aight hold up, uh here I go

(He beatboxes, they form a semicircle.)

JAH: uh, uh, check it, bus it, uh. it's da boy Jah, I'm on top of the game/ not gonna stop pumpin' rock Coke Cain/ and to any paper haters they can catch a shot to the brain/ young boy, lil ahk it's a shame/ but fuck it on my block it's all the same/ hip hop just a part of the game/ lil something on the side hustle/ not my main aim until I chill beside Russell/ my focus is to maintain/ still lemme explain/ I sell dope just to cope with the pain/ plus I flip that raw Coke Cain/ what cha need some weed? You know I got it/ flowin' straight to my pocket/ I stack up my profit/ the track get smacked up with hot shit/ I spit actual facts over beats/ just so we can eat in the streets/ me and my peeps never caught asleep with the heat/ rain, hail, snow, or sleet, ain't shit sweet! What!

DEX: Yeah! ain't shit sweet this ain't candy land/ I spit darts from the heart so you can understand me man/ I be bombin' all day that's the plan at hand/ you can always catch me with a can in hand/ except for the jakes, but this man never ran/ I don't hesitate to escape without fear/ I mastered the art of how to disappear/ ain't it clear I'm so sick wit' it/ plus I'm slick witted/ I'm a pro that know how to talk shit/ that's why I always get acquitted/ in court with a du-rag and a fitted/ you fags bullshitted/ you gonna get me pissed, you don't wanna see me vexed/ so I'm a give it to Chris you see he's next/ peace I'm a leave you my name it's the D to the E to the X

CHRIS: Aight well I guess I'm next to flex/ I grab the mike from Dex/ and ya know I'm red ta blast it like techs/ that's automatic I collect welfare checks/

from crack addicts some say it's a bad habit/ but I'm no fuckin' jack rabbit/ runnin' in a wheel, matter a fact/ I'm runnin' with steel/ cuz the way I feel is I need to make a meal/ and none of us got a deal/ so we just deal with the real/ fools get buried cuz we carry chrome/ of the top of the dome/ rockin' the microphone/ clockin' on the block till I might go home/ y'all fake motherfuckas is soft like foam/ the type that like soft serve in a cone/ y'all can all get served/ cuz ya getting on my Goddamn nerves/ word fuckin' herbs don't even deserve these superb words/ it's absurd I smoke herb get high and serve nerds/ you couldn't describe my actions with a thousand verbs/ aww shit go ahead Jay/ take it away what you got ta say/ before I rhyme all day

JAY: Yo, yo, I got flow, like a river/ I be making hoes knees quiver/ they be begging me please deliver/ like I'm UPS or FedEx/ we share bitches like he gets head next/ in this biz you can exchange brain for cooked up cain/ it's a shame but fuck it don't hate the player hate the game/ I ain't make the rules/ I just grew up to drop jewelz/ and ya know we all got tools/ that we ain't afraid to use/ my team will squeeze for the cheese/ nigga please/ I don't like to just dream about getting cream/ so I organize brothers like Kareem/ Jay's short for Jason, nahemsayin'/ like Jah's short for Jaheem, yanahmean/ and ever since my rodey brody copped the triple beam/ it's been all good in the hood/ I do the knowledge till it's overstood/ and never trust a digital/ I'm a criminal individual/ from the ghetto where it's dismal/ so my goal is putting digits on the left of the decimal/ point, ya get the point I stays on point/ even if I blaze a joint/ or a real big phat el/ to escape the fact/ that this ain't on tape is whack/ and even though we all rap well, we still trapped in hell/ fuck heaven

JAH: Yeah aight fuck heaven/ that's why we keep the spot open twenty-four seven/ just like a fuckin' Seven Eleven/ me and my faculty/ eliminate any muthafucka coming after me/ we shut you down and make you leave town like a factory/ that's exactly how it goes down actually/ so don't come back to Philly/ unless you want to get smacked silly/ with my all black automatic mack-millie/ this ain't the fuckin' Beverly Hillbillys/ all my real ones still feel me/ chill wit' me, still wit' me, still filthy/ come ride and rob and steal wit' me/ but never from me, unless you a dummy/ try and chump me, and I take half your head off like gumby/ ain't shit funny, nothing move but the money

DEX: Nothing move but the money/ from Monday, to Sunday/ and hopefully one day/ we can all be chilling without the gun play/ I know that some say I'm crazy/ cuz I think that way but maybe/ I been catchin' visions

lately/ precision decisions make me/ not a hater so don't hate me/ looking for some sing of hope/ I seen queens turn to fiends get in line for
dope/ but nope, I don't see no light at the end of the tunnel/ I only feel
aight at the end of a bundle/ it makes me wonder if somebody tryin' to
take me under/ the fuck type of life is this/ got me hype as shit

JAY: The fuck type of life is this/ let me get some rice and fish/ who the fuck
is nice as this/ maybe I can help bring to life your wish/ if you can assist
with the dish/ then I can dish an assist/ I know why these conditions exist
it's cuz the rich is too rich/ I don't miss, every shot is a swish/ I think you
get the gist, with just a flick of my wrist/ they be getting pissed/ I'm on
point pushing snow like Eric/ I got the best flow in America/ all the bitches
go hysterical/ I got 'em in foul trouble, plus I got myself a triple double/
back to the block where the rock is how I bubble/ like a goose down jacket,
I got the illest tactics/ that's where I hide the gun/ I'm the live-ist one/
like Allen muthafuckin' Iverson!

*(They all celebrate the cipher, and give each other props, this part can be ad-
libbed.)*

JAY: Ay yo, y'all see that game last night? A.I. was killin' em!!! What did he
drop like thirty-five? Forty points? He was on fire.

JAH: I know, I'm tryin' to go see them play the Wizards before Allen or Mike
gets hurt again. You know Jordan said he's gonna retire for real this time.

JAY: We should all get tickets together, I don't care who they play, I'll go see
them any night.

CHRIS: I gonna save up for something like that. Y'all be flossin'.

DEX: I know man, I thought I was finally gonna be able to cop some new Tims
for the winter time, I was planning on going shopping on Friday, I need
all types of gear, man, it's starting to get cold out here. Then my grandma
called me up, and you know she don't like asking for shit, so when she
do ask for something you know she really needs it. I go over her crib to
see what she needed, man, she cleaned me out! She had two shut off
notices about the electricity, and one for the phone. I dropped like $350
just on paying her late bills. It's all good though, of course I'm gonna help
her out — I mean, how's that gonna look, me out here rocking fresh gear
and new Tims, and I got grandma sitting at home in the dark with no
lights and no phone. I just gotta start saving up all over again that's all.

CHRIS: Damn, Dex, that's fucked up, I feel you though, I been struggling
myself. Plus Christmas is right around the corner, too. It's getting ugly.

JAY: I know last week was bad, we should be making like twice what we're making right now. I don't even know what's wrong, but we'll fix it.

JAH: Yeah I'm tryin' to find out, too.

(Enter Social Worker, Ms. Roberts.)

MS. ROBERTS: Chris hey Chris. Can I talk to you for a minute?

(Aside downstage.)

CHRIS: What the fuck are you doin' here?

MS. ROBERTS: I was on my way to your school to look for you, but here you are. I've been trying to contact your mother but I can't catch her at all. Where's your mom been?

CHRIS: Why do you keep botherin' her? She's working two jobs and she's sleeping. Let her rest.

MS. ROBERTS: But I was just at your house, and no one was home.

CHRIS: She's sleepin', she ain't gonna answer the door. And what are you going to do about our Access Card? We got cut off.

MS. ROBERTS: I know. And I can't get you cut back on until I talk to your mother.

CHRIS: That's going to be hard to do. She's doing telemarketing in the day, and working at the diner at night.

MS. ROBERTS: I've been to King Of Prussia. She isn't telemarketing. And I went to the diner and they say they haven't seen her in three days. Chris, you need to help me on this.

CHRIS: Bullshit. All I know is I put her on the bus every day.

MS. ROBERTS: Look Chris, I'm not the enemy here. I didn't take away your Access Card. I've been here from the beginning on you and your mother's side. All I need from you is a little help.

CHRIS: All I'm doing is helping.

DEX: Yo Chris, man, we got work to do.

(Chris turns to leave. Ms. Roberts grabs Chris by the arm.)

MS. ROBERTS: I know exactly what you're doing out here, Chris. You think you're helping her by working on the corner? You and your mom need help. I don't understand why you won't just let me do my job? She cares about you, and I know you care about her. So what's your problem with me helping you? I don't get it.

(Chris pulls away from Ms. Robert's grip.)

MS. ROBERTS: I'm not going to give up on you.

(Ms. Roberts exits.)

DEX: Chris?

CHRIS: What?

DEX: I'm not going to give up on you either.

(Dex reaches out to hug Chris.)

CHRIS: Get off me, man, stop playing.

(Enter Smokey. He hesitates, then tries to slip by unnoticed.)

JAH: Ah-hah look at you, Smokey, where you been at?

SMOKEY: Oh I been chillin'.

JAH: Nice shirt. Is that a curtain? What's up man, you coppin' or what?

SMOKEY: Naw I'm chillin'.

JAH: No? You don't need nothin'?

SMOKEY: No, I'm cool, Jah, for right now.

JAH: Smokey, why am I losing dough out here?

SMOKEY: What you talking about, Jah?

JAH: Don't play that dumb shit with me Smokey, I know you got your sources. I know you keep an ear to the street and an eye on the block.

SMOKEY: Oh not really.

JAH: I bet one rock you know why I'm losing dough and I'll bet another rock you know who else is getting that dough that I ain't getting.

SMOKEY: Uh uh — well there is this new spot on B Street.

JAH: B Street! Who is it!?!

SMOKEY: I don't know 'em but they look like them young boys from 8th Street.

JAH: 8th Street!!! Damn Smokey when they open up?

SMOKEY: I'm not sure Jah but I seen 'em since last week.

JAH: What they got out over there?

SMOKEY: Just ready rock and some weed for now but they said they gonna have H soon.

JAH: Anything else you think I should know?

SMOKEY: Well, um, the young boy had a nine. That's really all I know really.

JAH: Aight. Take this and get the fuck outta here.

SMOKEY: You said you was gonna give me two rocks?

JAH: I never said I was gonna give you shit. Take the one and get the fuck outta here before I take that one back. Lil punk ass bitch. Move, man, go!
(Smokey exits quickly. Jay has been listening in on them but the corner is busy right now, the rest of them are oblivious to what Jah has just learned.)

JAY: Ay what he say?

JAH: He said them young boys from 8th Street opened up shop on B Street and they pushin' rock and weed and they got plans to push H too and they strapped.

JAY: Aw fuck that shit, I'm a go ride past 'em right now.

JAH: Aight but don't do nothing till we plan something, man, we need strategy.

JAY: I know, Jah, I just wanna see if I recognize anyone. Yo Chris hold the rest of this bundle.

(Chris takes the rest of the bundle. Jay exits.)

DEX: I know a bunch of writers from 8th Street. I know some of 'em hustle a lil something but nothing big, no dope. Mostly just weed or wet maybe some pills or some shit.

CHRIS: That's dirty. I thought everybody knew this is where we eat at.

JAH: That's the thing about it, Chris, everyone does know that this is our shit all right around here. But you gotta expect heads to test you sometimes. The hard part is you gotta always stand true to your rep if you wanna keep what you got. But we're organized, we got leaders and systems and schedules and plans, don't worry about it. That's the difference between us and the rest— we got experience out here, ain't nothing new to us, it's using our experience as knowledge that separates us from the rest. That's why we're organized. That's why we're survivors.

CHRIS: So what are we gonna do Jah?

JAH: We're gonna wait. We ain't doin' shit till I say so, and me and Jay size 'em up, see exactly what we dealing with. But y'all can't talk to nobody outside of our circle, ya heard me Dex? You can listen but don't talk. Matter-a-fact please listen see if they are your graffiti peoples, or if not, they might know 'em. Keep your eyes and ears open but as far as any outsider is concerned we ain't got no problems. Everything is lovely, business as usual.

DEX: Aight I feel you Jah. I guess I could go by 8th Street later after this shift I'm supposed to go on a paint mission on Saturday with one of them anyway.

CHRIS: Where are you getting your paint from now anyway?

DEX: Cherry Hill. No cages and no cameras.

JAH: I hope you got a plan for if you get locked up in Jersey, 'cause don't call me. Especially if you get locked up for stealing paint or writing on walls. And don't call Jay either, we ain't got time for that little dumb shit.

DEX: Don't worry about me Jah, I got mad game, I can talk myself out of almost anything. Plus I'm not eighteen yet so I can get locked up as much as I want as long as it's all misdemeanors.

CHRIS: He's got a point.

(Jay returns.)

JAH: What's the science Jason?

JAY: All new faces to me, I ain't know none of them, I copped two nicks though, twist one.

(Jay tosses one bag and a cigar to Dex. He holds the other bag up and smells it then passes it off to Jah who also inspects it.)

JAY: We got a lot more problems that Smokey failed to mention. First of all, the H is already out there.

JAH: How many they got working over there.

JAY: At least two lookouts and about three kids on shift, but it could have been more, they're really busy over there. I mean they just pumping work out fast one kid servin' weed, one servin' rock, and one servin' the dope. They had cars pulling up down the block, coppin' right out of they window like fuckin' McDonald's drive-through. I didn't really think they were big-time like that, they killing shit over there.

CHRIS: So you didn't recognize anyone?

JAY: Naw, not at all, but I ain't really expect to, what fucks me up is none of them recognized me. I figured coming all the way across from 8th Street that somebody would be from around here or would have at least come around to scope out competition before opening up shop in someone else's hood. You know what I'm sayin'?

DEX: I don't think this weed is any better than our weed.

JAY: It's not any better because it's not any different from ours. It's the same weed, they got the same source.

JAH: Oh they're done, they're finished. It's over.

JAY: So what you wanna do to 'em, Jah, 'cause I can tell you what I wanna do to 'em.

JAH: Yeah you right, I'm a have to holla at the boy 'bout them thangs though.

DEX: Aight the el is ready. I'm not smoking though cuz I'm painting tonight, so who wansta spark it?
(Chris takes it from Dex.)

CHRIS: Lemme see that lighter too.
(Troy and Brody enter.)

TROY: Hold up Chris, don't light that shit around me I gotta take a pee-pee test!

CHRIS: Oh shit, nuh-uh! When did you get out?

TROY: I'm here now that's all I know.

JAH: What's the drills baby boy!!!

TROY: Just livin' ya know! I'm free and I'm hungry.

DEX: Damn Man it's good to see you! You got a lil big, you were working out inside?

TROY: Ain't much better to do. I was lifting every other day.

DEX: They got you doing some type of job program like job training, or place-ment, or some type shit like that?

TROY: I think they gonna try that shit on me I don't really know yet I gotta meet with my P.O. on Wednesday. But I'm not feelin' them, they not relatin' to my needs. I gotta feed my daughter. How's the spot doing?

JAH: It's been good while you was gone, we blew up a lil somethin', started getting the weed in bulk for half what we used to pay, we got rocks up now too. So we been bubblin'.

TROY: Damn, that's bangin'. So what's up with a shift? Let a brother live.

JAH: Yeah I could probably fit you in somewhere, but shit ain't real sweet right now. We got a minor setback we gotta handle first.

JAY: *(To Jah.)* You go ride around there and call what you see minor.

JAH: Damn Jay, I was just politickin' wit' the boy a setback is a setback. Small problems need small solutions and we need a big solution. But I ain't wor-ried about it it ain't nothing we haven't dealt with already. It's all apart of the game.

TROY: So what's the setback?

CHRIS: This squad of young boys is tryin' to hurt our pockets. Right around the corner on B Street.

JAY: What you mean tryin' — Chris, my pockets took a ass-whoopin' last week. Brody, what were the numbers?

BRODY: I don't remember the numbers but it was a drop of about like 40 per-cent of the monthly average.

TROY: How you know that shit Brody?

BRODY: I do the books now. I been doin' em.

JAY: He's not bad at it either.

TROY: So what y'all gonna do?

JAH: I'm gonna go holla at Kareem see if he wanna ride for us. If it's all good you can work the morning shift for him with Brody.

TROY: Aight that's peace.

(Jah begins to exit.)

JAY: Holla at the boy 'bout them heaters too.

CHRIS: I'm ridin' too if you need me Jay, I don't give a fuck.

JAY: Hell yeah we need you Chris, what about you Dex? You gonna ride for us?

DEX: *(Hesitates.)* Yeah. It's whatever.

(Dex takes the blunt back from Chris, lights the lighter. Lights out to black. Actors freeze. Dex holds the lighter for three seconds in the dark, then break. Scene.)

SCENE THREE

It's nighttime. Dex, Chris and Kareem are holding down the spot.

KAREEM: Naw Man you crazy. It ain't gonna happen. I think you right about what you said about private property but the rest of that shit just ain't never gonna happen.

DEX: You'll see, watch.

CHRIS: I can't believe y'all are still arguing about that shit.

DEX: Graffiti is gonna change the world. I'm doing another piece tonight. One by one till I got every roof on the EL line, the North Philly ones first, then the West Philly ones, too. Then after I king all the EL roofs I'm gonna hit the tunnels, then the Broad Street line too. I'm not gonna stop. I can't be stopped. Even if they ban the spray cans, I'll do it with roller paint. Tonight I'm going to hit Berks, and the York Dauphin stops.

KAREEM: You can't do that tonight.

DEX: Why not?

KAREEM: Cause you supposed to be at me and Jay crib at five o'clock A.M. Remember? The problem-solving team? Unless you weren't coming?

CHRIS: Oh yeah, he's right, you can't paint tonight Dex.

DEX: Aww fuck. That's right. I forgot that's all. I'm a be there. *(Pause.)* But I'm still gonna do that shit. That's my next mission. Watch.
(Enter Natashia and Marisol.)

CHRIS: Hey what's up.

NATASHIA: Hey what's up y'all.

MARISOL: Yo she just made the hottest single!

DEX: Word?

MARISOL: Yeah, she actually just did three tracks, but

NATASHIA: But the one is the one! I know exactly which one they gonna want for the radio, so I'm gonna release that one first. It's definitely a banger.

KAREEM: Naw naw, don't do it like that you gotta save the really hot shit for the album. Don't you hate it when you buy a record 'cause the single was banging but the rest of the jawn is a disappointment? Trust me.

CHRIS: Man don't listen to him, what the fuck does he know.

MARISOL: *(To Dex.)* Hey let me get two more bags of that weed. *(To Natashia.)* Then we even from earlier. That shit was pretty good y'all, I ain't smoked in a while anyway so it had me on my jawn.
(Dex gives her the weed. The girls start to roll a blunt and the boys also start to roll one of their own. They may ad-lib. Natashia rolls one and Kareem rolls the other one.)

CHRIS: You need a Phillie?

KAREEM: Naw I'm good.

DEX: What's that, a Dutch?

KAREEM: Naw. It's a Garcia Vega.

(Enter Raul Rodriguez.)

RAUL: Marisol!!!

(They all scramble to hide the blunts. Marisol goes downstage to him.)

RAUL: *(In Spanish.)* What the fuck are you doing here? Don't you know what this corner is? A respectable young woman like yourself doesn't belong anywhere near these people. This is a fucking drug corner!

MARISOL: *(In Spanish.)* Yeah I know where I am, I've been around these drug corners my whole life, just like you. What's your problem? We're just talking. These people are friends.

RAUL: *(In Spanish.)* These people are not your friends, they don't even respect each other, they don't even respect themselves. You are above them, you're too good for them. You don't want friends that are criminals.

MARISOL: *(Now in English.)* Look motherfucka, you ain't my father and who do you think you are telling me what to do and who I can and can't be cool with?

RAUL: *(In English.)* I'm just warning you, watch your back if you wanna hang out with a bunch of dirty thugs. And don't you have a job and a kid to be taking care of? It's one o'clock in the morning and you hanging out on the corner with teenagers.

MARISOL: Yeah I got a really fucking good job, and I never go out, my mom is with my son and I have earned the right to go out once and a while, it's my reward. This is the first time I've done anything fun at all in over a month, but the point is that it ain't none of your damn business in the first place! Comprende?

RAUL: I know I'm not your father and I'm not trying to be, but my family has always been tight with your family and it's my responsibility to watch out for you. I saw your brother go down the same path and look where he is now, there's only two futures for them, death and jail, and that shit is not a joke.

MARISOL: You've got some nerve, you are way out of line. Ever since you joined the force you've changed These are regular people that we all grew up with. I don't need to defend myself to you, I've already proved myself. I'm a grown woman, I know who I am, you're the one with the identity issues.

RAUL: It's for your own good. I don't care what you think, I don't want to see you on this corner again, it's not safe for you to be here. I know I'm not your father but I am an officer of the law, and you look high.

MARISOL: *(In Spanish.)* I already told you to mind your fuckin' business, leave me alone, Raul! If they are dirty thug criminals why don't you do something about it, almighty officer of the law!?! Get out of here.

RAUL: *(In Spanish.)* You better watch it girl, if I see you out here with them again I will do something about it. And your mother will hear about it too.
(Raul Rodriguez storms offstage.)

MARISOL: I can't believe him. What an asshole.

NATASHIA: What was he saying to you?

MARISOL: Nothing, don't even worry about it. Just go ahead and spark that el.

KAREEM: Fuck that dude, I can't stand him either.

CHRIS: I know, he thinks he's super cop or some shit.

MARISOL: He's so funny, when he ran out of shit to say, he said he was gonna tell my mom, then he ran away! Like a little boy.
(They all laugh.)

NATASHIA: Oh shit, that's funny. You wanna come back to my crib for a minute?

MARISOL: Yeah I guess so.

CHRIS: Oh I see, y'all ain't tryin' to chill wit' us?

NATASHIA: Come on now Chris, I'm tired, and all I wanna do is go to my own end, smoke my own blunt, listen to what I just did then pass out. Besides, it's getting fuckin' cold out here.

MARISOL: Ain't that the truth, it's brick out here. I'm feelin' you girl, that sounds like a plan to me. Let's roll.

NATASHIA: Bye, guys. Catch you next time. Bye, Chris.

CHRIS: Peace, Tash.
(Natashia and Marisol exit.)

DEX: NO GAME!!! Ha ha y'all got no game at all, nice try, Chris. Oh, y'all ain't tryin' to chill wit' us? The fuck was that? I had to bite my tongue not to step in there.

KAREEM: Hey I got game, my game is tight, but I ain't want to step on your toes, Chris, and my brother is rappin' to Marisol, so I was just chillin'.

CHRIS: Man, fuck y'all. I got game. Y'all bullshittin', acting like you the fuckin' mack. Y'all ain't got no game.

DEX: Dawg, I'm sorry, but they were tryin' to chill, until you fucked it up. Well you ain't really fuck it up that bad, but you didn't hook it up either.

CHRIS: They left cause it's fuckin' cold out here, man. Damn.

DEX: Aight, but you coulda tried to get 'em back to your crib, or you coulda tried to go to her crib and chill. Oh, I wanna hear your new songs, too,

Man it's like a thousand other things you could of done. It's not what you say it's how you say it. And no more free advice from Dr. Dex, from now on it'll cost ya.

KAREEM: He's learning, man. I think she does like you though. You'll get 'em next time, champ.

CHRIS: Man, fuck y'all I don't need no help. I get mad pussy, y'all don't get no pussy. I'm doing something different this time cause I think she might be a keeper.

DEX: Well, I wanted to speak up and help you out, but I was afraid she might fall for me, it happens all the time. But if you don't make a move in a week I'm not going to be so kind, she is too cute. If you sleep I'll creep.

KAREEM: Oh shit a challenge.

DEX: Naw, it's just a little extra motivation, Chris. I believe in you.

CHRIS: Aight whatever, we'll see.

KAREEM: My brother could probably run through both them chicks before you even get started. He's the real player. Nobody got game like him.

DEX: Aww stop jocking him. He ain't all that.

CHRIS: Yo Reem what's up with that blunt?

KAREEM: Oh shit, my bad. You smoking, Dex?

DEX: Am I painting tonight?

KAREEM: No.

DEX: Well then I'm smoking. You know my rules.

CHRIS: Lemme get that Reem. It's from my bundle, I get to spark it.

KAREEM: But I rolled it

CHRIS: Don't matter, I bought it I light it.

DEX: You gotta respect a man with rules. Give him his blunt.

KAREEM: Aight here. But I rolled it

CHRIS: Thank you, sir.

(End of scene, the lights fade and transition music comes over as they start to light the blunt.)

SCENE FOUR

Brody and Troy are working and playing spelling bee, it's around ten in the morning the next day. Lights fade up.

TROY: Spell . . . spell, *universe.*

BRODY: Um, *universe.* U-N-I-V-E-R-S-E. *Universe.*

TROY: Spell *distribution.*

BRODY: *Distribution.* D-I-S-T-R-A-B-U-T-I-O-N. *Distrabution.*

TROY: Naw. there's no *a* in *distribution,* it's D-I-S-T-R-I-B-U-T-I-O-N.

BRODY: Oh OK, I was close. What's the next one.

TROY: Can you spell, *felony?*

BRODY: *Felony,* T-R-O-Y-*(Laughs.)* sike-naw.

TROY: Naw, go head, spell *felony.*

BRODY: Uh, *felony.* F-E-L-O-N-Y. *Felony?*

TROY: Spell *problems.*

BRODY: *Problems.* P-R-O-B-L-U-M-S. *Problems.*

TROY: Naw its L-E-M, not L-U-M. Spell *narcotics.*

BRODY: *Narcotics.* N-A-R-C-O-T-I-C-S. *Narcotics.*

> *(Enter Customer, gives money, gets crack. Exits.)*

BRODY: Did you get into any beef in there? Did ya have to fight anyone?

TROY: Well, yeah . . . my second day, some knucklehead was grittin' on me, so I just rushed him, I started fucking him up. By the time I was done, everyone else had jumped in and was fuckin' him up, too. I guess no one liked him anyway. I got my props from the gate and I didn't have to fight after that. I seen some ill shit, though. Like this one dude, just shanked his cell mate in the eye, and popped out his eyeball, then left his other eye in, so he could watch him play with it, in the same cell sitting across from him. I seen crazy shit for real. I been in there twice, and I ain't never going back. It's hell. You know how we say this is hell on earth bein' here? Being here on the block or just growing up in the hood, struggling and suffering? Yeah, it's hellish, but prison is actually hell. Like you meet the Devil up in there. That pain never goes away, the whole time, till you walk out here again. Makes this shit not seem so bad. At least you can think for yourself out here, choose when to go in or out, eat your own shit not they shit, you know what I'm saying.

BRODY: Yeah, I feel you, but ain't nothin' promised out here. You can go in and out when you want, only if you got money to keep a crib. And you can eat what you want, only if you got money for food. I guess you end up risking the one freedom for the other freedom. If you gotta do illegal shit to eat food and pay rent, but you get caught and lose it all just tryin' to live in the first place.

TROY: That's true . . . I guess I learned how to not get caught more than anything else I learned inside. I didn't really think about it till now. I read mad books and tried that study shit but on the real the only things that I learned that matters that I consider valuable or useful in the real world was all the old heads that schooled me to the game. Learning something from everyone's story. Old heads be droppin' jewels on me. They put me Dee with how to not get caught again, skills that actually apply to my life and yours too. I'm gonna teach you some lil tricks so you won't have to go through what I went through to figure out the same shit.

(Chris and Kareem enter fast. They have big black bags they are trying to hide.)

TROY: What the fuck happened? What did y'all do?

KAREEM: We just took them motherfuckas out!!!

CHRIS: We got mad shit we took everything!

KAREEM: We got all types of money, bricks of coke, crack bundles, heroin, weed, guns

TROY: Yo, shut the fuck up man, what is you stupid stop advertisin'!!! You can go turn yourself in if you want, but I'm still on parole!

BRODY: Where's everyone else?

CHRIS: They comin' now we're supposed to meet them here.

KAREEM: Yo that shit was crazy dawg.

(Dex and Jay enter also carrying big black bags.)

DEX: Damn, Kareem what the fuck was that shit all about? I didn't know you was gonna start blastin' on 'em, you definitely didn't have to, we had 'em shook already

KAREEM: What the fuck's your problem? Dex why you bitchin' for?!

DEX: You didn't have to blast on 'em!!!

JAY: He did the right thing. Don't worry about it. It's over, shit happens all the time.

BRODY: What the fuck happened?!!

CHRIS: We ran up in they spot, took all they shit, Kareem told the boy don't move, he moved.

KAREEM: It's that simple, I banged him in his chest piece. That shit felt ill.

CHRIS: Then after Kareem shot the one boy, they all tried to break out, Jay banged on one of 'em too. I think after Kareem saw Jay blastin' he said fuck it and unloaded on all of 'em. That shit was a bloody mess, I think there was five of 'em.

DEX: Yeah it was five of 'em. Y'all killed all of 'em.

JAY: Brody help me organize all this weight, I wanna flip it as soon as possible.

BRODY: Aight here I come.

(Jay has opened the secret door and has collected all the new mystery bags.)
(Brody and Jay go inside.)

KAREEM: I feel like I'm the shit right now. I feel invincible.

TROY: You better calm down super man. Just as easy as it was for you to do what you just did, anybody could do that to you to all of us.

DEX: All I'm sayin' is you didn't need to, man, it was totally unnecessary.

KAREEM: Why the fuck not! Fuck them, I don't know them, they tryin' to get dough on our block, we own this strip, we run this shit! Fuck 'em. That shit felt good too.

DEX: Yeah, well, maybe I did know them, aight.

KAREEM: Aw you's a lil bitch, man, stop girlin'.

DEX: Man fuck you I ain't a bitch just cause I ain't a murderer. I don't need to hide behind triggers and bullets. I fight with my hands!

KAREEM: So what you sayin', motherfucka swing

(Dex takes a swing at Kareem, they fight. Troy breaks it up.)

TROY: Aight I'm done with your bullshit, you makin' the corner hot, man, you drawlin'.

Aight now, both of you calm the fuck down, and tell me what happened.

CHRIS: Well, Jay took us to some house on Second Street, we waited in the car Jason went in first he left the beeper in the car and told us to come running in when the beeper goes off.

KAREEM: The beeper goes off, and we rush the spot, it's all five of them in one room and Jay is blocking the back exit, we got the front.

CHRIS: It all happened so fast after that, we were trying to get them on the floor I think Jay wanted to tie 'em up but one dude kept creeping away toward the shelves and that's when Kareem started banging on 'em heavy first he just shot the one boy, then he just kept squeezing on all of them.

KAREEM: He was going for a gun, I saw it. What was I supposed to do? Huh? Let him get his gun? Naw Man fuck that shit, it was us — or them —. I did the right thing for all you know, I could of just saved your life man, and I'm supposed to feel bad about that? Fuck that.

TROY: So then what?

CHRIS: We started bagging up all they shit, we didn't stick around we cleaned 'em out and left real quick. Jay stayed behind a little longer I guess to make sure we didn't leave no evidence.

TROY: Y'all just left the bodies? Oh this is ugly and it's gonna get worse. I thought someone had some sort of master plan? That don't sound like best way to do it but fuck it now, what's done is done.

(Dex has been getting light-headed, he has been standing then sitting then standing then sitting and holding his head, this escalates to him passing out when he tries to stand one more time, the others catch him and try to hold him up or sit him down, then he wakes up enough to throw up.)

DEX: Oouwwhhla. *(Vomits.)*

END OF ACT I

ACT II

SCENE ONE

Quiet morning, very early, the streets are deserted. Enter Smokey, he looks around, paces a little. Then settles down to wait for the sellers.

SMOKEY: They call me Smokey, but I have a real name, it's Spencer. Yep Spencer Hamilton. That's me, or who I was rather. Now I'm just Smokey. That name used to mean something. Mr. Hamilton. I had whole classrooms full of bright and beautiful little children. Every day they would be excited to learn what Mr. Hamilton had to teach, and I would be excited to teach it to them. My father was a factory worker. He dedicated thirty-seven years of hard work to a company that shut down all production, closed the plant and relocated to some more cost-effective location. Probably Mexico or Indonesia, they never told us. I have fond memories of growing up in this neighborhood. I liked it. I watched it all change every step of the way. My father's plant wasn't the only one that did this, one by one they all closed. They used to have a saying that you could walk down American street and find a job in five minutes. *(Chuckles sadly.)* The factories are still there, they're just empty now. People like me use them for shelter. Last night I went into the same building that my father used to work at. I remembered the first time seeing the place from the inside. I was about nine years old when Dad gave me the grand tour of where Daddy worked. Most of the equipment was still there. I slept in the top boss man's old office, I wonder if he lost his job too, or if he got a promotion. They never told us. Mom couldn't earn very much with her limited skills, but she tried real hard. I told my pop to take the money that he was saving for my college funds and use it for the family. I told him that it was OK, and that I would just work extra hard through high school to make sure that I could get all the best scholarships. I was still gonna go to college no matter what, and eventually, I did. At first Pop didn't want to use the savings for the family, but as hard times got harder, and with little to no income, it became easier for him to see it my way. I was always studying. I kept my grades up. Dad was finding little odd jobs here and there, mostly physical labor, moving stuff. A few days of work here and there. Mom had an agency that sent her to faraway suburbs to clean big fancy houses. It was very sporadic and no fun at all, she hated it, but it was still better than nothing. I graduated with honors and moved out to State College. That's when Pop started drinking, well, really drinking, heavy. I had no idea. When I was away they pretended like everything was alright. Whenever I called, or came to visit it was all an act. Four years later, I've got my degree, and landed my teaching job. You can imagine my surprise to find out that they had gone completely broke and lost the house also. Mom left without saying good-bye. I had gotten the job! I was ready to give back now! Why did you wait so long just to give up at the finish line, MOM! We couldn't find her, she was gone. I wonder how many divorces are economic? I helped my father get back on his feet with an apartment. About six weeks later he disappeared. They found him dead in his car, wrecked, probably driving home from the bar. So all I had left at this point was a wonderful group of amazing children from eight o'clock in the morning to three o'clock in the afternoon. Mondays through Fridays. And health benefits. I got around to reading over my insurance packets and found out that I was covered for mental health. So I went to see a shrink. I don't know if it helped, I guess it was nice to talk to someone. He put me on some antidepressants. I told him that they made me feel funny, and weren't really working. So he took me off of them, and gave me some type of painkillers instead. Don't ask me why, I was in emotional pain not physical pain. Anyway I got hooked on the painkillers, then I ran out of refills. He said that I was never supposed to be on them in the first place, and that it was a mistake. So he wouldn't write me any more new ones, but that was what I wanted. After a few days of withdrawal it didn't take much to justify acquiring them through outside sources. On the street market I found even better painkillers, the best and strongest ones there are. That went on for months, still teaching. I would take them before work and become Mr. Happy-Mr. Hamilton, and on days I was out, or couldn't score, I was Mr. Mean-Mr. Hamilton. Then there was some sort of a drought or a crackdown or shortage and I couldn't get them. My usual dealer suggested in a joke you need to chill out, guy, smoke a joint or something weed is the natural painkiller I had tried it a few times in college, but it wasn't really my thing. I took his advice anyway and found a new escape. Then when the pills came back out on the street, I was now doing both popping the pills and smoking weed at the same time. I was running from something, running from life. I'm still running. One day I was smoking with some guys I had met on the streets, they didn't tell me but they had laced the weed with coke or crack, at first it made me sick, then soon I started to like it like that. Now I don't care about anything other than crack and coke in any form I can get it.

(It is five o'clock in the morning. Two Detectives enter drinking coffee. Smokey starts to move off but the Detectives call Smokey over.)

CIRILLI (OLD DETECTIVE): Hey you. *(Pause.)* Come here.

SMOKEY: *(Looks around.)* Who me?

CIRILLI: Who the fuck you think we're talking to.

SMOKEY: Who me?

CIRILLI: Get the fuck over here.

GRABANSKI (YOUNG DETECTIVE): I'm Detective Grabanski and this is Cirilli. *(Flashes his badge.)* We have a few questions we wanted to ask you.

SMOKEY: I ain't do nothing.

GRABANSKI: I didn't say you did anything. I just want to ask a few questions.

SMOKEY: About what?

CIRILLI: You know the drill — We ask the fucking questions you give the answers. *(Cirilli gives Grabanski a look.)* So, what are you doing out here this time of morning.

SMOKEY: I ain't doing nothing.

GRABANSKI: Yeah it looks like you've been doing a lot of nothing for a long time. What the hell are you doing sitting on this corner at five o'clock in the morning?

SMOKEY: Nothing. I got no place to —

GRABANSKI: Where do you live? Around here? You got any identification? Huh? No I.D.?

SMOKEY: Yeah, I'm from around here —

GRABANSKI: Around here where? You got proof of residence?

SMOKEY: Um no, um I'm homeless —

CIRILLI: You mean you're a bum? He's a bum kid. Let's get to the point.

GRABANSKI: Last night we had five young men murdered just a few blocks from here, what do you know?

(Smokey in shock doesn't say anything. Cirilli notices this.)

CIRILLI: What do ya know?

SMOKEY: *(Very quickly.)* Nothing.

CIRILLI: You're lying. We're going to send you ass away for acting on concert. That's twenty-five to life for each murder.

SMOKEY: On what grounds?

CIRILLI: Fuck the grounds. You know someone is going to help themselves out by giving you up. Do you think your words will hold up in court. Fucking junkie. It's five fucking o'clock in the morning and this guy is looking free bee. Bullshit. *(Grips Smokey.)* I'm tired and five fucking kids were killed last night on my watch and I'm going to get to the bottom of this shit, tell us what you know or you'll go down, it's simple. Help yourself out.

SMOKEY: I don't know much.

GRABANSKI: What do you know?

SMOKEY: I know people hustle here.

CIRILLI: What good are you? Give us a fucking name.

SMOKEY: I don't know nobody.

GRABANSKI: You know somebody. Give us a name.

SMOKEY: Jay. Jay!

GRABANSKI: Jay what? Jay who? What's his last name?

SMOKEY: I don't know.

CIRILLI: That's smart. Come on let's go. *(Starts to cuff Smokey.)*

GRABANSKI: Frank what are you doing. *(Pause.)* Frank.

SMOKEY: Smith! Smith!

CIRILLI: OK, Jay Smith now that'll work. I'm done with you, get the fuck out of my sight. *(Takes cuffs off and pushes Smokey away. Smokey exits.)* Don't you fuckin' undermine me when I'm dealing with a mope.

GRABANSKI: I just got this shield and I'm not gonna let you blow this for me!

CIRILLI: You don't learn. You ain't keeping that shield if you don't find out who put those bodies in that house.

GRABANSKI: Look, I really wanna get these fuckin' guys, and I want it to stick. This shit's gotta hold up in court, what's the point if it doesn't hold up in court?

CIRILLI: What? This is the way it gets done. I've been doing this fifteen years and it always holds up in court.

GRABANSKI: Frank, this is big, we need to do this right. We do a canvass of the neighborhood, we'll get our perps.

CIRILLI: This is the way it gets done. Just stick with me and you'll learn.

(Detectives exit.)

SCENE TWO

At this point customers are coming on stage. There is a light change to indicate that there has been a change in time. Troy, Jah, Chris, and Dex are dealing with the customers. Jane enters and walks over to Dex.

JANE: I need two.

DEX: Aight I got it. Where's your cash.

JANE: *(Takes a deep breath.)* Well I was hoping I could get it on the eye like last time.

DEX: I can't do it. You gotta ask him. *(Indicates Jah.)*

JANE: Why can't you just keep this between me and you. Can't you slide me two on the low?

DEX: My boss is right there. I can't do it. You gotta ask him.

JANE: *(To Jah.)* Dex said I should ask you if I can get two rocks on the eye.

JAH: Bitch what the fuck you think this is. I ain't giving you shit on the eye. Nobody gets credit out here. Yo get the fuck out of here.

(Troy whispers something in Jah's ear. They start laughing.)

JAH: *(Yells.)* Yo Chris come over here. Chris how old are you man.

CHRIS: Seventeen.

TROY: Have you ever had your dick sucked, man?

(Jane starts to get nervous.)

CHRIS: Yeah.

JAH, TROY, AND DEX: Get the fuck out of here.

CHRIS: I did. For real yo. For real.

DEX: Man when? When? You bullshitting.

CHRIS: Your mom.

(Dex doesn't say anything.)

JAH: Make you a deal. You take care of my boy and we'll take care of you.

(Dex pulls out the rock.)

CHRIS: I ain't going to do it here.

TROY: Naw Man you going to take it in the back.

(Jane is hesitant.)

JANE: Naw I don't do that.

TROY: Bitch you wanna get high or what.

JANE: Come on y'all please. You know I'm good for it.

TROY: What the fuck did I say.

(Pause. Jane goes in the room first. Everyone looks at Chris. Chris saunters into the room. Activity is going on and music is playing in the background for like three to four minutes. Door opens. Chris comes out smiling. Everyone is smiling at Chris. Jane's head is down. Dex gives her the two rocks.)

DEX: Yo come here.

(Jane looks up at him. He gives her two more and she leaves. Guys start to ad-lib.)

JAH: How was it?

TROY: Was it good?

DEX: Did she swallow?

CHRIS: Yo man. Get out of here.

    (Smokey enters.)

SMOKEY: Yo, you got that?

JAH: Yeah man, we got that for ya. How many you need?

SMOKEY: Uh, two, no wait three. *(Counts his money.)* How about a early bird special? I'll buy two, you give me three?

JAH: Don't start that shit, Smokey, I ain't in the mood, it's too early today. We make the deals not you, Smoke. Lemme get set up first. *(Under his breath.)* Early bird special motherfucka

SMOKEY: Alright, Jah, I'm sorry. Just two then. I got enough for two.

JAH: Aight here. *(Sells him the two.)* Wait, hold up Smokey, I got something for you.

SMOKEY: Really?

JAH: You ever tried dope?

SMOKEY: What, heroin? No I never tried it.

JAH: Well we havin' a special promotional offer for a limited time only. First two bags of H are free, that's a twenty-dollar value.

SMOKEY: Free!?! Twenty-dollar value!?!

JAH: Yeah man, but you gotta do it yourself, you can't have it if you gonna sell it or trade it for ready rocks. Ya heard?

SMOKEY: OK, yeah, sure, I'll try it.

JAH: Aight Smokey, I'll see you later.

    (Exit Smokey.)

JAH: He's lying through his teeth, I know he gonna get crack for that shit. He ain't gonna try it.

TROY: So why did you give it to him if you know he's lying?

JAH: Because he'll spread the word. Whoever ends up with it is gonna know where it came from and where to go back for more. Smokey's a good talker, he'll advertise for us and he don't even know that's what he's doing, he thinks he's getting over on us! Besides, Smokey's too smart to try that shit and get hooked on something new.

TROY: Oh, shit, that's funny. Damn, Jah, you learned some shit while I was gone.

JAH: Yeah man, it's been a crazy couple of years. But I'm still young in the game. I'm trying to figure this H thing out. It's a whole new world to me.

TROY: Yeah we gonna need to find a steady dope connect for now on. There's a lot of money in heroin man, much more than coke or any of that other shit.

JAH: I know, that's what they tell me.

TROY: I could find some connects for us. I could get weight no problem.

JAH: Word. Jay said he knows people that got it too.

TROY: I don't care where it comes from, we gotta get this money.

JAH: Straight up, fam, I'm tryin' to turn this brown into green right quick.

(Officer Rodriguez enters. Guys are gambling, making noise. Troy notices Rodriguez and vice versa. Troy goes over to Rodriguez.)

TROY: Yo whassup.

(Gives Rodriguez a hug.)

RODRIGUEZ: Whassup Troy.

TROY: Man you looking good. They give y'all some nice uniforms up there. Officer Rodriguez. How you been.

RODRIGUEZ: Been good. How you been Troy. Heard you got out a couple of days ago.

TROY: I been out for about a week.

RODRIGUEZ: So what you been up to.

TROY: Chillin'. Maintaining. Spending time with my daughter Brianna.

RODRIGUEZ: How old is she now?

TROY: She's almost three.

RODRIGUEZ: So you found work yet.

TROY: Aww Man please.

RODRIGUEZ: I'm serious. Troy.

TROY: What the fuck you mean did I find work yet? I just got out of jail, lemme breath a lil damn.

RODRIGUEZ: Fuck y'all looking at!?! Was I talking to y'all? Do I gotta run you all in for gambling on the corner!?! *(Pause.)* That's what I thought.

TROY: Raul what you want.

RODRIGUEZ: I just want to talk.

TROY: We talking now. Brody said you were looking for me.

RODRIGUEZ: I know you ain't out here doing the same shit.

TROY: Why you in my business.

RODRIGUEZ: Because you're out here doing the same shit that got you locked up the first time.

TROY: I don't do that shit no more.

RODRIGUEZ: That's bullshit and you know it.

TROY: Well fuck it. It's bullshit then.

RODRIGUEZ: You need to grow the fuck up. You don't learn do you? You got off easy man, you only did two out of the six years they gave you. Now you know if you get caught up in some shit again you gonna catch at least ten easy.

TROY: What the fuck am I supposed to do? Huh? Ain't nobody trying to hire an ex-con, how the fuck am I supposed to support my daughter? What you want me to work at Micky Dee's or some shit?

RODRIGUEZ: You're a father now, you got a daughter, and you know your brother looks up to you right? What kind of an example are you setting for your family?

TROY: Yo stay out of my family business.

RODRIGUEZ: What family business? You just got out of jail, you living off your mom, you got your brother out here doing the same shit you're doing, and how the fuck you taking care of your daughter?

TROY: What the fuck you know about my situation. Did you ever get locked up? Did you ever watch your child grow up in pictures? You don't know shit Raul! Remember when we used to feed you, but you stand up here in front of me in that cop uniform like you're better than me, like them other motherfuckers who want me to change but ain't giving me no fuckin' options. So don't say shit about my situation 'cause I remember yours.

RODRIGUEZ: So what about Brody. He's still young. He still has options. You gonna let him go down the same road you did?

TROY: Brody nineteen years old. He's a grown ass man. He can make his own decisions.

RODRIGUEZ: Be realistic Troy. He's nineteen but he's still a kid and you know he's following in your footsteps.

(Rodriguez gives Troy a disappointed look and leaves. Troy stands there thinking about what Rodriguez just said. Then turns around and he's back to normal with his boys.)

JAH: What he want?

TROY: Bullshit. He's just being Officer Rodriguez.

(Enter Natashia.)

NATASHIA: Hey Jah.

JAH: Oh, hey, Tash, what's up?

NATASHIA: Can I talk to you for a minute?

JAH: Yeah, of course. What's going on?

(They walk downstage together.)

NATASHIA: Well, basically I wanted to ask you if I could work for you?

JAH: What? You wanna hustle? Why? I thought you was about to get signed? What happened to the rap thing?

NATASHIA: Well it's still happening, but that's long term for me, I'm not even signed yet, I just have a demo in production. Nobody's paying me to do my demo. I need something more immediate.

JAH: Yeah but — are you sure you wanna do this? This shit is dangerous, ain't shit sweet out here, there's nothing glamorous about what we do. In fact it's the opposite, this shit is very ugly.

NATASHIA: I know how it is out here. I know exactly what I'm getting into. Besides, my mom just got cut off welfare, and my dad still don't have a job yet. I gotta do what I gotta do.

JAH: Damn, you are serious, aight, lemme see what I can do for ya.

NATASHIA: Aight, thanks Jah, I appreciate it.

JAH: It's all good, aight check it this is what you gonna do, take this pager, when we page you, just come here to the corner. You might have to start as a lookout but that's where everyone starts, that's where I started too. You cool with that?

NATASHIA: Yeah that's straight. Good looking, Jah.

JAH: Aight shorty holla back.

TROY: Aight peace Tash.

NATASHIA: Peace y'all.

(Exit Natashia.)

CHRIS: Ay what did she want?

JAH: Yo she actually just asked if she can work with us.

CHRIS: Damn, she looked stressed out, she ain't even say hi to me. So what did you tell her Jah?

JAH: Well she's really broke so I told her she can be a lookout or some shit. What else would I say? I gave her the extra beeper.

TROY: See, everyone's broke, there ain't no money coming in around here.

JAH: Only this drug money, and that welfare shit. And they cutting the welfare, it's almost finished. I don't know what the fuck they think is supposed to happen after all the welfare is gone, that's when shit's gonna hit the fan. It's gonna be crazy.

TROY: I'm on some shit right now where I don't even care about myself anymore; it's all about my baby girl, the next generation ain't got no choices, man, there ain't shit for the kids to do. No options, nothing positive. Everyone that I was cool with when I was locked up was in there 'cause they're poor, they already took my two years away from me that I can't get back. I wanna watch my daughter grow up.

(Enter Brody. Brody relieves Dex and Chris so they can take a short break. They will work back-to-back shifts. They both exit and go to the store. They must return soon.)

BRODY: What's up y'all.

JAH: What's up Brody.

TROY: I was just talking about you.

BRODY: Yeah? What you say?

TROY: I was talking about all the new youth, you're a part of a new era. You got class today?

BRODY: Naw, not today, I just gotta study. I registered for one more session of them classes, then I should be ready to take the real test.

TROY: Then you get your Good Enough Diploma, right?

BRODY: Yes, sir.

JAH: Then what?

BRODY: Well, maybe college.

JAH: College is hard Man you ain't even finish High School.

BRODY: I know Man that's why I'm taking my GED classes.

TROY: So, what school do you want to go to.

BRODY: Well, I'm going to go to community for two years. Then I'm going to a university. Shit my dream is UCLA it's in Cali. The program is great plus the jawns and the weather out there. But my money ain't that long. Then there is the University of Penn. And they say that the Warden Business School is the best in the country and that's right here in Philly and I could save so much money *(Customer comes in.)* living at home. But, I ain't even got my GED classes yet and my SAT scores weren't that great, but I can take those over again and I know if I can keep my grades up I shouldn't have a problem getting in to Temple. Then maybe Penn for grad school. Shit, I got a lot of work to do!!

TROY: Damn, Brody you put some thought into this why I was gone huh?

BRODY: Yeah, Man I been wanting to do accounting, I've been learning a lot doing the books here, and I've been learning a lot at those classes, too. I kinda like keeping track of numbers and money, it might sound boring to some people but its kinda fun for me. I'd be happy if I could just do that, maybe work at a bank or something.

JAH: So that's why you been taking them fucking classes. That's ill Brody; I never knew you had goals like that.

TROY: Goals are important, you gotta stay focused.

(Enter Chris.)

CHRIS: Yeooooooo.

(He gives everyone a pound.)

JAH: Yo, you working a double today?

CHRIS: Yeah, always.

JAH: Oh, you're early.

CHRIS: Yeah, I know. I only went to the store.

JAH: *(To Brody.)* You work today?

BRODY: Naw. I was just comin' to meet Troy. But I can work if you need me to, I need the money. You know I gotta pay for all these classes myself, they ain't free, and I still gotta eat, too.

JAH: Aight, hmmm . . . Chris, who you supposed to be working with?

CHRIS: Dex but he still gotta couple minutes to get back, he ain't late yet.

JAH: Aight, hmmm . . . Well, this is the deal; y'all two can work this shift, me and Troy going on a mission, and I got some other work for Dex, anyway.

(Enter Dex.)

DEX: What's up, Jah, I heard my name.

JAH: Yeah, I'm glad you could make it. I'm a pay you whatever they make today whatever you would have made here to stand over on B Street today and tell everyone who comes to cop, to come here. Don't say anything specific, just say that they moved here, you don't know anything else about it. And make sure you don't have anything on you, keep your body clean. Just send 'em over. Got it?

DEX: I gotta tell you something, Jah. It's important.

JAH: What?

DEX: I just went by Jay and Kareem's crib, I wanted to talk to Kareem, but anyway, I just kept going right past the crib cause there were detectives just chillin' in cars in front of the house.

TROY: What?!! Are you sure?

DEX: Yeah, I know DT's when I see 'em.

JAH: Fuck.

BRODY: Do you think they're home?

JAH: I dunno, but it don't even matter.

TROY: Fuck man, I hate when shit gets hot like this.

JAH: Chill out Troy, it's nothing. Dex, you still do what I said alright? *(To Brody and Chris.)* Y'all still gonna run this shit here. Just use the safe system, hide shit, please, and try to only serve regulars. Well, fuck. Forget that, you're gonna have to serve new people the dope, damn. Just use your judgment. If you have to, you can even ask a motherfucka straight out "Are you cop?" There's a law where they gotta tell you, they can't lie about that shit. Aight so y'all cool?

BRODY: Uh I guess so.

CHRIS: Yeah we'll be aight Jah, but you should probably be around today just in case.

JAH: Yeah I'll be back, or Jay, we'll be around today. What about you Dex? You got the easy job, you cool with that right?

DEX: Yeah it's all good.

JAH: Yeah of course it's all good, you getting paid to not hustle! I wish I had your job today! Ha ha. Come on Troy, lets go cop some brown bricks.
(Jah, Troy and, Dex exit.)

CHRIS: Damn Man sometimes I hate this fuckin' job.

BRODY: Yeah me too.

CHRIS: I hope nobody gets locked up.

BRODY: Yeah me too.

CHRIS: We ain't even got no hammer out here right now do we?

BRODY: What are you crazy Chris? You think I'd be out here without protection?
(Brody shows Chris where he hides his gun.)

CHRIS: Oh good. Is that yours?

BRODY: Yeah, Troy gave me that when he got locked up. At first I wasn't down with it, but now I don't do much without it. I really wish we had more lookouts more often. I remember when I first started we only sold weed and we always had a lookout for every shift. Now I don't know what the fuck is going on.

CHRIS: Fuck it, we'll get through it.
(Chris and Brody continue to work the corner, customers enter, buy, exit, music over.)

SCENE THREE
Later that day. Natashia, Chris, Kareem, and Jay are all working and chilling.

NATASHIA: They put what on it?

JAY: Formaldehyde, sometimes even ammonia.

CHRIS: Damn, that's nasty.

NATASHIA: Does this weed got that shit on it?

JAY: I dunno, sometimes. That's why I rarely smoke the corner weed.

NATASHIA: How can you tell?

KAREEM: 'Cause it smells funny, and it makes your head hurt. You know how sometimes you smoke a blunt and it gets you really, really high, but it only lasts like a half hour, and then you get a headache all day? That's cause it's some dirt-ass weed that wouldn't even get you high, so they have to treat it with somethin'.

JAY: Sometimes a really big batch will get treated in bulk, but other times small-time kids just spray whatever they got around the house you know, Raid, roach spray, Windex, whatever.

NATASHIA: So what do you smoke?

JAY: I rarely smoke at all anymore. When I do smoke, it's strictly that hydro shit. It's much more expensive, but it lasts longer, you can make a small amount go a long way.

KAREEM: Word. I'm sayin' though, heads be sleepin' on that killa chronic.

JAY: But for real, Natashia, heads be sleepin' on them cigarettes they got all them nasty chemicals in 'em, even more then whatever else type shit.

(Enter Marisol.)

NATASHIA: Hey what's up girl?

MARISOL: Hey what's up Tash. What you doing here?

NATASHIA: I'm working here now, gotta get paper. What you doing here?

JAY: Hey Ma

MARISOL: Jay, lemme rap to you for a minute

JAY: Yeah no doubt, what's going on?

(They go downstage together.)

MARISOL: Jay I gotta be straight up wit' you

JAY: I was gonna tell you something too

MARISOL: Oh, well, OK, then you go first.

JAY: I just was gonna tell you that I been thinking about you a lot, and that don't usually happen to me. Not like this. I think your mad cool, you ain't like most other jawns, you really got your shit together. And I think I like you.

MARISOL: Oh man, this is exactly what I was afraid of. Jay I don't know how to say this but —

JAY: What? What's the problem?

MARISOL: This might not make any sense to you but I like you too, and that's why I can't see you anymore.

JAY: What? That don't make no sense.

MARISOL: I know but listen, I've been through a lot already and I just can't right now.

JAY: What do you mean? I still don't understand, you just said you like me too —

MARISOL: I know, I do but, it's just that I've been down this road before. I don't want to hurt you and I can't let myself get hurt again.

JAY: Aww come on wit' that shit

MARISOL: Aight I'm sorry, I'm a break it down, basically, if I catch feelings for you I'm not gonna want to see anything bad happen to you. And you are living your own life, your own style, and that's fine but if you wanna be with me I can't be getting stressed out about you on the block. I've been there and done that already. That's why my lil man ain't got no daddy right now.

JAY: You buggin' girl, you act like this all I'm gonna be my whole life.

MARISOL: No that's not what I'm sayin', I'm sure you could do anything that you put your mind to, but I'm saying that if you get out the game it has to be for yourself, not for me.

JAY: Ain't nothing gonna happen to me out here, I got this shit locked down. My squad is tight, they got my back. I got it all under control baby, this is the way I'm gonna get out, I gotta stack my money up right so when I do get out, it's for good and I don't have to come back, yanahemsayin'?

MARISOL: I do believe in you Jay, I just can't go through that with you right now, I hope you can understand.

JAY: I understand what your sayin' but ain't nothing bad gonna happen to me out here. I promise. Besides I know you could use a little extra support, I make a lot of money doing this.

MARISOL: No I don't. I do just fine on my own.

JAY: Well what the fuck am I supposed to do? I run this whole shit right here, and I'm fuckin' good at it. I came a long way to be in charge of something, this is all I know. I don't like this shit, I don't wanna do this, I hate this fuckin' game! But its all I got. It's mine. I made it out of nothing.

MARISOL: Jay, I'm sorry, I know you gotta do what you gotta do, so make your moves. Just be careful. And when you do get out, I'm a be here. Aight.

JAY: Aight. Whatever.

MARISOL: Good-bye Jay. *(Starts to walk.)* Peace Tash.
    (Enter Buckshot.)

JAY: Yo, Buckshot, what's up.

BUCK: What up Jay.

JAY: Everything is everything.

BUCK: It's been one minute dawg.

JAY: Yeah, I ain't seen you in a minute. You been good?

BUCK: Maintaining. Yourself?

JAY: Same. How is your little sister.

BUCK: She cool she just started college.

JAY: Oh yeah what school is she going to?

BUCK: She going to Columbia up in NYC.

JAY: Damn, I know that's hurting your pockets.

BUCK: Yeah but that's my little sister I gotta take care of her. How things round here?

JAY: Everything's good same shit. We had a little drama but its cool now. Jah was just asking about you the other day.

BUCK: Yeah. Damn how is everybody.

JAY: They good. And you know Troy just came home.

BUCK: Old head Troy that use to shoot people in the ass with a BB gun?

JAY: Yeah. That's how you became BuckShot.

BUCK: I was walking home from school minding my own damn business and BAM! I felt this hard sting on my ass and that shit was no joke! I was rubbing my ass and when I looked up I saw Troy with a BB gun laughing with his boys and still pointing the gun at me. He asked me if I was alright, and I was like naw motherfucka that shit hurt! Next thing you know he reloaded and then cocked it and started bucking at me again. I took off running and never even looked back. Fuckin' Troy man.

JAY: Damn that shit was funny, we talked about that shit for weeks.

BUCK: That shit was funny to y'all but I still got the scar from that. *(Beat.)* Yo I need to pick up a couple crack bundles.

JAY: I thought you got out the game. I heard you were working with hot electronics and burnt out cell phones?

BUCK: Still am but the money ain't coming in fast enough. And I'm out there in the suburbs and the demand for ready rock is big out there. There's some lawyer's wife out there that's strung the fuck out every day, she's on the lookout for some crack, but I tell her I don't do that no more, but I can't keep turning this money down and I gotta pay for Mia's college too. Besides, you get addicted to drugs not burn out cell phones.

JAY: Do they fuck with heroin out there.

BUCK: Yeah they fuck with that more than the rock. The suburbs got the money. The biggest consumers of crack, heroin, or whatever drug will fuck you up in a heartbeat are people in the suburbs. You see them fools driving their Volvos coming in the hood looking for some shit, if it wasn't for the suburbs we wouldn't be getting the same cheddar like we getting now.

JAY: You damn right, a lot of them fools are in-the-closet drug addicts.

BUCK: Heroin is big out there right now, people looking for it like hotcakes.

JAY: Well we just got some H in, you want some of that?

BUCK: Yeah lemme get two of them, and two of the rocks.

JAY: Aight, I got you.

(Jay exits.)

KAREEM: You coppin' bundles Bruce Lee?

(Buck stares at Kareem.)

KAREEM: What you gonna do with those bundles?

BUCK: You really shouldn't ask people's business you get fucked up like that.

CHRIS: Damn dawg, you gonna let him punk you like that?

KAREEM: Shut up Chris, I can handle mines. Yo Mister Lee —

BUCK: You Kareem ain't you?

KAREEM: How you know me?

BUCK: How many Chinese people use to live on your block?

KAREEM: You can't be Buckshot!

(They greet and shake hands.)

BUCK: It's all good young blood, damn man, is it me or did you get uglier?

NATASHIA: Kareem you gonna intro —

KAREEM: My bad, yo Buckshot this is Natashia and Chris. Buckshot is like a brother, his family came over from China and his parents worked all the time so my moms would take care of all of us together.

BUCK: What's up little lady? What are you doing out here?

NATASHIA: Just chilling and working.

BUCK: Aight. Be safe out here.

CHRIS: She is safe out here!

BUCK: Chill son you ain't even safe out here.

(Jay enters.)

JAY: Aight you good right here.

BUCK: What's the damage?

(Jay whispers something in Buckshot's ear. Buck pulls out a fat stack, gives Jay some money.)

JAY: Aight good looking.

BUCK: Yo be safe out there dawg.

JAY: I will man.

(Enter Ms. Roberts. Jay sees her and gives Chris a look and a gesture, Chris quickly takes her off to the side, they begin to whisper.)

KAREEM: Yo Buck it's been too long, you know you family right?

BUCK: Of course Reem. You need to come holla at me.

JAY: I will Man I just been busy.

BUCK: Same number same crib.

JAY: Aight my nigga.

BUCK: My Chink.

(Buckshot exits.)

MS. ROBERTS: Look Chris. she missed her last two appointments with me, and I need her signature for some forms so I can get your benefits back on.

CHRIS: Well can I just sign for it then?

MS. ROBERTS: No, I'm sorry, it has to be her. Where is she? I still haven't heard from her.

CHRIS: Ahg. I already told you. She's gonna call you as soon as —

(Enter Cirilli and Grabanski.)

CIRILLI: Jason Smith!?

JAY: Who you?

GRABANSKI: Jason Smith huh? We need to ask you some questions.

JAY: Naw, who are you?

GRABANSKI: We're detectives from the homicide division, I'm Grabanski, and this is my partner officer Cirilli. We don't have time to play games.

JAY: What are you talking about? I ain't do nothing.

CIRILLI: That's not what I heard. You wanna come down to the station and talk about what you didn't do?

JAY: Am I under arrest?

GRABANSKI: Not yet.

JAY: Well then I ain't going nowhere.

CIRILLI: Alright tuff guy. Then we can do this right here. Grabanski make a report, we're gonna get a statement.

(Grabanski gets paperwork ready, with pen and clipboard.)

MS. ROBERTS: Chris what's going on?

CHRIS: I have no idea.

MS. ROBERTS: Those are detectives they said they are from homicide

GRABANSKI: OK Jason, do you have I.D.?

JAY: No.

GRABANSKI: Of course not. Alright, where were you yesterday morning?

JAY: Here.

GRABANSKI: You got an alibi?

JAY: I was wit' a chick.

GRABANSKI: That's convenient.

CIRILLI: Get to the point Grabanski!

GRABANSKI: You know anything about the murder of five young men on Second Street?

JAY: I think I saw something about that on the news.

CIRILLI: Ah BULLSHIT!! This motherfucker's lying! Fuck this shit, nobody's going anywhere until we get a statement from all of youz!

MS. ROBERTS: Oh my god Chris, do you want me to talk to them? This sounds serious, maybe I could help.

CHRIS: Naw chill. Don't worry about it.

GRABANSKI: You sure you don't know anything?

JAY: I told you. Only what I seen on the news.

CIRILLI: *(To Natashia.)* And what's your name?

NATASHIA: *(Looks at Jay. Jay nods yes.)* Natashia

CIRILLI: *(To Natashia.)* What are you doing out here?

CHRIS: *(Leaves Roberts, steps to Cirilli.)* Yo she's with me.

CIRILLI: *(To Chris.)* Shut the fuck up. I wasn't talking to you. *(To Natashia.)* So this is your boyfriend, huh?

NATASHIA: Nuh-uh.

CIRILLI: What?

NATASHIA: No, Officer.

GRABANSKI: Natashia, you got any I.D. on you?

NATASHIA: No.

(Grabanski is taking notes.)

GRABANSKI: What's your last name? Natashia what? Are you from around here?

NATASHIA: *(Hesitates.)* Um, yeah, not too far from here

CHRIS: You ain't gotta tell 'em shit Tash!

CIRILLI: *(Grabs Chris.)* Fuck you kid! I'm in charge here!

MS. ROBERTS: Whoa! Get the hell off of him! What's the matter with you?

GRABANSKI: Look lady this is serious shit, why don't you mind your business.

CHRIS: I ain't do shit!

CIRILLI: Motherfucker get against the wall. Get against the fuckin' wall asshole.

(He grips Chris up and throws him against the wall. Starts to frisk him.)

MS. ROBERTS: He is my business, so this is my fuckin' business!

GRABANSKI: This is police business. *(Flashes badge.)* Who the hell are you anyway?

MS. ROBERTS: I'm Josephine Roberts and I'm department of social services. And that's Chris he's one of my clients and he's not mixed up in any —

CIRILLI: Well, well. What do we have here — oh shit! I hit the jackpot! Wow, six, seven, eight bags of crack! What do you get for this, Grabanski?

GRABANSKI: Well, because it's bagged up separately, we can charge you for distribution

CHRIS: Naw! Ms. Roberts that ain't mine! He just planted that shit! I swear!

CIRILLI: You lying piece of shit! *(He smacks him across the face, Chris stumbles.)*

GRABANSKI: Shit Frank! The fuck are you doing?!!

JAY: Why don't you leave the kid alone.

CIRILLI: *(To Jay.)* What the fuck did you say?

JAY: I said leave the kid alone. He said he don't know nothing.

GRABANSKI: Frank I think that you

CIRILLI: Shut up rookie! *(He starts toward Jay.)* Look I'm a tell you mother-fuckers. I need to know something before I leave this fucking corner.

MS. ROBERTS: Are you alright Chris? *(Chris nods, as he gathers himself.)*

JAY: The only thing I heard was that those dudes over there on 8th Street had owed some dudes some money.

GRABANSKI: What dudes?

JAY: I don't know. I never seen them before.

GRABANSKI: Jason, I hope that you are not lying to us.

CHRIS: Ain't nobody lying to you.

CIRILLI: Who the fuck do you think your talking to? This is enough for a felony! *(Holds up Chris' crack bundle.)* I'd shut the fuck up if I was you.

MS. ROBERTS: How do I know you didn't just plant that on him?

CIRILLI: Look lady don't play stupid. I don't need to plant shit. I'm investigating murder here. These kids have crossed the line.

MS. ROBERTS: I think you just crossed the line. These kids are human beings and that's not the way they deserve to be treated.

CIRILLI: I don't give a shit. I'm not their social worker. Let me tell you something. Yesterday I had to tell five mothers that their sons were murdered. Where were you? *(Pause.)* Right, nowhere. Come on Grabanski let's go, I'm done.

GRABANSKI: But I only got two of the statements and —

CIRILLI: Fuck the statements kid. We got enough for now. Let's go. And fellas, look forward to seeing you again.
(Detectives exit.)

MS. ROBERTS: Chris let me help you. I can help you.

JAY: Don't nobody need your help. Just get the fuck out of here. Chris ain't talking to nobody right now.
(Jay stares at Roberts. She stares back then she turns and exits.)

JAY: WHAT THE FUCK?!!!

CHRIS: God Damn!!

JAY: How the hell did they know my name?

CHRIS: I don't know but he took the rest of my shit.

NATASHIA: What's going on? *(No one answers.)*

KAREEM: Jay, what the fuck we gonna do now?

JAY: Chill! Let me think for a second!!

NATASHIA: *(To Chris.)* What the fuck is going on?

CHRIS: What you think going on? The cops tryin' to the find the boys who did it.

NATASHIA: Did y'all do it?

CHRIS: It don't matter if we did it or not, the cops still comin' round here askin' questions.

NATASHIA: I ain't getting locked up for some shit I ain't do!

KAREEM: Nobody said you did shit.

NATASHIA: Then why the cops question me and they ain't say nothing to you.

KAREEM: Man, shut up.

NATASHIA: Kareem, don't tell me to shut up cause you ain't have shit to say when the cops were here.

CHRIS: I know you ain't say shit.

KAREEM: What am I suppose to say they ain't ask me no questions.

CHRIS: Why didn't they ask you no questions huh?

KAREEM: What the fuck you tryin' to say?

JAY: Calm down. Ain't nobody snitchin'. And Natashia nobody getting locked up the cops don't know shit if they wouldn't have left on that bullshit story I gave 'em.

(Enter Smokey.)

JAY: What's up Smokey, what you got on my lunch?

SMOKEY: I dunno, Jay, what you got on my turbo?

JAY: I'll set you up with a crack blunt if you set me up with lunch.

SMOKEY: Jay, I didn't even eat today, how am I supposed to feed you?

JAY: It don't matter anyway, you know I ain't givin' you shit right?

SMOKEY: Yeah I know.

JAY: And I probably wouldn't actually eat anything you gave me anyway. So what the fuck you need man, you got some money?

SMOKEY: Do y'all got two corners now?

JAY: Why?

SMOKEY: 'Cause I just seen uh what's his name? The young kid, who I see always writing on shit.

JAY: Dex?

SMOKEY: Yeah, Dex, that's what he writes, right? Well I just seen him hustling on the other corner, that B Street spot. He was just talking to the police.

KAREEM: What you say Smokey!?! Something about Dex talking to the police!?!

JAY: Chill out 'Reem, I got this. When you see that Smoke?

SMOKEY: Just now on my way here.

KAREEM: Yo I knew he was a snitch!!! That little motherfucka!!!

JAY: Yo Kareem you gotta watch your fuckin' temper man, it's very counter-productive!! How many times do I gotta tell you, always remain calm, no matter what! Damn!

CHRIS: Yeah Kareem, chill out dawg, this is business. You can't be wilin' out all the time. Not here.

KAREEM: Aww shut the fuck up Chris, you don't know shit!

JAY: Yo damn Kareem, chill, sit down and relax. I said I got this.

(Kareem sits down, but he does not relax.)

JAY: Smokey, what else you got to tell me?

SMOKEY: Uh, that's it, I guess.

JAY: Aight well make yourself useful, either buy something or get the fuck out.

(Smokey buys one crack rock from Chris, and then exits quickly and quietly.)

KAREEM: See Man you can't trust nobody, I knew he didn't have no fuckin' heart! I'm a fuck that kid up for real this time! Watch!

CHRIS: All Dex does got is heart. Why you always hating on him all of a sudden? You just said yourself that you can't trust nobody, and you gonna trust Smokey the fuckin' piper over Dex? He ain't even do nothing man.

NATASHIA: Yeah Kareem. You didn't think of it like that now did you?

JAY: Look. Kareem. I'm not even worried about if he's snitching or not, I'm much more concerned about the fact that Smokey said he was selling shit over there. He's supposed to just send 'em over here, and he's supposed to keep his body clean. If he's selling over there, then he fucked up bad. Real bad. Not only cause he violated his orders, but because that's basically like doing the same exact thing that the other corner kids was doing that started this whole shit. But it's even worse cause it's Dex, if it's even true. I'm gonna go straight to the source right now, 'cause I never believe secondhand stories, always go to the source. And always take Smokey and any other addict at face value. Just calm down Bro, I'll be right back.

(Jay exits.)

KAREEM: I don't give a fuck, Dex is my man, but he been getting on my nerves lately. And you need to stop telling me what to do Chris; you wouldn't even be out here if I didn't put you on.

CHRIS: OK, true, you did put me on cause that's your brother, but you know I would have had put you on if that was my brother that ran shit. And you think I need to stop telling you what to do? I'm only telling you what to do cause you need to fuckin' do it man! I'm just tryin' to look out for you and yours. You know it's your crib that's got undercovers parked in front of it right? Not mine.

KAREEM: You're Goddamn right I know it's my crib that's under surveillance!!!

Why the fuck you think I'm so hype about a motherfucka snitching in the first place! Me and Jason, that's family that's all we got is each other! We got the most to lose out of all a y'all! We got them bodies on Second Street; we got all the weight in the crib!

NATASHIA: Yo chill chill chill cops right there!

(*Rodriguez enters stares at them and crosses. They all pause and back off a little. Raul exits.*)

NATASHIA: Yo, y'all gotta squash this dumb shit right quick cause this corner is probably under surveillance too, and we wouldn't even know it. Besides, Kareem, we all got a lot to lose, not just you and Jay, aight? You the only one blowin' up the spot anyway!

KAREEM: Shut the fuck up BITCH!

NATASHIA: What the fuck did you just say?

CHRIS: Now you crossed the line you stupid motherfucka! Don't you ever disrespect her again!

KAREEM: The fuck you gonna do about it, tough guy?

CHRIS: I will fuckin' destroy you!!! Just not here! Not now you stupid fuck!!! Why you always startin' shit!! You need to fuckin' think, you're acting retarded!

KAREEM: Man fuck you Chris, whatever, bring it motherfucka, I'm right here! And fuck you too bitch the fuck is you staring at? Y'all be bitchin' about how your parents can't find jobs shit we can't even find our parents!!! And your mom gets high Chris now what! Oh oops, you didn't know your mom smokes? You didn't know you mom's a fuckin' crackhead? She cops her rock from me, from right there. She cops from all of us when she know you ain't working.

CHRIS: Ay yo, chill, what the fuck is you talking about? You trippin' Kareem. That shit ain't even funny, dawg, I don't know how you could even joke about that shit.

KAREEM: Oh, I'm joking? I'm trippin'? That shit is for real dawg, you best believe it. None of them had the heart to tell you, you should be thanking me for my honesty, I know the truth hurts dawg, but it's still the truth. You can't blame them for not telling you though, plus she made us all promise not to tell you. I made her promise that she would tell you, but I guess she didn't keep hers, so I ain't keep mine. I knew she couldn't tell you that though, I mean how do you tell your son that? But I thought you would catch it on your own, I mean, you spend all day around crackheads; I figured that you'd recognize the symptoms when you live with one.

CHRIS: Stop fucking with me Reem.

NATASHIA: What are you talking about Kareem, you really sold Chris's mom crack?

(Enter Jah.)

KAREEM: Yeah so did all of us, and you would too if you were on a shift without Chris. It's not personal, it's just supply and demand.

CHRIS: Is it true Jah?

JAH: Is what true? *(Glares at Kareem, Kareem just shrugs.)* I can't believe you told him that.

KAREEM: I can't believe nobody else told him. He deserves to know. I would want to know.

(Now it has fully sunk in for Chris that this is not a joke.)

NATASHIA: Oh my God, Chris, I'm so sorry. *(She hugs him.)*

CHRIS: How long has she been getting high?

JAH: Where's Jay at?

KAREEM: *(To Chris.)* For like a few months now. *(To Jah.)* He went to go see what's the deal with Dex, cause Smokey said he saw him selling shit on the B Street corner and he said he saw him talking to the police.

JAH: I can't believe you told him.

CHRIS: I can't do this anymore. I gotta go, I can't even be around this anymore. *(Chris pulls out his bundles and stares at it for a moment, and then he snaps and throws it. Jah scrambles to pick up the little baggies of crack. Chris exits.)*

NATASHIA: I gotta go, too, this ain't right, here y'all. I don't know I might be back, I might not. I gotta figure some shit out.

(Natashia tosses her weed bundle. Kareem catches it. Natashia exits.)

JAH: Wait, what the fuck just happened? And what was that about Dex selling on the other corner?

KAREEM: Jay went to check on him mad long ago, I don't know what the fuck is up. He might Is that them? Over there? I don't know if he was selling, that's up to you if you believe Smokey or not. I believe he was talking to the police though, and who knows what that punk said. He could be trying to take us all down.

JAH: Yeah that's them, I think. I think they are coming here.

KAREEM: Yo man, I can't have no rats around me, the stakes is too high.

JAH: Settle down, I'm sure Jay is figuring out the real deal. Don't jump to conclusions.

KAREEM: Why does everyone keep telling me to settle down, to chill the fuck out, man, you need to calm down yourself. I am fuckin' calm! I am fuckin' chill! What the fuck! Shit! Man, I'm just dealin' with these things, I don't want to go away, I don't want Jay to go away either.

JAH: Whoa easy, ain't nobody going away, Kareem. It's all good.

KAREEM: WHY ARE COPS SITTING IN FRONT OF MY HOUSE!?!?

(Enter Dex and Jay. Kareem makes a run at Dex, Jah is there to grab him.)

KAREEM: WHY ARE YOU TALKIN' TO THE COPS?!! WHAT THE FUCK DID YOU TELL THEM?!! WHAT DID YOU SAY?!! I'M GONNA KILL YOU IF YOU FUCKIN' SNITCHED!! I'LL FUCKIN' KILL YOU!

DEX: Oh man, you have lost it. You are out of your fuckin' mind.

JAY: Come on, I got him. Let's go, Kareem, let's go.

(Jah turns him over to Jay; he starts to walk him away.)

KAREEM: I'm sorry.

(Kareem sits down.)

JAH: Ahh, who got the weed, I need a blunt right now. Got-damn I hate this fuckin' job.

JAY: Please. Somebody twist something.

JAH: Yeah for real, who got the weed? I'm gonna roll one. Kareem, lemme see the weed.

(Kareem has his head down; he hands over the whole bundle that Natashia gave back without looking up. Jah takes the bundle, and gets out two nicks. He stashes the rest of the bundle.)

JAH: Aight who got a blunt? *(Pause.)* Alright then I'll be right back. You want something Kareem? Soda, juice, water? No? Nothing? Aight I'll be right back.

(Jah exits.)

DEX: I don't think I can do this anymore, Jay. Not with him treating me like this.

JAY: I understand. I might give him a break. Well you can always work here if you need to.

DEX: Thanks, Jay. Take care of that guy. He needs some help.

JAY: Thanks, Dex. Peace.

(Enter Chris in a crazed frenzy with gun drawn. He storms right up to Kareem and puts it to his head.)

CHRIS: What else did you forget to tell me, Kareem?

KAREEM: *(Looks up, a little bit out of it.)* What?

CHRIS: Don't play that shit Kareem she told me everything. Now I want to hear it from your own mouth. What part did you leave out? Say it. Say it. Tell me what you did, Kareem.

JAY: Put the gun down, Chris.

DEX: Chris, please don't do this.

CHRIS: Not until he tells me what he did with her. Just fuckin' say it Kareem.

KAREEM: I'm sorry, Chris, please don't do this. I'm sorry, OK.

JAY: Put that gun down, Chris

CHRIS: NO! It is not OK, you have to say it, Kareem, just say that shit!

KAREEM: Come on Chris, damn.

(Enter Jah with blunt.)

CHRIS: Just fuckin' say that shit!!!

JAH: Whoa SHIT!

(He drops his blunt and pulls out his gun.)

KAREEM: Aight! Damn, Chris! I fucked her! Aight! That's what you wanted to hear?! That's what you wanted me to say? I fucked her!

(Kareem pulls out the hidden corner gun from under the steps where he is sitting, as he jumps up. Jah still has his gun drawn, Jay pulls out a gun, too. Dex is caught right in the middle of this, and he is the only one with no gun.)

DEX: Oh my God, what the fuck.

(Black out. With a few gun shots — freeze in the dark scene.)

SCENE FOUR

Music and lights fade up, down, no music, still in dark, shadowed figure walks on, does tag in spray paint. Exits. Slow fade, lights come up. Kid 1 comes out, looks around the corner, signals and waves Kid 2 and Kid 3 on to the corner. Kids 2 and 3 are young and small, but Kid 1 is the youngest and smallest of all of them. After Kids 2 and 3 take their position, Troy strolls out onto the corner. He is dressed much nicer than when we last saw him. He pulls out a wad of money, speaks softly to Kid 1, breaks off some money from his stack, walks away, exits stage left. Beat. The new boys settle into their shift, and begin passing the time.

KID 2: Spell *economic.*

KID 3: *Economic.* E-C-O-M-O-N-I-C. *Economic.*

(Kids 1 and 2 look at each other, shrug it off. Enter Customers, Kids sell drugs.)

KID 2: Spell *financial.*

KID 3: *Financial.* F-I-N-A-N-C-I-A-L. *Financial.*

KID 2: Spell *Revolution.*

(Fade to black, music up.)

END OF PLAY

MIDNIGHT

By David Epstein

For Beth, Laura,
and my amazing mother and father

BIOGRAPHY

Born in the Chicago area, David has run the gamut from stagehand to producer. He graduated from Tisch School of the Arts at NYU where he received the award for Outstanding Achievement in Drama along with his BFA. He continued to train professionally at the Lee Strasberg Institute, which led to commercial, regional, and international acting work. As a writer, he did (as the play suggests), nearly win a contest in the third grade for creating a story about "a kid with his toy car," and he has since written plays and adaptations in collaboration with various theater companies in the city. In 2001, he served briefly as a "non-official consultant" (whatever that means), for an up-and-coming Hollywood screenwriter. This experience was the inspiration for *Midnight*. In 2002, he helped form the award-winning Invisible City Theatre Company that currently holds residency at Manhattan Theatre Source. David would like to send a shout-out to the energized and talented artists who manage that space. *Midnight* is David's first full-length play and was the vehicle for his New York City directing debut. He has since written and directed his modern dramas, *Strange Attractions* and *Drinking and Diving*, which both premiered in 2004, and he is working on his fourth play, *The Buddy Picture*. Other directing highlights include Shelagh Stephenson's *The Memory of Water*, Tom Stoppard's *Arcadia*, and the new drama, *Airport Hilton*, by Anthony Jaswinski. David is a member of SAG, AEA, and the Dramatists Guild, and he is proud to be included in this collection.

ORIGINAL PRODUCTION

Invisible City Theatre Company, David Epstein and Elizabeth Horn Artistic Directors, first presented *Midnight* on October 23, 2002, at Manhattan Theatre Source. The play was directed by its writer, lighting by Joe W. Novak, the set was designed by Dara Wishingrad, costumes by Adrienne Blount, and stage managed by Sarah Elliott. The cast was as follows:

THEODORE STINTZ	Gerry Lehane
DENNIS DEAN	Dan Patrick Brady
EVELYN MARYWEATHER	Christina Wollerman
TONY SIMPOLINI	J. T. Patton
JAMES HALLOWAY	Paul L. Coffey
MOISHA ADELSTEIN AND PAULO	Jono Jarrett
MAX ADELSTEIN AND RALPH	Jeffrey Evan Thomas
HARVEY GOULDENBURG	Dennis Tiede
FLORENCE	Elizabeth Horn

CHARACTERS

JAMES HALLOWAY: Hollywood director, forty
EVELYN MARYWEATHER: Mr. Halloway's assistant, thirty
DENNIS DEAN (DEANZIE): Mr. Halloway's lawyer, sixty
TONY SIMPOLINI: Unknown playwright, thirty
THEODORE STINTZ: Head butler at the Ritz (British accent), forty
MOISHA ADELSTEIN: Jewish Mobster (Russian descent), thirty
MAX ADELSTEIN: Moisha's giant cousin and strong-arm, thirty
HARVEY GOULDENBURG: Hollywood producer, fifty to sixty
FLORENCE: Harvey's buxom lackey, nineteen
PAULO AND RALPH: Bellboys at the Ritz, twenties

For the sake of economy, the actors cast as Paulo and Ralph can also play
Moisha and Max.

SETTING

The play is set in New York City during the winter of 1954.
The action takes place in the Presidential Suite of the Ritz Carlton Hotel
over the course of a weekend.

TIMELINE

ACT I: Friday afternoon
ACT II: Saturday morning
ACT III: Saturday night

YIDDISH TERMINOLOGY

Nishtekeit: a nobody
Meshugener: crazy man
Shmegegi: a fool

Midnight

FRIDAY AFTERNOON

The penthouse is the most luxurious room in the hotel. A bay window over-
looks a wintry Central Park. The main entrance is beside it. Between the two
is a grandfather clock. At left is a quaint dining room set with a long table-
cloth, a door to the guest room and a hallway that leads to the rest of the suite.
At right, steps lead to a sunken lounge where couches surround a coffee table.
There is a bar with a big cabinet and a courtesy phone. A painting of the
park hangs above and hides a steel safe built into the wall. Swinging doors
lead to the kitchen.

Enchanting period music precedes the scene: A spotlight rises upon a Variety *magazine that is being read by Theo, the dry and refined butler. The rest*
of the suite illuminates revealing two bellboys hard at work: Paulo shines Theo's
shoes while Ralph is placing the last of the flowers.

RALPH: We're out of roses, Mr. Stintz.

THEO: Just use what you have, Ralph.

PAULO: So who's it going to be, Mr. Stintz?

THEO: I'm afraid I don't know what you mean.

PAULO: This weekend, who's in the suite?

THEO: Well, I haven't been told yet, and even if I had been —

PAULO: I know, I know. You wouldn't tell me.

THEO: Now you're learning. Let this be a day long remembered. Paulo can learn.

RALPH: I bet you see some pretty interesting stuff living way up here with the
up-and-crusties.

THEO: Not at all. I serve drinks, I open doors, I bring out dinner. Beyond that
I am quite frankly told to make myself scarce. No boys, I'm afraid life in
the penthouse is just as dull as life in the lobby. In fact the only difference between you and I is I have the trust of a company that intends to
keep me on for a while, whereas you boys have —

RALPH: Diddley-squat?

THEO: Not the phrase I'd use to describe it, but in essence.

PAULO: There are movie stars, though?

THEO: Sometimes, yes.

PAULO: So the tips must be pretty good then.

RALPH: "Pretty good," don't be an idiot.

THEO: You know how I feel about street talk, boys.

PAULO: I'm just saying the tips must be good, OK?

RALPH: You're a genius. How'd you figure that one?

THEO: That will be all, Ralph. Paulo will learn all too quickly that the hotel is a stressful environment. The last thing he needs is some smart talker giving him the brush simply because he is trying to find his way.

RALPH: Sorry, Mr. Stintz.

THEO: Not to me.

RALPH: Sorry, Paulo.

THEO: Very good. We may make head butler out of you yet.

(Checks his watch.)

Now then, be a lad and help me into this.

(Ralph guides Theo into his jacket.)

PAULO: So, tell me, Mr. Stintz. How do you become head butler?

THEO: Oh, it's very simple. By taking it in the gut on a daily basis until that glorious morning when you wake up miraculously immune to the life of servitude because you recognize the illusion of it.

PAULO: *(Not getting it.)* Oh.

THEO: OK. He should be up any moment. *(Snaps them to attention.)* Ralph, you'll be upstairs with me for the early evening and Paulo you'll work the party on twelve. And don't let me catch either of you loafing about in the hall begging for handouts. I won't tolerate that sort of behavior.

PAULO AND RALPH: Yes, Mr. Stintz.

(Paulo exits through the main door. Ralph picks up the Variety.*)*

RALPH: Your trade paper, sir.

(They share a brief glance. Theo crosses boldly and snatches the magazine.)

THEO: Do a dust off.

(He exits to the kitchen. The bellboy exits to the hall. It is then that Tony Simpolini runs into the suite. Tony is tough and street-smart with curly, greasy bangs. He carries a mangled manuscript complete with coffee stains, tire tracks, and cigarette burns. He is out of breath and frantically searching for a place to hide. He hears whistling in the hall and quickly stuffs himself inside the bar cabinet. Ralph enters just as the cabinet slams shut. The bellboy looks sharply at it and goes to investigate. Just before Ralph can open it, Dennis Dean [Deanzie] enters through the main door. He wears a trench coat and carries a briefcase.)

DEANZIE: Excuse me, I'm looking for Mr. Stintz?

RALPH: He'll be right out, sir.

DEANZIE: May I?

RALPH: Yes, of course.

(Deanzie sets his briefcase down and makes a drink at the bar. Ralph continues to glare at the cabinet as Theo enters with an outstretched hand.)

THEO: Mr. Dean, I presume. How do you do?

DEANZIE: Ah, Mr. Stintz.

THEO: Please, call me Theo.

DEANZIE: Management told me I could find you here to run over some last minute details, if that would be all right?

THEO: Yes, of course.

DEANZIE: OK, Theo, we're short on time so I'll just get to it.

THEO: *(Slightly annoyed.)* By all means.

DEANZIE: *(Taking notes.)* Tell me, how long have you been in the service industry?

THEO: Fifteen years last month.

DEANZIE: And how many of those have been spent at the Ritz?

THEO: Twelve, I believe.

DEANZIE: Where'd you start?

THEO: Mail room, sir.

DEANZIE: Yes, I remember the mail room.

THEO: We all have a mail room to look back on. It doesn't matter who you are.

DEANZIE: That we do.

THEO: Ahem.

(He snaps at Ralph who, by this time, has wrapped his hand around the cabinet handle and is about to open it.)

RALPH: Pardon me, sir. All done here.

THEO: Very good.

(Guides Ralph to the door.)

RALPH: You, um, may want to check the cabinet for —

THEO: I think I can manage, thank you, Paulo. Stay by —

RALPH: The front desk, yes sir. And it's Ralph.

THEO: Whatever.

(Shuts the door on the bellboy.)

DEANZIE: You run a pretty tight ship.

THEO: This is the Ritz, sir.

DEANZIE: I take it you can tell me who I am then?

THEO: *(In one breath.)* You are a lawyer, Mr. Dean, who is party to a preferred client of the hotel and are here to have the waitstaff sign a letter of agreement to ensure the privacy of that client. Otherwise known as a silencer note.

DEANZIE: Hey, you know your stuff. My client will be impressed with you. He's a very particular man. Likes things a certain way.

THEO: Of course.

DEANZIE: So I've got to ask you, Theo, and it may seem like a strange question, but the man I work for insists on knowing certain things about the people who are wandering around his world.

THEO: I see.

DEANZIE: Are you an actor, Theo?

THEO: Is that the question?

DEANZIE: It's strange, I know. But you must understand my client is very influential in the entertainment industry and has, in the past, run into a few characters. Actors specifically. Not character actors —

THEO: I know what you mean, sir.

DEANZIE: Right. Anyway, couple years back one of these thespians managed to give my client a pretty good scare.

THEO: I see.

DEANZIE: Your basic harassment, breaking and entering. After the trial my client adopted some new rules, one of which is that if he isn't doing something involving the picture then there'd better be no actors around. This includes when he goes to restaurants, parties, and of course —

THEO: Hotels.

DEANZIE: That's right. Only problem is that in most of these places actors make up 90 percent of the staff so you can imagine that we run into our fair share of problems.

THEO: It seems odd.

DEANZIE: Believe me, it is.

THEO: But doesn't your client deal with actors every day?

DEANZIE: It's complicated. He's got no problem with working actors, you see. He's friends with many stars. It's the out-of-work ones he can't stand. Fringe performers looking for a break. And ever since the incident my client has had . . . Problems.

THEO: Oh, dear.

DEANZIE: So Theo, "To be or not to be?"

THEO: Well, Mr. Dean, I admit that the voice I use with you here is not the one I use in my private life, and I think that in many ways I do play a role at the Ritz, but to say I am an actor in the true sense of the word, is incorrect.

DEANZIE: Well said. But, you never know. Robert Mitchum was a stagehand, didn't know a lick about acting and look at him now.

THEO: I suppose anything's possible.

DEANZIE: You think?

THEO: No, sir. I postulate.

DEANZIE: *(Laughing.)* Oh, yeah, Jimmy's gonna like you. Now, are there any other staff members who will be up here?

THEO: They'll be in and out, but never when your client is present.

DEANZIE: And where are your quarters in case I need you?

THEO: Down the hall, first door on the right.

DEANZIE: And the safe?

(Theo opens the painting above the bar. Deanzie refers to a slip of paper containing the combination and puts folds of money in. He then hands Theo a document.)

DEANZIE: Now that the preliminaries are through let's get down to the wear and tear. That promissory "ensures that you will not mention to any persons that you know of my client's whereabouts, and hereby attest to any and all —"

THEO: *(Agitated as he signs the contract.)* I understand, Mr. Dean.

DEANZIE: Ah, yes. I forget myself. This is old hat to you. Very good. My client's name is Halloway. James Halloway. The name ring a bell?

THEO: I can't say that it does.

DEANZIE: He directs movies. He made *A.W.O.L.? Blinded by Glory?*

THEO: The war pictures?

DEANZIE: That's the one.

THEO: Yes, I quite enjoyed those films.

DEANZIE: He was nominated for *Glory.* He also did *Target Gunner. Tail Gunner. Belly Gunner. Son of a Gunner.* The list is long.

THEO: Obviously a talented man.

DEANZIE: Oh, he is. Though not without his idiosyncrasies.

THEO: We are all a victim to that, if I may say.

DEANZIE: Indeed. OK, Theo, that should do it. I left the dinner details at the front desk. Oh, yeah, I meant to ask. Is there a reunion this weekend? There seemed to be a group gathering in the lobby.

THEO: Well, the banquet halls do get rented out.

DEANZIE: Oh, nothing like that. Just a group. Interesting looking fellows. I suppose they would best be described as . . . Religious. *(No response.)* Not important. Well, I can't think of anything else. He should just about be on his way up. I'll wait for him in the hall.

THEO: Very good, sir.

DEANZIE: Nice talking to you, Theo.

THEO: And you, Mr. Dean.

(As Deanzie exits, he makes room for the bellboys who arrive with luggage.)

PAULO: Where to, Mr. Stintz?

THEO: Master bedroom.

(They exit to the hallway. Theo pulls out a hand-mirror and combs his hair.)

THEO: Stop admiring the room, boys. Leave the luggage by the bed and disperse.

(The boys beeline to the main door.)

PAULO: Good night Mr. Stintz.

THEO: Good night, Paulo.

RALPH: Good night, Mr. Stintz.

THEO: Good night, Frank. Stay by —

RALPH: The front desk yes, sir. And it's —

THEO: Whatever.

(Theo shuts the door on Ralph and exits to the kitchen. The bar cabinet yawns open. Tony gets out. He stretches and stares at the decrepit folder in his hand. He places it on a nightstand and looks to the window. Voices suddenly rise from the hall. Tony scrambles back into the cabinet just as Jimmy Halloway enters followed by Evelyn Maryweather and Dennis Dean. Jimmy is tall and menacing with a dopey, boyish allure that somehow exists all at once. Evie is strikingly beautiful underneath her reading glasses, with a wit to match.)

JIMMY: Boy, I tell ya', if I don't get on another plane for the rest of my life it won't be too soon.

EVIE: You mean, it will, Jim.

JIMMY: It will what?

EVIE: Be too soon.

JIMMY: For what?

EVIE: For getting on a plane. What you said infers that you want to head back to the airport and jump on the first plane you see.

JIMMY: That's not what I said.

EVIE: Then I guess it doesn't matter.

JIMMY: If you're going to orbit around me like some fancy pants English teacher, then I'd say it does matter, Evelyn.

EVIE: I'm sorry. I didn't realize I was *orbiting.*

(She inadvertently places her belongings on top of Tony's manuscript.)

DEANZIE: Well we're here now so we can all relax.

JIMMY: Hey, I'm relaxed. Don't I look it? What about you, Eve, you relaxed?

EVIE: Comatose.

JIMMY: See. Situation normal. Maybe you need to relax, Deanz. You damn well better with what I'm shelling out. Where is the service in this joint anyway? I thought a penguin came with the room?

EVIE: You haven't been here ten seconds and already you need someone to fetch something.

JIMMY: That's right.

EVIE: There's a bar right there, Jim. Why don't you fix yourself a drink? Or go to the bar in the lobby.

JIMMY: I'm not going down there, I just got up here. Besides, I don't want people to recognize me.

EVIE: No one's going to recognize you. This is New York. The people — Don't care.

THEO: *(Enters with Cabernet.)* Good evening, Mr. Halloway. Welcome to the penthouse.

JIMMY: Weren't you supposed to say that when I came through the door?

DEANZIE: Take it easy.

THEO: I was retrieving wine, sir.

JIMMY: Fine, pop 'em. Jack and ice for me. Deanzie.

DEANZIE: Gin Split.

> *(Theo offers to Evie who declines. He moves to the bar. Jim is at the window.)*

JIMMY: New York, New York, huh?

> *(Studies the city and grows weary.)*

I hate this place. What do you think, Deanzie?

DEANZIE: *(Pulls out a deck of cards.)* It's crowded.

JIMMY: Yup. Way too many people crammed in this town. Why anybody would willingly choose to live in a cesspool like this is beyond my understanding.

EVIE: They say it's an acquired taste.

JIMMY: What is?

EVIE: City life.

JIMMY: Who says that?

EVIE: The locals. They say you learn to love it.

JIMMY: Oh, that's reassuring.

EVIE: You know, it wouldn't hurt to see the sights this time around. The museums, Central Park is supposed to be lovely —

JIMMY: It's twenty degrees, Eve, we're not going to some park.

EVIE: I don't mean this very second, Jim.

> *(Jim moves to Theo and examines him like a cop giving a shakedown.)*

EVIE: Personally, I love it when we visit. A thousand city blocks crammed together on one tiny island and the whole thing somehow fits. All the clubs and theaters in Times Square. Jazz on every corner.

DEANZIE: Sounds like you're talking about a night life. If only I could remember what that was.

EVIE: Yeah, well. Who can?

(Looks to Jim who still hovers.)

Jim, what are you doing?

DEANZIE: Jim?

EVIE AND DEANZIE: *Jim?*

JIMMY: What? Do you need me for something?

EVIE: Yes. That's why you respond when we call your name.

DEANZIE: He's fine. Everything checks out.

(Jim fixes Theo's collar and examines his nameplate.)

JIMMY: Theodore, huh?

THEO: Theo's fine, sir.

JIMMY: That's false advertising, you know.

THEO: I suppose it is. Perhaps one day they'll have a nameplate that simply reads "Butler."

JIMMY: *(Odd-beat.)* Can I ask you something, Theo?

THEO: By all means.

JIMMY: And be honest with me because I'll know.

EVIE: Jim —

THEO: Sir?

JIMMY: Are you an actor?

EVIE: I can't believe it! You're out of your mind, do you know that?

DEANZIE: What do you make me come up here for if each and every time —

JIMMY: I'm just checking, OK?

DEANZIE: Well, don't check, how about that?

JIMMY: That's easy for you to say.

EVIE: It's embarrassing.

JIMMY: To who? You?

EVIE AND DEANZIE: Yes!

JIMMY: No! If anything it should embarrass me. You can never be too safe.

EVIE: Safe about what?

JIMMY: We don't know these people. They could be dangerous.

EVIE: Maybe you're dangerous. You ever think about that?

(Resigned, Jim turns to the butler. Deanzie and Evie give up.)

JIMMY: So?

THEO: As I stated earlier to Mr. Dean, I am not now, nor have I ever been a member of the theater community. Though, if I may say, I do see the pictures when I have the time, and as a member of the world outside of entertainment, where the thing that matters most is punching out at the end of the day, I do enjoy your pictures every much, sir.

JIMMY: Oh, you're good. This guy is good.

DEANZIE: I told you.

JIMMY: So which ones?

THEO: I'm sorry?

JIMMY: Which of my films did you like?

THEO: I liked *A.W.O.L.*, sir.

JIMMY: You *liked* it?

THEO: Yes. I thought it made a bold statement.

JIMMY: Bold? I'll take bold. Vague but positive. And you're sure you're not an actor?

EVIE: He's not an actor! He's not an actor! How many times does he have to say it?

JIMMY: I said I'm checking.

EVIE: At least look for the signals before you start interrogating everyone you meet.

JIMMY: Oh, there are signals now?

EVIE: Do you see him drooling, shaking in his pants, bumbling over his words? Do you hear him telling you you're a genius?

JIMMY: No.

EVIE: Then he's *not* an actor.

JIMMY: Fine. But I don't interrogate everyone.

EVIE: Yes you do.

JIMMY: Deanzie, do I —

DEANZIE: You do, Jim.

JIMMY: That's right. Go on. Consort. What the hell do I pay you people for?! *(Ruins Deanzie's solitaire game.)* Tell me something, Theo —

EVIE: Here we go.

JIMMY: You're the head butler here?

THEO: I am, sir.

JIMMY: And I take it you have a sizable staff of penguins to manage? Bellboys, maids, and the like?

THEO: At times, sir, yes.

JIMMY: Now let us imagine you gave one of these staffers a bad deal one week. I'm sure it's happened to you.

THEO: Indeed.

JIMMY: Right. Maybe he served the wrong brand of booze and you had to let him go. Right? Or maybe you didn't even know the guy. Maybe he was just some person who applied for a job and you turned him away cause he didn't have the right credentials. You with me?

THEO: To the last, Mr. Halloway.

JIMMY: Now, picture this person taking such quick offense to your decision that before you can say "restraining order," his devout belief that you are the source of all his problems causes him to break into your home, hide in a bedroom closet wielding a nine-inch hunting knife, just waiting for you to return.

THEO: How grisly.

JIMMY: But he doesn't attack head on.

THEO: No?

JIMMY: Oh, no. He waits some more. Until you're in bed, when it's dark, and you're tired, and there is nothing but the sound of gentle wind —

(Deanzie insinuates "wind.")

JIMMY: And then, twelve o'clock strikes on the grandfather clock . . . Dong . . . Dong . . . Dong . . . D —

EVIE: Can you just get through this?

JIMMY: *(Wraps an arm around Theo.)* What do you think happens next?

THEO: I hate to guess.

JIMMY: He attacks with intent to kill.

THEO: A morose scenario to say the least, Mr. Halloway.

JIMMY: Morose times twelve. Now, assuming you are crafty enough to even survive such an event, how could you face your workers, how could you face *people* the same way again knowing full well that, at any moment, someone out there may snap and strike over something that, to you, seems . . . Stupid?

THEO: I'm afraid I don't have an answer for that, Mr. Halloway.

JIMMY: Neither do I. And that's my dilemma.

THEO: I suppose all one can do is be on their best behavior.

(They look to each other.)

Your drink, sir.

JIMMY: If you could bring out a hot rag then that will be all.

THEO: Of course. And thank you for the . . . Thought-provoking story.

(Rolls his eyes as he exits.)

EVIE: Are you done?

JIMMY: I don't want the man thinking I'm crazy.

DEANZIE: Well, you're off to an excellent start.

JIMMY: All right. What have we got? Tell me about my weekend with the illustrious Harvey Gouldenburg.

EVIE: *(Opens the schedule.)* Thank you. He lands tomorrow afternoon and should arrive late in the evening.

JIMMY: We got something prepared for that?

EVIE: Like what?

JIMMY: Three-piece band?

EVIE: Gouldenburg's a serious man, Jim. He wants to conduct business.

JIMMY: You're damn right he does. This is how you make things happen. Harvey Gouldenburg is the guy who sets the standard, isn't he, Eve?

EVIE: He's the hot ticket this year.

JIMMY: And the studio lets him produce whatever he wants! Oh, we're going to turn things around in here boy! This is my year. I'm telling you, this is my year!

EVIE: Now, we have nothing planned for this evening —

JIMMY: Let's keep it that way.

EVIE: But the studio did send invites for shows tonight.

JIMMY: Shows?

EVIE: Plays, Jim. Theatrical events.

JIMMY: *(Not enthused.)* Great.

EVIE: Here are the programs.

JIMMY: Chekhov, Chekhov, Strindberg, Chekhov, Shakespeare, Chek — Is that all they do out here? Aren't there any writers left in this world? Forget tonight. What about tomorrow?

EVIE: The day is clear until the meeting. I have your script notes for *The Great War.* You said you wanted to go over them in the morning.
(Theo enters from the kitchen and gives Jimmy the steaming rag. Jimmy puts it on his eyes. Theo exits.)

JIMMY: What else?

EVIE: That's it.

JIMMY: Good. So just Harvey. Convince him I'm the man to direct *The Great War,* make things happen.

DEANZIE: You might close the deal tomorrow.

EVIE: Depending on how he plays his cards.

JIMMY: Oh, I'll play my cards. Everyone knows I'm the best director at the studio for war pictures. They think because my last three didn't do so hot that suddenly my talent has dried up. Everyone forgets I was under contract. They made me make those comedies. Didn't matter if the director's heart was in the picture. Film it, print it, brand it with my name. That's how things get done. Personally, I didn't think those comedies were that bad. *(Looks to his unresponsive comrades.)* Are you dolts listening to me?

EVIE: Of course we're listening.

DEANZIE: You know we agree with you.

JIMMY: *(Tosses the rag to the bar.)* Comedy. What do I know about comedy?

DEANZIE: Exactly.

JIMMY: I didn't come from a bloodline of circus performers.

EVIE: You came from drunks.

JIMMY: That's right. I came from a world of drama and hard liquor. That's the world I know. I would kill to do a script that had depth like that. I mean, *Blinded by Glory,* there was some gutsy stuff in there, but just once I'd like the opportunity to direct something, I don't know . . .

EVIE: Soft.

JIMMY: No. Not soft. Soft means fluff, Evie, and fluff means *crap.* I mean something that does justice to my name. Something close to the hearts of the people who pay to sit in front of that silver screen. Where the characters come out in the first act and, zap, they're defined, each with a story about life and hardship and love.

DEANZIE: Maybe we should put a camera on you.

JIMMY: I mean it. If I found a script I believed in I'd back it myself.

EVIE: You would?

JIMMY: But you can't find that anymore which is what I'm saying. A mediocre script is practically gold nowadays. The studios will have you film a bar of soap if they thought there was a script in it. Competition is growing. Television is on the rise. Oh, what's the use? You're right, Deanz. I just need to relax. Just lie down and relax.

EVIE: So, should I confirm you for one of these productions?

JIMMY: Evelyn, I'm not sitting through three hours of trying to figure out the difference between Ivan Ivanovich and Stepan *Stepanovitch* Ivanovich.

EVIE: Some of these shows are modernized to make it easier for —

JIMMY: For what? Morons like me?

EVIE: All right. If you don't want to see any of these, can I suggest something?

JIMMY: What?

EVIE: There is a new theater in the city called — *(Reaching for her notes.)* The Thespian Studio. Word has it that —

JIMMY: Thespian Studio?! God! I really do hate this town.

EVIE: It's supposed to be good, Jim. They're in the process of developing a whole new technique of performance —

JIMMY: Now what does that mean? It's no science. What does an actor do aside from memorizing lines and saying 'em? And half of 'em can't even do that. *(He and Deanzie toast.)*
Thespian Studio. Pfh. In three months it'll be an abandoned building, you wait.

EVIE: So, that's a 'no,' then?

JIMMY: Yeah. A 'no.'

DEANZIE: Aw, why don't you go, Jim? You might find some talent for *The Great War,* let Harvey know you're thinking. You've got nothing else. You should check it out just to see what —

JIMMY: Fine, fine, fine, fine, fine. Book the seats.

EVIE: I already did.
(Reveals tickets.)

JIMMY: I'm not saying I'm going, Eve. I've got to build up some strength for that. But I'm telling you, if I get there and am accosted by a single actor who thinks he'd be perfect for some role that doesn't even exist, I'm going to be very upset. I'm taking a nap.

EVIE: It will have to be a short one.

JIMMY: Fine. Wake me when food comes. *(Exits to the kitchen then returns.)* Where's my room?

DEANZIE: *(Points the way.)* End of the hall.

JIMMY: *(Stops and turns to her.)* Eve?

EVIE: I've got calls.
(Jim exits, sour with her response. Evie goes to the bar and makes a drink.)

EVIE: I swear. He thinks my primary function in life is to serve.

DEANZIE: This is a pressure point. He's got to make this deal.

EVIE: I know. I'm being selfish aren't I? Demanding respect from my boss.

DEANZIE: I think he's more than that.

EVIE: Is he? I wonder, Deanz, I really do. Sometimes I'd like to take that drink he's always got in his hand and throw it in his face.

DEANZIE: Look, I guarantee you when this weekend is over things will be different. He'll have a contract, he'll have his director's chair. He'll be happy.

EVIE: And I'll have to sit next to him on-set and fetch coffee while he flirts with the lead.

DEANZIE: Nobody said it was easy. Just give it one more shot.

EVIE: One more shot. Isn't that what you said the last time? *(Smiles to herself.)* It's a man's world, Dennis. Jim can do whatever he wants.

DEANZIE: Have things been good?

EVIE: "Good?" Sure, why not?

DEANZIE: He doesn't go out anymore?

EVIE: I don't know.

DEANZIE: He's getting his head straight, you know that. That's Jim's way. Even before the crap he pulled. He's a complicated man.

EVIE: Oh, please. You can't convince me of that.

DEANZIE: Maybe that actor *did* mess with his head somehow.

EVIE: We're up to six today.

DEANZIE: It wasn't six.

EVIE: The driver to the airport, the stewardess on the plane, the driver from the airport, the bellboy who took the luggage, the bellboy in the service elevator and just now with the butler. Six. And the day isn't over yet.

DEANZIE: All right. So maybe the road is a little longer than we thought.

EVIE: A *little* longer? We've got a budding nutcase on our hands. You know what he needs? A psychiatrist.

DEANZIE: Dear lord, I hope you never mention that to him.

EVIE: I did.

DEANZIE: Evie —

EVIE: It's almost 1955. In our business seeing a psychiatrist doesn't mean you are an insane person. You'd be surprised how many of his associates see one.

DEANZIE: Well, what did he say?

EVIE: What do you think? I tell ya', he's lucky we stick around. You're like a father to him. His only friend.

DEANZIE: Come on, Jim's got friends.

EVIE: And I can't even count the number of times I've had to pull the shoe out of his mouth. Last week he told Vince LaMare from Paramount that, and I quote, "The French are decent people, if they bathed more they *might* be taken seriously."

DEANZIE: That's kind of funny.

EVIE: Mr. LaMare is from Paris, Deanz. And I'm left to say, "Oh, Mr. Halloway didn't mean it Mr. LaMare. He just has an abrasive sense of humor." Meanwhile, Jim is staring out the window with a oafy smile slurping down lobster with butter all over his face.

DEANZIE: I don't get you.

EVIE: No?

DEANZIE: That's right. Why do you have all this steam to let off? You're a beautiful woman —

EVIE: Oh, Deanz.

DEANZIE: You're smart, you're successful, but you're not happy.

EVIE: I used to be.

DEANZIE: Hold on there. I'm the old fart who should be talking about all the "used to be's" in this world. Maybe you need a new job. You ever think about that? I know some people that would be glad to have you and they probably pay better than Jim if you can believe it.

EVIE: I know people too, Dennis. Did he put you up to this?

DEANZIE: Well, cripes, Evie, no, I . . . Thanks a lot. I should just keep my mouth shut. I'll live longer with you two around.

(He plops into the couch. Evie crosses to him, pulls off his hat and kisses his forehead. Before Deanzie can speak, she places the hat over his face then exits to the bedroom. Deanzie rubs his temples as Theo enters to clean.)

THEO: Are you all right, Mr. Dean?

DEANZIE: Headache.

THEO: Would you care for aspirin?

DEANZIE: No, that's fine. I've got some downstairs. Mr. Halloway will be expecting dinner shortly.

THEO: It's on the way up, sir.

DEANZIE: Very good. Well, good night, Theo. Break a leg.

THEO: *(Gives an abrupt look.)* Thank you, sir.

(Deanzie exits. Theo disperses to the kitchen. Tony again slides out of the cabinet. He peruses through Evie's belongings until he finds his mangled manuscript. He carefully sets the dirty pages upright against the back of the couch. A knock comes at the door.)

RALPH: *(Offstage.)* Room service.

(Tony shuffles under the table as Ralph enters with a bread basket and silverware. He sets them down then exits. Tony sneaks out and quickly pockets all but one piece of bread. He darts back to his hiding place just as Ralph returns. The bellboy sets salads then notices the near-empty bread basket. He turns ominously to the cabinet and goes to it. He opens it with an "aha" — but it is empty. Theo returns and stares at the bellboy.)

THEO: Billy? What are you doing?

RALPH: I was . . . I think someone . . . My name is —

THEO: Enough. I'll inform our guests that dinner is served. Put the main course in the oven.

RALPH: Yes of course, Mr. Stintz.

(Theo exits to the hall, Ralph to the kitchen. Tony climbs from under the table with bread stuffed in his mouth. He grabs a salad then runs back into the

cabinet. Ralph returns just as the cabinet slams shut. The bellboy walks deter-
mined to the bar and rushes to the handle, he opens it halfway, revealing Tony
inside. It is then that Theo enters yet again, angry at the sight of his preoc-
cupied staff. Tony is just out of sight.)

THEO: Come on, come on, let's go!

RALPH: But, Mr. Stintz!

THEO: But nothing, Michael! A guest is on his way out. Close the cabinet!

(Ralph does so.)

Get back downstairs and stay by —

RALPH: The front desk. I know.

*(Theo slams the main door on the bellboy. The butler straightens the table as
Jimmy enters in a sporty suit.)*

THEO: Good evening, Mr. Halloway. Lobster is on the way and here is your
garden salad appetizer for two . . . One.

JIMMY: Kinda chintzy on the bread, don't ya' think?

THEO: Oh, I believe you're right. I'll send for more.

JIMMY: Forget it. Dinner is going to be short.

(Theo exits.)

JIMMY: Hey, Evie, you eating or what? Evie? *(Dials phone.)* Yeah, give me Henderson, 5214 . . . Hey, it's me . . . Jimmy . . . A few hours ago . . . Tonight
is my only night . . . I got tickets for some Actor's Studio . . . Thespian
Studio, Actor's Studio, what's the friggin' difference? How many studios
can one town have for God's sake . . . Well, I want to see you and I know
you like that kind of thing . . .

(Evie enters in an understated gown looking gorgeous.)

JIMMY: I think I can suffer through two hours of melodrama . . . How is seven
thirty? . . . See you then. *(He hangs up and notices her.)* Looking fancy.

EVIE: Who was that?

JIMMY: Old friend, lives in New York, wants to get together. Yada-yada-yada.

(They sit for dinner.)

EVIE: Oh. I didn't hear the phone.

(Jim takes her salad.)

EVIE: How do you know her?

JIMMY: Evelyn, why do you automatically assume —

EVIE: Because when you describe this person you describe them genderless. It
doesn't take Sherlock Holmes.

JIMMY: What's with the get-up?

EVIE: We're going to the show.

JIMMY: We?

EVIE: I got tickets for us.

JIMMY: Oh, you got the tickets.

EVIE: I ordered the tickets.

JIMMY: That's right, you ordered them and if I go out I need you by the phone.

EVIE: For what?

JIMMY: In case Harvey's people call.

EVIE: The meeting is set. They would have cancelled by now if they were pulling out.

JIMMY: I guess I wasn't clear.

EVIE: Deanzie can do it. He doesn't have plans.

JIMMY: Deanzie's not my assistant.

(He keeps eating. Evie finally gets it. She takes off her shoes and crosses away.)

JIMMY: You eating?

EVIE: You took my salad.

JIMMY: Lobster is coming.

EVIE: I hate lobster. You know I hate lobster and somehow that's all we ever eat in these joints.

(Grabs the theater tickets.)

I guess you'll be needing only one of these then.

JIMMY: Let me have 'em.

EVIE: You don't need them both, Jim.

JIMMY: Evelyn, give me the damn tickets.

EVIE: No!

(She holds them tightly until Jim forcefully takes them. He is ashamed as he exits the suite. Evie falls into the couch, sobbing silently. Theo enters with an empty tray.)

THEO: The lobster is ready miss, would you like me to —

EVIE: You can throw it out.

THEO: Very good.

(He cleans up then notices she is crying. He rolls his eyes before handing her a handkerchief.)

EVIE: Thank you.

THEO: If there will be nothing more, I'll be downstairs getting stock for tomorrow. It may take time. Will that be all right?

(Evie nods. Theo bows and exits with the full tray. Evie reaches into her purse and pulls out a note pad. She crosses to the table and begins to write. The bar cabinet opens. Tony is about to step out when — a knock comes at the door. Evie sets down her pen and goes to answer. The door opens to reveal Moisha Adelstein, super short, and his bodyguard Max, super tall. They are

dressed in thick brimmed hats, black suits and have curly sideburns. Your basic
Rabbi gangsters. [Klezmer music can accompany their entrance.] Tony again
hides himself away.)

EVIE: Yes?

MOISHA: Hotel security.

EVIE: Yes?

MOISHA: We received call.

EVIE: You must be mistaken.

MOISHA: No mistaken. We weer' notified by front desk. Get call all night. A
vagrant has invaded premise.
(They enter the suite.)
We take little of time. Quick check of all room.

EVIE: But there was no call from here. Let me phone the front desk and
straighten this out. This can't be standard procedure.
*(Max takes the receiver from her and hangs it. Eve turns and finds herself
face to face with Moisha.)*

EVIE: Are those standard security suits?

MOISHA: We look for person.

EVIE: Yes, I got that part.

MOISHA: Young man, curly Q, yay tall. Calls himself writer? You know who
I talk about?

EVIE: No, I'm afraid I spend my time with older man, yay tall, calls himself
"director." Similar, but not the same. You know, you aren't supposed to —

MOISHA: Man we look for is dangerous. Crazy. Meshugener.

EVIE: Meshi? I'm sorry? Mushu . . .

MAX: Shmegegi.

MOISHA: *(Glances to his partner.)* We weer' hired by Bellevue to bring back by
all mean. Avoid embarrassment to hotel. Tell me Ms. —

EVIE: Maryweather.

MOISHA: You have seen no person?

EVIE: No. I have seen no person.

MOISHA: No one has made contact with you?

EVIE: Look, no one has been up here, no one had made any calls, OK?

MAX: No one?

MOISHA: Excuse me.
(He pulls Max aside and quietly addresses him.)

MOISHA: What do I tell you? What do I say? If we both talk what is lost? Tell
me what is lost if we both talk?

MAX: "The impact?"

MOISHA: *(Gestures "exactly.")* Now go. I have no patient to look at you.

MAX: But —

MOISHA: *(Slaps Max's hand away.)* No.

MAX: Please, I —

MOISHA: *(Slaps hand again.)* No.

MAX: Moisha —

MOISHA: *(Another slap.)* That's three!

> *(Like a hurt dog, Max proceeds to check each room — entering and exiting.)*

MOISHA: Forgive intrusion. Just doing job. If you see person, keep distant at all cost. Very dangerous. I have men stationed in lobby. If you have question or information regarding this Nishtikeit please direct to them.

EVIE: Oh, I will. *(She breaks away.)* So, you boys are from Russia I take it?

> *(The mobsters freeze and look at her.)*

MOISHA: No, we are not from Russia.

MAX: Nooo . . .

MOISHA: We come from . . .

MOISHA AND MAX: Utah/Florida.

MOISHA AND MAX: Florida/Utah.

MOISHA: Utah Florida. It's a lovely little town you've never been. Lots of oranges and skiing. Well. Thank you for your hospital'. Now, we weel' go. Max.

EVIE: Very good. Sorry I couldn't be of more assistance.

> *(She shuts the door on them, perhaps smiles at the oddness of it, then gets back to work. After a beat, Tony slips out from his hiding place. She finally notices him.)*

TONY: How ya' doin?

EVIE: Oh, my god. You're the, you're the . . . Curly Q!

TONY: Stay calm. I ain't gonna hurt ya'.

EVIE: What are you doing here?

TONY: I'm hidin' from those men.

EVIE: The orderlies? You're the meshi, mooshu, shmegoogly —

TONY: I'm not what ya' think. And they sure as hell ain't orderlies. Listen to me, Evelyn —

EVIE: He knows my name! How do you know my — ?

TONY: Cause I've been trapped in that friggin' cabinet for an hour, that's how! There was no otha' way.

EVIE: I don't know what you want but you better get out of here! The butler will be back and he's going to be angry with you —

TONY: *(Snatches her from the phone.)* I said calm down! Lowa' your voice! I promise, I won't hurt ya'. Listen to me! They don't work for no hospital. They've had this place staked out all day.

(Brings her to the window.)

Ya' see those men down there? Those men carry guns. They know I'm here and the want me out so they can kill me! How many orderlies in this world wear hats like that? If he had any connection to the hotel he wouldn't 'a asked ya' for your name, Evelyn. He shoulda' known it. New York is strange but it ain't *that* strange. I'm gonna let go-aya'. I won't lay a hand on ya'. Ar-right? Nod ya' head so I know ya' listenin'.

(She nods. Tony lets go and she tries to run. He grabs her again.)

TONY: No! Let's just siddown', we'll wait, then I'll be gone. Good. That's real good. *(Grabs his script from the couch then checks the suite.)* I'm no thug, OK? I got nothin' on me. No weapons. You can frisk me if you like.

EVIE: Look, I have money in my purse. I can get it for you and then you can move on to the next room.

TONY: I'm no thief, Evelyn! I don't wantcha' money. All I want is for ya' to wait and stay calm!

(Paces then takes her pad.)

EVIE: Hey! Give me that!

TONY: No! Siddown'! Sit!

(She does. Tony leafs through her writing and becomes intrigued.)

TONY: Fancy. These are like . . . What do ya' call 'em?

EVIE: Poems?!

TONY: You like to write, huh? Whad'ya know about that? It's a small world ain't it?

EVIE: Tiny.

TONY: You know, I like to write.

EVIE: You don't say.

TONY: In fact, I consida' myself to be a writa'. It's true, ya' know. I am a writa'. I mean, I do write.

EVIE: Oh, I'm sure. With diction like that it's really no wonder.

TONY: I see. You think if a guy says he's a ditch digga' then he musta' dug the Erie Canal, right? Well, it don't really work that way.

EVIE: I *don't* really care.

TONY: Well, I *do* write. In fact, I wrote this. *(Reveals his dirty script.)* It's a play I wrote myself.

EVIE: All by yourself?

TONY: That's right.

EVIE: Wow.

TONY: I also happened to take second place in a writing contest at my old school, P.S. 121 in'a Bronx. And that was in'a third grade.

EVIE: For Pete's sake.

TONY: No, don' say that like it don' mean nothin'. That story almost got published in *Highlights for Children*. It's about this kid, right, who was always playing with his toy car which had the number five on it, right? And this kid, he took that car everywheres' he went. Then, one day, the kid's father brings him to the racetrack. And the kid, of course, he's rootin' heavy for car number five, right? So the race goes and goes, twenty laps, fifty laps, a hundred laps, until at last, it's the final stretch. Car number five is neck and neck for the championship prize. The kid is squeezin' his toy car on the sideline for good luck then, woops, a minor miscalculation by da' driva' and, whamo! Car number five goes topplin' over sideways, flippin' and flyin', this way and that, then it smacks on'a concrete like a pancake and woosh! The whole thing goes up in'a huge explosion! Smoke and flame everywhere. Silence falls onta' da' crowd. The toy car slips out of the kid's hand and falls onta' da' dirt. Pretty ironic, don't ya' think?

EVIE: It's brilliant.

TONY: But? You think there should be more.

EVIE: Look, I'm not getting into a conversation with you about this or anything else, OK?

TONY: Hey. Fine. whateva. You know, I think I'm being pretty decent about all'a this. I know I ain't supposed to be here but I ain't gonna hurt ya'. Ya' don't wanna' talk, ya' don't wanna' talk. Seems to me like you're dyin' for some decent conversation after what I heard. I mean, sittin' alone in Manhattan on'a weekend don't seem like a whole barrel of laughs to me, but, you know, suit ya'self.

EVIE: *(Silence before she submits.)* So, what happens to the kid?

TONY: The kid?

EVIE: The kid, the kid!

TONY: I don't know, I don't know. That was how it ended.

EVIE: It's not very happy.

TONY: Does everything have to be rainbows and sunshine?

EVIE: No, but the general rule is to walk away from a story having learned something.

TONY: All right. Maybe the kid goes home and stares long and hard into the mirra' only to realize that, maybe, five ain't his lucky number after all.

EVIE: Look, how much longer is this going to last? Those men have probably gone by now.

TONY: A few more minutes, a'right? You know, I'm not really like this. I mean, if you knew me —

EVIE: I don't know you.

TONY: I know, that's why I'm sayin' "if" —

EVIE: But I know why you're here so don't bother explaining it. What? You think you're the first person to try and sneak in here with the next great American screenplay?

TONY: No —

EVIE: You think if he came walking in that door, he'd strike up a conversation and be willing to listen to a story about a kid with his toy car?

TONY: No, I —

EVIE: Look at you. Look how you're dressed. Your manuscript is in no condition to be put in the hands of a man like James Halloway. *(Reading:)* "An Italian Female Immigrant Farmer at the Dawn of the Industrial Age." Is that a synopsis?

TONY: It's the title.

EVIE: *(Stares at him for a moment.)* Oh, yeah. Jimmy'd call the cops the second he laid eyes on you. Who knows. With your troubles maybe that's just what you want and damnit, it makes me wonder if he's right for God's sake and he really isn't being too paranoid about weirdos like you.
(Tony tries to speak.)

EVIE: I don't want to hear about it Mr. Burglar Writer Man! No-names like you are all under the impression that because you recorded your thoughts or because you appeared in your high school's production of *Our Town,* you can hop a bus to Hollywood and jump headlong into the business.

TONY: I'm from the Bronx.

EVIE: Are you listening? Breaking into this suite isn't helping you, Bucko!

TONY: My name is Tony.

EVIE: It's been tried before and I'm sorry to inform you this is not how things get done!

TONY: Oh, yeah, then what's the trick?

EVIE: *(Gets in his face.) The trick,* Tony from the Bronx, is about gaining the trust of people who have more power than you, more everything! Success doesn't depend on your ideas or how creative you are, but on whether or not you order the same wine as the producer you sit with for lunch because if you do, that must mean you have good taste! It's a crapshoot, and you're playing with people who make a sport of throwing promises into the wind simply because they can, and I assure you not one of these egomaniacs will ever hold true until you learn to stroke him in just the right way which is an art form in itself ten times more complex than writing! You have to forget everything you know about logic and right and wrong until you are as smooth talking, sharp shooting and cutthroat as the rest of them! That is the trick, Mr. Burglar Writer Man, cut and print! *(She sits, thinks, stands.)* At the rate you're going, I imagine you'll soon be in prison, or you will probably be . . . I mean you'll be —

TONY: Dead? Go on, say it. Look lady, I'm sorry I busted in here. I really am. I had no otha' choice. I'm at the bottom of my rope and I didn't know what else to do. I tell ya', if I'da known you'd be rev'd up to make this big speech, *believe me I'da gone someplace else.* But I didn't just wake up this mornin' and decide to break in here, a'right? I been trying for weeks to get this script out there. I sent it through the proper avenues, to the studios. But nobody eva' called. They didn't even send it back.

EVIE: To whom exactly did you send it?

TONY: What do you mean, "Whom"? The studios. Like Universal Studios?

EVIE: You addressed it to "Universal Studios."

TONY: Well . . . Yeah.

EVIE: *(Covers her face.)* Look, you had to have some brains in order to know that Mr. Halloway would even be here.

TONY: It just happened.

EVIE: You happened to meander into the room of a famous director?

TONY: I recognized him at the airport. I was about to hop on a plane as a last —

EVIE: Recognized him from where?

TONY: He did a shoot a few years back in *Variety.*

EVIE: And you remember that?

TONY: I never forget a face.

(Theo enters the main door carrying a kilt and a blonde wig.)

THEO: Oh, forgive me, I . . . Management need extra hands at a costume party on twelve and I . . . *(He fashions the wig then quickly takes it off.)* Excuse me.

(Theo exits to the kitchen. Evie breaks away from the table but Tony's voice stops her.)

TONY: Don't rat me out, Eve. I'm harmless I swear.

EVIE: Then why are these people after you?

TONY: I owe money. They are loan sharks from out by me. I came up with the idea for my script, I knew it was good, I mean it is good —

EVIE: *(Warning him.)* The butler is coming.

TONY: I needed the money to take a break from the pizza shop so I could write.

EVIE: *(Wryly.)* The pizza shop?

TONY: That's right. You gotta problem with that?

EVIE: No. I —

TONY: I thought I had a few weeks but the Rabbi cut my time. I gotta pay by midnight tomorra' or I'm as dead as —

THEO: *(Returns from the kitchen.)* Please, forgive my interruption. Is everything OK, Ms. Maryweather?

EVIE: Yes. Our guest was just leaving.

THEO: Well, if you won't be needing me I'll be in my quarters. Sir.

TONY: Good night.

(Theo exits out the main door. Evie crosses away from her assailant.)

TONY: Thanks. I owe you. You know. I think I know that guy. The butler, he is —

EVIE: It's time for you to go. If Mr. Halloway comes back things could get out of hand. The last thing he needs are stranger ideas than the ones he's already got.

TONY: Right. Look, Evie —

EVIE: Just get out!

(She rushes to hit him but Tony grabs her wrist. He wraps his free arm around her waist and pulls her close.)

TONY: You know, this may be my last one.

(He kisses her. Evie struggles for a moment then succumbs. The clock chimes as he dips her. They kiss passionately until Tony finally breaks away. He struts to the door, smiling as he exits. The lights change as swelling music ensues [perhaps "Rhapsody in Blue"]. Evelyn leans against the door posturing with sensuality. She goes to the table and finds the dirty script. As the music reaches a sultry climax, Evie turns the first page and begins to read. Blackout.)

END OF ACT I

ACT II

SATURDAY MORNING

Lights up. Deanzie is at the table with the paper. Theo is pouring him a drink.

DEANZIE: The market is all over the place.

THEO: Indeed.

DEANZIE: You own stock, Theo?

THEO: Five hundred shares in the Ritz Carlton Company. Christmas bonus last year.

DEANZIE: No kidding. Any openings in this joint?

(Jimmy enters the suite in shorts and a sweater. He goes straight to the bar.)

THEO: Good morning, Mr. Halloway.

JIMMY: Morning. I thought you'd be sleeping in.

DEANZIE: Are you kidding? Tonight's the big meeting. I have to keep you happy for the rest of the day. How was the show?

JIMMY: Good.

DEANZIE: What?

JIMMY: Is that so strange?

DEANZIE: Coming from you.

JIMMY: When something is good, it's good. I'm not going to be a jerk about it simply because I have problems.

DEANZIE: Tell me about it.

JIMMY: There was one guy who really stuck out.

DEANZIE: Oh, yeah?

JIMMY: Stole the show. I mean this actor, he brought you right there, you know? Just a small role at the top, but whew, he was something. Tell you the truth he looked kind of familiar but he was wearing this blonde wig so it was hard to tell.

DEANZIE: What was the part?

JIMMY: Oh, he played this violent ex-con fresh out of Leavenworth named . . . What was it? McLurey. Boy, was he creepy.

(Theo stops his work and stares briefly at the audience.)

JIMMY: He had this perfect Scottish accent. Half the time you couldn't even understand him but it worked. Kept ranting about throwing people out of windows.

(Theo darts out of the room.)

DEANZIE: Charming.

JIMMY: I waited to talk to the guy but he left before curtain call.

DEANZIE: Did you get his name?

JIMMY: I forgot the program. Evie'll pick one up before we leave.

DEANZIE: I'll bet she had fun. She loves that avant-garde stuff.

JIMMY: *(Downs his drink.)* Evie didn't go.

DEANZIE: Oh? Was she not feeling well?

JIMMY: No, she was fine. And I don't want to hear about it, got me?

DEANZIE: *(Examines Jim narrowly.)* I swear. I swear, Jim, if I had the strength I had ten years ago I'd pop you one right in the kisser, I would!

JIMMY: I just said that I —

DEANZIE: An imbecile!

JIMMY: Lower your voice, would you?

DEANZIE: Who'd you go with?

JIMMY: *Person.*

DEANZIE: A person. Did this person have breasts?

JIMMY: Oh, what does it matter? I went out.

DEANZIE: And she knows? *(Digests Jim's glare.)* When are you going to learn? Don't you understand that you need her?

JIMMY: How do you know what I need? Huh, Dennis? I don't keep you around to tell me who is right for me and who is wrong. Contrary to public vote, you are not my father.

DEANZIE: You're so cotton-picking dense. I'm talking about your business, you moron. Are you so blind you think she has nothing to do with that? You think you do all this on your own? Evie represents you, she makes all the preliminary friendships, she siphons through the crappy scripts, she placates the studio heads at your parties.

JIMMY: You the head of her fan club now?

DEANZIE: Look how you got this Harvey meeting. Never even met the girl and the biggest man in Tinseltown took it upon himself to call *her* up, probably to offer her a job. He didn't ask for you, Jim. Not until she talked you up like you are some sort of genius or something, which, contrary to the popular vote, you are not!

JIMMY: One more word from you, Dennis, and —

DEANZIE: And what? I'm a lawyer. I'll sue your ass for every dime and I know exactly how many dimes you got left, Jimbo. *(This gets Jim's attention.)* That's right. She's not made of rock and steel, not the way she plays off. She tries to be strong but you're too much. She's a daisy and you're a . . . You're a friggin' bulldozer, and I can't stand around and watch while you roll over her again. I know Evelyn, Jim. I'm her friend.

JIMMY: Yeah? Well, that's all you'll ever be.

(This hurts Dennis. He gathers his belongings quietly and stops at the door.)

DEANZIE: You know something? It wasn't that actor that turned you into this person that no one can touch.

JIMMY: Is that right?

DEANZIE: That's right. Success, Jim. You haven't tamed it, you see? It's tamed you.

JIMMY: Thanks for the fortune cookie, Mahatma.

DEANZIE: You're gonna lose her, my friend. If you haven't already.

(Deanzie exits. Jim's anger rises until he punches like a child into thin air. Evie enters from the hallway in a robe. Tony's script opened in one hand, a box of tissue in the other. She has been crying. She sits at the table and reads with her back to Jim. It takes him a few tries before the words come out.)

JIMMY: We've got a big day ahead of us, huh?

(She blows her nose.)

JIMMY: Evelyn, I understand you're upset.

(Evie sniffles.)

JIMMY: And maybe what I did last night was wrong. What I did to you I mean. I mean . . . Maybe it was wrong. I don't want my emotions to distract me and I forget sometimes the things I do, the things I say, well, they have an effect.

(She bursts into tears.)

JIMMY: Oh, Evie. Don't do that. I've hurt you, I know, but nothing happened last night. I care about you Eve and I . . . That's what I want to say. I understand you need time to sort all this out. That's fine. I'm here for you. Are you going to be all right? Evie? Evelyn?

(She turns to him in a haze.)

JIMMY: Are you going to be OK?

EVIE: *(Tears billowing.)* Yeah . . . How've you been?

JIMMY: Well, I'm fine.

EVIE: That's good. I'm sorry, Jim. It's just that, if you knew . . .

JIMMY: Knew what? Tell me.

EVIE: I mean, she is so sad. So sad. Oh, God.

(More tears.)

JIMMY: I know. I know she's sad, kiddo.

EVIE: I mean, she worked so hard for so long. All of her life.

JIMMY: I know she did.

EVIE: And what did she get in return? What did the world ever bring her?

JIMMY: Grief?

EVIE: Yes! It breaks your heart doesn't it? I can't seem to let it go.

JIMMY: We'll get through it, I promise we will.

EVIE: Don't get me wrong . . .

JIMMY: No, no —

EVIE: It's going to take work.

JIMMY: Everything does —

EVIE: I mean . . . It needs a rewrite. A complete overhaul. But the structure and the story . . . I've never read anything like it. *(Laughs through tears.)* I'm sorry, did I . . . ? Were you saying something?

JIMMY: Forget it.

EVIE: No, is there something on your mind?

JIMMY: I said forget it.

(Studies her.)

So what's it about?

EVIE: What?

JIMMY: That.

EVIE: This?

JIMMY: Yes.

EVIE: Nothing.

JIMMY: You just said it was the best thing you ever read.

EVIE: You wouldn't like it.

JIMMY: Why not?

EVIE: I think you know.

JIMMY: No, Evelyn, I don't.

EVIE: Well you should. It happens every Monday afternoon when the manuscripts come in. If I love a script and beg you to read it, you will hate it on principle, because I'm a woman, or because I'm not enough of a woman. I mean, who knows what goes on in that complicated brain of yours. But if I tell you I think you'll hate a script, for whatever reason, you end up loving it.

JIMMY: I don't think so.

EVIE: Good. Then do yourself a favor and don't read this script. It lacks honesty, integrity. In fact, it's not even a story. It's just a mishmash of words on paper with a comma sprinkled here and there —

JIMMY: *(He snatches the script.)* Jesus, you could catch a disease from this thing.

EVIE: It's seen a lot of offices.

JIMMY: "An Italian Female Immigrant Farmer at the Dawn of the Industrial Age?" What the hell kind of title is that?

EVIE: A bad one. I'll give you that.

JIMMY: Tony . . . *Simpa Low Knee?* Is that Cherokee Indian?

EVIE: Simpolini, Jim. It's Italian.

JIMMY: It's just a play.

EVIE: Yes, Jim. *Hamlet* is just a play. That didn't stop, oh, what's his name, Olivier, from giving it a try. *Arsenic and Old Lace* is just a play.

JIMMY: No, that's a film with Cary Grant.

EVIE: It was a play first.

JIMMY: So you found something. Good. I'll read it on the plane tomorrow.

EVIE: It doesn't belong to the studio. He's East Coast and may be back to pick it up.

JIMMY: What? You're telling me this Navajo was here?

EVIE: Oh, what do you care? I don't have to explain anything to you. Not after last night. That was the straw that broke the camel's back. I mean the camel, Jim, if you stop to look at it, it's pretty much dead.

JIMMY: Evelyn, come on. You heard what I said. I told you what I thought.

EVIE: Wow. What an accomplishment.

JIMMY: Everything's fine. We're at the pressure point with Harvey coming, that's all. It's like we're waiting in limbo in the second act for this cataclysmic event and we're all getting a little nuts. There's a storm brewing on the horizon and —

EVIE: For God's sake, this isn't a movie. We're not discussing plot.

JIMMY: I know this isn't a —

EVIE: We're talking about our lives.

JIMMY: I know what we're talking about. I'm trying to make a point.

EVIE: Yeah, yeah, you and your points. You'd be lucky if an English professor could make sense of 'em.

JIMMY: What's gotten into you? Give me something I can work with here or why bother with this?

EVIE: Do you remember when we met, Jim?

JIMMY: Yes.

EVIE: You found me in the literary department. I was what, twenty? And you helped me, gave me a job. Taught me to walk the rope of a Hollywood lunch. Made me good at what I do.

JIMMY: I made you the best.

EVIE: And I believed that the sun rose and set with you. You sure had me convinced of it.

JIMMY: But . . .

EVIE: But I don't see you like that anymore.

JIMMY: Yeah. I'm trying to figure out why that is.

EVIE: Oh, I know why. I know now. *(They lock eyes.)* It's the way you look at me.

JIMMY: How do I look at you?

EVIE: It's the way you talk to me. The way you treat me.

JIMMY: Evelyn —

EVIE: It never seems to get through your head that I'm a woman now and am able to deduce things *at least* as fast as you. I am no longer that little girl. I no longer emulate you, I don't look up to you, I don't even know if I like you.

JIMMY: What is this, Evie's coming-of-age hour?

EVIE: Oh, Jim.

JIMMY: Yes, OK, you've changed, Eve. You don't think I see that? Believe me I see it. But I've changed too. I have. In fact, we've changed, you know why? Because that's what people do, Eve. They change. But you only knew me a short time before the attack. I was a *much* different guy back then.

EVIE: Oh, yes. The attack, the attack. The horrible attack. How could you have survived such an ordeal?

JIMMY: Hey, don't make it sound like that, OK? We're talking here. What happened that night changed my life forever.

EVIE: Why, Jim? He went to jail.

JIMMY: But the scars remain.

EVIE: What scars, for the love of Pete! You had a bruised knee and a swollen thumb.

JIMMY: Emotional scars, Evie. You of all people should understand that. It was your idea I see some headshrinker.

EVIE: A psychiatrist, which you never did.

JIMMY: I deal with the attack my way.

EVIE: Oh, what's to deal with? Some actor broke into your house and wrestled with you for one minute on your bearskin rug while you beat him over the head with a script. To tell you the truth I can't believe the struggle lasted as long as it did. That actor, he was what, a midget? You're practically twice his size.

JIMMY: He was carrying a ten-inch hunting knife, Evie!

EVIE: You know, every time you tell that story the knife gets a little longer. Have you noticed that? In the police report it's probably described as a plastic spoon.

JIMMY: All right, you know what? Give it a rest, would you? I've got things on my mind and I don't —

EVIE: Oh, yes, the big important man. Do you know what you really are, Jim?

JIMMY: Does my response even matter?

EVIE: One big baby. Everybody has to say everything just the right way. Everybody has to laugh at all your stupid jokes and if you scrape your elbow we have to make a holiday out of it so every year we can look back and remember the strength it took for you to endure such unending agony. Going out?

JIMMY: You're crazy if you think I'm going to listen to this.

EVIE: Oh, don't worry. One of these days you won't have to. I just might make a change around here.

JIMMY: Fine, Eve. Whatever you want to do, we'll do.

EVIE: I'm making a change, Jim.

JIMMY: I said fine! You want to start writing your little poetry again then go right ahead.

EVIE: Who said I ever stopped? Maybe I'll move to New York.

JIMMY: *(Laughs.)* Fine, move to New York.

EVIE: I don't need your permission.

(He tries to touch her.)

EVIE: No, Jim.

JIMMY: Come on, Eve.

EVIE: No!

(She slaps him hard across the face. Jim backs away. He puts on his coat then exits the suite. Evie has a sense of victory on her face. After a moment, a knock comes at the door.)

EVIE: Oh, give it a rest. The dumb clod. You're not going to make me feel —
(She opens it to reveal Tony. He is in new clothes and is groomed.)

TONY: How ya' doin'?

EVIE: You know you managed to leave your script. Guess that was part of the plan, huh? Can't get Halloway, then get his assistant. Kiss the girl, dump the script, come back in the morning for the review?

TONY: Not afta' what ya' said last night.

EVIE: I'm trying to forget last night if you don't mind.

TONY: You was right about me, ya' know. It's hopeless. I don't know how things work. I should stick to flippin' pizza and forget this idea that I can somehow get out'a'da Bronx.

EVIE: Well, what are you doing here? Isn't it dangerous for you to be out and about?

TONY: The place has cleared some. Two of 'em are still parked arounda' corner to keep an eye, but I figure it was safe enough for me to sneak in and apologize, to you, I mean, like a gentleman or whateva'. And to, ya' know —

EVIE: You're welcome.

TONY: Right. And I wanted to give ya' somethin'.

(He hands her an envelope. Evie reads something tender and kind.)

TONY: I found change in a telephone booth to pay for'da card but the pen unfortunately had to be swiped from'da gift shop. Well, it was nice knowing you. Thanks for saving my life and everything.

(Moves to the door.)

EVIE: I read your script.

TONY: Garbage, huh?

EVIE: No. It looks like garbage. I mean, I've read scripts that stunk before but never one that actually had its own scent.

TONY: What'd'ya think?

EVIE: It's good.

TONY: Yeah?

EVIE: Yes. In fact, as much as I hate to say it, it's more than good.

TONY: No kiddin'?

EVIE: No, no kiddin'. It needs work. A lot of grammatical errors, more than I've ever seen. And you've got to change that title.

TONY: You don't like, "An Italian Female Immigrant Farmer at the Dawn of the Industrial " —

EVIE: It's a drop wordy. Titles need to be catchy. Two words that hook us into the story.

TONY: Oh, OK. How 'bout "Immigrant Farmer."

EVIE: One word.

TONY: "Farmer"?

EVIE: It doesn't matter. Are you for real?

TONY: I'm standin' here, ain't I?

EVIE: Tony . . . You say you wrote this but, honestly, I listen to you —

TONY: Eve. I may *sound* stupid, but I ain't no chump.

EVIE: Right.

TONY: When I was a kid I was the only guy in the neighborhood who didn't go to Times Square to pick people's pockets. I was always sneakin' in the stage door of the Barrymore to catch the show. Lot'a good that did me.

EVIE: Wait. (Leafs through the script.) That scene, when she's on the prairie, "Martha sticks da' shovel in da' dirt. She goes to da' farm and finds it on fire. Storage lost, a harvest she single-handedly labored over is —"

EVIE AND TONY: "Lost in da' plumes'a smoke."

EVIE: You did write this.

TONY: Look, Evelyn, about last night.

EVIE: I told you I was trying to forget that.

TONY: No, I have to say this. I think I stepped ova, ya' know, like those lines they have . . . The, uh . . . What are they called?

EVIE: Boundaries?

TONY: Yeah, I may have stepped ova' 'em.

EVIE: You did.

TONY: Yeah, 'ats what I thought. And it was wrong'a me.

EVIE: It was.

TONY: And I'm sorry for that. Things were pretty crazy. *(Gets close to her.)* And also, last night . . .

EVIE: Yes . . .

TONY: It's funny but, I could have sworn —

EVIE: Uh-huh.

TONY: When I kissed you —

EVIE: Really?

> *(They are entwined in a passionate embrace. Deanzie enters drunk, bottle in hand. The lovebirds scramble.)*

DEANZIE: Hello. Oh, *hello*. Company, my dear?

EVIE: Yes. Tony Simpolini, meet Dennis Dean. Jimmy's lawyer.

DEANZIE: Nice to meet you, kid.

TONY: Mr. Dean.

DEANZIE: So where is he?

EVIE: Out pondering greatness.

DEANZIE: Good. Let him take his time. I could use the peace.

EVIE: Amen to that.

DEANZIE: And what's your story son?

EVIE: Tony's a writer here in New York.

DEANZIE: A writer? Better get him out. When you're living under this roof only one creative person is allowed at all times. And how do you two know each other if you don't mind my asking?

TONY: Oh, last night I broke inta'da suite and took Ms. Maryweather hostage.

DEANZIE: *(Laughs drunkenly.)* And you write spy novels I gather?

TONY: Plays.

DEANZIE: With the studio?

EVIE: Tony freelances.

TONY: What she means is that I'm broke and out of a job.

DEANZIE: Money and the arts don't have much in common, kid. Aside for the lucky few.

TONY: Yeah, I'm just learnin' that.

EVIE: Well, you won't be out of a job forever.

TONY: That's right. I'll be dead and buried before I make it to the unemployment line.

EVIE: We are going to sell your script.

TONY: Oh, really? *Really?*

EVIE: Tony, I have an address book a mile long and every name in it is connected. Hopefully it won't come to that. Hopefully we can make things happen with who we know.

TONY: Who do we know? I don't know anybody.

EVIE: Have you forgotten why you came up here in the first place?

TONY: Yeah, but afta' everything you said —

EVIE: Oh, forget what I said.

TONY: I don't know. He makes movies about glory and honor and all that. My script is about an Italian female immigrant farmer at the dawn of the industrial age. Very borin' to a guy like Halloway. No explosions. No bombs dropping. Besides, it's just'a play.

EVIE: Now you sound like him.

TONY: What does 'at mean?

EVIE: It means plays are transcribed every day. Where do you think the studios get their stories? Sooner or later every good play becomes a mediocre movie.

DEANZIE: From what I'm hearing it sounds like a hard sell. No offense kid.

EVIE: But you haven't read it, it's very good.

DEANZIE: Oh, I'm sure it is.

EVIE: Will you then? Come on, Deanz, I need backup on this. He's always talking about producing his own picture and this could very well be it.

TONY: I think I should get going.

EVIE: You're not going anywhere. Sit down.

DEANZIE: Atta' girl.

EVIE: And no smart talk out of you.

DEANZIE: Sorry.

EVIE: Read this as fast as you can and don't skim. Please, Dennis.

DEANZIE: How can I say no to you?

> *(She hands him the script.)*

> Yuck . . . What is this?

EVIE: Don't mind the stains, after a while you begin to appreciate them. I'll set you up in there. *(To Tony.)* Don't go anywhere.

> *(She exits with Deanzie. Tony checks out the window as Theo enters and cleans.)*

THEO: Good evening.

TONY: How ya' doin'? *(Studies him.)* Say, uh, do I know you?

THEO: Sir?

TONY: I know you from somewheres don't I?

THEO: We met briefly last night.

TONY: No, no. Because even then I knew I knew you. What's your name? Wait, don't tell me. Stintz, right? Theo Stintz? You played King Lear at the Thespian Studio!

THEO: Oh, no. I'm afraid not.

TONY: No, no, I never forget a face. My name's Tony. Tony Simpolini. I'm a writa' here in New York.

THEO: A pleasure. Though I must say you have me mistaken with another actor — person.

TONY: Come on, I know it was you. You was really good in that show. I mean it. I was on the edga' my seat even from the back row.

(Theo looks around to make sure no one is listening. His accent suddenly becomes blue-collar New Yorker, ten times thicker than Tony's voice.)

THEO: Well, t'anks, t'anks a lot. Dat's real nice'a'ya to say. Dat was a pretty grueling production actually. King Lear can take a lot out a'ya.

TONY: *(Double takes.)* Where you from, Stintz?

THEO: Yonka's, born and bred.

TONY: Yonka's? What's wit'da voice?

THEO: Well, trut' is, I used it when I applied for da' job, convinced management I was from England, ya' know, give myself dat' air'a elegance. And ever since dat' day I haven't been able to use my natural voice cause they got a strict "no actor policy" here at da' Ritz. Da' staff is convinced I'm from West Bambridge just south'a London and to tell ya' da' trut', I don't even know if there is such a place as Bambridge just south'a of London. I t'ink some of the bellboys are gettin' wise.

TONY: Say, that's dedication. No wonder you belong to the Thespian Studio. You doing anything now?

THEO: Closed a show last night actually. *Scottish Luck?*

TONY: Oh, yeah, yeah. I heard'a it. I tried to get tickets but I couldn't scrounge up the cash. You know it costs almost fi' dollars to see a Broadway play. Fi' dollars!

THEO: Well, it's a precursor'a things to come.

TONY: It sure is . . . How do ya' mean?

THEO: I mean theater prices'll keep goin' up as long as'a competition keeps growin'.

TONY: Competition?

(Evie peeks out from the hallway.)

THEO: Television, Simpolini. People don't need to leave da' house no more to be enta-tained, they just go to the livin' room.

TONY: Yeah, you know I know a guy with two televisions. I mean, he stole 'em but —

THEO: Of course you do. And dat's exactly why stages are empty and movie studios are foldin' by da' numbers. The audience just ain't there no more. *(Evie exits.)*

So, Hollywood sends its key players to the Big Apple wit' bundles of cash in their hand, people like this Halloway, and they scramble to buy out all'a talent before da' television heads do da' same thing. Talent which rightly belongs to the theater.

TONY: Sounds complicated.

THEO: Yeah, well, maybe. I mean, don't get me wrong, I like da' pictures, are you kiddin'? I love 'em! I put my life on the line just'a get an audition. That's boo-koo dollars. I just can't help wonderin' where things are going. I mean try to imagine Bra'way fifty years fr'now, right? You're standing on Times Square on New Year's Eve and da' clock is about to chime midnight. And the people are cheerin' as you look down'a strip to a total of maybe ten theater marquees, which will be all dat's left by then, and da' only shows you see playin' are *revivals!* Think about it. A Bra-way so friggin' dead'a ideas they're still putting up productions'a *Oklahoma,* or *Kiss Me Kate,* for Chrissake!

TONY: Hey, hey. Now, wait'a second, Stintz. Those shows are enta-tainin'. They're good. I mean, don't get me wrong —

THEO AND TONY: They ain't Shakespeare.

THEO: *(As if asking "You see?")* Eh?!

TONY: *(As if replying "No.")* Eh.

THEO: *(As if asking "You don't?")* Eh?!

TONY: *(As if saying "Maybe I do.")* Eh . . .

THEO: *(As if saying "Come on!")* Eh!!

THEO AND TONY: *(As if coming to a mutual understanding.)* Ehhh!!

THEO: All I'm saying is dat' one day Bra'way'll be so starved for talent it'll have nothin' to fall back on but "da' show," you know? Da' sets and costumes'll become so friggin' bizzaro that ticket price'll go trewda' roof. I mean they'll have plays where the entire cast jumps around on pogo-sticks or wears rolla-skates for God's sake, you know, crazy stuff. There'll be pratfalls and mistaken identities, people hidin' in cabinets to keep away from da "bad guys."

(He and Tony share a brief, mechanical glance with the audience.)

THEO: It'll be one endless vaudevillian nightmare. All da' while real theater will be pushed so far aside dat' you'll have to go down a darkened back-street basement just to find it. And shows that are considered mainstream will be re-vamped versions of the movies cause dat's exactly what the the-ater is competin' against! Mark my words, one day some moron is gonna trow' down a million dollars to create da' staged musical version of *Bridge on the River Kwai!* They'll have a river, they'll have a bridge and every night it'll explode. Trow' in a couple songs, add an exclamation point to the title, and you're looking at the future of theater. But let me tell you some-thin' Simpolini. That ain't the worst of it.

TONY: No?

THEO: As'right. One day, artistic inspiration will be such an idea of the past that they'll just put ten people together in a living room or on'a bus or some deserted friggin' island and they'll just . . . Film it.

TONY: And?

THEO: And that's it.

TONY: Come on, Stintz. What would be the point of that?

THEO: I have no idea. But audiences will be so starved for a sense of da' raw human emotion that they'll be fighting to watch. All of this, my friend, leaves us right where we are. *(Another glance to the crowd.)* All I can say is I pray I don't live to see da' day when every play ends with people hold-ing guns to each others' heads until da' good guys break in and save da' day. I really do —

(Evie enters. Theo's accent shoots back to British.)

THEO: — Believe that at the current rate of the New York stock, the annual presumption of the four-point-four ratings of any conglomerate can be beneficial to those who hold shares, given, of course, that the market is stable and healthily rising. So my advice to you, Mr. Simpolini, is sim-ply this . . . Government bonds.

TONY: *(Beat.)* The hell you talkin' about?

EVIE: Hi.

TONY: Oh. Hey.

THEO: Well, I humbly thank you, Mr. Simpolini, for a most pleasurable dis-cussion of today's market. I shall now disperse and make my exit. That is to say, take my cue. I shall simply leave.

(He exits.)

TONY: And I thought I had a lot on my mind. The butler takes the cake.

EVIE: You must be tired. You can nap here.

TONY: Evelyn —

EVIE: When was the last time you slept on a bed? You can pay them as soon as we sell your script.

TONY: These people don't work that way. I'm puttin' you in danger the longa' I stay.

EVIE: You have until twelve.

TONY: They could come any time. The Rabbi found me in Manhattan one day afta' I left the neighborhood. One day! And here I thought I'd be a needle in a stacka' hay.

EVIE: The Rabbi is the man I met?

TONY: That's what he calls himself. His real name is Moisha Adelstein, from Little Ukraine. Just a street thug. That getup he's got on is his gimmick. Everybody in his neighborhood is a Hasidic Jew so Moisha and his crew use the frock to stay sorta underground.

EVIE: Seems like more of a pain than it's worth.

TONY: Look, don't ask me. All I wanted to do was stop by and thank you, and now I've done that.

EVIE: Wait! What if this Moisha does know you're here? Maybe the reason he hasn't come for you is that he thinks you are getting the money. I mean this is the Ritz. If he saw you leave then come back, he's bound to think that you know someone. And besides, if you're going to make a clean get-away you'll need to rest.

TONY: Evelyn, why are you so nice to me? Nobody has eva' been so —

EVIE: I know. That's why you've got these troubles. It's why we all do. Come on.

(She points him to the guest room. He exits. Evie sits at the table and calls to the kitchen.)

EVIE: Mr. Stintz? Theo?

THEO: *(Enters.)* Ms. Maryweather? How may I be of service?

EVIE: King Lear?

THEO: *(Picks up the phone.)* Would you like me to find where it's playing? There are several productions currently headlined on the strip. I could easily acquire reservations for your party —

EVIE: King Lear . . . Thespian Studio . . . You.

THEO: *(Sets down the phone — New York accent returns.)* I suppose da' gig is up.

EVIE: That's right it is. I'm going to keep my mouth shut, OK? But you owe me, understood? How much experience do you have?

THEO: I've been around the block. At the studio I was voted best nonwork-
     ing actor.
EVIE: Well, it's a start. Now listen, people are coming here tonight and some
     of them aren't necessarily "guests," if you catch my meaning.
THEO: I think I unda-stand.
EVIE: We're going to have to keep on our toes. I guess in your language that
     means —
THEO: We improvise.
EVIE: Exactly. Come with me and I'll explain!
     (They exit to the kitchen. Up-beat jazz fills the room. Blackout.)

INTERMISSION

ACT III

SATURDAY NIGHT

Lively Klesmer music fills the stage then cuts off. Lights up. Deanzie is on the couch weeping out of control over Tony's script. He sheds long, loud, and pathetic tears. He blows his nose on the pages, wipes it, then bursts into more tears. Evie sits beside as Deanzie leafs through the script and points to the text.

DEANZIE: "Lost in da' plumes of smoke . . ." *(He bursts into even more emotion and manages to gain his composure through the following.)* Of course you were right. Gouldenburg's war script is like *The Howdy Doody Show* compared to this. It's raw, to the heart. When she goes back to the farm to find that it's burning down 'cause that moron dropped a cigarette in the hay, my God. *(More uncontrolled tears.)* Jimmy has got to get his hands on this.

(Tony enters from the guest bedroom.)

DEANZIE: Look who it is. Odets himself. Great story, kid.

TONY: Thanks Mr. Dean. Evie, I gotta go.

EVIE: You still have time.

TONY: No. It's late. It ain't safe no more.

DEANZIE: Safe?

EVIE: He's just being funny.

TONY: I think it would be best if I tried to get to Grand Central. That's my only hope.

EVIE: Where will you go?

TONY: Anywhere but here.

DEANZIE: What's going on?

TONY: I owe money, Mr. Dean.

DEANZIE: Don't we all? How much?

TONY: Seventeen hundred big ones.

DEANZIE: That's a lot of bananas. You paying off a student loan?

TONY: Naw, nothin' like that. I owe the mob.

DEANZIE: The mob?

TONY: That's right.

DEANZIE: The *mob* mob?

TONY: *Yeah, yeah.* They were here last night looking for me.

DEANZIE: What?

EVIE: Oh, he's just fooling.

DEANZIE: Fooling?

TONY: No I'm not. It's a long story, Mr. Dean.

DEANZIE: Story?

TONY: Yeah. I gotta get out of here before they stop by again.

DEANZIE: Again?

TONY: *(Confused.)* Yeah . . .

(A knock comes at the door. Tony rushes to the cabinet and is about to hide.)

JIMMY: *(Offstage.)* Hey, open up. It's me for God's sake.

DEANZIE: Eve, think about what you're doing.

(Deanzie opens the door. Jim enters.)

DEANZIE: You forget the key?

JIMMY: Obviously. Harvey call?

EVIE: Nothing's changed. He should be here soon.

DEANZIE: Where have you been?

JIMMY: I took a walk. Am I allowed to do that or have you got more to say?

DEANZIE: It's good to see you back, that's all.

JIMMY: Who is this?

EVIE: Tony Simpolini, meet James Halloway. Remember that script I showed you?

JIMMY: You mean, the one that smells? How could I forget?

EVIE: I thought you could take a look at it before the meeting.

JIMMY: Evie tells me you stopped by last night.

TONY: I was just on my way out.

EVIE: Just read the first act, Jim. I'm recommending it to you.

JIMMY: So? Let's see what all the fuss is about.

(She hands him the script.)

JIMMY: No money in plays kid. Got to write for the big screen if you want to make a life of it. All right. Well, right off the bat every word in your opening description is . . . misspelled.

(He looks warily to Eve. She gestures for him to continue.)

JIMMY: And what kind of first line is this? "We're out of wheat"? That doesn't work kid, a beginning has got to hook you by the —

(Jimmy gets quiet. The others watch as he finishes the first page and starts with the second.)

DEANZIE: That's when you get us, right from the start.

EVIE: Exactly. You stamp out Martha to us in the first description and she unfolds from there.

TONY: I can't believe you think it's good.

DEANZIE: Modesty.

EVIE: When she makes her way to Nathaniel's farm because she has finally figured out his true identity.

DEANZIE: *(Getting emotional.)* And he has to tell her about the accident in the field when he dropped the baby headfirst against the anvil!

JIMMY: Do you mind?

EVIE: Sorry.

DEANZIE: Sorry, Jim.

JIMMY: I'll take it inside. Tell me when Harvey buzzes.

DEANZIE: Sure thing.

(Jim exits.)

EVIE: If he stays long enough for Jimmy to finish, then maybe —

DEANZIE: No maybe, Evelyn. Even if he loves it, it takes time to negotiate these deals. You know that.

EVIE: He'll have no chance if he leaves.

DEANZIE: That may be the case, but we have business tonight. Harvey, Evie. Harvey is coming.

TONY: He's right. There's nothin' more you can do. Good-bye, Evelyn. I'll try and contact you as soon as I'm safe.

(The two lovebirds share a heartfelt moment. Tony opens the door and is face to face with Moisha and Max. Max grabs Tony violently.)

DEANZIE: Hey!

(Moisha gives Deanzie a punch to the gut. He falls to the floor.)

TONY: Take it easy! You said I had until midnight!

MOISHA: I did. But I keep close eye. Debt cause man do strange thing.

TONY: I thought I lost you.

MOISHA: Almost, but when you come back to hotel you ruin chance of that. Not so smart me think.

EVIE: Are you people crazy? You can't stay!

MOISHA: Ah, Ms. Maryweather. How nice to see. We have no intention of stay. I think it odd you not know curly-haired nishtekeit when I question yesterday. Make things difficult, yes? We wouldn't be back if you just tell truth.

EVIE: I didn't know and I certainly wouldn't have told the likes of you.

(Moisha pulls her to her knees.)

TONY: You bastard!

MOISHA: Maybe you come back for a reason, eh?

TONY: Go to hell!

MOISHA: Where is my money? Do you see the pain you cause friends?

TONY: I don't have your money.

MOISHA: That is no good, Simpolini. For a moment I thought you would, how they say, "pull through."

TONY: I'm happy to disappoint you. Let's get it ova' with. Take me and leave these people alone.

(Moisha thinks this is a good idea. He tosses Evelyn aside while Max pushes Tony to the door.)

EVIE: The money will be here!

TONY: Evelyn, don't —

MOISHA: You can vouch for him?

EVIE: Yes, I can.

TONY: No, she can't.

MOISHA: The writer seems to think no.

EVIE: I work for James Halloway the Hollywood director. He will pay Tony's debt.

DEANZIE: Evelyn!

MOISHA: Well where is he?

EVIE: In the next room talking with the bank.

(Moisha nods for Max to check it out. Max simply nods back. Moisha gestures again and Max returns another nod. He doesn't get it. They continue this way until Moisha loses his patience:)

MOISHA: Max! Go find him!

EVIE: Wait a second. Don't tell me this is how you boys do business. A deal is a deal. You said twelve o'clock. Isn't it enough that you barged in here? Are you not men of your word?

(Max looks to Moisha for orders. Moisha tells him to continue.)

DEANZIE: Now hold on a cotton-picking minute! Mr. Halloway isn't some two-bit Joe off the street. You got me? He's a very powerful man who knows people in very powerful places —

EVIE: Senate, congress.

DEANZIE: *(Shares a doubtful look with Eve.)* That's right! And if you bust in there and try to muscle him tonight, he will use all of his power to seek you out and make your life a living hell first thing tomorrow morning. So please, consider this.

(Moisha signals for Max to stop his investigation.)

MOISHA: We weel' wait.

(He pulls out a gun and motions for everyone to sit. Max grabs Evie and Deanzie and sits between them on the couch.)

MOISHA: *(Continued. In Tony's face.)* Well, well, well. We are here. Face-to-face. A couple of silver spoons, no? You know, I never like you. Not when we weer' kids and not now. You sit in doghouse you call apartment and eat crumbs while you work to make money to buy typing paper. That is what you do. That is life. So I had Max do you favor.

TONY: What's that?

MOISHA: The typewriter, it go to bottom of East River. After tonight, you won't be needing. Not that it did you good in first place.

EVIE: Look, can't you just wait in the lobby?

MOISHA: No one talks to you Minnie Mouse so do my ears favor and shut up!

TONY: Good ol', Moisha. Always had a way with women.

MOISHA: And you should watch what you say. This is not game of stickball.

TONY: At this point what difference does it make what I say? You know, all the guys in the neighborhood were hope'n you'd make it trew'da cracks. You used to be OK. I guess you're workin' for the old man full-time now, huh?

MOISHA: Tell me, Tony. Are you the lefty or the righty?

TONY: Lefty.

MOISHA: Max, break his hand. His right hand.

(Max grabs his left hand.)

MOISHA: The opposite one from the one he said!

(Tony yelps as his fingers are brought to the breaking point. Suddenly, Jimmy enters. He wipes tears as he reads the script. He crosses to the bar, oblivious to the situation, pours a drink and downs it. Moisha signals for Max to stop, the gun is put away. Jimmy finally turns to the room.)

EVIE: *(Announcing.)* Mr. Halloway!

JIMMY: Oh. You're here.

MOISHA: I am.

JIMMY: No one told me you arrived.

MOISHA: Perhaps we came too soon.

JIMMY: No, no. It's an honor to meet you. You have all my respect.

EVIE: Jim —

JIMMY: I have to tell you I truly enjoy what you do. And I also want you to know that I think you and I are going to have a strong relationship, business and otherwise. I didn't expect you to be so young and so . . . Jewish.

EVIE: Jim!

JIMMY: But judging from the great things I've heard about you, that you are a one-of-a-kind kind of guy, it's no wonder you're dressed up for Halloween.

DEANZIE: Dear God.

JIMMY: Listen, I'm in the middle of a read. I hate to keep you waiting, but this . . . Do you mind if I take just a few minutes to skim the rest? Rest assured, we will do business in just a jiffy.

MOISHA: We will discuss writer, no?

JIMMY: Simpauloanee here? I thought we were discussing direction, but, whatever you want is fine. You're in charge.

MOISHA: Good, then my mind is clear.

JIMMY: Great. So make yourself comfortable and I'll be with you in a flash.

MOISHA: By all mean.

(Jim buries his head back in the script and walks off the way he came.)

EVIE: Are you satisfied? I told you he would vouch for Tony. Now can we please be civilized about this?

(A knock comes at the door. Evie and Deanzie share a petrified look.)

MOISHA: Answer. But remember before you forget, I watch close. Don't try anything with humor.

(Evie nervously goes to the door. She opens it to reveal the round Harvey Gouldenburg making out with his buxom girl of the week, Florence. She giggles as she chomps gum.)

EVIE: Mr. Gouldenburg.

HARVEY: In the flesh.

EVIE: You're early.

HARVEY: Evelyn Maryweather. You are more beautiful than what the boys on the golf course say.

(He storms into the room.)

EVIE: Please, um, come in.

(Harvey slaps Evie's butt and smiles.)

FLORENCE: Harvey!

HARVEY: Take it easy, Flo, take it easy. This is New York, it's the custom.

FLORENCE: It's your custom.

HARVEY: Can it. *(They growl at each other.)* How ya' doing, how ya' doing. Good to see you all. How is everybody? *(Studies Moisha and Max.)* Well, well, well. What do we have here? Let me guess. The robes say to me . . . Investors.

DEANZIE: This isn't happening.

EVIE: How about a drink, Mr. Gouldenburg?

HARVEY: Sure. Hey, what about you boys? Evie, call down for some Manachevitz for the boys here. *(Slaps Moisha and Max on the back.)* I tell ya', if I don't step foot on another plane in this lifetime it won't be too soon.

FLORENCE: It wasn't that bad.

HARVEY: Does somebody hear a bird chirping? Chirp chirp, chirp, chirp.

FLORENCE: Come on, Harv. I'm tired'a talking.

HARVEY: That's just how I like it, Hummingbird.

FLORENCE: And you promised we'd go dancing.

(She pulls off her mink scarf and reveals her skin-tight dress.)

HARVEY: I did, didn't I? *(He kisses and dips her.)* The brain power is amazing. A never ending fountain of information. Gonna make a star out of her one day.

FLORENCE: So you keep telling me.

(Harvey slaps her butt and the two of them moan in excitement.)

MOISHA: Max, show Mr. Goldenbreasts a seat.

HARVEY: No, hey, I been on my behind all day. I sat and I sat and I —

(Max grabs Harvey by the neck and throws him into a seat.)

HARVEY: Hey, that's quite a grip you got there, Schlomo. See Flo, customs.

EVIE: Welcome, Mr. Gouldenburg . . . The situation is . . . Let me say that it really is an absolute —

HARVEY: Evie — *(He gently smacks her cheek.)* Don't say another word, the pleasure is all mine. *(Clenches tightly on her thigh.)* They tell me you've become quite the expert at bringing together the heavy hitters.

(Slaps her hard on the back.)

DEANZIE: Mr. Gouldenburg, you have no idea.

HARVEY: Say. You got any food in this place? Some nuts or something? My stomach is acting up.

FLORENCE: That's what happens when you eat the rabbit food, Harv.

HARVEY: Hey, Flamingo Lady, pipe down.

EVIE: Food should be up shortly. In fact the butler —

HARVEY: Good. Flaberbaum, that's my doctor, he's got me on one of them strict veggie diets now and sometimes a head of broccoli . . . Has more power than you think.

(No one knows what to say. Harvey slaps his own thigh and rises.)

HARVEY: Ooh, I'm excited. I'm telling you, this town is like another country, right? All the different people, all the nooks and crannies. All the oddball cultures.

EVIE: Well, it is an exciting place. Never quite know what'll happen next.

FLORENCE: Exciting, yeah, I give you that, sister. Except for this yawn, of course. All he ever does is go to meet'n, after meet'n, after meet'n, after meet'n, after meet'n, after meet'n, after meet'n —

HARVEY: You'll have to forgive my darling bud. I found her at the mental institution and she has an undying condition of the yap. It never takes a nap.

FLORENCE: Yeah, look who's talking about talking.

HARVEY: Flo!

FLORENCE: *(To the Rabbis.)* So. You boys know of any good clubs around here? But like, good ones, not some speakeasy. We hear the jazz is from this place they call . . . Harem.

EVIE: That's Harlem.

FLORENCE: Say, I like this look you boys have here. Very South American. You look like Zorro. Hey Harv, doesn't he look exactly like Zorro?

HARVEY: Hey, Woodpecker, can you give it a rest for ten seconds?

FLORENCE: I wonder if they sell these at Macy's. Turn for me. Turn.

(Max spins fashionably for Flo.)

DEANZIE: Are you two . . . ?

HARVEY: Are you kidding? *(Slaps Deanzie's back.)* So, where's Jim? I look forward to finally meeting him. Kind of amazing that we miss each other. We do live in the same zip code for God's sake.

EVIE: Actually, he's on with the coast stamping out the details of another contract.

HARVEY: Contract? I didn't realize. It was my understanding Jim was working on nada-mucho-pucho as they say down south. On the road to H.B. city.

EVIE: H.B.?

HARVEY: Has Been.

DEANZIE: Oh, no, not Jimmy. Are you kidding? H.B.? That's funny. Isn't that funny, Eve?

(They both laugh nervously. Deanzie encourages Tony to join in.)

DEANZIE: Jim's always got something up his sleeve, Mr. Gouldenburg. Even when he doesn't know it.

EVIE: He sure has. He should be out soon.

HARVEY: Well, I can't wait for that.

MOISHA: Neither can I.

HARVEY: Now, Evie, tell me, who is everyone? I'm looking around this room thinking I'm supposed to be at a meet'n but instead I'm feeling guilty for not going to temple.

HARVEY: *(To the Rabbis.)* Did my mother send you?

(Slaps his leg and laughs, everyone follows suit.)

EVIE: Well, this is Dennis Dean, Jimmy's lawyer.

(Harvey retracts his extended handshake, leaving Deanzie in the wind.)

HARVEY: Eh, a bloodsucker, good to know ya'.

EVIE: And this is Tony Simpolini. A writer.

HARVEY: Simpolini? Yeah, yeah. I like your work.

(Gives a hearty handshake.)

TONY: Um, thanks.

HARVEY: You got the Oscar for writing *Winter in Sicily*. Right?

TONY: No, I can't say I did.

HARVEY: Well, you should have for Chrissake! *(Slaps Tony's shoulder.)* So, I guess you all know who I am.

FLORENCE: Harv. Hello?

HARVEY: Oh, right. I almost forgot. This is my pet parakeet, Petunia.

FLORENCE: Florence. Hiya.

HARVEY: Can it. Now, what about these guys? How you hooked up to the Jimster?

EVIE: Oh, they're just associates. Pay them no mind.

HARVEY: Pay them no mind? These two and I are practically — paesan!

(Silence.)

That's a joke, people. *(More fake laughter.)* So you're a Rabbi?

MOISHA: Some would call me that.

HARVEY: Some? Ha! What do you know? I guess the tribe is more liberal in the east. I thought it was the other way around. See, the Rabbis by me don't really go the traditional route. They all got winter homes and sunglasses, fast cars and modern temples made of glass. I like this painting. Besides, it's L.A. Way too hot to be running all over town in those heavy robes. You'd probably sweat like a pig in that getup. Whoops, did I say pig? Sorry, Rabbi. We'll call it a horse. OK, so let me guess, why would Halloway have a Rabbi in his suite? Why would Halloway have a Rabbi in his suite? It's an odd one, ain't it, Flo?

FLORENCE: *(Zero interest.)* It's killing me, Harv.

HARVEY: I think I got it. Let me take a stab. You are here . . . To collect donations. Am I right? Am I right?

(Harvey laughs at his own idiocy and smacks his knee with joy. He then gives Moisha a slap on the back. Moisha stands abruptly and reveals the gun.)

HARVEY: Whoa! I'm just kiddin', padre!

MOISHA: I am out of my patient!

HARVEY: See, Flo, crazy customs. What's real, what's not? Who knows?

MOISHA: Shut up fat man!

HARVEY: Hey, now wait a minute. That's not very funny. I try to stay fit. I eat well. My mom said I was big boned —

MOISHA: It's not meant as a humor, you house! Now keep mouth shut!

HARVEY: All right, all right, take it easy, Rabbi. He's a real live wire, ain't he, Flo?

FLORENCE: Harvey, I think this is real.

HARVEY: Well of course, Israel. It don't take science to see these guys ain't from Australia.

FLORENCE: Not Israel, you dumb clod. Is real. As in, real.

HARVEY: What are you saying?

FLORENCE: Are you mental or something? Real, real, real, real, real, real, real, real, real, real, real —

HARVEY: *(Suddenly understanding.)* Evelyn, is this —

MOISHA: This is real fat man! This is real gun! This is real bullet!

EVIE: Mr. Stintz?!

MOISHA: You be quiet, girl. *(To Tony.)* Maybe I should blow brains out here and now, save myself gasoline. What do you think, Max?

MAX: But we have full tank . . .
    (For a moment all eyes are on Max.)

EVIE: Mr. Stintz! Mr. Sti — Mr. McLurey, Mr. McLurey!

MOISHA: For the last time I say be quiet!
    (Suddenly, a prideful Scottish marching anthem begins to play loud bagpipes. The characters are unsure of where the music is coming from. The main door swings open and the lights change.)
    (Theo boldly steps in wearing his costume from the Thespian Studio: Blond wig, kilt, plaid hat — Scottish. He is menacing and hard to understand through a thick brogue.)

THEO: Aye! What is it then?! Well? What have you to say for yourself? *(Signals for the music to cut, which it does.)* I know it's no matter to you but I was trying to take a dump out in the service lavatory and I'd like to get back to me business if that isn't all right with you for the love of friggin' St. Sebastian.

EVIE: I . . . We . . .

THEO: "I, we"? *(Grabs her neck.)* What then lass? Cat gotcher-tongue? I want to know what all the damn ruckus is about and if you don't talk I swear to the Lord in heaven who protects us that I'll toss you straight out that window like a pretty polly!

TONY: If you let go of her then maybe she could speak.

THEO: Zip it, Shakespeare!

DEANZIE: *(Realizing.)* Theo?

THEO: *(Grabs Deanz by the throat.)* No one calls me by that! No one not ever! Not you, or you, or you. Have you got me? Have you got me old man?

DEANZIE: I got you, I got you.

THEO: Damn right you do and ya' won't get rid'a me! *(Pushes him to a seat.)*

Now, before I grab somebody by their bleedin' knob and toss 'em clear through that window, what in the name of all lovin' Christ is going on? I see the regular cast of characters. And I see old man Gouldenburg and his child bride, as expected. Though, it's hard to imagine what these two look like under the sheets. I mean, let's face the bagpipes folks. Let's wake up and smell the whiskey. There is something crass in the image of a five hundred year old humpback whale mating with a newborn gazelle still wet from birth.

EVIE: Let's not get carried away Mr. Mc . . . Theo.

THEO: *(Grabs her again.)* What did you say?! What did I finish jabbering about not two bits ago, aye? What is my name, eh?! What is it, littl'un before I nail you to a plank and send you up the Hudson!

TONY: He really is good.

THEO: Zip it, boy! Not another peep or it'll be out the window with the lot of yeh'!

FLORENCE: Harvey, is he some sorta' . . . pirate?

MOISHA: Yes. What the hell are you?

THEO: Well, right. What do we have here? The newest members of the O'Vatican friggin' church I take it? The name's McLurey it is, case you haven't been listenin'. Francis, Ian, William, Wallace, Rob, Roy McLurey the fourteenth. Descended from the original line of McLureys back in the homeland as it is.

EVIE: This is . . . He is Mr. Halloway's personal bodyguard.

THEO: That's right, I'm a full-blown bodyguard and with me it's always personal. I was born and bred to guard the body of anyone who can match me price and let me tell yeh', in my country there is no bodyguard that is more trained than the man who stands before ye' now, shy and silent as an oak.

HARVEY: *(To Florence.)* Shy?

THEO: I've grown shy havin' to spend most me life in a Turkish prison. Let me ask you something, you black robed heap of wet dung, do you know what they do to yeh' in Turkey if you dress up like a holy man? If you impersonate a man of the cloth? *Answer me or I swear to all the saints and Devils that I'll grab your beard-ridden skull and chuck you clear out that window!*

MOISHA: I can't understand what you even say.

(Gestures that the situation is 'over his head.')

THEO: They cut your diamonds off in Turkey, that's what they do. Then they tie your hands to your feet, behind your back, and leave you on the roof of a four-story building so you can either roast to death, which is always pleasant, or you can roll yourself overboard and end it all. So, the moral of the story, the lesson that is to be taken with yeh' to ponder on in the wee hours of the night is simply this, don't — move — to Turkey.

HARVEY: Well. Thanks for the good time, people. Evie, it's been great. I think me and my gazelle will be heading out now. Come on Bambi, we have reservations —

THEO: Sit down!

HARVEY AND FLORENCE: OK.

THEO: Now. I'll ask it one more time before I get angry. What in the name, of all loving Christ —

MOISHA: We have no business with you. We leave now.

THEO: Not with Shakespeare. He stays until midnight. Wasn't that the deal?

TONY: That was da' deal Mr. Adelstein had made with me, as'right Mr. McLurey, and I think it's only fair that —

THEO: All right, all right, Shakespeare. No need to recite a friggin' monologue. Yes or bleedin' no will do good and proper.

MOISHA: That was deal. But we go now.

(Moisha and Max aim their guns.)

THEO: Oooh, I see yeh got yer' pee-shooters aimed at me, do yeh? I've had many weapons pointed in my direction. I'll start by saying that.

MOISHA: No. This is where you stop.

THEO: You willin' to bet on that? I swear it's out the window with the both of yeh'.

MAX: Stay where you are.

THEO: Look into me eyes and say that. Make me believe you are goin' to shoot 'cause I don't think ye' got the spirit.

MAX: Stop moving!

THEO: *(Prances in a Scottish half step.)* Is that what you really want me to do? I spend the last five years o' me life in an American prison and you want to be the first person to give me an order since I got out?

DEANZIE: How many prisons you been to?

THEO: Shut up you!

EVIE: Gentlemen please!

MOISHA: Max! Shoot him!

(Max goes to pull the trigger. The room gasps. Theo starts to laugh.)

THEO: Yer safety's on. You boys are top-notch low-level thieves, aye? Your safety. Here, let me show you.

MOISHA: Max, no!

THEO: *(Consoles Max and takes the gun.)* See, the safety, it's this button right here. Ha-ha!

(Points the gun at Max who runs out of the suite in fear. Tony thinks fast. He spins out of Moisha's grip and begins struggling for the other gun. The fight for the weapon comes center stage. The gun begins to shake in their hands à la the ending of every 'cop' movie ever made. It is a very long, silly moment. Finally, Tony gives Moisha a knee to the gut and gains control.)

TONY AND THEO: Freeze!

TONY: Now, Mr. Adelstein, I think it's about time you left. I'll come up with the money in a few weeks. You can wait for me to —

JIMMY: *(Enters.)* What is going on out here? *(Notices Theo with the gun aimed at Moisha.)* You're from the Actor's STUDIO!!!

(Jimmy cracks Theo across the face with the script! He takes the butler down and beats him with it. The gun is lost in the confusion, the wig goes flying.)

EVIE: Jimmy, no!

JIMMY: I knew you were an actor! I knew I recognized you! Going for my producer, huh? Harvey Gouldenburg is an important man you son of a — Take that, and —

(Jimmy helps Moisha off the floor. The Rabbi has reclaimed the gun.)

JIMMY: I'm so sorry, Mr. Gouldenburg. Are you all right? *(To Evie.)* Psychiatry, huh? There's your psychiatry.

DEANZIE: Jim, you don't understand!

JIMMY: I understand just fine —

(Moisha puts the gun to Jim's neck.)

JIMMY: I understand Mr. Gouldenburg is upset. You're in shock, Harv, that's all. I've done extensive research on the subject and what you are feeling now is perfectly natural. Nine times out of ten a good "massage" will cure that right up.

DEANZIE: Jim! This is Mr. Gouldenburg!

JIMMY: What?

HARVEY: How ya' doing, Jim?

EVIE: It's what we've been trying to tell you.

JIMMY: Then who the hell is this?

TONY: *(With the gun still poised to fire.)* He's a debt collector, Mr. Halloway.

JIMMY: Jesus, kid, put the gun down.

TONY: I'm afraid I can't do that.

JIMMY: Evie, I'm a little confused.

MOISHA: *(Tosses Jim aside and aims at Tony.)* Go ahead! Let's shoot each other.

Just like in movie, no? And what an audience you have. Now put gun down before you make me kill you in front of people.

FLORENCE: This is getting exciting.

HARVEY: Would you shut up you magpie!

FLORENCE: Oh, I should shut up? 'Israel,' Harvey, and I should shut up? For God's sake!

HARVEY: One more word you ignoramus and I'll —

JIMMY: Hold on everybody, just hold on! Simpauloanee, I don't know what you got us into but you have some explaining to do.

EVIE: He owes money, Jim.

JIMMY: How much? How much, for God's sake?

MOISHA: Seventeen hundred dollars, Mr. Hollywood. And for pain and suffering of having to partake in little circus, he owes three hundred more.

JIMMY: Wait. Everybody just wait. I'm going to do something here and I don't want anyone to get excited. OK? I advise you all to stay calm. Deanzie, open the safe.

(Deanzie does.)

JIMMY: Harvey, welcome. *(They shake hands.)* As you can see I'm in a pretty difficult circumstance.

HARVEY: Yeah. Maybe we should postpone. My corns are killing me.

JIMMY: If I was in a different frame of mind I'd agree. But I would appreciate it if you could stick around. I promise that I'll make it worth your while. Man to man.

MOISHA: This becomes tiresome.

JIMMY: Deanzie. Gimme' five grand.

(Deanz quickly hands him the cash. Meanwhile, Evie grabs the manuscript and waits for the next command. Jimmy turns to Tony and throws an arm over his shoulder.)

JIMMY: Come here kid. Come on, take a walk with Uncle Jimmy. Come on, put the gun down.

(Tony, frazzled, steps away with Jim.)

JIMMY: That scene, when she sticks the shovel in the dirt. That is really something. And then she goes back to the farm and you have that great description. What is it?

EVIE AND DEANZIE: "Lost in da' plumes'a smoke."

JIMMY: And I love the way you used really bad grammar to let us see how uneducated your characters are. It's brilliant. Damn brilliant.

MOISHA: *(Points at his gun.)* Ahem!

JIMMY: Hold your robes! *(To Tony.)* Where in God's good heaven did you come up with that?

TONY: Well, when I was a kid, my building caught fire. I remember my motha' was standin' on the street watching them put it out. I think most of what I wrote came from that.

JIMMY: It all boils down to our mothers, doesn't it?

(Everyone nods.)

HARVEY: It does, it really does.

JIMMY: Now listen, kid. I'm buying your script and I want you to transcribe it from a play into a movie. Deanzie will set up the paperwork if you're interested. If not, you can always head out with this clown.

(He offers two folds of money. Tony takes it.)

JIMMY: Now give me the gun, kid.

(Tony reluctantly hands the pistol to Jim who then turns to Moisha and hands off the rest of the cash.)

JIMMY: Are we clear? Everybody happy? Then you can go.

(Moisha turns to leave.)

JIMMY: But before you do, I want to ask you something.

MOISHA: And what is that?

JIMMY: Do you want to know how I know you are stupid?

EVIE: Jesus, Jimmy, just let him go.

JIMMY: No, no, don't worry, Eve. I'm going to say the right thing here. Nobody invited this guy and I want him to know how I know he is stupid.

MOISHA: *(Aims at Jimmy.)* I warn you, you should not say such —

JIMMY: I know you are stupid because you, a businessman — *(Pushes Moisha's gun aside.)* Didn't have the brains to simply take a look at what this kid is doing. He's talented, you know that? And that means something where we come from. Right? *(Everyone nods.)* And another thing. You have no right to be dressing up like this. It's an insult to people who really do have the faith. It's people like you that give a bad name to criminals all around the world. *(Dramatically.)* Now take your hat . . .

(Jimmy pulls Moisha's hat off. The "curly sideburns" are stapled to it.)

JIMMY: And get out of here!

(Jimmy pushes him out and slams the door. Everyone is joyous.)

DEANZIE: Bravo! Belisimo! Extroardinario!

(The happiness is short lived as Harvey is guiding Flo out.)

JIMMY: Harvey. Wait. You said you'd stay.

HARVEY: This is a bit much for me, Jimbo. I like how you handled that, no wonder you make the war pictures, but I need to check my blood pressure. Look at me Flo, I'm breaking out in hives.

FLORENCE: You look fine.

(Jim rushes to him and throws an arm around his shoulder.)

JIMMY: What's your favorite drink?

HARVEY: Awe, really. Enough is enough.

FLORENCE: Gin, straight. That's his juice.

JIMMY: Mr. Stintz?

(Theo pops out from behind the dinner table wearing a sour look and a black eye.)

JIMMY: If you would, and some niblets for everyone.

(Theo is almost at the kitchen.)

JIMMY: Oh, and Stintz. Sorry I mugged you like that. You had me fooled. What'd'ya say we screen-test you for my next picture? I think we can find a part for him somewhere, right, Eve.

EVIE: I think we can manage it.

THEO: No kiddin'?

JIMMY: No, no kiddin'.

THEO: Mr. Halloway, I don't know what to say. Are you serious? That would be, I mean, I can't believe you'd —

JIMMY: Food, Stintz, food. You're not a working actor yet.

THEO: Right, food, food.

(Theo darts to the kitchen. Deanzie is having Tony sign forms at the table.)

JIMMY: *(To Harvey.)* Now, I don't want to waste your time, Harvey, so I'm going to be blunt because after all this, you deserve it.

HARVEY: Flo, my pills.

(She pulls a pillbox from her cleavage.)

JIMMY: We talked about signing me as the director for *The Great War.*

HARVEY: Well, we had discussed it —

JIMMY: Before we take it any further I want you to know that I'll have to decline on that.

HARVEY: Then I'm at a loss. What am I doing here if —

JIMMY: *(Evie hands him the play.)* I've recently purchased a script that I believe is worth your having a look at. It's called, "An Italian Female Im . . ." *(Thinks.)* The Immigrant. It's called *The Immigrant.* Now, you give me an hour of your time and if you don't like what we've got, we separate with a handshake. OK? Come on. We'll sit on the balcony and look at the park.

HARVEY: It's cold out, Jimbo.

(Slaps Jim's back.)

JIMMY: It's heated, Harv. This is the Ritz. *(Returns the slap in mutual admiration.)* Now, imagine farmland as far as the eye can see. It is the dawn of the industrial age. A strong immigrant is plowing the cornfield. She's no beauty queen, her qualities lie deep within.

(He, Harvey, and Flo exit down the hall. Theo returns with a tray of snacks. Evie takes it and sets it down.)

EVIE: You think you overdid it, Stintz? I told you to stall those guys, not enrage them. You almost got shot.

THEO: I'm sorry, Eve. It's my training. You know what our motto at da' studio is? "If it ain't real, it's crap." I only hope it was worth it.

EVIE: Well he did offer you a part.

THEO: My God, he did didn't he?!

EVIE: I mean it won't be a lead or anything.

THEO: Who needs a lead? It's always the supporting role dat' you remember.

EVIE: Why don't you take the night off? We'll take care of you.

THEO: Tanks', Evie.

TONY: Hey, Stintz. Thanks. Thanks for stickin' ya' neck out.

THEO: Hey, we all have our own motivation. Don't you forget what we talked about now.

TONY: It was a little over my head, but —

THEO: Ah, you heard me. End'a'da twentieth century, Times Square, midnight. We'll be old and broken then, but you'll remember.

(Theo exits to the kitchen.)

DEANZIE: *(Spent of emotion.)* I feel like we just said good-bye to the Scarecrow. The things people do for their craft.

(Tony and Eve embrace.)

DEANZIE: Well, I suppose we should get out there. Help Jim along.

EVIE: He's doing fine by himself.

DEANZIE: *(Weighs her statement.)* You done good cookie. You know I love you.

EVIE: I know. I love you too.

DEANZIE: Nice meeting you kid. Take care of her.

(He walks off somberly, turns to Eve, winks and exits.)

EVIE: Well, Tony. Last night you were on the verge of becoming a hardened criminal and tonight you're practically a Hollywood success. Not much difference between these two things.

TONY: Eve. I gotta lot I want to say. I wish I could start all over, pretend I met you in a different place.

EVIE: And you will.

(Goes to kiss him.)

TONY: Wait. You don't know what ya' getting into.

EVIE: I know enough.

TONY: You know my script.

EVIE: I know how I felt after you kissed me. I want to feel that way again. Especially now that you've taken a shower.

TONY: Evie, it's me. Can't you see I have nothin' to offa'. If you saw where I lived, believe me, you'd think twice.

EVIE: I don't care.

TONY: Well it's a dump. The toilet is out in da' hall and I share it with all the tenants on da' sixth floor. A walk-up, I might add. I can't snap my fingas' and make people clean my shoes. This is all da' money I have to my name. Don't get me wrong, I'm not complainin'. I'm just not good enough for you.

EVIE: Tony. I've got too many people in my life who tell me what I want.

TONY: Yeah? Well, what *do* you want?

EVIE: I want to pick up where I left off, no compromises. I want to stay in New York. I want to go to the shows and see the buildings and quaint corners and I want to do all that with you.

TONY: You do?

EVIE: Why not? And besides, Mr. Burglar Writer Man. You think I don't make a living?

(She takes the money and tosses it to the table. They kiss. The clock chimes. Jimmy arrives and watches them.)

JIMMY: Simpolini.

(Tony scrambles.)

JIMMY: What do you think you're doing?

TONY: I, uh . . . leavin'.

JIMMY: Stop.

(Gets in Tony's face.)

Shouldn't you be doing something right now?

TONY: Well, if I'm gonna fight you, Mr. Halloway, I better start by praying to —

JIMMY: Gouldenburg is waiting to hear the pitch. Well? What are you standing there for? Get in there.

(Tony exits down the hall in a happy strut.)

JIMMY: You like this fella? Stupid question.

EVIE: Jim, I'm sorry, I —

JIMMY: Don't apologize. Let me do the talking. You're used to that, right? I want to thank you, Eve. Thanks for setting this up. You saved my hide once again, didn't you? Look. Whatever happens, just, try not to remember me as a bad man, OK?

EVIE: Oh, Jim, you're not bad. You're not.

JIMMY: Then why am I losing everyone?

EVIE: You don't lose them Jim. You push them away.

JIMMY: Why do I do that?

EVIE: Jimmy, you can't get caught up in the smooth talk and the sharp shooting and the idea that everybody wants something from you —

(Jim tries to interrupt.)

EVIE: No matter how true it may be. You have to succumb to it.

JIMMY: English, Eve.

EVIE: I'm saying, because people need something from you is the best reason to give it. You helped people tonight, didn't you? Doesn't that make you feel good? Isn't that proof of something? Not everyone is out to get you, Jim. Especially not the ones who are close.

JIMMY: You know what? If Gouldenburg bites, and he's already nibbling, you are going to be associate producer on this thing.

EVIE: Oh, Jim, don't —

JIMMY: Why not? It's fair. You set the meeting. You found the script, you deserve a shot. Just do me a favor before you disappear into New York for the winter. Get your associate producing butt in there and make sure your wonder boy doesn't louse this whole thing up.

EVIE: Oh, Jim!

(She goes to hug him but Jim puts up his hands in humble protest.)

JIMMY: Call me when you get back in town.

(Evie exits. Jim exhales and smiles to himself. Meanwhile, Florence enters with a smirk. Jim finally notices her.)

JIMMY: Hi.

FLORENCE: Hi.

JIMMY: You want a drink?

FLORENCE: Whiskey, straight.

JIMMY: Have a seat.

FLORENCE: I like your movies.

JIMMY: Yeah? Thank you. That means a lot to me.

FLORENCE: You're welcome.

JIMMY: And, uh, which ones?

FLORENCE: What?

JIMMY: Nothing. So . . . you're Harvey's assistant?

(Florence smiles and blows a bubble. It pops. Blackout.)

END OF PLAY

SPANISH GIRL

By Hunt Holman

This play is dedicated to Phoebe

ORIGINAL PRODUCTION

Spanish Girl was first produced by Second Stage Theater in their New Plays Uptown Series, July 2002. It was directed by Erica Schmidt with the following cast:

BUCKY . . . . Joey Kern
CHET . . . . Nate Mooney
JOLENE . . . . Jama Williamson
SKYLER . . . . Ari Graynor

Sets . . . . Michelle Malavet
Costumes. . . . . Juman Malouf
Lights. . . . . Shelly Sabel
Sound . . . . Bart Fasbender
Stage Manager . . . . Jennifer O'Byrne

CHARACTERS

BUCKY: Twenty, college guy
CHET: Twenty, roommate
JOLENE: Twenty, girlfriend
SKYLER: Sixteen, summer love

TIME

The present.

SETTING

A shitty attic apartment in a small college town. There are three openings in the upstage wall. The one upstage right has a door in it, which opens to Chet's room. The one upstage center opens onto the staircase down to the door leading out, on the ground floor. The one upstage left leads to Bucky's room, and it is blocked by a tie-dyed sheet hung over a curtain rod. There is a refrigerator stage right of the door to Chet's room. On the stage right wall, there is a window looking out on trees and houses, and an efficiency-style kitchen. On the stage left wall, there is a door leading to the bathroom. Down center there is a table with chairs, piled high with Chet's Greek books, and other flotsam. There is a stuffed chair down left, facing the table.

Spanish Girl

Bucky and Chet sit at the kitchen table of a shitty attic apartment. There is a square of orange light on the wall behind them, from the sun setting outside the window.

BUCKY: She had green eyes and blonde hair that shone in the sun and she walked toward me down this gravel path and my mouth fell open, or whatever. I could feel my butt hole yawning open in fear and shock at the sight of her, she was so beautiful. She was looking at me and she smiled, and her teeth were terrible.

CHET: How terrible?

BUCKY: You could pass a quarter between two of them. And the edges were black. Like she could floss with like, a shoelace.

CHET: Dude. Heinous.

BUCKY: But we went through this month of lingering stares before we arranged to have the same day off, not together, it just happened that way. All our days off everyone just sat on this crappy beach on the west side of the island and got shitfaced at ten in the morning, then slept all afternoon. Woke up at dinner time hung over and sunburned. And I took her off into the woods and we made out, like behind some log.

CHET: How glamorous.

BUCKY: And I whispered into her ear, "Te Quiero . . ."

CHET: What does that mean?

BUCKY: I don't know. It's like, I love you, or I want you, or something. Professora Herrick told us it was what romantic Spaniards said to their amorosas, so I thought maybe it might get me into her pants.

CHET: Did it?

BUCKY: No. She said she didn't believe me.

CHET: Smart girl.

BUCKY: But she was a really good kisser.

CHET: What about her teeth?

BUCKY: Forgot all about them. You know, like, as long as she wasn't smiling . . .

CHET: Man, that's gross.

BUCKY: It was a hot sunny day. I was drunk.

CHET: I'd be afraid they were contagious.

BUCKY: Not after you heard her accent.

CHET: Spanish accent?

BUCKY: Very Old World. Something about a woman with an accent, and like, cheekbones, just. I don't know. It's like a big pile of cash. I just. I can't help myself.

CHET: But you didn't get in her pants?

BUCKY: We were in the woods, behind this log. There were sticks and bugs and dirt.

CHET: Sounds perfect.

BUCKY: People back at the beach started to wake up.

CHET: Sunburned and hung over . . .

BUCKY: They wanted to go for pizza. They started calling our names. So, we walked out.

CHET: Did they applaud?

BUCKY: No. See, because I was already having this torrid affair with this other girl, who like, nobody thought I should be with her.

CHET: Why not?

BUCKY: Well, because she was seventeen.

CHET: That's a good age.

BUCKY: At a summer camp? Hello. It's illegal.

CHET: Big deal. That's the call of the wild. If she's not ready at seventeen, there's a problem.

BUCKY: Well, she was actually sixteen.

CHET: So what? People are supposed to do that! It's the meaning of life, man.

BUCKY: Well. The truth is, Chet. She was fifteen.

CHET: Fuck.

BUCKY: But a very developed fifteen.

CHET: My sister's fifteen, man. That's gross.

BUCKY: She was a camper. I was a counselor. I couldn't keep my hands off her. And she loved me, too. I know she did. She was mature in every way, and knew how to express herself. She was a full-grown woman, ready for life and love, and we fucked every chance we had, and I'm telling you, Chet. If anyone found out. I'd be in less trouble if I killed her.

CHET: Other people knew about this?

BUCKY: A few might have suspected. I don't know.

CHET: And they didn't do anything?

BUCKY: Let me explain to you. This was a summer camp. A couple of hundred people, all but about four of whom are under twenty-five. All marooned together in the woods on this island. It's like, if you tried to throw out everybody who was enjoying some kind of forbidden fruit, like sex or pot or whatever, there wouldn't be anybody left.

CHET: So you walked out of the woods with Spanish Girl.

BUCKY: Nobody said anything. They didn't know the play. See, they couldn't say it was bad to cheat on Skyler, because that would mean our relationship was legitimate. This was all kind of too much of a moral quagmire for a bunch of sunburned, hungover people, so everyone just sort of went for pizza.

CHET: It might be too much of a moral quagmire for me, too.

BUCKY: Whatever you're thinking, it wasn't like that.

CHET: Yeah it was. It was exactly like that. Because I'm thinking of my sister, and her friends. They're all fifteen, too. They can't chew bubble gum, because it sticks to their braces. That's what you had in your mouth, OK.

BUCKY: I have to start at the beginning.

CHET: No. you don't.

BUCKY: It wasn't like that. It was innocent. It was like anyone else. I liked to talk to her. She was cute. She had curly hair. Big brown eyes. She was just my type. I liked to tease her. She laughed at my jokes. It was fun. We were friends. The sun shined when I looked at her.

CHET: Oh, man. Don't describe it like that.

BUCKY: Why not? We were friends. Isn't that what it feels like? When you have a friend who understands you, who makes your heart feel less alone? That was her. I can have that with anyone. It's not wrong.

CHET: I'm not saying it was wrong. I'm just saying, it's not who I would choose.

BUCKY: Choose has nothing to do with it. I didn't choose anything. We were alone. Our eyes locked. Bang! We were making it.

CHET: Oh, Jesus.

BUCKY: Hey, man. Age is a number. It's arbitrary. It has nothing to do with experience, with your heart. Some people at fifteen might not be ready. She was.

CHET: What does your girlfriend think about this?

BUCKY: She'll never find out.

CHET: You sure?

BUCKY: Not a chance.

CHET: What, after all this passion? No love letters? No visits?

BUCKY: Nope. I dumped her.

CHET: You dumped her?

BUCKY: Dude. She was fifteen.

CHET: I hope she took it well.

BUCKY: She got used to the idea.

CHET: I suppose. I mean. If you had to get involved with her at all.

BUCKY: I did.

CHET: If you say so.

BUCKY: You can't judge me. If my love is dirty so is everyone else's.

CHET: But the best thing would be to cut her off gently and firmly and not leave her with any illusions. Not try to spare her feelings. Be as open and honest as you can. Let her know where she stands. Not leave anything behind that's going to fuck her up later on. You did that, didn't you.

BUCKY: Well . . .

CHET: It's like low-impact camping. You pack out what you packed in. You leave no trace on the landscape. The people who come after you, don't even know you were there. That's what you did, right?

BUCKY: Well . . .

CHET: Come on, man. Tell me that's what you did.

BUCKY: It sort of was.

CHET: Oh, shit.

BUCKY: I mean, how it happened was. At first it was so hot. But then after a while, like three or four days, the pure animal pleasure of it kind of died down a little. And, like, more and more too, something was happening where she like, wanted to talk all the time. Before, that was great, because I thought she was so funny and smart. I mean, she laughed at my jokes. She liked the same music. But now, she didn't want to talk about that stuff anymore. Stuff that was fun. Because it was like, since we had sex we weren't friends anymore. And that's when I realized, "Hey, kid. You're only fifteen years old. Get away from me, man!"

CHET: Good for you.

BUCKY: You think so?

CHET: Yes. That was the right thing to do.

BUCKY: No it wasn't.

CHET: OK. The right thing would have been to never lay a finger on her. But since you missed that particular exit, the next best thing would be to put it behind you.

BUCKY: It didn't happen like that, though.

CHET: Bucky. Shit.

BUCKY: These teenage girls, man . . .

CHET: Don't even tell me.

BUCKY: It's not my fault. It's like, once they get an idea in their heads. It's not my fault.

CHET: How did it happen, then? If you know it's wrong, and you're not a complete shit, you'll put a stop to it!

BUCKY: That's exactly what I said! I said it's wrong! We should stop!

CHET: And that was the end of it.

BUCKY: Well . . .

CHET: Bucky. Tell me that was the end of it.

BUCKY: I can't.

CHET: Tell me anyway.

BUCKY: But that wasn't the end of it.

CHET: You said all the right things!

BUCKY: She didn't believe me.

CHET: But that's true! That's what you're supposed to say!

BUCKY: She said she didn't care if it was wrong. She didn't care what anyone thought.

CHET: Did you bring up her future?

BUCKY: She said her future was with me.

CHET: Oh, fuck. Mayday! Mayday!

BUCKY: She said I shouldn't do the right thing with her. She said the right thing was wrong. She said all that really mattered was that I loved her.

CHET: No, you didn't.

BUCKY: Yes I did! Of course she was right. I loved her. I loved her desperately. She said she knew I did, and why was I a slave to rules when all I really had to do was love her. She said, "Look at the stars! Look at the moon!"

CHET: Oh, shit.

BUCKY: And the old magic came back. We made love all night. In the middle of the soccer field, under a full moon, we literally fucked all night. It was the most beautiful thing I've ever done. Bar none. The best few hours of my life. I'll never forget it.

CHET: Then you didn't dump her.

BUCKY: Yeah I did.

CHET: After that?

BUCKY: I had to!

CHET: So you told her. After that. After what you just described, you told her what.

BUCKY: I didn't tell her anything.

CHET: You didn't?

BUCKY: No! I couldn't talk to her. I tried that once already. You see where that got me. No. I could see that conventional methods were not going to work. I had to make her hate me.

CHET: So you made out with this other chick behind a log?

BUCKY: It was the right thing to do!

CHET: Did it work?

BUCKY: I guess so. I don't know. I was pretty upset, walking to the bus, on the last day of camp. I couldn't stop kissing her. Part of the reason was God-damn Skyler kept on looking over at me, like she expected some kind of good-bye gesture, in front of all those people? So I had to keep my nose buried in the Spanish Girl, just playing tonsil hockey for everything I was worth, till, I was looking over Spanish Girl, sort of around her head, so I could see when Skyler finally gave up and got on her bus. That was a little depressing. I didn't feel too good about that, but what was I supposed to do? Just sweep her off her feet, right there in public, in front of everyone? I knew I couldn't control myself with her. I knew if I said one word to her I'd end up sticking my tongue down her throat right in the middle of the driveway with everyone watching, so no. I had to be good. I had to deny everything, and show a little self-control. For once. And it worked. She turned away. She got on the bus. The end. And I was so happy. I was so relieved, to have escaped. That some of that relief trans-mogrified itself into affection for Spanish Girl. Because, I'll tell you, I was having a hard time tearing myself away. She was standing in the sunshine on this country road. Sunlight in her hair. I could see the outline of her legs through the fabric of her skirt. And I thought, Christ, where am I going? I belong with her. And I stood and looked at her a minute, and at the exact moment where I was like, fuck this, I'm staying, at that exact moment, she SMILED.

CHET: Oh no.

BUCKY: And I saw her TEETH. And I turned right around and got on that bus. Summer was over.

CHET: Lucky you.

BUCKY: No shit. I really dodged two bullets there in the space of like, a week. And I think even though there wasn't any deeper, like, we didn't have much in common. Like, for example, English. In spite of all that, I think the prize for Girl of the Summer goes to Ingrid, because she helped me do the right thing, she had a really hot accent, and best of all, she went back to Spain, which is a very long way away.

(A knock at the door, downstairs.)

JOLENE: *(Chirpy.)* Hello!

CHET: Come on up!

BUCKY: Don't say anything to her about this, OK?

(Jolene enters.)

JOLENE: Don't say anything to me about what?

CHET: Little surprise Buck has for you.

JOLENE: Did you get me something sweet?

BUCKY: Uh. Yeah. Sure.

JOLENE: You're too late if it's a corsage. I got my own. See?

BUCKY: You didn't have to do that.

JOLENE: Yes I did. I knew you'd get the wrong thing.

BUCKY: I have one for you.

JOLENE: Let me see it.

BUCKY: It's in the fridge.

(Bucky crosses to the fridge.)

JOLENE: You're not dressed. Why aren't you dressed?

BUCKY: Chet wouldn't let me. Kept talking my ear off. Here's your corsage.

JOLENE: Yeah. See. This is why I bought my own.

BUCKY: What's wrong with it?

JOLENE: It's cheap. You can keep it. I got my own, exactly the kind I wanted. Gardenia, worn on the wrist. It's big, trashy and smells like a French cathouse. You want a whiff, Chet?

CHET: No thanks.

JOLENE: Don't stand there gaping. Go get dressed.

BUCKY: What am I supposed to do with this?

JOLENE: Maybe one of your other girlfriends can wear it. Go on. Shoo.

(Bucky puts the corsage back in the fridge, and exits to his room.)

JOLENE: And don't pout! Jesus Christ, Chet. Sometimes I don't know how you can live with the guy.

CHET: I'm not his girlfriend.

JOLENE: Lucky for you. Do you like my dress?

CHET: Sure.

JOLENE: You didn't say anything.

CHET: It's beautiful.

JOLENE: I thought maybe you didn't notice. Nobody else does.

CHET: How could I miss it? You look spectacular.

JOLENE: Keep it coming.

CHET: That dress is sumptuous.

JOLENE: I know. I bought it in Seattle. With a credit card. I got my own. Do you have your own yet?

CHET: It's just for emergencies.

JOLENE: That was the deal I had with mine, too. So I got another one.

CHET: You can do that?

JOLENE: This is college! They hand them out like candy here. You should get one.

CHET: I don't know.

JOLENE: You totally should! They are the cat's pajamas. It's like free money. I got the dress, the shoes, the purse, and the earrings all in one swell foop. You only have to pay these people like, ten dollars a month. You can buy whatever you want, and they pay for it.

CHET: I don't think it's that simple.

JOLENE: You can't argue with the results.

CHET: Nope. I sure can't.

JOLENE: Are you coming to the dance?

CHET: No.

JOLENE: Why not?

CHET: I have work to do.

JOLENE: It's Friday night. You have all weekend.

CHET: I have a lot of work.

JOLENE: College is not about work. It's about meeting the right people, so you don't have to work.

CHET: I don't have a date.

JOLENE: There's lots of people without dates! You can come stag.

CHET: I don't want to do that.

JOLENE: You should come! I know lots of girls who are coming without dates. They want to drink and dance. They'll be looking for company. You should come.

CHET: Maybe later.

JOLENE: You should see how beautiful the courtyard looks. I strung Christmas lights and paper lanterns from the doorway of the Music Hall out to all the trees in front. It's the first year anyone has ever extended the decorations outside. I got the idea from a 1920s yearbook picture I saw when I was doing research. You see? I did research! I crossed every I and dotted every T. The president himself has already congratulated me, on achieving a major revival of the Fall Formal. There's even a jazz band playing swing music. You have to come!

CHET: It is a perfect night for it.

JOLENE: There are luminaries up the front walkway. I chose the Music Hall because it's the only Beaux Arts building left on campus, and it's not the gym, so you don't have to take your shoes off. This is not your usual lame ass college dance. This is the Great Gatsby! Do you promise you'll come?

CHET: Later.

JOLENE: Don't forget, now. I'm holding you to this. If you don't show up by eleven I'll send Bucky to come get you. I know how you operate. You smile and nod and agree to anything, just so people like me will leave you alone, and let you get back to your Latin.

CHET: This is Greek.

JOLENE: Same diff. Look at those letters! You are going to ruin your eyes. You know, they put all those books into English, to save people like you the trouble, so you'd have more time to come to dances.

CHET: I said I'd come.

JOLENE: That's not good enough! I require absolute obedience! You may think Greek homework is a good enough excuse to skip the Barn Dance, or the Halloween Toga, but as long as I'm Social Chair, if you don't show up for the Fall Formal, Chet Hopkins, you better be dead. Is that clear?

CHET: Yup.

JOLENE: Good. And if you want to get laid, bring some flowers.

CHET: That's all it takes?

JOLENE: A handful of daisies will get you under the dress of any unspoken for sophomore. They're young enough nobody's tried that on them yet. Just steal some out of the neighbors' yard. Cut them, and clean them up so they look nice. Sidle up to some sweet young thing and ask where she's been all your life. After a few drinks you can sperm to your heart's content. Now you have to come to the dance, because I gave you the secret password. Everyone must come to the dance! I am Social Chair! Hear me roar!

(Bucky returns, dressed for the dance.)

JOLENE: Change your shoes.

BUCKY: No.

JOLENE: You are not wearing sneakers to my Fall Formal.

BUCKY: They're not sneakers.

JOLENE: They're not acceptable, is what they are not.

BUCKY: They are hiking shoes.

JOLENE: Change them.

BUCKY: I don't have to!

JOLENE: Bucky. Now! They are not appropriate.

BUCKY: I don't have any others.

JOLENE: You have a pair of loafers that you are putting on right now.

BUCKY: No.

JOLENE: Take them off! Now! Off! Off! Off!

BUCKY: Jesus . . .

   (Bucky exits.)

JOLENE: I'm not sorry! This is my big night! My name is all over this thing! Everyone's judging me on the basis of how it goes! I will NOT lose points because my boyfriend felt like being different!

CHET: Yeah, Bucky!

JOLENE: Nor will I lose points because his roommate felt like doing homework! It is time for a little law and order around here! You will be at the dance by eleven, or I'll send someone to come get you.

CHET: And I should bring daisies.

JOLENE: If that doesn't get you laid, I'll eat them for breakfast.

   (Bucky returns, loafered.)

JOLENE: Well, that's some improvement, anyway.

BUCKY: They're too small. They pinch like hell.

JOLENE: Welcome to my world, honey. Let me look at you. Oh, come here. You haven't buttoned your collar —

BUCKY: I don't want to!

JOLENE: Yes you do.

BUCKY: It's too tight!

JOLENE: I don't care! You are not meeting the president of this college like some kind of Bohemian ragamuffin. You are buttoning your collar!

   (Jolene buttons his collar.)

BUCKY: OW!

JOLENE: Shut up. That doesn't hurt.

BUCKY: Yes it does!

JOLENE: Oh, you're such a poser. Leave it.

BUCKY: I can't breathe!

JOLENE: LEAVE IT, or I'll break your kneecaps. You can open it after we have our picture taken.

BUCKY: Pictures?

JOLENE: Yes, pictures. And you can spare me the condescending attitude. We need to have pictures, so we can remember happily my night of triumph.

BUCKY: Remembering is what you do with your brain, not a camera.

JOLENE: Am I forcing you into something you don't want to do here?

BUCKY: No.

JOLENE: Because I can just go dance all night with Dirk and Justin. They don't give me any shit. They don't have to sneer and pout about some pretentious outsider trip that, I have a news flash for you, Mr Che Guevara, if you were half the outsider you like to think you are, you would never have gotten into this college, OK? So you might as well come down off your high horse and have your picture taken, because you are as bourgeois as the rest of us, and trying to pretend you're not, just makes you look pathetic.

CHET: Yeah. Bucky.

JOLENE: Don't be smug. You're coming, too.

CHET: If I finish my work.

JOLENE: No ifs! I have homework too, you know. I probably have more homework than you, because I have a real major, that might even land me a job someday, unlike some people. Everyone knows poli sci is the toughest department on campus, but I'm still going to the dance. Why? Because I want to? No. Because I have to. If I have to, so does everyone.

BUCKY: Yeah, Chet.

JOLENE: I am so SICK of unappreciative people thwarting my will! Why can't you just do what I say? Don't you know I'm always right?

BUCKY: Yeah, Chet.

JOLENE: I am talking to you!

CHET: Yeah, Bucky.

JOLENE: Oh, fuck this shit! Good-bye!

(Jolene stomps down the stairs.)

BUCKY: Will you hurry up and come, so I'm not stuck there?

CHET: Dude. Wild horses couldn't drag me to that shit.

JOLENE: *(Downstairs.)* Are you coming?!!

CHET: Hey. Nice shoes.

BUCKY: Jesus . . .

(Bucky exits down the stairs. The door downstairs slams. Chet sits at his table and resumes working. His mind soon wanders, however, and it is not long before he is staring at the wall with his mouth open. Then he snaps out of it. He tries to return to work, but finds he can't. Another idea has hold of him now. Suddenly Chet leaps up from the table and runs down the stairs. We hear the door slam. Chet is gone a long time. Then he comes bounding back up the stairs with a fistful of daisies, which he drops in the kitchen sink before exiting to his room to get dressed. While the stage is empty, someone knocks on the door downstairs. Chet emerges from his room, with a clean shirt and tie on but no pants, looking puzzled.)

CHET: They're a little early.

(Chet looks at his watch. The person downstairs knocks again.)

CHET: Come on up!

(The door opens and closes. Someone walks up the stairs.)

(Chet realizes he has no pants on, and dives back into his room. Skyler appears at the top of the stairs.)

SKYLER: Hello?

(Chet enters, with pants on.)

CHET: Hi there. Aren't you a little early?

SKYLER: For what?

CHET: Never mind, never mind. It's OK. So. Are you one of the famous sophomores?

SKYLER: The who?

CHET: The sophomore girls, on the Social Committee. Jolene sent you over to fetch me.

SKYLER: No.

CHET: You're not a sophomore?

SKYLER: Nope.

CHET: Are you sure? You look like a sophomore. You look like a cute sophomore.

(Chet grabs his flowers.)

CHET: These are for you. You want to bust a move?

SKYLER: No thank you. I'm looking for Bucky. Do I have the right place?

CHET: Yup. I'm Chet. I'm his roommate.

SKYLER: I need to see him real bad. I'm Skyler Henderson.

CHET: That name kind of rings a bell somewhere. Why is that.

SKYLER: I know him from this summer at camp.

CHET: Right . . . Oh God.

SKYLER: Can I come in?

CHET: Shit!

SKYLER: Excuse me?

CHET: I mean, sure.

SKYLER: I'm sorry to drop in on you like this, out of the blue.

CHET: No, it's all right. Please come in. Put your backpack down.

SKYLER: I would've called first, but this time yesterday I didn't know I'd be here, either.

CHET: Is something wrong?

SKYLER: No. Nothing is wrong. I just. I need to see Bucky. Real bad. Something has come up which requires his attention.

CHET: What is it?

SKYLER: I just have a little problem. It's a family problem, and a medical problem. And Bucky's involved, too. But it's not a problem, not really. It's really the best thing that's ever happened to me in my life. It has set me totally free of everything I wanted to be free of, irrevocably, so I can never go back. It's so liberating. I've never felt more alive. I've never felt more beautiful. I've never felt more real, as a woman. It's like my life just started.

CHET: Could you tell me what it is?

SKYLER: Haven't you guessed yet? I'm pregnant.

CHET: Oh, God.

SKYLER: Why do people react like that?

CHET: I don't know what else to say.

SKYLER: You should. It's good news.

CHET: Then congratulations.

SKYLER: Thank you. You're the first person who's said that.

CHET: Nobody else was happy for you?

SKYLER: What do you think?

CHET: I'm guessing no.

SKYLER: My mother immediately wanted to take me to the clinic for an abortion. Do not pass Go. Do not collect two hundred dollars. She didn't want to hear about it. She just made the appointment. I called my dad and told him the whole story, because I thought he would at least listen to my side of things. He didn't. He sat with my mother behind a closed door. They wouldn't even let me talk to them! They came out and proclaimed their decision, that they made, without asking me at all. He took her side! He said I should have the, the procedure! He even said I had to tell him where Bucky is, so he could have Bucky arrested!

CHET: Uh. He's not home right now.

SKYLER: Don't worry. That's not going to happen. If I'm old enough to get pregnant, I'm old enough to make my own decisions. I don't need them. All I need is Bucky.

CHET: I'm sure he'll help you any way he can.

SKYLER: I knew he would. That's why I came.

CHET: He'll give you money. He'll take you to the clinic.

SKYLER: What clinic?

CHET: It's over by the hospital. You wouldn't think they'd have one here because it's such a small town. But there's a college here, too. So I guess they're kind of busy.

SKYLER: I'm not going to a place like that.

CHET: You're not going to keep it, are you?

SKYLER: Of course I am. Bucky and I are running away. We're going to start a new life together.

CHET: OK. You should go home now. Right now.

SKYLER: The morning sickness started. I threw up in the bus station, so hard I couldn't even stand up. I think I passed out for a minute. My head was resting on the seat. Filthy seat. My tongue was out. I almost missed my bus.

CHET: I know, because I've ridden it before, there's another bus that leaves, nine o'clock tonight, back to Seattle. You should be on it.

SKYLER: I can't.

CHET: You're going to have to.

SKYLER: I don't have enough money!

CHET: I'll give you some.

SKYLER: No. Let Bucky give it to me. After he sees me. If he wants me to go, I will.

CHET: I can't let Bucky see you.

SKYLER: What do you have to do with it?

CHET: He can't control himself around you.

SKYLER: Oh. So you're one of those people.

CHET: One of what people.

SKYLER: One of those people who know everything.

CHET: I'm not like that.

SKYLER: Oh yeah? What are those books?

CHET: That's Greek. That's my homework. I'm a classics major.

SKYLER: Am I interrupting you?

CHET: No. I'm going to a dance. That's why I'm dressed up.

SKYLER: There's a dance tonight?

CHET: The Fall Formal.

SKYLER: I think I walked past that.

CHET: That's where Bucky is.

SKYLER: I didn't see him.

CHET: He must've been inside.

SKYLER: I didn't see anyone. It didn't look like anyone was there. Like nothing had started yet.

CHET: It started, all right. It's been going for a long time. I have to get over there.

SKYLER: Do you have a date?

CHET: I'm going stag.

SKYLER: Why don't you take me?

CHET: I don't think that's a good idea.

SKYLER: Yes, it is. Then I can see Bucky.

CHET: No. That's a bad idea. Definitely.

SKYLER: I have to see him!

CHET: You can't see him, all right. He's with his girlfriend.

SKYLER: Ingrid is here?

CHET: Who?

SKYLER: His girlfriend, Ingrid.

CHET: No. His girlfriend's name is Jolene.

SKYLER: Never heard of her.

CHET: They've been going out for two years. She's a heavy hitter. Smart, sexy, great résumé. He's desperately in love with her.

SKYLER: I don't believe that! He can't be!

CHET: He was just telling me an hour ago.

SKYLER: Then why did he want me all summer? Until that snake in the grass Ingrid. If he's so in love with this chick, why was he with me?

CHET: I don't know. He thought you were cute. He was passing time. Whatever.

SKYLER: You don't know anything about it!

CHET: He just told me the whole story.

SKYLER: He doesn't know the whole story. I just told you the whole story!

CHET: Look, I don't wish you any ill will. All I'm saying is, you have some romantic picture in your head, of him and how he's going to respond. That's not Bucky. He won't respond the way you want him to. You should get out of here, before he sees you. Go back home. Have a good, long think, if this is really what you want to do. If it is, then write him a letter. Give him some warning. Let's try to do things rationally, and reasonably. You can't put a guy on the spot like that!

SKYLER: I don't think I like you, Chet. You're not a very open person.

CHET: I'm just trying to protect you.

SKYLER: You're a defeatist. And you're a coward. And when Bucky hears about this . . .

CHET: He's not going to hear about it.

SKYLER: Yes he is. I'm going down to that dance, right now, with you or without you, I will see Bucky face-to-face!

CHET: I can't let you do that.

SKYLER: I'm not getting back on that bus!

CHET: You have no right to intrude! Not on Bucky! Not on Jolene! Especially not on Jolene! She is the Social Chair this semester! Do you know how hard she worked to put this together? You have no right to come here uninvited, with your bad news, and ruin everything! I won't let it happen.

SKYLER: It's none of your business.

CHET: If I have to stop you physically, I'll stop you. You are not going to that dance.

SKYLER: I'll see you later.

CHET: If you leave this apartment, you'll go to the bus station!

SKYLER: Then I won't leave the apartment. This room is Bucky's?

CHET: Hey! You can't go in there!

SKYLER: Maybe I'll put on one of his shirts. I love his shirts . . .

(Skyler exits to Bucky's room.)

CHET: Young lady! You come out of there this minute!

(Bucky enters.)

BUCKY: Oh, good. You're dressed.

CHET: What? What're you doing here?

BUCKY: Relax, man. It's time to come to the dance.

CHET: What do you mean? I'm relaxed! I'm perfectly relaxed!

BUCKY: So let's go.

CHET: I'm ready to go! I have been!

BUCKY: Are you all right?

CHET: Yeah! I'm fine! I should be asking the questions. You weren't supposed to come get me till eleven.

BUCKY: We have to go now.

CHET: Is something wrong?

BUCKY: Yeah. There's nobody there.

CHET: Nobody where.

BUCKY: At the dance. Nobody came. It's a total washout. Jolene's standing there with the president and a bunch of deans. That band's not even playing. I think a couple of them went home already. It's a big, flat flop.

CHET: We have to save it! We have to round up more people!

BUCKY: We can try. I don't know, though. It doesn't look like swing dancing has hit Walla Walla yet. I think she's trying to impose some big city fad here. People resent it. They don't want to be told how to dress and where to stand. They just want to drink their beer.

CHET: Maybe you don't. But I bet lots of people appreciate a strong, attractive leader like Jolene.

BUCKY: Maybe you can help me find those people, then. Because none of them came to the dance.

CHET: She looks beautiful tonight, doesn't she.

BUCKY: She did.

CHET: She glowed, when she walked out of here. Like an absolute angel.

BUCKY: She doesn't anymore. Her temper has kind of taken its toll. On her looks, I mean.

CHET: She has a right to be upset! After all the time and effort she poured into the planning. To be insulted and ignored like this? I'd be pissed off! Wouldn't you?

BUCKY: I wouldn't presume to tell people what to do.

CHET: Only because you have no ideas. She does! I'm surprised you don't take this more seriously. Wake up, man! Isn't she your girlfriend? Your one true love? Your heart's delight?

BUCKY: Well. She is my girlfriend.

CHET: Shouldn't you be helping her, then?

BUCKY: I don't know, Chet. I don't think I want to be under her thumb anymore. I think I want to break up with her.

CHET: You can't do that!

BUCKY: Yeah I can.

CHET: You can't do it tonight!

BUCKY: I'm not going to do it tonight. Sometime soon, though. Maybe Sunday, after I do my laundry at her place. Get one last load done.

CHET: Look, Bucky. This is Jolene, man! Beautiful, smart, funny Jolene! Are you sure you want to just, bounce her out of your life like this?

BUCKY: I don't love her anymore.

CHET: That's always the first thing to go.

BUCKY: No. I mean, I really don't. I think I hate her. She's mean. And childish. And bossy.

CHET: How are you going to do anything without her? You can't get out of bed in the morning!

BUCKY: I'll have to find a way.

CHET: No. See. That takes character. Character is exactly what you do not have. If you had character, you would stand by her. You would not fuck around. You would not get fifteen year olds pregnant!

BUCKY: What?

CHET: OK. That's a bad example.

BUCKY: What're you talking about? Nobody's pregnant.

CHET: I know. It's all just a big, silly joke.

BUCKY: It's not very funny.

CHET: Yeah. Just like you breaking up with Jolene. That's not very funny, either. Now let's go back to the dance, and forget this conversation ever happened.

BUCKY: I'm changing my shoes first.

(Bucky crosses to his room.)

CHET: No! You can't go in there!

BUCKY: Why not?

CHET: You just can't. Don't ask questions, OK?

BUCKY: Why can't I go in my room?

CHET: Skyler's in there.

BUCKY: Who?

CHET: Your teenybopper girlfriend came home to roost. And you know what else? She's pregnant. I'll get your shoes for you.

BUCKY: Wait. Who's in my room?

CHET: If she doesn't see you. More importantly, if you don't see her. If you go home with Jolene tonight, then I can get rid of her. She goes home to Mommy on a bus and gets an abortion. This whole mess gets forgotten, like it never happened.

BUCKY: Skyler's in there, huh.

CHET: She's in there. She's pregnant. She thinks you're going to save her.

BUCKY: Maybe I am.

CHET: No, you're not!

BUCKY: This is perfect! It's my escape from everything!

CHET: OK. Let's think about that for a minute.

BUCKY: She's pregnant? She's carrying my child?

CHET: Be very careful now, Bucky. Your whole future is riding on this.

BUCKY: I can't think about it that way.

CHET: You have to!

BUCKY: I can't separate or speculate or try to plan what's best. All I know is, when I see her. When I smell her or touch her or hear her voice. I don't know anything else. There's only her and I want her close to me, I want to bathe in her for the rest of my life.

CHET: That's why you should go back to the dance.

BUCKY: I can't do that. I'll never see her again.

CHET: That's why you have to go.

BUCKY: I can't run away from her.

CHET: She has a chance to get out of here clean, before that baby is born and her life is completely ruined. Let her take it. You take it too. Just walk away. Turn your back on this. We'll forget it ever happened, and get on with our lives. Isn't that what you want?

BUCKY: I want Skyler!

(Skyler enters. She's sleepy, disheveled, wearing a flannel shirt of Bucky's over her clothes.)

SKYLER: Bucky?

CHET: Run.

SKYLER: Bucky? Is that you?

CHET: I said, Run, Goddamn it.

(Skyler runs into Bucky's arms.)

SKYLER: I was asleep. I didn't know when you'd be back.

BUCKY: You're so warm.

SKYLER: I need you, Bucky.

BUCKY: I know you do. I'm here.

SKYLER: I have to tell you some news.

BUCKY: I know.

SKYLER: No!

BUCKY: Chet told me already.

SKYLER: I didn't want you to find out like that! I wanted it to be happy!

BUCKY: It is. It is happy.

SKYLER: Don't send me away.

BUCKY: I'm not going to.

SKYLER: We have to save this baby. It's yours too. You have to help me.

BUCKY: I will help you. I just need a little time to absorb all this.

SKYLER: There isn't much to absorb, really. There's me. There's the baby. We're in love. That makes everything very simple, doesn't it?

BUCKY: I hope so.

SKYLER: What do you mean, you hope so? There's nobody else who's important in this.

CHET: There's Jolene.

BUCKY: No, man. I'm dumping her.

CHET: You are not!

SKYLER: He never loved her. I heard him say it.

CHET: Yes he did!

BUCKY: That was a long time ago, man.

SKYLER: You don't love her now. She's not holding you here. There's nobody else. There's no Ingrid. There's only me.

BUCKY: That's right.

CHET: Oh, fuck.

SKYLER: So we know what we'll do, then. There's you and me and the baby. I'll move in here . . .

CHET: Now wait a minute!!

SKYLER: I'll get a job and pay my way. We can save up and move to a new place when the baby's born. That's seven months away. There's plenty of time for you to finish school. In the evenings we'll take long walks and love, like we used to. This town is so beautiful. I walked all the way here from the bus station. With the leaves piled in the yards, the orange light on white houses, it's so beautiful it almost made me cry. But I think that's because you were here.

CHET: The baby's due when?

SKYLER: Late April.

CHET: Perfect! Right in the middle of orals! You want to deal with that?

BUCKY: Chet . . .

CHET: You'll have to move. You can't live here. I won't stand for it. I don't know about you, but I intend to pass my orals with distinction!

BUCKY: So do I.

CHET: How? You'll have three mouths to feed. You have no means of support.

BUCKY: We'll find a way. People have done it on less than we have.

SKYLER: People who weren't even in love. People who married because they thought they had to, not out of free choice like we are.

CHET: Choice? What choice?

SKYLER: The choice to keep the baby.

CHET: Choice? That's not a choice! That's cowardice! That's lack of nerve!

SKYLER: It is not cowardice to bring a child into the world.

CHET: Yes it is.

SKYLER: It's the bravest thing you could possibly do!

CHET: You're not ready!

SKYLER: No one is every ready.

CHET: That's not true! People are ready. When their careers have reached a certain point. They have some money in the bank. Some health insurance, for Christ's sake. They are ready to settle down and start a family. You are not ready. You have nothing.

SKYLER: We have love.

CHET: No. You're just too cowardly to admit the obvious pathetic truth, which is that you have fucked up, horribly, and now, because you won't admit that, you can't screw up enough nerve to take the only way out, and have an abortion.

SKYLER: I think that's cowardly.

CHET: It is not cowardly to recognize necessity.

SKYLER: Necessity is all in your mind! It doesn't exist! We're free to choose what's necessary and what's not!

CHET: You call this free? This is a jail sentence you're talking about. You didn't come here because you're free. You came here because you're pregnant.

SKYLER: I came because I could've stayed in Seattle, and let my parents rail-road me into that procedure. And deny that there was any possibility that Bucky could love me, or that I could love him, or that we could raise this child together. But instead I chose, freely, I FREELY CHOSE, to believe in that chance. To be open to the change. Love changes things. You can choose to be open to this. To let love do its work. Or you can choose to pretend it's not there. It doesn't exist. And nothing changes. And you really are in control of your life.

CHET: That's the truth!

SKYLER: Maybe for you. But I'm not. I can't be. I choose to let love rule. I have to, because the other choice is death. Right, Bucky?

BUCKY: Oh. Yeah. Sure.

CHET: You're a fucking joke. Wait'll Jolene hears this.

BUCKY: She's not going to.

CHET: Yeah she is. I'm going to find her and tell her right now.

BUCKY: We won't be here when you get back.

SKYLER: Where are we going?

BUCKY: I'm going to take you down to the bus station.

SKYLER: I'm not getting on another bus!

BUCKY: Relax. We're getting on it together.

CHET: Where do you think you're going?

BUCKY: We'll go to my parents' house in Ellensburg.

SKYLER: Ellensburg?

BUCKY: That's the best thing to do right now. We can't stay here. Chet is right. It'll be impossible to go to school here, with you living here too.

SKYLER: I won't get in the way.

BUCKY: It's not that. Back in Ellensburg we can stay with my parents. I can finish up my degree at the community college, and work full-time.

SKYLER: In Ellensburg?

BUCKY: Yeah.

SKYLER: But. Isn't Ellensburg kind of a dump?

CHET: Yeah, it is. Literally.

SKYLER: I thought so. The bus stopped there. Doesn't the bus stop there?

CHET: Yeah. Right across the highway from the slaughterhouse.

SKYLER: We could smell it. It stunk. The drive said it never goes away.

CHET: He's right.

BUCKY: My parents live on the far end of town. You can't smell it there.

SKYLER: The far end of town?

CHET: It's right by the dump.

BUCKY: It's not right by. It's not next to it. Jesus.

SKYLER: That's were all the trucks were going.

BUCKY: What trucks?

SKYLER: There was this huge line of garbage trucks all chugging up the same freeway exit. They crossed over the pass with us from Seattle. The bus driver said they were overflow garbage trucks, full of trash from Seattle they had no room for in the dumps there, headed for a bigger dump in Ellensburg.

CHET: The one right by his parents' house.

SKYLER: Bucky! Gross!

BUCKY: There is nothing wrong with my parents' house! We'll be fine there. If you've got a better idea, I'd like to hear it.

SKYLER: We could stay here.

BUCKY: No, we can't.

SKYLER: Just for a few days. Just to plan and organize and figure out what we want for each other.

BUCKY: Can't we do that in Ellensburg?

SKYLER: Shouldn't we have some alone time first, so we can show a united front? I mean, who knows? Maybe your parents will react the same way mine did.

BUCKY: No they won't.

SKYLER: You can't predict that.

BUCKY: They were in exactly the same situation. How do you think I was born? They'll be happy and ready to help, because that's how everyone treated them.

SKYLER: Was your mom this young?

BUCKY: Practically.

SKYLER: I don't know, Bucky. I mean, don't we have a lot of things to figure out before we're ready to settle down?

BUCKY: Like what?

SKYLER: Like is Ellensburg really the place we want to raise the child?

BUCKY: I don't see why not.

SKYLER: Because there's a slaughterhouse and a dump!

BUCKY: So what? In this town there's a prison. Can you tell the difference?

SKYLER: The prison doesn't smell!

BUCKY: I just want to go there to make a clean break, so I can think clearly.

SKYLER: Do we have to do that in Ellensburg?

BUCKY: I don't trust myself to do it here.

SKYLER: There's just so many other places I want to see, all up and down the coast, like Portland, San Francisco, Vancouver B.C. . . .

CHET: How are you going to do that with a baby?

SKYLER: We'll find a way.

CHET: With a screaming kid who's sick all the time, and you have no way to make money. What're you going to do, Bucky?

BUCKY: I can work for my dad.

CHET: Then you're stuck in Ellensburg.

SKYLER: I don't want that to happen.

CHET: Look. You've both proved your good intentions, OK. We all know you'd rather not have the procedure. You hit all the bases. Fine. Now go home to your mother and solve this problem before it ruins your life.

SKYLER: What do you think, Bucky?

BUCKY: I don't know. This is not really a decision I was ready to make tonight.

SKYLER: Let's not make it, then.

BUCKY: What are we going to do?

SKYLER: I'll just stay overnight. We can sleep on it, and talk in the morning.

CHET: What about Jolene?

SKYLER: You can forget about Jolene.

BUCKY: I have to break up with her first.

CHET: You should go back to the dance.

SKYLER: No!

BUCKY: Stay here. Don't answer the door.

SKYLER: Where are you going?

BUCKY: I don't know.

SKYLER: I want you to stay with me!

BUCKY: I can't leave her without saying something.

SKYLER: Then I want to come with you!

BUCKY: I won't be gone long. You sat on the bus seven hours, right? You can wait a little bit longer. We'll be right back. We'll go to the dance. We'll take care of business. We'll be back before you know it. OK?

SKYLER: OK.

BUCKY: All right. Jesus. Let's go find Jolene.

(A knock at the door.)

CHET: She just found us.

BUCKY: Don't answer it. She'll think we're not home.

JOLENE: *(Chirpy.)* Hello!

BUCKY: Shit! Everybody hide!

JOLENE: Bucky? Chet? Are you up here?

(We hear Jolene climbing the stairs.)

SKYLER: No! I want her to see my face!

BUCKY: Can we do this my way, please . . .

(Jolene enters.)

JOLENE: Do what your way?

BUCKY: Jolene! Hi, sweetheart! How's the dance going?

JOLENE: It's going fine.

BUCKY: See? Just like I told you. It's a huge hit.

JOLENE: You were just there two minutes ago.

BUCKY: Wall to wall. It's a mob scene.

JOLENE: Hey. Why aren't you dressed?

SKYLER: Excuse me?

JOLENE: I was very clear on the dress code. Hello? It is not Woodstock Night. This is the Fall Formal. That means a little black dress. If you need an example, you can just copy me. Now run along and change. You're dismissed.

BUCKY: Jolene. She's not a sophomore.

JOLENE: She's not?

BUCKY: No!

JOLENE: Is she your date?

CHET: No.

JOLENE: Who is she, then?

CHET: Ask Bucky.

JOLENE: Why would he know?

BUCKY: OK. Promise you won't get mad.

SKYLER: My name is Skyler.

JOLENE: And what are you doing here?

SKYLER: I'm carrying his baby.

JOLENE: Carrying it where?

SKYLER: In my uterus.

JOLENE: And how did it get there? Bucky?

BUCKY: I have no idea.

SKYLER: I got pregnant because Bucky and I made love last summer. Several times over several weeks and we never used anything. Ever. We made love in a state of nature. We have a baby now. We're in love. We're running away. And we're never looking back! Right, Bucky?

BUCKY: Uh. Yeah. Sure.

JOLENE: OK. You lost me. You're pregnant.

SKYLER: Yes.

JOLENE: Because you had sex with him.

SKYLER: Many times. In many places. In many different ways . . .

BUCKY: OK! OK! We get it!

JOLENE: Let me get this straight. He took his penis. And he put it in your vagina. And he rubbed it back and forth. After probably not an immense amount of foreplay, if we're talking about the same person. And neither one of you was using anything, so now you're knocked up.

SKYLER: You left out the love. But I guess that's to be expected.

JOLENE: I don't buy this for a minute.

SKYLER: That doesn't make it go away.

JOLENE: We'll see about that, honey. You're trying to tell me, that one of your sperm you squirted into her. See, I can't picture this at all. Actually found its way through her cervix? Because I'm telling you, in my mind. You squeeze them out. They're as stupid as you. They start swimming the wrong way.

BUCKY: My sperm know how to swim!

JOLENE: OK. Let's just for a moment get our bullet points up on the dry erase board, please? Thank you. You have this baby, that is sort of this sexually distributed amalgamation of the two of you, which is frightening, and it's proliferating inside you like strip malls in a suburb, and you're just going to let it?

SKYLER: Yes.

JOLENE: You're not going to do anything about it?

SKYLER: No!

JOLENE: You're just going to let it go on getting bigger and more alive every day?

BUCKY: Uh. What else would we do?

SKYLER: Nothing!

JOLENE: Forgive me. That's not entirely true.

SKYLER: Bucky, no!

BUCKY: What? I just asked a question!

SKYLER: She wants to take it away from us !

BUCKY: Relax. It's just words. What can they do?

JOLENE: That's the $100,000 question, isn't it?

BUCKY: You're not changing my mind, Jolene. For once in my life, I will not have my spirit crushed by you. This girl has brought me a beautiful gift. Along with the baby. Along with her love. She's brought me freedom from you.

JOLENE: So she's going to have the baby. And you're going to have it with her.

BUCKY: That's right!

JOLENE: So when she gets large, and starts craving stuff, and throwing up . . .

SKYLER: I'm already throwing up.

BUCKY: Uh. You are?

SKYLER: It only lasts three months.

BUCKY: Three months?!

JOLENE: And going to childbirth class. And seeing a doctor all the time. Do you have health insurance?

SKYLER: I'll be seeing a midwife.

JOLENE: Ahhh, a midwife! So you'll be doing it without drugs.

SKYLER: Of course.

JOLENE: You're going to face that kind of pain alone?

SKYLER: I'm not alone. I've got Bucky.

BUCKY: Yeah! She's got me!

SKYLER: He'll be right there with me, in the birthing room.

BUCKY: Wait. I have to be in the room?

SKYLER: You're my birth partner.

BUCKY: I thought I waited outside.

JOLENE: That's if you do it with drugs.

BUCKY: We can do it with drugs.

JOLENE: No. See. For that you need a doctor. For a doctor you need insurance.

BUCKY: I don't have insurance.

JOLENE: Then you're going to be her "birth partner."

BUCKY: Skyler! I don't have insurance!

SKYLER: We don't need it. We're going to a midwife.

BUCKY: Don't we go to a hospital?

SKYLER: No. We have the baby at home.

BUCKY: At home?!!

CHET: Over my dead body, man.

SKYLER: That's how a midwife does it.

BUCKY: But Skyler, you don't understand. My home is here. We can't have a baby here. This place is a dump!

SKYLER: Or we could go to the birth center. They have rooms, too.

BUCKY: That'll cost more money.

SKYLER: It doesn't matter. We'll find it somewhere.

BUCKY: And you don't get any drugs.

SKYLER: I don't want any. I can do it without drugs.

BUCKY: Skyler. Childbirth hurts.

SKYLER: What do you know about childbirth?

BUCKY: I know it hurts. And I don't want to see it.

SKYLER: It's beautiful.

BUCKY: It's all blood and guts —

SKYLER: There's no guts. There's hardly any blood.

BUCKY: And placenta. And cords.

SKYLER: You can cut the umbilical cord yourself.

BUCKY: No thanks!!!

SKYLER: That's why you go to class. You watch a video.

BUCKY: And screaming. And pain. A lot of pain.

SKYLER: So you actually know what it is you're talking about. Then people like her will have a much harder time playing you.

BUCKY: She's not playing me! I know what I'm talking about! I'm supposed to pace outside the door! That's my job! I hand out cigars! And get slapped on the back! I'm nobody's "birth partner"!

SKYLER: Except mine.

BUCKY: I don't know, Skyler. This changes things.

JOLENE: And if you think that's bad. Then you have to take the damn thing home. And feed it every two hours, and wipe its ass and listen to it scream all night . . . .

BUCKY: OK. I don't want to take it home!

CHET: Damn right. You're not bringing it here.

JOLENE: And the worst part of all is, there's no going back. You can't return the damn thing to the store, if it doesn't fit. You are stuck with it for life.

SKYLER: That's just a really stupid way to look at it.

JOLENE: You don't have it yet! You don't know!

SKYLER: I can't wait to love someone that much. A chance like this only comes once, maybe twice in your entire life. How many people do you know who can't live without you?

JOLENE: Bucky. Chet. The sophomores.

SKYLER: No. I mean really can't live. I mean would die if you left them. Actually die, so you'd be prosecuted. I know the answer. None! You could disappear right now, and absolutely nothing would change, because you're not that important. I'm about to be that important to somebody. I'm about to have that much power. I can create life. I'm the luckiest woman on earth.

JOLENE: You may be. But he isn't.

BUCKY: Yeah, man. I'm not even a woman.

JOLENE: He's just a guy who fucked you. Now get lost.

SKYLER: Is that what you want, Bucky?

BUCKY: I don't know, man.

SKYLER: I'm going.

BUCKY: No! Skyler! You can't do it alone!

SKYLER: Yes, I can. I have to now.

BUCKY: Please don't go.

SKYLER: You don't know if you want me to stay?

BUCKY: When you put me on the spot, of course not! I'm frozen in the head-lights. But when I have to watch you walk away. I can't let that happen, either. I don't want to be without you. Please stay. I'll do whatever you want.

SKYLER: Then don't listen to her.

BUCKY: I'm not going to!

SKYLER: All right.

BUCKY: I just want to hear what she has to say.

SKYLER: You don't need to!

BUCKY: Except she's really smart. She might know something we don't.

SKYLER: We don't need to "know" anything!

BUCKY: What about insurance? No drugs? Me being in the birth room?

SKYLER: If we love each other, we'll find a way.

BUCKY: I don't know, man.

SKYLER: Then we must not love each other.

BUCKY: No! God, no! Of course not! God, Skyler! Of course I love you! With all my heart, I love you.

SKYLER: Doesn't that make it possible, then?

BUCKY: When you're talking about all this other stuff I have to do, no. It doesn't.

(Skyler takes off Bucky's shirt. Drops it at his feet.)

SKYLER: I guess this is yours.

JOLENE: Are you leaving now?

SKYLER: I don't have any money.

JOLENE: Bucky?

BUCKY: Uhhhh . . . I don't actually have any either, man.

JOLENE: Has it really come to this?

BUCKY: What? I spent it all on your stupid corsage.

CHET: I'll give her some.

JOLENE: No. I want to do it.

(Jolene gets money out of her purse. Hands it to Skyler.)

JOLENE: The first thing you need to do, honey, is get a credit card. Now good-bye.

SKYLER: I have no idea where to go.

JOLENE: Back where you came from. To Mommy and Daddy.

SKYLER: I don't want to let them be right.

JOLENE: But they probably are right.

SKYLER: I don't care. I don't want to let them win.

JOLENE: Nobody is winning or losing anything. We're all just setting our lives right again, after a sudden gust of wind blew them all over. Now you've probably wandered an awfully long way from home, haven't you? I'll bet they're worried sick.

SKYLER: They want me to have an abortion.

JOLENE: That's not necessarily a bad thing.

SKYLER: How can you say that?

JOLENE: Lots of people have them.

SKYLER: Lots of people smoke! That doesn't make it right! Lots of people drive drunk! They tell lies! They make you feel wanted and loved and at the exact moment you need them most, they yank it all back again and pretend you don't exist . . . .

JOLENE: Skyler. Let's try to be adult about this.

SKYLER: Anything lots of people do, is pretty much guaranteed to suck!!

JOLENE: Skyler. You're a smart girl.

SKYLER: Am I?

JOLENE: Of course you are!

SKYLER: I was beginning to wonder.

JOLENE: And you know every single person in that phrase "lots of people" is actually a single person, just like you, or me. And neither of us does things mindlessly, for no reason. So why would anyone else?

SKYLER: I don't know.

JOLENE: It might just be a case of people who think something is evil, don't really know anything about it. Because they've never had to live with it. You and I know that's not true. Because we have.

SKYLER: Had to live with what.

JOLENE: I was hoping this wouldn't come up. But I've lived with it.

BUCKY: What?!

JOLENE: It seems horrible at the time. But you can actually do what your heart tells you. Even if it seems impossible, do it anyway. You'll survive.

SKYLER: What did you do?

JOLENE: I didn't keep it.

SKYLER: I don't know if I could do that.

JOLENE: I didn't know, either. But I did it. And I lived to tell the tale.

SKYLER: I guess I should be getting home.

JOLENE: Yes. You should. You really don't want to miss that bus. It's the last one of the night.

(Skyler gathers up her things and exits. The door downstairs slams. Jolene turns to Bucky.)

JOLENE: Are you ready to go?

BUCKY: Go where?

JOLENE: To the after party.

BUCKY: You're going to have an after party?

JOLENE: Of course. Why wouldn't we?

BUCKY: The dance was a flop.

JOLENE: The dance was not a flop.

BUCKY: Nobody came!

JOLENE: That doesn't matter. We got some nice shots for the newspaper.

BUCKY: But nobody came!

JOLENE: We don't have to describe it that way, if we don't want to.

BUCKY: But, Jolene. Nobody came.

JOLENE: Nobody knows what happened. They know what they read in the paper. Monday morning, people who had no idea this was happening tonight, people who weren't even in town, probably, people who left to go skiing. They'll see those pictures in the paper, and tell everyone what a great time they had at this dance.

BUCKY: What about tonight?

JOLENE: That's why we have the after party! We all go to the Green Lantern. Talk up how great the dance was. Who's going to say any different? They don't know. They weren't there.

BUCKY: But it's not true.

JOLENE: It will be Monday. That's all I care about. Now chop chop. We have to go.

BUCKY: I don't think I want to.

JOLENE: Bucky, Bucky, Bucky. What you want is really the least of my worries right now.

BUCKY: You better move it on up the list.

JOLENE: What you want, is not a flea on the ass of my worries right now.

BUCKY: I don't feel like going.

JOLENE: Do you think I felt like doing what I had to do tonight?

BUCKY: Nobody put a gun to your head.

JOLENE: The night of the dance! The most important night of the whole year for me, you choose to introduce me to your, your, I don't even know what to call her! She makes me so angry! You make me so angry! I should've thrown something at you! I should've run from the room screaming! God knows I wanted to. But, as usual, if I walked away, who was there to take my place? Nobody. So I bit back my feelings. I swallowed my pride. And I handled it. In spite of everything I had breathing down my neck I cleaned up your mess and put her back on the bus. Now you owe me one, you little fuck. You are going to that bar with me tonight, and you are going to look happy!

BUCKY: When did you have an abortion?

JOLENE: Oh, Bucky . . .

BUCKY: Answer the question.

JOLENE: I never had one.

BUCKY: What?!!

JOLENE: Come on. Think. Am I the kind of slob who has problems like that?

BUCKY: No.

JOLENE: I never had one.

BUCKY: Then why did you say you did?

JOLENE: She was looking at me as a kindred spirit, as a sister, to see what I would do. So I lied. I told her what she wanted to hear, which is that she'll live through it. And she will. But she needed to hear that from some-body who'd been there. And we didn't exactly have anyone handy, so. Somebody's got to do it. Why not me, you know? I do everything else around here.

CHET: Oh, man. You're going straight to the top some day.

JOLENE: That's right. Hillary Clinton better watch her ass. Now let's go.

BUCKY: I can't believe you lied.

JOLENE: Go get her! If you're so upset! If this isn't exactly what you wanted, chase her down! There's still time!

CHET: That bus hasn't left yet.

JOLENE: Every second you sit there pouting she gets further away, and that's exactly what you want, you piece of shit, isn't it. Let's go.

BUCKY: I'm not going anywhere with you.

JOLENE: Isn't it a little late to be digging in your heels?

BUCKY: I should have never come back here. I should have stayed with Span-ish Girl. I should've taken her to a dentist . . .

JOLENE: Spanish Girl? Who's that?

CHET: His summer love.

JOLENE: There's another one?!

CHET: This was his other summer love.

JOLENE: She better not be pregnant. I can only do that once a night.

CHET: No, man. She went back to Spain.

BUCKY: We don't know that for sure!

CHET: Where else could she be?

BUCKY: On her way here.

CHET: Oh, man. No way!

BUCKY: She has the address. And if she shows up, I'll go with her. In a heart-beat! You see if I don't! I want no part of this place! It's a nest of vipers! People like me don't belong here! People with a conscience, and a heart! People who care about right and wrong!

JOLENE: Should I run out and get Skyler for you?

BUCKY: No.

JOLENE: Are you sure? Apparently I can talk that chick into anything.

BUCKY: No.

JOLENE: Because if there's someplace you'd rather be, you should go there.

BUCKY: There's no place I'd rather be. Damn it.

JOLENE: Then let's go to the dance.

CHET: All right! This is going to rock! Where's my flowers?

BUCKY: In the sink. I never touched them.

CHET: Friends, if I don't get laid tonight . . . I don't know how to finish that sentence.

JOLENE: I'll eat your flowers for breakfast.

CHET: You're on!

BUCKY: Use a condom.

CHET: Duh. What do I look like? You?

BUCKY: I'm going to change my shoes.

(Bucky exits to his room.)

CHET: So tell me, Jolene. Are there any sophomores who are just really, really slutty? I mean like trash slutty. Because I want to meet them first.

JOLENE: They all are.

CHET: That's what I like to hear.

(Bucky returns with his other shoes. Sits at the table to put them on.)

BUCKY: Do we have to go to this thing?

JOLENE AND CHET: Yes.

BUCKY: That's not the answer I'm looking for.

JOLENE: I want you to see it.

BUCKY: I did see it! It's a flop!

JOLENE: No. I want you to see me save it.

BUCKY: Do you really think you can do that?

JOLENE: I got rid of that girl, didn't I? Now for an encore I'll go save the dance. Maybe then you'll love me, do you think?

BUCKY: I'm never going to hear the end of this.

JOLENE: Do you think you'll ever love me, really?

BUCKY: We'll be eighty years old. With our grandkids! You'll still be beating me over the head. "Do you remember the time in college?"

JOLENE: Maybe I'll show up pregnant next time. Introduce you to my new Luh-Var.

BUCKY: You better not.

JOLENE: What would you do?

BUCKY: Kill you.

JOLENE: No. Really. What would you do.

BUCKY: I don't know.

JOLENE: Would you fight for me?

BUCKY: Do you mean with my fists?

JOLENE: Would it even occur to you to do that? Or would you just curl up and die?

BUCKY: I know you wouldn't get pregnant.

JOLENE: Wouldn't I?

BUCKY: No. Because you're not the kind of slob that has those problems. Are you.

JOLENE: Maybe I should be. Seems like that's your type.

BUCKY: Are you, Jolene.

JOLENE: You know what? This corsage looks a little droopy. Where's the one you got me?

BUCKY: In the fridge.

JOLENE: I think I better put it on.

BUCKY: I'll get it for you.

JOLENE: Throw out this old thing. It's too delicate. I need an action corsage.

BUCKY: Maybe they make one out of hemp.

JOLENE: Why hemp?

BUCKY: Because it's tough and useful.

JOLENE: Just like me.

(Bucky replaces the corsage.)

BUCKY: Just like you.

JOLENE: Now I'm ready to save the world. Mmm, this smells good . . .

BUCKY: You coming, Chet?

CHET: You better believe it.

JOLENE: Don't forget your flowers.

CHET: Oh, right . . .

(As Chet grabs his flowers from the sink, Jolene quite impulsively takes Bucky's face in her hands and kisses him.)

JOLENE: This is going to be the best night of my life . . .

(She hurries out, followed by Bucky and Chet. We hear the door downstairs slam. Blackout.)

END OF PLAY

HOMEBOUND

By Javon Johnson

For Frank "Pop" Mundy, Lummie Young III, Keltrus Lindsey,
and Rodriquez Cowens

BIOGRAPHY

Javon Johnson is a native of Anderson, South Carolina. He is a founding member and resident playwright for Congo Square Theatre Company of Chicago, Illinois. He is also a member of the Dramatist Guild, the Writer's League of America, Screen Actor's Guild, Actor's Equity Association, a MFA graduate of the University of Pittsburgh, and a BA recipient from South Carolina State University.

Johnson is the recipient of several awards and honors including 2004 Black Theatre Alliance Lorraine Hansberry Award for Best New Play, 2003 NOW Professional Theatre Playwriting Award, 2001 Jefferson award nomination for best new play. 2001 and 1999 recipient of the National Project Award sponsored by Pierians, Inc. Pittsburgh Chapter, 2002 Chicago's African-American Alliance Award for Best Lead Actor in a Play, 2001 Chicago's Black Theatre Alliance's Paul Robeson Award for Best Lead Actor in a Play, 2000 participant at the Sundance Theatre Laboratory, 1999 finalist for the Allen Lee Hughes Fellowship at Arena Stage of Washington, D.C., 1999 Theodore Ward Playwright Award, 1999 Pittsburgh Playwright Award, 1999 Finalist for the National Play Award, 1999 second place recipient of the Lorraine Hansberry Award, 1998 Lorraine Hansberry Award, 1998 Yukon/Pacific New Play Award, 1998 Kennedy Center Fellowship to attend the Eugene O'Neill National Playwrights Conference, publication by Dramatic Publishing Company, and 1998 Best One-Act Play in the American College Theatre Festival Region II Competition.

He has had play readings at Lanford Wilson's Playwright's Retreat, Kennedy Center, Alabama Shakespeare Festival, National Black Theatre Festival, New Jersey Repertory, The Edward Albee Theatre Conference in Valdez, Alaska, the Whitefire Theatre and Stage 52 in Los Angeles, CA, CAP21 and Lab Theatre Company in New York.

Productions at the Grahamstown Festival in South Africa, St. Louis Black Repertory, Victory Gardens Theatre and Congo Square Theatre of Chicago, Studio Theatre of D.C., Horizon Theatre of Atlanta, National Black Theatre Festival of Winston-Salem, N.C., featuring Malcolm Jamal Warner, Studio 52 in Los Angeles, New Jersey Repertory Company, Dunbar Repertory Theatre of New Jersey, Kuntu Repertory Theatre, Columbia College, Pittsburgh's New Voices, and H.E.R.E. Theatre of New York. Johnson also served three consecutive years as a panelist alongside Ed Bullins, Bill Hoffman, Michael Warren Powell, and others for the Edward Albee Theatre Conference in Valdez, Alaska. He has also taught acting and stage combat at the University of Pittsburgh and Freedom Theatre.

Some of Johnson's acting credits Cinque in *Amistad Voices* for Duncan Chernin Center for the Arts, the Provost in *Measure for Measure* for Pittsburgh Public Theatre, Asagai in *A Raisin in the Sun* for City Theatre, Guy in *Blues for an Alabama Sky* for Kuntu Repertory Theatre, Cory in *Fences* for Hilton Head Playhouse, Young Ali in *Ali* for Congo Square Theatre, Wendal in *Before it Hits Home* for Congo Square Theatre and Jazz Actors Theatre, Pericles in *Pericles,* Macbeth in *Macbeth,* and Joe in *Pill Hill.* He has performance experience with theater greats Delroy Lindo, Ella Joyce, and August Wilson. Film credits include Calvin, Sr. (Ice Cube's father) in *Barbershop 2,* Louis Price in *The Temptations* for NBC, Gangster in *Dogma* for Askew Films, and Sportin' Life in *Porgy: A Gullah Version* for SC Educational Television.

He has also been featured in *USA Today Weekend Magazine* as the protégé of August Wilson — May 2001, *Black Voices Quarterly* — Summer 2001, and the cover issue of *American Theatre Magazine* — Oct. 2002 and *Black Mask* — October 2003.

ORIGINAL PRODUCTION

ETA Creative Arts Foundation Production, ETA Theatre, Chicago, Illinois, March 6 thru April 20, 2003, producer Abena Joan Brown, artistic director Runako Jahi. It was directed by Derrick Sanders, with the following cast:

DARNELL AKA "SPIT" . . . . Demetrius Thornton
JAY AKA "SMOKE" . . . . Darnell Brown
RAYMOND AKA "PISTOL" . . . . Taj McCord
CALVIN AKA "KANE". . . . . Ethan Henry
VOICE OF MS. BRADY . . . . TaRon Patton

Stage Manager . . . . Carol Woolfolk
Technical Director. . . . . Darryl Goodman, Sr.
Costume Designer . . . . Karen Nolan
Set Designer. . . . . Logan Shunmugam
Sound Tech . . . . Carl Cohen
Light Tech . . . . Regina M. Davis
Dramaturg. . . . . Paul Carter Harrison

CHARACTERS

DARNELL "SPIT": Sixteen-year-old black male
JAY "SMOKE": Fifteen-year-old black male
RAYMOND "PISTOL": Sixteen-year-old black male
CALVIN "KANE": Seventeen-year-old black male

SETTING

A boys' home in Anderson, South Carolina. The room should have a "boot camp" feel to it with four bunks with simple white sheets and pillows. There's a small lamp and dresser by each bunk. There's one desk that sits downstage and off center. A study lamp also sits on the desk. There are closet doors, one with a mirror on the outside. A window with bars is mounted upstage of the bunks. The walls may be fence or bars themselves. There's also an intercom located near the main entrance. The walls of the dorm could be a huge fence appearing as a cage.

TIME

Contemporary

Homebound

PROLOGUE

The stage is dark. We hear Raymond's voice over the house speakers.

RAYMOND: Some things happen because they happen. Others happen because they must. Sometimes they change people. For better or worse, whatever happens . . . there's always a reason.

ACT I

SCENE ONE

Lights rise. Spit lies in his bunk reading an adult magazine and fondling himself. All lights are out except the lamp near Spit's bunk.

After a moment, Smoke enters through the front followed by Raymond. They watch Spit for a beat. Smoke slams the door shut startling Spit who quickly puts the magazine away and stands embarrassed.

SPIT: Dang it, man! Don't you know how to let somebody know you coming?

SMOKE: Don't you?

SPIT: *(Beat, obviously not liking the joke.)* Where Kane at?

SMOKE: I dunno.

SPIT: Ms. Brady came by here looking for him. I told you he's gonna get us into trouble!

SMOKE: I can't be watching after Kane all the time. He don't listen to me nohow.

SPIT: He don't listen to nobody! I'm tired of washing somebody's dirty draws cause of him! *(Notices Raymond standing by the door.)* Who's he?

SMOKE: This our new roommate . . . Raymond. He's from Friendship Court. *(Spit crosses to Raymond, staring at him with each step. Raymond seems a bit uncertain as Spit now stands in his face. After a moment.)*

SPIT: Spit. *(Beat.)* Spit!
(Raymond spits on the floor. Spit and Smoke are repulsed.)

SMOKE: Nah man, he means his name is Spit. That's what we call him.

RAYMOND: *(Wipes away the spit with his shoe.)* I'm Raymond.

SPIT: Yeah, I heard that. What you in for?

RAYMOND: I shot somebody.

(Beat. Smoke and Spit look at each other then back to Raymond.)

SMOKE: You kill 'em?

(Raymond does not respond.)

SPIT: You like shooting at people?

SMOKE: You like shooting people, we gonna call you . . . Bullet.

SPIT: Nah, Pistol.

SMOKE: Yeah, that sound better.

RAYMOND: My name Raymond.

SPIT: Well, you Pistol now. Whatever you was out there don't count in here. Tell him Smoke.

SMOKE: In here you become whatever you need to be to stay alive.

(Raymond starts to sit on Kane's bunk. Spit points to another one.)

SPIT: That's your bunk right there.

(Raymond crosses to the other bunk.)

SMOKE: That used to be Emilio's bunk.

RAYMOND: Who's Emilio?

SPIT: Hispanic boy used to be here. They had him in here for hot-wiring cars.

SMOKE: He ain't even have no license.

RAYMOND: *(Sits on his bunk.)* Where he at now?

SPIT: Oh, he dead now.

(Raymond quickly jumps up from the bunk.)

SMOKE: Drank a whole can of Drano. If I was gonna take myself out I know I wouldn't be burning up my insides like that. Might take some sleeping pills or something, but I ain't drinking no poison.

RAYMOND: What he do that for?

SPIT: You stay here long enough . . . you'll figure it out.

SMOKE: The bathroom's over there and I guess you know the kitchen's the next dorm over.

RAYMOND: You said your name was Jay. Why he call you Smoke?

(Smoke looks at Spit then back to Raymond. Without responding, he exits into the bathroom.)

RAYMOND: Something wrong with him?

SPIT: Smoke been here for awhile. Longer than most people here I know. Him and Kane been here the longest.

RAYMOND: Kane?

SPIT: That's Smoke's crazy brother. Real name's Calvin. Most people don't come here until they thirteen. They been in here since they was about nine or so. Kane been out before, but he keep coming back. I don't think they can breathe without each other. That's Kane's bunk over there.

RAYMOND: Curfew's at ten.

SPIT: Kane don't care nothing about no curfew. That's why he ain't never gonna get outta this place.

RAYMOND: What about your friend . . . Smoke?

SPIT: Ain't nobody friends here. You just bunk with somebody and that's it. Just like boot camp. People come and go. Besides, there ain't nothing wrong with Smoke except he don't like to talk about what he in here for.

RAYMOND: He kill somebody?

SPIT: If Smoke wanna tell you what he did you let him tell you. That's his business and I don't mess in nobody's business but my own. Live longer that way.

RAYMOND: *(Beat.)* What you in for?

SPIT: Man, I shouldn't be in here. Been here two years and that girl out there telling lies on me . . . said I raped her. That ain't the first time she said no. That was part of what we do. She say no, I push harder. Started seeing her when she was thirteen. She the kinda girl be young but look old cause of puberty. Her mama found out she been having sex and she started talking about I took it. There should be something against that. Girl cry rape and everybody just accept it. Don't care what really went on, all they know is you took it. You could be doing it for three days straight, she say no, you don't stop, now you done raped somebody. I'm telling you there should be something against that!

(Smoke reenters from the bathroom. Raymond watches as Smoke lies in his bunk and pulls the covers over his head. He then turns to Spit.)

RAYMOND: Why they call you Spit?

SPIT: You ask too many questions. The light switch over there.

(He lies on his bunk. Raymond looks around for a moment then settles at his bunk after inspecting the sheets. He takes off his shoes and shirt, turns out the light, and lies down. Kane enters through the front and stumbles on Raymond's suitcase.)

KANE: What the hell? Spit! Spit, keep your shit off my side!

SPIT: *(Turns on his lamp.)* That ain't my shit.

KANE: Well, who's shit is it then if it ain't your shit?

(Raymond turns on his lamp. Kane turns and looks.)

KANE: Who the hell is that?

SMOKE: *(Turns on main light.)* He from Northside. Friendship Court.

KANE: Yeah, I know where that's at.

SPIT: This Kane. The one always getting us into trouble.

KANE: What you talking about? Ms. Brady been by here?

SPIT: You know she been by here.

KANE: I ain't been here to know she been by here! Damn! What she say? The kitchen or the trash yard?

SMOKE: Another week of laundry duty.

KANE: Ah hell, that ain't nothing. I'll take that any day.

SPIT: I ain't gonna be doing too much more of this for you. You need to stay here after curfew.

KANE: Don't you start with me, Spit. You don't tell me what to do. I come in when I say it's time for me to come in. Ms. Brady or nobody gonna tell Kane what to do. *(Crosses to Raymond and sniffs him.)* You a virgin? *(Raymond does not respond.)* Niggah, I said is you a virgin? You know what the poon-tang look like?

SPIT: Leave him alone, Kane.

KANE: Nah Spit, you know the rules. This dorm for men only. He a virgin he ain't no man yet.

SPIT: What difference it make? He tell you he ain't no virgin how you gonna know if he ain't? You gonna give him some?

KANE: He got to tell me. *(To Raymond.)* You a virgin? Lot of them Friendship boys is virgins. What about you, partner? You ever get you some . . . or you like your honey with nuts?

SMOKE: That's enough, Kane. He ain't done nothing to you.

KANE: *(Beat.)* Friendship Court, huh? Me and Jay from the Earl Homes. You know about the Earl Homes?

RAYMOND: I been there.

KANE: Then you know not to fuck with me and not to put your shit on my side.

RAYMOND: Sorry.

(Moves suitcase.)

KANE: How old are you?

RAYMOND: Sixteen.

KANE: Alright, I'm the oldest. This how it work. You earn your stripes around here. I do what I wanna do. You got a problem with what I do you come to me about it. Jay my little brother. Don't fuck with him. Spit ain't no blood to me. Whatever goes on between you and Spit is between you and Spit.

RAYMOND: I just wanna go to sleep.

KANE: What you doing here? Probably one of them pretty boys, stole some candy or some shit, huh?

RAYMOND: I shot somebody.

KANE: *(Beat.)* You shot somebody. *(Pulls out a knife.)* Well, I don't care who you shot. Don't fuck with me . . . or my little brother.

SMOKE: Go to bed, Kane.

KANE: I'm going to bed. Just gotta set things straight with my man . . .

RAYMOND: Pistol.

KANE: *(Beat.)* Pistol. Yeah . . . Pistol. *(Beat.)* We straight now.

(Puts the knife away as everyone once again tries to settle. He then pulls money from his pocket.)

Got forty dollars, Jay. Here's your twenty.

SMOKE: Go on, Kane. Go to sleep.

KANE: Take your money, niggah.

SMOKE: That ain't my money.

KANE: What you mean it ain't your money? My money is your money, you know how it go.

SMOKE: Go to bed.

KANE: I'll go to bed after you take your money!

SMOKE: I ain't gettin' in trouble with you! Go on! Leave me alone!

(He turns off his lamp. Kane throws money at him.)

KANE: That's your money! *(Beat.)* Me and you a team!

(He turns out the light and lies in his bunk. The only light is the lamp at Raymond's bunk. Raymond sits. He takes out a Bible then turns to the audience.)

RAYMOND: My mother was the only thing that stood between me and the end of the world. She give me this Bible. Told me there was hope where there is none . . . and that if I could take one step to find it, I'd be that much closer to coming home.

(He opens the Bible and reads as the lamp fades.)

SCENE TWO

Following morning. Raymond is still reading when Spit enters from the bathroom. He has just showered and has a towel around his waist.

SPIT: You Jehovah Witness or something?

RAYMOND: This my mama's Bible.

SPIT: You go to church, too?

RAYMOND: My mama used to take me to church.

(Spit turns upstage and drops the towel. Raymond turns away as Spit puts on his underwear.)

SPIT: Yeah, I ain't the Bible type. Ain't too much into God and stuff. Rev. Sewell always preaching that stuff, but I see it like this. If it ain't in front of me then it just ain't.

RAYMOND: You gotta die.

SPIT: *(Puts on his pants.)* I figure you dead the day you born. I mean you born to die right? If God set everything up, he set up when and how you gonna die. *(Puts on lotion.)* I figure the minute you born, you just here waiting around for the day God got set for you. Ain't that what that Bible say?

RAYMOND: I'm just on the creation part. I ain't got to death yet.

(Spit offers Raymond the bottle of lotion. Raymond simply stares.)

SPIT: My back. *(Beat.)* It's hard to get to. *(Raymond is not willing.)* C'mon man, I got your back you got mine. You need that in here.

(Raymond finally takes the lotion and rubs it onto Spit's back.)

SPIT: Couldn't sleep last night, huh?

RAYMOND: Hard to sleep in here.

SPIT: Don't let Kane get to you. He talk a good game, carry that knife around, but all he do is bark and sell drugs.

(Raymond has had enough as he steps away and crosses back to the table. Spit puts on his shirt.)

SPIT: How much time you get?

RAYMOND: As much time as my mama say it takes.

SPIT: *(Puts on socks and shoes.)* My mama in jail. She got caught shoplifting. She ain't do nothing but try to feed me and my sister. I ain't talk to my mama since I been in here.

RAYMOND: You ain't got no daddy?

(He stares at Raymond for a moment. This is obviously something he doesn't want to talk about.)

SPIT: You gonna like it here. Seventy-Five C the best dorm on the yard. We got a shower, got our own hot water heater. Kitchen right next door. *(Goes to window.)* You can see everything from where we at. That's the basket-ball courts to the left. We usually go down there before we go to work.

RAYMOND: Work?

SPIT: I got trash and yard duty. Smoke work in the kitchen at lunch and Kane usually do the laundry. They probably going to put you in the kitchen.

RAYMOND: Why the kitchen?

SPIT: This dude Smoke used to work with got stabbed to death. Look, Ms. Brady's dorm right over there. She be watching us all the time. I think that's how she be knowing Kane be sneaking out.

RAYMOND: What about the guards?

SPIT: Paychecks. Ms. Brady the only one who cares. That's the infirmary over there. You don't want to go in there. They just make you sick. Yeah, you really gonna like it here.

RAYMOND: How can you like being locked up?

SPIT: If you say you locked up, you ain't gonna like it. If you say you just taking a break, then you can get used to it. Hey, come here. *(Raymond joins him at the window.)* Ms. Brady nice ain't she?

RAYMOND: She . . . she nice.

SPIT: Got some big titties. I'm a tittie man. How about you?

RAYMOND: *(A bit uneasy.)* I dunno . . . I guess I like the titties.

SPIT: I like the thighs too, but Ms. Brady got some nice titties. Make me wanna be a baby all over again, but she mean though. Strong, too. She grabbed Kane one time and threw him to the floor like he wasn't nothing.

RAYMOND: What she do that for?

SPIT: Kane put his hand on her butt. She smacked him, too. He won't do that no more, but I tell you what. Had it been me . . . I would've put my hands on her titties.

RAYMOND: Counselors ain't supposed to hit us.

SPIT: You'll find out real fast about the rules in here. They don't work like they do on the paper. They just write that down for your parents. Let them think you safe. They do what they wanna do to you in here. *(Beat.)* Why you like shooting at people?

RAYMOND: I don't like nobody to talk about my mama.

SPIT: I don't like nobody to talk about my mama either, but hell, I ain't gonna shoot nobody if they talk about her. Might beat the crap out of them, but I ain't gonna shoot them.

RAYMOND: My mama been through too much. Her and my daddy used to fight sometimes but they don't fight no more.

SPIT: You kill him?

RAYMOND: *(Beat.)* I don't let nobody mess with my mama cause she an angel. You ain't suppose to mess with God's angels.

SPIT: Man, I wish there was a God. I wish he was black, too. White God wouldn't make no difference. Be just like it is now. People just waiting to die.

(Raymond takes a picture from his pocket.)

SPIT: What's that you got?

RAYMOND: Picture of my mama.

SPIT: Word? Let me check that out.

(He reaches for the picture. Raymond pulls it back.)

SPIT: C'mon man, I ain't gonna do nothing to it. I just wanna look at it. *(Uncertain, Raymond hands him the picture.)* This your mama? *(Raymond nods.)* Damn man, if God's angels look like that, hell ain't no place for me! *(Raymond grabs him violently.)* Hey! What you doing, man? Get your hands off me!

RAYMOND: Give me my mama's picture!

SPIT: *(Shoves Raymond away.)* Here! Take it! *(Throws the picture.)* Don't you be grabbing on me like that! Something wrong with you?

RAYMOND: Don't you talk about my mama!

SPIT: I ain't! I just said she fine! That ain't talking about her! I was saying something nice about the lady! You want me to say she ugly or something?
(They stare at each other. Smoke enters through the front hiding something beneath his shirt.)

SMOKE: What's going on?

SPIT: Ain't nothing going on! This fool just bet not grab on me no more!

SMOKE: *(Beat.)* They got blueberries today.

SPIT: Blueberry? You ain't sneak me none out?

SMOKE: You know they watching us, man. We can't sneak nothing out no more.

SPIT: You watch this fool, Smoke. Something wrong with him.
(He exits through the front. After a moment.)

SMOKE: Spit messin' with you? *(Raymond does not respond.)* You don't want no blueberries?

RAYMOND: Blueberry what?

SMOKE: Muffins. Everybody like the blueberry muffins. You better get you some now. They don't last too long.
(Raymond does not respond as he opens his Bible.)

SMOKE: Why you always reading that? They gotta Sunday School class every week. Everybody gotta go to that. Why don't you just wait until Sunday? That way you don't have to waste your time reading it now.

RAYMOND: My mama give this to me. She want me to read it that's what I'm gonna do.
(Smoke takes muffins from inside his shirt and eats.)

RAYMOND: Why you ain't say nothing?

SMOKE: Spit gotta get his own muffins.

RAYMOND: Yesterday Spit told me what he in for. You just went to the bathroom.
(Smoke stares at Raymond. After a moment, he gathers his muffins and exits into the bathroom.)

RAYMOND: What's wrong with these people?

(Kane enters through the front.)

KANE: Jay? Yo, Jay! *(Sees Raymond.)* What you looking at?

(Raymond turns away. Kane goes to bathroom door and knocks.)

KANE: Hey, Bruh!

SMOKE: *(From bathroom.)* What?

KANE: Ms. Brady full of it! She say I gotta do the laundry all by myself!

SMOKE: Do it then!

KANE: That's the whole yard! You gotta help me! I can't do all that by myself!
(Beat. He knocks on the door.) Yo, Jay! Man, you hear what I'm saying?

SMOKE: I'll help you alright! Just stop banging on the door!

KANE: Damn right you'll help me! We blood! Blood stick together!
(He crosses to his bunk and removes a bag of cocaine from a slit cut into the side of the mattress. He feels Raymond watching him.)

KANE: You snort?

RAYMOND: *(Turns away.)* Nah.
(Kane places some cocaine into a smaller bag then puts it into his pocket. He replaces the larger bag inside the mattress.)

KANE: Then this ain't got nothing to do with you. You bustas from Friendship shady. I get busted I know where you at.
(He starts to exit.)

RAYMOND: You like this place?

KANE: Say what?

RAYMOND: Spit say you keep coming back. I thought maybe you like it here.

KANE: Let me tell you something. I'm the oldest in this camp. I know how
things work. It don't make no difference where you at. Rather you in here
or out there, you gotta do what you gotta do. Them people out there don't
accept that. See, I'm the type got something on my mind I act on it. You
know, like instinct. I let my natural instinct guide me. I ain't gotta listen
to nobody.

RAYMOND: You gotta listen to your mama.

KANE: My mama dead. Both my parents dead. *(Beat.)* Ain't you gonna say something?

RAYMOND: What?

KANE: Niggah, I just told you both my parents dead. You just gonna sit up
there and not say nothing?

RAYMOND: How they die?

KANE: *(Stares at him.)* Tell my brother I'll be back.
(He exits through the front. Smoke reenters from the bathroom.)

SMOKE: Where's Kane?

RAYMOND: Just left.

SMOKE: You wanna go play some ball? They gotta pick-up game in the courtyard. Start in about a half hour if you wanna go.

RAYMOND: You ever read the Bible?

SMOKE: What?

RAYMOND: My mama ain't dead . . . but if she did die, I'd probably just read
the Bible. *(Beat.)* You wanna read mine?
*(The silence is uneasy. Smoke exits through the front. Ms. Brady can be heard
through the intercom.)*

MS. BRADY: Seventy-Five C, pick up. *(Beat.)* Seventy-Five C, pick up. *(Raymond looks around the room.)* This Ms. Brady. Jay, Calvin, Darnell. If y'all
in there, let Raymond know his mother is down here to see him.

RAYMOND: *(Searches for the voice.)* My mama?

MS. BRADY: Tell him to come down to the main office.

RAYMOND: Ms. Brady! It's me, Raymond!

MS. BRADY: I know he likes muffins, so you might find him at the cafeteria.

RAYMOND: *(Finds the intercom.)* Ms. Brady! I'm right here! Tell my mama I'm
coming! Ms. Brady!

MS. BRADY: He has four minutes to get down here.

RAYMOND: Mama, I'm coming!

MS. BRADY: Y'all have a nice day.

RAYMOND: No, wait a minute!
(Spit enters through the front eating muffins.)

RAYMOND: Ms. Brady come back! Tell my mama I'm coming! I'm coming right
now!

SPIT: What you doing, man?

RAYMOND: I gotta go see my mama! How I get to the main office?

SPIT: Go down by the kitchen and cut a left. Hey! You want a muffin?
(Raymond exits.)

SPIT: Something wrong with him. He ain't gonna make it.
*(He suddenly realizes he may be alone. He looks out the windows and closes
the door. He also checks the bathroom then pulls an adult magazine from his
mattress.)*
Hey, baby. Nah, I was gonna call you, why you fussin' at me? Forget you
then, I don't need you. I'll just turn over to page forty-seven. *(Turns page.)*
Page forty-seven . . . yeah, there you go.
*(He takes off his pants, gets lotion, and lies in his bunk. Kane enters through
the front counting money. He notices Spit and watches.)*

SPIT: I don't too much like white girls, but baby you got some nice titties. Big butt, too. Must eat some collard greens or something. Come here and let me . . .

KANE: *(In girl's voice.)* Oooh.

SPIT: Oooh, yeah. That's what I'm talking about.

KANE: Please stop.

SPIT: Oh c'mon baby, I ain't gonna hurt you.

KANE: No.

SPIT: Yeah.

KANE: Oh, no.

SPIT: Oooh, yeah.

KANE: Oooh, yeah, rape! Rape! Somebody help! You going to jail, niggah!

SPIT: *(Jumps to his feet in panic.)* Rape? No, I ain't rape nobody! I ain't touched nobody! I ain't done nothing!

(Kane breaks into laughter. Spit snaps out of it and stares at Kane. Once again he is embarrassed.)

KANE: Why you always doing that, man? I can get you a woman. Get you a real woman. All you got to do is wait for the truck like last time.

SPIT: This ain't your business, Kane! Leave me alone!

KANE: You oughtta do it in the bathroom you don't want me to talk about it! All out here in the open! I don't wanna see that shit! You need to wash your sheets!

SPIT: Go on, Kane! I ain't playing with you!

KANE: Man, I can get you a woman. We just gotta hop on the truck. We can go tonight if you want.

SPIT: I don't need no woman!

KANE: Oh, you just scared you gonna go crazy again. Start touching yourself and moanin'. You remember that? Girl just standing there, just talking to you. Ain't took nothing off and you grabbing yourself, moaning like you a cow. Wouldn't no girl talk to you after that.

SPIT: You don't know what you talking about!

KANE: Is that a white girl? *(Grabs magazine.)* Spit! What you doing jackin' off on a white girl? *(Distracted by the photo.)* Damn, she got some big titties though.

(Spit grabs his magazine back, gets lotion, and exits into the bathroom.)

KANE: Man, don't be wasting your stuff on that white girl! We can get you some sistas over there at the Girl's Home. Three or four at a time. You know how we do. All we gotta do is get on the truck. We can do it tonight! Truck come around about eight. Get you a real woman. I had me one of them sistas, you know what she did to me? She tied me up with her panties, some of them wasn't even hers. Poured sugar all over me and called me her Sugar Daddy. She was spanking me and rubbing me all over. Tossin' my salad! Hey man, you need something like that! C'mon and go on the truck with me tonight! *(A loud moan sounds from the bathroom.)* Alright then, go on and spit! Just don't spit on the floor. You spit on the floor you clean that shit up!

(Raymond enters through the front carrying a shoe box.)

KANE: What's up, partner? What you got there?

RAYMOND: This from my mama.

KANE: Your mama got you some new shoes?

RAYMOND: It's a care package.

KANE: What kinda caring stuff in there?

RAYMOND: Stuff my mama put in there. Stuff for me.

KANE: Hey man, I don't want your little box. I'm just trying to conversate with you. Remind me not to say nothing next time. *(Beat.)* Why you so tight on your mama anyway? You sixteen, you know how to shoot a gun. You ain't no virgin like you say, why you so tight on your mama?

RAYMOND: My mama all I got. Can't imagine what I'd do without her. How you do it?

KANE: *(Beat, shuffles a deck of cards.)* You play cards? *(Raymond nods.)* What you play? Gin-Rummy, Tunk, Spades, or what?

RAYMOND: Spades.

KANE: Alright, we playing Knuckles.

RAYMOND: I don't know how to play that.

KANE: All you gotta do is be a man. You a man, you can play. Pick a card. *(Raymond takes a card.)* What you got? *(Raymond shows him the card.)* Five. Alright . . . I gotta take me a card. *(Picks a card.)* Two. Alright, that mean you get to hit me. *(Extends his fist to Raymond.)* Go on.

RAYMOND: Go on and what?

KANE: Hit me. You gotta hit me five times cause you won that one.

RAYMOND: I don't wanna hit you.

KANE: But that's how you play the game. You a man, hit me. *(Beat.)* Look punk, take the cards . . . the whole deck, and hit me across the knuckles with all you got . . . five times. Then we pick again. First person give up lose. *(Beat.)* C'mon now, hit me . . . or I hit you.

(Raymond picks up the deck of cards and strikes them across Kane's knuckles.)

KANE: That's all you got? Harder! *(Raymond strikes him again.)* C'mon chump, harder! *(Strikes again.)* You swinging like a sissy! Thought you said you

ain't no faggot! *(Strikes again.)* Man, you hit like a mama's boy! Ain't
nobody's mama here! Swing, niggah, swing!

*(Raymond hits him violently. Kane quickly grabs him by the shirt. Raymond
grabs Kane by his shirt. They stand off as Spit reenters from the bathroom.)*

SPIT: Hey, what y'all doing?

KANE: Playing Knuckles!

SPIT: Y'all about to fight over playing Knuckles?

KANE: This niggah hit me!

SPIT: I thought that's how you play Knuckles. Ain't that how you play?

KANE: *(Releases Raymond's shirt.)* Pick your card. *(Raymond does not respond.)*
I said pick your card! I ain't quit!

*(Raymond picks his card and lays it on the desk. Kane picks his card and lays
it on the desk. Raymond extends his fist to Kane who strikes his knuckles hard.
Raymond reveals no sign of pain.)*

KANE: One! *(Strikes him again.)* Two! *(Strikes again.)* Three!

SPIT: Stop messin' around, Kane!

KANE: That's four!

SPIT: Kane!

KANE: Five-six-seven . . .

SPIT: *(Grabs Kane.)* C'mon, man! Stop hittin' him like that! You see he don't
wanna play!

KANE: *(Throws the deck of cards at Raymond.)* You touch me again! One more
time you got to touch me! One more! And you see what I do to you!
*(Beat. Raymond crosses to his bunk and picks up his care package. Kane pushes
Spit away.)*

KANE: Get your hands off me! You been in there spittin', I don't want your
hands on me either!

(He exits through the front. After a moment . . .)

RAYMOND: You know he got drugs in here?

SPIT: Who?

RAYMOND: Kane.

SPIT: Everybody on the yard know Kane got drugs in here. That's all he do is
sell drugs. I don't know how Ms. Brady don't know about it.

RAYMOND: How he get them in here?

SPIT: We got a truck come by every other day. This dude from the east wing
know this guy drive the truck. Whatever you need, you can get it off the
truck. You just gotta wait a day or so.

RAYMOND: How far the truck go?

SPIT: It don't go no farther than the Girl's Home, but this dude that drive it, he go pick up whatever you need.

RAYMOND: You can get me to the truck?

SPIT: You got something you need?

(They stare at each other as the lights fade.)

SCENE THREE

Two weeks later. Raymond sits outside the dorm on the front steps staring at the dark sky. Inside, Spit is connecting the alarm clock to an extension cord. Kane and Smoke are asleep. After a moment, Spit enters from inside the dorm carrying the alarm clock.

SPIT: Eleven forty-eight.

(He sets the clock near the door then sits a little too close to Raymond. Raymond slides away. After a moment.)

SPIT: I can't believe Smoke about to turn sixteen. He don't act like he twelve yet. *(Beat.)* You look like you sad.

PISTOL: Just thinking about my mama.

SPIT: She see you kill him?

PISTOL: Who?

SPIT: Your daddy. *(Beat.)* C'mon man, we ain't gotta be friends but you gotta talk to somebody. *(Raymond does not respond.)* Alright, but the nights don't get no shorter.

(He starts to go back into the dorm.)

RAYMOND: We was on our way to church. *(Beat. Spit turns back.)* Me and Mama. Dad, he tired, he just come home from work. Two stoplights from the house I say, "Mama, you forgot your Bible." She looked at me like she didn't want to go back and get it. Another light come by and I say, "Mama? You forgot your . . . " Before I could finish what I was saying she turned the car around. We pull up in the driveway and it wasn't empty and we ain't got but one car. We only got one car. *(Beat.)* Mama ain't say a word. She just pulled in, went inside, and I waited. Sitting there listening to the car. The engine got this rhythm I ain't never heard before. Never paid attention to it, but sitting there waiting, I could hear it. Repeating itself, slowing down and speeding up, but it was a rhythm. That rhythm had to happen to keep it running. Smooth and quiet. Then I looked at the house and I thought inside that house is a rhythm. And when I saw that woman, pretty woman, but not my mama, when I saw her run outside and get into her car, I knew that rhythm inside that house had stopped. I knew those crashes against the walls and those screams weren't about smooth and quiet and I wasn't going to sit there and wait for it to repeat itself. I ran into the house. I stepped inside and there was my mama. Glass on the floor and she bleeding. There was this picture we had of me, her, and my daddy. Big picture with this crystal frame and my daddy hit her across the face with it. That was the first time I hated my dad. First time I ever hit him. *(Hands him a photo.)* That was after the stitches. Three months later my mama tried to kill herself. See everybody was talking about her. Calling her names. She couldn't even go to church without somebody looking at her like she was sick. Even the preacher who would always throw her a smile turned away. She slit her wrist. Would've died if I didn't see the blood coming from under the bathroom door. I drove her to the hospital. I sat there and waited for those doctors to say she was going to be alright then I went home and I shot my daddy. I knew he was sleep, I knew he had a gun and I knew he was never going to repeat himself. I pick up my mama's Bible and I take it to her. Somehow she must've knew I needed it cause she wouldn't take it. She just opened it up and told me to read. *(Beat.)* Now, I'm here, man. Now I'm here.

SPIT: *(Beat. He hands Raymond the photo back.)* Sometimes you gotta be some place else to get to where you need to be.

RAYMOND: I don't think this right. All them stars up there and we're in here. That don't seem right.

SPIT: I blame that on my granddaddy.

(Hearing the boys outside, Kane awakes.)

SPIT: I'm telling you man it's my granddaddy's fault. There's something he didn't tell my daddy that he needed to tell me to keep me from going through this shit. Somebody dropped the ball somewhere.

RAYMOND: It just ain't right Smoke gotta celebrate his birthday in a place like this.

SPIT: Gettin' old in here ain't no blessing. You get old in here and they send you off to the bricks.

RAYMOND: The bricks?

SPIT: The bricks is where you go when you turn eighteen.

(Kane enters from inside the dorm.)

SPIT: You about to turn eighteen ain't you, Kane? *(Kane presents his middle finger.)* We call it Hell's Dungeon. That's something Rev. Sewell said one time. They say people dying every day in there.

KANE: People dying every day everywhere.

SPIT: They say the minute somebody die a baby born at the same time. I heard that from my grandmama. She called it the crossing of the souls. That's why I don't believe in all that heaven and hell talk. I think people just change bodies when they die. I mean, if you think about it. When you born, you can't do nothing right. Can't talk, can't use the bathroom for yourself, gotta learn how to walk and how the world works. Somebody else gotta feed and bathe you. That's the same thing happen when you get old. You forget how the world works. Your legs can't walk no more, you dooky all over yourself. I think that's just getting you ready to be born all over again.

RAYMOND: You are born all over again. Into the Kingdom of God.

KANE: Will y'all niggahs shut up?

RAYMOND: Why you always calling us niggahs?

KANE: What niggah?

RAYMOND: Why you always calling us niggahs? You say you don't like white people, but you calling us niggahs like we slaves.

KANE: What you think you is? You think you something other than a niggah? You here like everybody else here, but you always gotta be in the middle of something. White people on one side or the other, but you gotta be caught between African or Afro something. Every year we changing up. Gheri curls, jelly shoes, parachute pants, from Hilfiger to hilniggah, horse weave to cow weave. We don't know what we wanna be. You ask somebody black who they are. What they say? "I got Indian in my blood." Them girls over at the Girl's Home always talking about they got Indian in their blood. Ain't none of them just black cause what that mean? Nothing. See, you're a niggah cause you don't know who you are.

RAYMOND: Yeah, but white people don't call white people cracker. We calling each other niggah like we don't know what it mean. Nah Kane, you're a niggah cause you don't know that you're a niggah. And as long as you keep thinking the way you thinking you're always gonna be a niggah.

(A long beat as Kane and Raymond stand eye-to-eye. Spit tries to break the tension.)

SPIT: It's almost twelve o'clock. *(Beat.)* You ain't got nothing to worry about, Pistol. You got two more years before they ship you off.

RAYMOND: I ain't gonna be here that long.

KANE: They ain't shipping me nowhere. I'm gonna get outta here. Maybe catch the truck or something.

SPIT: You know the truck don't go but to the Girl's Home and back.

KANE: Well, they ain't taking me to the Dungeon!

SPIT: Man, you gonna alert the guards! Shut up!

(They freeze as a security light flashes by.)

KANE: Y'all gonna stay here until I get out. They ain't gonna put me in that place. Y'all gonna stay here with me and we all gonna leave together.

SPIT: What you talking about, Kane? You older than everybody.

KANE: Y'all ain't gonna let them take me! Put me in there so they can do things to me. I know what they do. That cat, Roc, from Seventy-Two B been in there nine months. The only reason he ain't dead now is cause he doing all the killin'. They say he ain't been to sleep the whole time he been in there. Say the Dungeon make you like that. Kill all your nerves to where you can't feel nothing. Can't see nothing but blood and death. Say every minute you breathing, you just going crazy. Ain't nobody sane. Everybody just like animals . . . living off their instincts.

RAYMOND: That's why I pray.

KANE: Pray? *(Beat.)* Man, what the hell am I going to pray for? I used to get down on my knees every night hoping some blessing would fall down on me. Until I opened my eyes and hell's right there in front of me. Caging me in, making me feel black. This world ain't nothing but space. You gotta live in it or die in it. The last time I got down on my knees I stood up before I got to Amen. I got to occupy my space . . . or die trying.

SPIT: But your time running out.

(The alarm clock sounds. They stare at it then rush into the dorm. Spit turns on light. Kane snatches the bedsheets off of Smoke who is asleep in his underwear. Kane and Spit drag Smoke to the desk and lay him on his stomach.)

SMOKE: What y'all doing? Why y'all grabbing on me?

KANE: It's your birthday take it like a man! Spit, grab his legs! I'm going first!

(Spit grabs Smoke's legs. Kane moves upstage of the desk and strikes Smoke's butt.)

KANE: One mamajama! Two mamajama! Three mamajama! Four mamajama!

SMOKE: Owww, that shit hurt!

SPIT: Let me get mine, Kane!

KANE: Five mamajama! Six mamajama!

SPIT: C'mon, Kane! My turn!

KANE: Go ahead! I got my six!

SMOKE: Owww! Y'all let me go, man!

RAYMOND: I think we should let him go.

KANE: Shut up and hold him! Go on, Spit! Get yours!

(Raymond trades places with Spit.)

SPIT: Six mamajama!

SMOKE: Nah . . . nah . . . that's seven! Y'all messin' up!

RAYMOND: He's right! That's seven!

SPIT: Alright. *(Strikes him again.)* Seven mamajama!

SMOKE: Nah, that's eight!

KANE: Seven, eight, it don't make no difference! Hit him, Spit!

SPIT: Nine mamajama! Ten mamajama!

SMOKE: Owww!

SPIT: Eleven mamajama! Twelve mamajama!

KANE: Hey, it's Pistol's turn! Pist gotta get his!

RAYMOND: That's alright. Y'all go ahead.

SPIT: Nah, Pist. You family, too. Hit him up!

KANE: What number we on now?

SMOKE: Sixteen! Y'all on sixteen!

SPIT: Pull his draws down, Kane!

SMOKE: Nah . . . nah! Y'all gonna see my ding-dong!

KANE: Man, we ain't worried about seeing your ding-a-ling! We got the same
thing you got! Ain't nobody here no fag! *(Pulls Smoke's underwear off his
butt.)* Go on, Pist! Get you some bare naked ass! *(Beat.)* Niggah, what
you waiting on?

SPIT: C'mon, Pistol! You number thirteen!

RAYMOND: *(Strikes Smoke.)* Thirteen.

SPIT: Mamajama! Thirteen mamajama!

KANE: Yeah and hit harder!

RAYMOND: Fourteen . . . mama-jama. Fifteen mamajama.

KANE: One more, niggah! One more!

SPIT: This everybody! Hands up! *(Spit and Kane raise their hands high.)* C'mon,
Pistol! Get your hand up! This the last one! *(Raymond raises his hand.)*
Hands . . . down!

SPIT/KANE: Sixteen mamajama!
(Kane and Spit strike Smoke. Raymond lowers his hand to his side.)

SPIT: Pull his draws up.

SMOKE: *(In tears.)* Don't y'all touch me!
*(He pulls his underwear up and sits in the chair at the desk, but jumps up
suddenly.)*

SMOKE: Owww . . . shit!

KANE: *(Laughs.)* Now, that's what I call a hot ass.

SPIT: Yeah, you might wanna let that cool off before you do that.

RAYMOND: *(Puts a pillow on the chair.)* Try that, Smoke.
(Smoke eases himself onto the pillow.)

KANE: Boy, I can't wait 'til you turn seventeen!

SPIT: Hey, Pist! Why you bail out on us, man? You ain't follow through on sixteen.

RAYMOND: He was crying.

KANE: You let me worry about my brother. He cry all the time. Jay just soft like that. He gonna be a man though, cause Jay ain't no virgin. Ain't that right, Bruh?

SMOKE: Y'all hit me too hard.

SPIT: That's just a part of gettin' old, Smoke. You hear old people talking about how bad they hurt all the time.

RAYMOND: *(Takes a bag from beneath his bunk.)* I got you some muffins. I got you blueberries. Tried to get you sixteen, but they had their eyes on me. I couldn't get but four. Guy on the truck got me the candles.

SPIT: *(Pats his back.)* Hey man, that's alright. You alright with me, Pist.

RAYMOND: *(Hands muffins to Smoke.)* Happy birthday.

KANE: Speech! Speech . . .

SPIT: *(Joins in clapping and stomping his feet.)* Speech! Speech . . .

SMOKE: Y'all gonna make Ms. Brady come down here! Stop shoutin'!

KANE: Give us a speech then, niggah!

SPIT: What you gotta say, Smoke? Me and you the same age now!

SMOKE: Alright, alright! *(Thinks for a moment.)* Today . . . I'm sixteen years old and thanks to my brother and my roommates, my black ass hurt like hell.

(They all laugh.)

KANE: Ah, go on, man! If it was my birthday, y'all be doing me the same way.
(Raymond strikes a match. Smoke screams in fear.)

SMOKE: Ahhhh! Ahhhh!
(He throws himself from the chair and crawls into a corner. Kane smacks the match from Raymond's hand.)

KANE: Niggah, what you doing?

RAYMOND: I'm just lighting the candles so he can blow them out!

KANE: Jay, don't like fire!

RAYMOND: Well, I didn't know!

KANE: It's cool, Bruh! There ain't no fire.

SMOKE: I seen it! I seen it! It was burning!

KANE: Nah, it ain't nothing, Bruh! Pistol was just messin' with you! There ain't no fire nowhere! Come out the corner!

SMOKE: I seen it! It was burning like the house!

KANE: There ain't no fire, Jay! It was just make-believe! Now c'mon!

SMOKE: Mama! Get Mama, Kane! You gotta get Mama and Daddy!

KANE: Shoot Jay, stop it!

SMOKE: Ahhh, Mama! Daddy . . . I see the fire coming! I ain't mean nothing! We was just playing! I ain't mean to make the fire come!

KANE: Look what you did, niggah! You see that? Got my brother all upset!

RAYMOND: I didn't know! How was I supposed to know?

KANE: *(Tries to lure Smoke out of the corner.)* C'mon, Bruh. Now, I told you there ain't no fire. The fire gone now. Get off the floor.

SMOKE: I seen it, Kane! You seen it, too!

(The sound of crackling fire can be heard as the lights shift to flames.)

SMOKE: You see the fire like I see it! It's burning everything up! *(Crawls on the floor.)* Get down, Kane! You gotta get down on the floor when the fire come! Mama, you gotta get up! You and Daddy gotta get outta the bed! The fire coming! *(Pulls Kane to the floor.)* Get down, Kane! You gonna burn up if you don't get down! Ahhh, my shirt! My shirt on fire! Mama, I'm burning! Ahhh! I'm burning up, Daddy, help me! The fire got me! Get the fire off my back, Mama! The fire burning me up . . .

KANE: *(Cradles Smoke.)* Nah, it's OK, Bruh. There ain't no fire. It's all gone now. Everything's alright now.

SMOKE: Mama?

KANE: Mama's right here, Jay. She's gonna take care of you. Me and you.

SMOKE: You gotta get Daddy, Kane! You gotta get Daddy! The fire going to get him!

KANE: Daddy's right here. Daddy got your hand. You feel Daddy's hand?

SMOKE: Daddy got my hand? I feel my Daddy's hand. Hey Bruh, Daddy here. Daddy, you alright? You ain't let the fire get you?

KANE: No, the fire didn't get Daddy.

SMOKE: You OK, Mama?

KANE: Mama's fine, baby. You just having one of them dreams.

SMOKE: I was dreaming the fire burn you and Daddy up.

KANE: You was just dreaming, Jay. The fire all gone now. You rest your head on Mama. Go on to sleep now . . . Mama and Daddy alright . . .

(Lights shift as they now sit in a pool of red flames. Kane hums and rocks back and forth with Smoke in his arms as Raymond and Spit look on.)

(Lights fade.))

SCENE FOUR

Lights rise. The boys all return from Sunday School service. Each enter carrying a program. All except Raymond have been undressing along the way. Some carrying ties with shirts unbuttoned. Raymond carries another shoe box.

SMOKE: Kane, help me loosen up. Thing almost made me pass out.

KANE: Your birthday was over a month ago. Loosen up your own tie.

SPIT: You almost passed out cause you was sleeping.

KANE: I don't understand why we gotta wear a tie nohow. A tie around my neck that's the same as a rope, but we still gotta get dressed all up to listen to all them lies Rev. Sewell be saying.

RAYMOND: Rev. Sewell know what he talking about. I read it in the Bible.

KANE: *(Drinks a soda.)* Ain't none of that stuff real. You let white people tell you anything. They tell you they gonna give you equal opportunity you gonna believe that, too. The white man can't tell me nothing.

RAYMOND: The Bible black with white pages.

KANE: Niggah, what that supposed to mean? The Bible black with white pages. That don't prove nothing. What color the Bible is ain't got nothing to do with it. It's what they talking about. What they telling us that count. Rev. Sewell talking about stealing and drugs ain't got no morals to it. You hear him say that, Smoke?

SMOKE: I fell asleep on that part.

KANE: He come talking about, "You steal from thy neighbor, you doing drugs, you going to hell." That's all white people do is steal. Hell, it's a white man drive the truck who bring me the drugs. So, what he talking about? People kill me talking about heaven and hell. We in hell right now. Eternal Fire, burning of the flesh. I'm telling you, hell done turned over and got us killing each other. We ain't gotta worry about what the white man do cause whatever he needs to be done, we doing it ourselves. So, the white man ain't got nothing to do with me. He don't bother me, I don't mess with him.

SPIT: You pay taxes don't you?

KANE: Niggah, I sell drugs. How you gonna pay taxes on drugs?

SPIT: Don't you sell drugs to keep from working so you don't have to pay taxes? Everything you do the white man got something to do with. You in the situation you in right now cause of something the white man had to say about it.

KANE: That's a bunch of bull, Spit. I'm saying I ain't gotta deal with him straight up. That's what I'm trying to communicate to you.

SPIT: Don't matter how you deal with him. You gotta deal with him one way or another.

KANE: I'm getting around the system. I sell drugs, I get the profit. Ain't too much we can get a hundred percent on, but I get what I'm supposed to on that.

SPIT: You still gotta pay taxes.

KANE: I ain't gotta pay shit.

SPIT: What you think you paid on that drink you drinking? The sign say ninety-nine cents. What you pay? A dollar and five. That's another six cents.

SMOKE: At least.

KANE: First off, I didn't pay for the drink. I jacked it from the kitchen. Second, all y'all niggahs tired. And I ain't listening to nothing you fishes got to say cause y'all on dry land.

RAYMOND: *(Rambles through his care package.)* I don't know why everything gotta be about the white man anyway. Why we can't just move on?

KANE: I don't care about it. It's them tired niggahs.

SPIT: What you standing there talking about why we can't move on for?

RAYMOND: The world here for everybody. We living in it together. The Bible say . . .

KANE: Oh hell, the Bible say. The Bible say all kinds of things. You know, I liked it better when you wasn't talking much. You done got comfortable in here and now can't nobody shut you up!

SPIT: Pistol, you telling me you like white people?

RAYMOND: I'm just saying God made everybody. If you look back to the beginning, we come from the same place.

SMOKE: Pistol? What you think Rev. Sewell meant when he said evil is black and total damnation is without light?

KANE: I think he was talking about black people.

SPIT: What if you wanted to be president? There ain't no black presidents.

RAYMOND: I'm just saying every time something come up the white man come up with it. We can't even sit here and look at each other without talking about the white man. I get so tired of hearing people talking about what chances they didn't have . . . what chances I ain't gonna get. Half the brothers on the streets now, on the streets cause that's where they comfortable.

KANE: You saying I ain't responsible?

RAYMOND: I'm saying if the white man didn't exist you wouldn't be using him as an excuse for what you doing.

KANE: Nah . . . I see what you getting at. This niggah done got pasty on us. Don't nothing stick to him but the high and the mighty. I been in the bathroom after you, niggah. Your shit smell like shit just like everybody else.

SMOKE: Chill out, Kane.

KANE: What's up, Pist? You a pasty niggah?

RAYMOND: You stop calling me niggah.

KANE: Oh, I see. Now you ain't even a niggah at all. You just sittin' up here with a bunch of other niggahs just pretending you a niggah. You ain't no better cause your mama send you stuff. Hell, I can buy my own toothbrushes and shit paper. I don't need my mama looking after me.

RAYMOND: *(Stands.)* You talking about my mama, niggah?

KANE: Oh, now I'm a niggah. Damn, ain't you special.

RAYMOND: You saying something about my mama?

SPIT: Hey, y'all chill out!

KANE: Everybody know Pist a mama's boy! Everybody know Mama come running when baby Pist come calling!

RAYMOND: You talking about my mama?

KANE: I'm talking about what I said.

RAYMOND: You say something about my mama?

KANE: Yeah, I said something about your mama!

RAYMOND: *(Beat. Takes a gun from his mattress.)* Go ahead, niggah! Say something! Say something else about my mama!

SMOKE: Pistol, where you get that?

RAYMOND: I got it off the truck! Now this niggah ain't gonna say nothing else about my mama!

SPIT: Put that away, man! You gonna get yourself in trouble!

RAYMOND: What you talking about, Kane? You saying something?

SMOKE: He ain't saying nothing, Pistol! You know how he do!

SPIT: Ms. Brady come in here we gotta be cool! *(Beat.)* Pistol, c'mon, man!

KANE: Nah, y'all back up! *(Beat.)* What you gonna do, Pist? You gonna shoot me with that thing?

SPIT: Pistol, it ain't worth it! You about to get out of this place! C'mon man, you know your name on the list! You gonna be able to see your mama! Don't you want that? Don't you wanna see your mama? C'mon, Kane ain't saying nothing! He just talking!

(After a moment, Raymond puts gun away and tends to his care package.)

SPIT: Man, I done told you about messin' with him! You know he'll shoot anybody talk about his mama!

KANE: I wasn't talking about his mama! Just trying to tell him something about how things work for people who ain't got it like him!

SPIT: Well, everybody don't see things the way you see it! You can't expect that! That's that man's business what his mama do!

SMOKE: Pistol, you gotta get rid of that gun.

KANE: I'm sick of this place. Walls caving in around me. You niggahs stealing my air with all this bitch talk. I'm getting outta here.

SPIT: How you gonna leave? Your time ain't up.

KANE: All I gotta do is jump the fence. That ain't nothing but a leg up. Jay can give me a leg up.

SMOKE: My time coming up soon. Dr. Chisholm say I'm getting better. I ain't messing it up for you.

KANE: What you saying, man? Me and you come in here together. Now you don't wanna help me out?

SMOKE: I'm always helping you out! That time you snuck that girl in here, what I do? I covered for you! That time Ms. Brady say you set off that fire alarm, I lied for you then! I would've been outta here a long time ago if it wasn't for you!

KANE: Man, have you lost your damn mind? Me and you is blood, niggah! There's more between us than anybody else in this hell-hole and you talking like you don't know me!

SMOKE: We came here together, but you got more time than me.

KANE: But you ain't seventeen!

SMOKE: I ain't gettin' in trouble for you no more, Kane! I just ain't!

KANE: *(Beat.)* Ain't that some shit! All y'all niggahs done turned pasty!

RAYMOND: The Bible say you gotta have knowledge to survive.

KANE: You saying I'm stupid?

RAYMOND: You scared you can't make it out there.

KANE: Niggah, I been out there before! That ain't nothing new to me! There ain't nothing out there bad enough to keep me in here!

RAYMOND: Then why you still here?

KANE: Cause my brother here! I ain't leaving my brother. And you better watch your mouth cause I'm telling Ms. Brady where you keep that pistol at!

SPIT: Ah c'mon, Kane. Ain't nobody told Ms. Brady you got them drugs in here!

RAYMOND: Maybe you should read the Bible. That'll tell you how to make it out there.

KANE: That Bible ain't nothing but stories somebody made up. Some white man creating the world with apples and snakes. What kinda bull is that? Boats floating around and people walking on water! If that shit was real people wouldn't be in the situation they in today cause whoever this white man is wouldn't let it happen that way! If he God and all!

RAYMOND: Everybody don't follow God. That's why we in this situation. You follow God, you ain't gotta worry about nothing.

KANE: I ain't hearing this. Spit, you hear this niggah talking about if we follow God?

SPIT: There ain't no God. Just people waiting to die.

KANE: Jay, you hear that? You hear this crazy fool talking about God? This niggah go around shooting at people and he talking about following God! You believe that?

SMOKE: I dunno.

KANE: What you mean you don't know? You always sleeping in Sunday School! What you talking about you don't know?

SMOKE: I mean, I dunno! How you explain how everything got here? Something had to happen! Somebody had to do something!

KANE: I don't believe this!

SMOKE: I'm saying, Kane! How you explain all this? Mountains and the oceans and stuff! That stuff had to come from somewhere!

KANE: Ain't no white man made it!

SMOKE: Well, how it get here?

KANE: It was just here! Like me, you, and everybody else! We just here breathing! Ain't no explanation for it!

RAYMOND: *(Reads Bible.)* "And God said, 'Let the waters under the Heaven be gathered together unto one place, and let the dry land appear:' and it was so. And God called the dry land Earth; and the gathering of the waters called He seas: and God saw that it was good."

KANE: That don't mean nothing cause somebody wrote it! You can't prove where them words come from! That's like if the world was to end right now and the only thing that's left is one of Spit's magazines. What's gonna happen? Whoever comes across that magazine gonna think that's heaven. They gonna think God's a nasty woman with big tits. Everybody be running around naked, humpin' each other, and putting on clothes would be a sin!

SMOKE: Well, something had to happen! It had to come from somewhere!

KANE: Ain't nothing happen except this niggah rubbing off on you! He come in here with all that Bible talk! You ain't think nothing about God until this niggah come in here!

SMOKE: I think about God all the time. I think about life. The stars and the moon.

KANE: Bruh? The stars and the moon?

SMOKE: I think about Mama and Daddy. How they burn up in that fire. I think about that all the time.

KANE: Shut up, Jay.

SMOKE: How they was sleeping and they wouldn't wake up.

KANE: Jay, I said shut up about it, alright!

SMOKE: The whole room burn up. I remember that.

KANE: You don't know what you talking about!

SMOKE: There gotta be a God. If there ain't no God where Mama and Daddy at? *(Beat.)* Say, Kane? Where they at if there ain't no God? Where they at, huh? They burn up in that fire. That ain't hell is it? Mama and Daddy ain't in hell, but they gotta be somewhere. Like the clouds and the moon. They gotta be somewhere right? You tell me. Where they at? If there ain't no God like you say, then you tell me where Mama and Daddy at!

KANE: I don't know! *(Beat.)* I don't know.

(He crosses to his bunk. There's silence as Smoke stands looking at them all.)

SMOKE: God somewhere. He gotta be.

(No one can respond. After a moment, the intercom sounds. We hear Ms. Brady.)

MS. BRADY: 75 C pick up. 75 C pick up. *(Beat.)* I don't like repeating myself.

(After a moment, Spit finally crosses to the intercom and pushes a button.)

SPIT: We here, Ms. Brady.

MS. BRADY: You boys get enough gospel this morning?

SPIT: Depends on who you asking.

MS. BRADY: Ummm humm. Well, make sure you check the list. I left an envelope in the desk. *(They all look at the desk.)* Those of you who's time is coming up can start working on your essays. The sooner you turn them in the better. Raymond, your mama's looking forward to you coming home. Dr. Chisholm is seriously considering your recommendation. Don't let this essay get in the way.

RAYMOND: I won't, Ms. Brady.

MS. BRADY: Calvin?

KANE: Yes ma'am?

MS. BRADY: Don't you let time run out on you. *(Beat.)* You boys get yourselves ready. We have a yard meeting in ten.

(The intercom sounds off. There's silence as they all stare at Kane. Kane crosses to the desk and removes the envelope from the drawer. He looks at it for a moment, then offers it to Spit.)

KANE: Open it.

SPIT: You open it.

KANE: Jay, open it.

RAYMOND: Why you scared to open it?

KANE: I told you I ain't scared of nothing! I just want somebody else to open it, that's all!

SPIT: I'll open it. Ain't nothing but a piece of paper.

(He opens the envelope. He reads. He smiles then suddenly stops. He drops the envelope back to the desk.)

SPIT: I'm uh . . . I'm going to the meeting. C'mon Pistol.

PISTOL: What's up?

SPIT: C'mon.

(He exits. Raymond reads the letter, looks at Kane, then exits. Kane sits as Smoke reads the letter. He then turns to Kane.)

SMOKE: You going to the meeting? *(Kane does not respond.)* I don't wanna be late.

(He exits. Outside he can be seen as he turns back to look through the window at Kane who sits alone inside the dorm. Kane looks up.)

KANE: I've waited for you. I've prayed for you, but my name ain't on the list. God helps those who help themselves right? Well, I can't help that I'm here. I can't help that my parents are dead. I can't help that I can't do this all by myself, but I am. "He might not come when you want him to, but he's always on time." *(Stands.)* But God, I don't think me and you in the same time zone! You working on when the time is right, I'm working on when the time is right now! And right now my time is running out! *(Beat.)* So Amen to you, God. If all it's gonna take is for me to drop down on my knees then here I am . . . *(Drops to his knees with arms out.)* . . . and I say it. *(Beat.)* Amen.

(He drops his head into his hands. Smoke turns away from the window and exits the yard. Lights fade.)

INTERMISSION

ACT II

SCENE ONE

One week later. All lights are out except for the study light at the desk. Smoke, Raymond, and Spit are asleep. Kane sits at desk writing. He seems to be having difficulty. After a moment, he crosses to Smoke's bunk.

KANE: Hey, Bruh . . . Bruh!
(Aims Smoke's lamp at his face and turns it on.)
Bruh!
(Smoke suddenly wakes up and immediately pushes the bright light away from his face.)

SMOKE: What?

KANE: How you spell *resentment?*

SMOKE: Spell what?

KANE: *Resentment.*

SMOKE: R-E-S-I-E-N-T . . . M . . . something.

KANE: Is it M-I or M-E?

SMOKE: M something. I'm sleep. Ask, Spit.
(He turns his lamp back off. Kane crosses to Spit's bunk. He aims Spit's lamp at his face and turns it on.)

KANE: Hey, Spit! Get up!

SPIT: *(Pushes the bright light from his face.)* For what?

KANE: I need to know how to spell *resentment.*

SPIT: Ask Smoke.

KANE: I did. He don't know.

SPIT: I don't know either. Sound it out.

KANE: It all sound the same. I can't tell if it's supposed to be I or E.

SPIT: *(Turns lamp off.)* Man, c'mon. Ask me in the morning. I can't think right now.

KANE: *(Turns lamp back on.)* I can't wait until the morning! *(Pulls bed sheet off Spit.)* How you spell it?

SPIT: F-U-C-K-Y-O-U.
(He turns off his the lamp and pulls the bed sheet back over his head. Kane looks at Raymond's bunk, but goes back to the desk and sits. After a moment, he decides to cross to Raymond's bunk. He aims Raymond's lamp directly at his face and turns it on.)

KANE: Hey, Pist, let me ask you something.

RAYMOND: *(Hiding from the light.)* I told you I don't snort.

KANE: It ain't about that. Jay wanna know how to spell *resentment*.

RAYMOND: Who wanna know?

KANE: Jay. For his essay.

RAYMOND: Smoke sleep.

KANE: He told me to get it for him. How you spell it?

RAYMOND: R-E-S-E-N-T-M-E-N-T.

KANE: *(Writes.)* E-N-T. Cool.

(*He crosses back to the desk and writes. Raymond heads for the bathroom.*)

RAYMOND: What you doing?

KANE: Helping my brother write his essay.

RAYMOND: Smoke wrote his essay already. He wrote it last week.

KANE: I'm proofreading it.

(*Raymond looks at Kane then exits into the bathroom. Kane reads and writes.*)

KANE: On behalf of Seventy-Five C and the Boy's Home, I like to show my resentment for my actions. Me and my brother would like to go home to make this world a better place.

(*Raymond reenters from the bathroom and looks on.*)

KANE: My friend Raymond and I been reading the Bible. It has helped me out a whole lot.

RAYMOND: You ain't on the list.

(*Kane glares at Raymond then continues to write.*)

RAYMOND: What you doing, Kane? You wasn't on the list.

KANE: I told you I'm proofreading this for Jay.

RAYMOND: They ain't gonna take it.

KANE: I told you it ain't for me!

SMOKE: Hey, y'all be quiet.

KANE: *(Beat.)* What you care? You ain't got but fourteen days. What you care what they take from me? You homebound.

RAYMOND: *(Gets Bible.)* There's this story in the Bible.

KANE: Here you go.

RAYMOND: This woman couldn't have no babies and the man Abraham . . . Abram, that's it! He wanted babies. So, his wife told him to sleep with the maid. They did it, but when the maid got pregnant she started disrespecting the woman. So, the woman started disrespecting her back and blaming the man . . . Abram. So, then the maid run off, but she run into this angel. The angel told her she had to go back and have the baby, but she had to stop treating Abram's wife like that.

KANE: I told you that's a bunch of bullshit, Pist.

RAYMOND: Nah, it ain't. I asked Rev. Sewell what it was all about. I asked him wasn't it wrong for that woman to make her husband sleep with the maid, but he said that ain't the meaning of the story. He say it's about faith.

KANE: Man, this ain't making no sense. What this gotta do with me?

RAYMOND: Rev. Sewell say it don't do no good to run away from nothing. He say the story mean you gotta face what you fear head up and adjust to it. Running away from your problems don't fix nothing if you ain't got faith.

KANE: I ain't running away.

RAYMOND: You running away from the Dungeon.

KANE: I ain't!

SPIT: Hey, man! I'm trying to sleep! Shut up!

KANE: *(Loud whisper.)* I'm just writing this essay so I can get outta here, too! Y'all ain't leaving me here!

RAYMOND: But your name not on the list. They ain't gonna take it if you not on the list.

KANE: I don't give a damn what they take! I ain't staying here! I'm sick of this place!

RAYMOND: Then get outta here, Kane, and stop using your brother as an excuse!

KANE: Excuse? You think I'm in here losing sleep over a damn excuse? Niggah, you don't know me.

RAYMOND: I think you're in here losing sleep over the truth.

KANE: I'm in here cause both my parents is dead!

RAYMOND: People dying every day everywhere.

KANE: But they ain't dying in their sleep! Not when their oldest son is in the next room trying to be a man! *(Beat.)* You do things when people say don't cause that's what makes you, but what I become, huh? Sitting there on the edge of the bed striking a match . . .

(The lights shift as Kane sits on the edge of his bunk. He pulls out a box of matches and a cigarette. He strikes a match waking up Smoke who rolls over.)

SMOKE: Bruh? Hey man, what you doing?

KANE: Nothing. Go to sleep.

SMOKE: Let me try it.

KANE: Jay, go back to sleep.

SMOKE: Let me try it or I'm telling Mama.

KANE: I said no, Jay! Now go back to sleep!

(He puts the cigarette out and lies in his bunk. After a moment, Smoke picks up the cigarette and strikes a match. Hearing the match, Kane puts the pillow over his head. Smoke lights it and takes a long drag. He then starts to cough.)

KANE: That's what you get.

(*Smoke now starts to choke as he drops the cigarette behind the bunk. After a moment, Kane rolls over sniffing the air as smoke rises from behind the bunk.*)

KANE: Jay?

(*He sees Smoke choking and the smoke rising from behind the bunk and immediately jumps to his feet.*)

KANE: Jay, where is it? I see smoke, Jay, now where is it?

(*Still choking, Smoke is unable to respond as Kane searches for the cigarettes. He crawls under the bunk. The lights shift as Smoke lies back in his bunk and Kane emerges from the other side of the bunk. He turns to Raymond.*)

KANE: Before I could even get to where it was it was too late. Seems like every way we turned there was fire. I could've sworn I was in hell man because those flames looked like they had eyes and they were coming after me. We get out. Mama and Daddy still in their sleep and we standing there watching them go up in flames.

RAYMOND: That's why you don't call him Smoke?

KANE: You get in here, man, and you feel like you gotta talk to somebody, but all you really gotta do is survive it. I told somebody and they told everybody else. They started calling him Smoke, saying he burned up his family. He was just trying to be like me. So, I ain't got no right to call him Smoke.

RAYMOND: But that ain't no right to be here. Shouldn't have to spend all this time paying for an accident.

KANE: Jay got violent, started seeing things. My grandma couldn't handle him and everybody made him out to be crazy. They kicked him out when he broke this teacher's arm pulling her to the floor trying to get her out the fire. Nowhere to go but here.

RAYMOND: But you had a choice.

KANE: He is my choice. Every second I spent out there I was wondering what they was doing to him in here.

RAYMOND: You started selling?

KANE: Stealing, whatever I had to do to get myself into trouble. Counselor's said it was some kinda post-traumatic something, but I had to. I wasn't going to stop until they put me with my brother. What else I have?

RAYMOND: But you didn't stop. You still selling.

KANE: Out there I was selling . . . in here . . . I'm surviving. (*Beat.*) Now they trying to kill me.

RAYMOND: (*Beat.*) Maybe you should read the Bible.

KANE: Read the Bible for what? The Bible ain't gonna save me.

RAYMOND: But it can change you. Listen to this.

KANE: Dammit, Pist! I ain't got time for this!

SPIT: I'm gonna sleep in the bathtub! Y'all making too much noise!
(He exits into the bathroom carrying his blanket and pillow.)

RAYMOND: Says here on page twelve. Genesis, chapter nine verse six, "Whoso 'sheddeth man's blood, by man shall his blood be shed: for in the image of God made he man."

KANE: So!

RAYMOND: So, I ain't gonna shoot nobody no more!
(Disturbed, Smoke rolls onto the floor and under his bunk where he continues to sleep.)

KANE: I'm gonna show you. I'm telling you that Bible ain't nothing! I'm gonna show you right now!
(Grabs Raymond's gun from beneath his mattress and puts it to Raymond's head.)

KANE: Alright, you say it's all about faith? Well, we gonna see what it's about. You take this gun and put your faith in the Lord like Rev. Sewell say.
(Places the gun on the Bible in front of Raymond.)

KANE: We gonna see if this Bible changed you. We gonna see if this God you talking about for real cause you wasting my time! Now let's see . . . you got faith?

RAYMOND: I believe in God.

KANE: Your mama believe in God . . . or is she just a whore? Hum? I can't hear you, Pist! I said is your mama a stinking whore?

RAYMOND: Don't talk about my mama.

KANE: What's the matter? Ain't you a changed man?

RAYMOND: Don't say nothing about my mama!

KANE: Did I say something about your mama? Oh, I did say whore didn't I?

RAYMOND: *(Grabs the gun.)* What you saying, Kane?

KANE: There you go! You getting the spirit now! C'mon, Pist! You a man of God, ain't you got faith?

RAYMOND: "Whoso 'sheddeth man's blood, by man shall his blood be shed!"

KANE: C'mon, Pist! God waiting on you to do your thing! C'mon!

RAYMOND: "For in the image of God made He man!"

KANE: Make your mama proud, Pist! Make that stink whore a righteous woman!
(Smoke wakes up and moves from beneath his bunk.)

RAYMOND: "Whoso 'sheddeth man's blood . . . "

KANE: Whoso sleepeth with Pistol's mama shall have the best of all whores!

RAYMOND: Shut up about my mama!

KANE: C'mon, Pist! Pull the trigger! Pull it, niggah! Pull it!

SPIT: *(Reenters from the bathroom.)* Man, what's going on out here?

KANE: *(Chants.)* Let's go, Pistol! Let's go! Pull the trigger, man! Pull it!

SPIT: Put it down, Pistol! Man, all you got is seven days! Put it down!

KANE: And God said let there be whores and then there was whores! And God said this is good and he called the whores Pistol's mama!

RAYMOND: I'LL KILL YOU SON-OF-A- . . . !

KANE: Well, c'mon! *(Beat.)* What you gonna do, niggah? C'mon! *(Beat.)* Pull the trigger, man! I'm standing here! C'mon and pull the trigger! *(Beat.)* God don't like evil! That's what Rev. Sewell say! You gotta get rid of evil! You gotta get rid of me! *(Pleading.)* C'mon and shoot! I ain't no good for nobody. Burn up my family. Sell them drugs. I ain't no good for nothing. You gotta get rid of me. You gotta do God's will. Cause I ain't nothing! I ain't shit to nobody!

(Kneels at Raymond's feet as if this was his moment of judgment.)

KANE: God gotta get rid of me. C'mon, Pistol. Let God do what he gotta do. C'mon . . . c'mon and shoot me . . . c'mon, man . . . shoot me . . . right here . . . *(Points to his head.)* please shoot me . . . shoot me right here . . . c'mon, Pistol, please . . . right here. *(Beat.)* What you doing, Pistol?

(Overcome by tears, he puts the barrel of the gun to his forehead.)

KANE: C'mon man, right here! Shoot me, dammit! Shoot me! *(Beat.)* Shoot me right here. *(Beat.)* Please.

(Fighting the temptation, Raymond holds the gun to Kane's forehead. They all freeze. Raymond addresses the audience.)

RAYMOND: I shot him. I felt myself pull the trigger more times than I had bullets. I know I shot him . . . but when it was all over he was still there. Begging me to get rid of God's evil, but I was standing in God's grace. And it was by the grace of God and the pure fear I saw in Kane's eyes that I couldn't pull that trigger. Through all that evil he was good . . . he just didn't know it.

(After a moment, Raymond lowers the gun. He then hands it to Spit.)

RAYMOND: I don't need it no more.

(Spit takes the gun and starts to exit. As he passes by Kane kneeling with his head pressed against the floor, Kane suddenly snatches the gun from Spit's hand.)

SMOKE: Kane!

(Kane seems a bit delirious as he wards off the others and backs himself into a corner.)

SMOKE: What you doing, Kane?

KANE: You see it, Jay?

SMOKE: See what?

KANE: The fire. You see it like I see it.

SMOKE: I don't see nothing.

KANE: I see it. I see what I did.

SMOKE: C'mon, Kane.

KANE: Total damnation without light. That's what Reverend Sewell say. *(Beat.)* If there ain't no light . . . then why do I still see it? *(Beat.)* I don't want to see it no more, Jay.

SMOKE: You don't have to. I'm gonna stay with you. We all gonna stay. Ain't that right, Pistol?

PISTOL: That's right.

SMOKE: C'mon Bruh, me and you a team.

(He cautiously reaches for the gun and pulls it from Kane's hand. Kane collapses into Smoke's arms. Smoke helps him to his bunk and tucks him in. Spit takes the gun and exits through the front. There's a moment of silence as Raymond looks at Smoke. Beat, Raymond crosses to his bunk and lies down.)

SMOKE: Why you ain't shoot him?

RAYMOND: Cause God made him. Every man got a piece of God in him.

SMOKE: God out there somewhere. I ain't know it before, but I know he was in that fire, too. He take my mama and daddy to heaven. That's how I know they ain't in hell. I seen it. Didn't see it, until I started believing what you and Rev. Sewell was saying. That fire was burning and them angels and God come. They pick my mama and daddy up and lifted them right out that fire. They wasn't even burning none. Then I seen God's face. Maybe it was the smoke or something, I ain't sure, but . . . He look black to me.

(Spit reenters through front.)

SPIT: I got rid of the gun. *(Beat.)* Smoke, you alright?

SMOKE: I'm gonna stay here with my brother. Y'all go ahead. Me and Kane gonna stay together.

SPIT: What you talking, Smoke? You been here all this time now you just gonna throw it away cause of him?

SMOKE: I gotta stay with my brother.

SPIT: You stay with your brother. All three of y'all can stay here if you want. Can't you see this place stepping on our brains? Look what it's doing to Kane. That list say I got one month and two days and that's how long

I'm staying here. I'm getting outta Seventy-Five C. Y'all ain't gonna see me no more. Stay here if you want, but I'm gone!

(He lies in his bunk and turns out his lamp. After a moment.)

SMOKE: What you gonna do, Pistol? You gonna leave, too?

RAYMOND: I can't stay in here, Jay. I'm going home and be with my mama.

SMOKE: *(Laughs.)* This place getting to you too, man. You just called me Jay.

RAYMOND: *(Beat.)* I don't have the right to call you nothing else.

(Smoke stops laughing as they look at each other. He watches Raymond pull the cover over his head and turn out his lamp. Beat.)

SMOKE: I'm gonna stay here with my brother. Wait for God and his angels to come back. *(Beat.)* They out there somewhere . . . they gotta be.

(He turns out his lamp. The lights fade.)

SCENE TWO

Following day. Kane still lies in his bunk. Smoke and Raymond are playing cards at the desk. Spit is heard singing in the bathroom.

RAYMOND: Give me one.

SMOKE: *(Deals him a card.)* I'll take two. *(Takes cards.)* What you wanna bet?

RAYMOND: I bet you Spit ain't never gonna stop singing.

SMOKE: If I was getting out early I wouldn't stop singing either. He don't know how lucky he got it.

RAYMOND: Lucky? How you figure he lucky? His grandmama just died.

SMOKE: I ain't mean he lucky cause his grandmama just died, but he lucky cause they letting him out because of it.

RAYMOND: I got a full house. What you got?

SMOKE: Dang it, three of a kind. Wanna play another one?

SPIT: *(From the bathroom door.)* Hey, Pistol! Help me out with this!

RAYMOND: Man, you doing all that singing and you don't know how to put on your own tie?

SPIT: C'mon man, I gotta look fancy. *(Raymond helps Spit with his tie.)* I want them boys from the south wing to shit on themselves when they see me stroll through that gate. Pay them back for eating up all the muffins.

RAYMOND: There. Now you looking good. What you say, Jay?

SMOKE: Yeah, he looking real good. Real sharp.

SPIT: You damn right I look sharp. Clean as spit, too.

RAYMOND: Clean as spit?

SMOKE: Spit clean?

SPIT: Y'all know what I'm saying.

(*He exits back into the bathroom.*)

RAYMOND: I'm glad Spit getting out. I think that girl lied on him. I don't believe he raped her.

SMOKE: Dr. Chisholm say Spit got a sexual problem.

RAYMOND: How you know that? Spit tell you that?

SMOKE: Yeah, he told me.

RAYMOND: I never would've told you nothing like that.

SMOKE: Well, he didn't tell me straight up. I heard him talking about it in his sleep. (*Beat.*) I heard him say, "You're hurting me. Make it stop."

RAYMOND: That could've been anything, Jay.

SMOKE: Could've been . . . if I didn't hear him say, "Daddy."

RAYMOND: (*Stares at Smoke for a moment.*) Maybe, you shouldn't be telling me this! Spit might not want me to know about all that.

SMOKE: Ah, he homebound now. It ain't gonna make no difference who knows about it. He ain't gonna be here to face up to it.

SMOKE: Pick your cards.

RAYMOND: (*Deals.*) What's the game?

SMOKE: Five card stud. Nothing wild but the one-eyed jack. I'm gonna beat you this time.

RAYMOND: (*After a moment.*) Kane been in that bunk all day. You think he gonna be alright?

SMOKE: There ain't no hope for him.

RAYMOND: That's your brother.

SMOKE: Still ain't no hope for him.

RAYMOND: You giving up on him?

SMOKE: He don't listen to me. All I can do is just stay with him.

RAYMOND: Sometimes it's the simplest thing that can change people.

SMOKE: I see how that Bible changed you last night.

RAYMOND: The Bible ain't simple.

(*Beat. Spit reenters from the bathroom, still singing.*)

SPIT: Y'all don't know what I know. See, I know what the birds know. I know what it feels like to be caved in then set free. I'm like the runaway slave crossing over to that great land of freedom!

RAYMOND: You ain't free yet.

SPIT: Oh, I'm free. Got the papers to prove it. (*Holds up a letter.*) Feast your eyes on the prize! (*Notices Kane.*) Damn, Kane still sleep?

RAYMOND: Didn't even go to breakfast this morning.

SPIT: Kane don't never miss breakfast. Even when he stay over at the Girl's Home he don't miss out on breakfast. Y'all sure he ain't dead?

(They look at each other then suddenly jump to their feet and back away. A long silence as the boys try to figure out who's going to check.)

SPIT: Go on, Smoke. He your brother.

(Smoke slowly crosses to Kane's bunk.)

SMOKE: . . . Kane, you up?

SPIT: He breathing?

SMOKE: I think so.

RAYMOND: Check and see.

SMOKE: Kane, you breathing?

SPIT: If he ain't breathing he ain't gonna tell you.

RAYMOND: Put your hand on his nose and check.

SMOKE: *(Puts his hand to Kane's nose.)* Yeah . . . he breathing.

SPIT: He just sleeping hard. Better leave him alone. 'Specially after last night.

RAYMOND: C'mon Jay, let's finish this hand. *(Crosses back to the desk and shuffles cards.)* How many you want?

(Smoke stares at Kane as Raymond deals.)

SPIT: I wonder what made Kane act like that? You think he really wanted you to shoot him, Pistol?

RAYMOND: *(Beat.)* How many cards you want, Jay?

(Not responding, Smoke continues to stare.)

SPIT: Seem to me he done gave up. Like he'd rather die than turn eighteen. If I was in his shoes, I'd go ahead and turn eighteen then decide rather or not I wanted to die. That way I know I ain't made no mistake.

RAYMOND: It's a mistake either way. God forgive you for everything but that.

SMOKE: Give me one . . . nah, nah, hold on. Let me think.

SPIT: *(At mirror.)* Hey, when I get out, I'm gonna tell everybody about you guys. Tell them I had two of the best friends anybody could ever have at Seventy-Five C.

RAYMOND: But there's three of us.

SPIT: Some people you just can't get along with, but I ain't worried about that. *(Makes his bunk.)* I'm gonna have the whole world to choose from.

RAYMOND: Yeah . . . just make sure you don't come back.

SMOKE: Give me two cards, Pistol.

RAYMOND: You sure?

SMOKE: Yeah . . . what? I can't have two cards?

RAYMOND: Just making sure that's what you want. You might need more time to think.

(Smoke glares at Raymond. Raymond deals him the cards.)

SPIT: Nah, I ain't never coming back to this joint. The only time I'm ever gonna see Seventy-Five C again is when I got my eyes closed. Caught up in some dream somewhere, but it's gonna be different, see. Seventy-Five C gonna be like a mansion with all kinds of girls running all over the place. Some with big titties, some with long legs. Running around in nothing but g-string draws and coconut butter dripping off their thighs. I'm gonna do every last one of them. And if they say no, I'm just gonna push harder. Push it and push it 'til they can't take it no more!

(Raymond and Smoke remain silent with a look of discernment.)

SPIT: Ah c'mon, man. I'm just trippin' with y'all. I ain't gonna do nothing like that. I ain't touching nothing got titties and smell like flowers. As long as I got my magazines I ain't gonna need no woman until I'm about thirty or something. Won't nobody be saying Darnell Perry's name and the word *rape* in the same breath ever again. I'm through with it.

RAYMOND: Amen to that.

SPIT: That's right, brother. That's right. Amen to that.

(After a moment, the intercom sounds and Ms. Brady is heard.)

MS. BRADY: Seventy-Five C, pick up. *(Beat.)* Seventy-Five C, pick up.

SPIT: *(Into intercom.)* Hey Ms. Brady, this Spit . . . I mean Darnell!

MS. BRADY: Darnell, you ready? The car be out front in five minutes.

SPIT: Hell yeah, I'm ready! I'm clean as spit, too!

MS. BRADY: You going out into the world, Darnell, but you don't forget, you can always come back here. You watch how you talk to people. Raymond, your mother's dropping you off a package, but she can't stay. I'll call you to pick it up. Calvin missed breakfast this morning. He sick? *(Beat.)* I don't like repeating myself.

SMOKE: I think he's . . .

RAYMOND: Tired. He's just tired, Ms. Brady.

MS. BRADY: Well, you tell him to go see Dr. Chisholm just in case. Darnell, I'll see you in five minutes. The rest of you get that room straightened up. Inspection's at five.

SMOKE/SPIT/RAYMOND: *(Military-like.)* Yes ma'am, Ms. Brady!

(Intercom sounds off.)

SPIT: Well fellas, guess this is it.

SMOKE: I'll wake Kane.

SPIT: Nah, let him sleep. Just give him this when he wakes up.

(Rips a page from his adult magazine and hands it to Smoke.)

SMOKE: What's this?

SPIT: Page forty-seven. Tell him that's a real woman. He'll know what I'm talking about. *(Turns to Raymond.)* Man, I wasn't sure if I was gonna like you, but you turned out an ace. What you got? Six days now?

RAYMOND: Plus three.

SPIT: Well hell, give me a call. I don't know where I'm gonna be staying, but this where I'm gonna be for the funeral. *(Writes down a number.)* Maybe we can get together, shoot the breeze.

RAYMOND: You hang with me people might think you reading the Bible or something.

SPIT: Nah, you cool. I just have to hook up with you on Sunday's only, that's all. *(They laugh. Beat.)* Guess this is it.

RAYMOND: Guess so.

SPIT: *(Beat.)* Alright, then.

(He takes one last look at the dorm then exits through the front. Raymond crosses back to the desk with Smoke. They continue to play cards. Seconds later, Spit reenters.)

SPIT: Hey, I almost forgot. *(Beat.)* I love you cats.

RAYMOND: *(Beat.)* We love you . . . too, Spit.

SMOKE: Yeah . . . we love you, too.

(Spit exits through the front.)

SMOKE: Man . . . Spit almost made me cry. *(Beat.)* What you gonna do when you get out?

RAYMOND: Go back to school maybe. Make something outta myself.

SMOKE: I don't like school.

RAYMOND: I don't either, but I gotta do something for my mama. Buy her a house or something. We ain't never lived in no place that ain't have no roaches. If I can get her something better than that, I'll be satisfied.

SMOKE: I wish I could do something for my mama. My daddy, too.

RAYMOND: Best thing you can do is pray and forgive. You forgive yourself and God'll take care of the rest.

SMOKE: Man, I bet you gonna be a preacher. The way you been talking in here, I bet I'm gonna get out and find you standing in front of some pawnshop preaching the word. "Amen, my people! I know cause I done strayed! I have sinned! I have dwelled in the house of Seventy-Five C! But now I'm walking in the house of the Lord!" *(Laughs.)* I bet you gonna sound just like that. Like Rev. Sewell except with a little soul.

RAYMOND: Maybe I'll sound like Dr. Martin Luther King. "This will be the day when the gates of heaven will open up and all men will be free! Free at last! Free at last! Thank God Almighty we're . . . "

(Kane awakes. Raymond and Smoke watch in silence as he exits into the bathroom.)

SMOKE: I don't know what I'm gonna do without Kane.

RAYMOND: Maybe Ms. Brady'll take his essay.

SMOKE: I'm so used to this place, but I'm more used to my brother. I don't even know if I could make it out there without him. *(Beat.)* I'm just gonna stay here. Maybe start reading the Bible like you. See if God got something for me. See if he wanna change me like he changed you.

RAYMOND: God got something for everybody. You just gotta want what he got.

(Kane reenters. Smoke crosses to him.)

SMOKE: Hey, Bruh? Spit told me to give this to you. He said to tell you that this a real woman. He said you'd know what he's talking about.

(He offers the magazine page to Kane who ignores it and lies back on his bunk. Beat. Smoke lays the page on Spit's bunk then gets the basketball.)

SMOKE: I'm gonna play some ball. You wanna go?

RAYMOND: Yeah.

SMOKE: *(Crosses to Kane's bunk.)* Hey, Bruh? We gonna play some ball. You wanna go? *(Beat.)* Hey, Bruh?

RAYMOND: Let's go, Jay. He don't wanna play.

(After a moment, they exit through the front. Kane sits upright in his bunk. He crosses to the window and looks out. He then looks at the magazine page Smoke left on Spit's bunk. After a moment, he lets it fall from his hands to the floor. He then sits on the edge of his bunk. Beat. He removes a bag of cocaine from the slit in his mattress. He then crosses to Raymond's bunk and retrieves the Bible. He then goes back to his own bunk and sits. He opens the Bible and the bag. The cocaine on one thigh and the Bible on the other. He snorts as he reads.)

KANE: "Whoso 'sheddeth man's blood, by man shall his blood be shed: *(Snorts.)* for in the image of God made he man. *(Snorts.)* And you, be ye . . . fru . . . fruitful *(Snorts.)* and . . . and mmm . . . mul . . . multiply; bring forth . . . bring forth . . .

(Snorts then stops reading and throws his head back, really feeling the affects of the drug. He then lifts his pant leg and removes a small bag of pills from his sock.)

Bring forth . . . light into this total damnation. *(Hesitates, but swallows a pill.)* Set free that which is caged. *(Swallows another.)* So that I may see . . . *(Swallows another.)* . . . smell . . . *(Swallows another.)* . . . feel something . . . something better than me. *(Swallows several.)* Better than who

I am . . . because I ain't nothing but black. *(Beat.)* I wanna go home. God, please, help me home.

(He closes the Bible then crosses to the window. He looks out. After a moment, he begins to have convulsive reactions to the drugs. He desperately struggles to breathe. His body begins to stiffen as it shakes uncontrollably. This seizure-like reaction continues for a moment, then it suddenly ceases. Kane's body has now gone limp and lifeless as he drops the Bible to the floor. Moments later, Spit is heard over the intercom.)

SPIT: Seventy-Five C, pick up! Hey, this Spit! Smoke, you and Pistol still there? *(Beat.)* It don't matter, this for Kane anyway. Kane, I know you in there! You might be sleeping, but I just wanted to say . . . you alright! Don't worry about the Dungeon. Ms. Brady say if you keep your act together until November she gonna try to work something out! You hang in there! I'm gonna write you guys soon, alright? Hey, I gotta go, but Kane . . . I want you to know . . . I love you, too. See ya!

(The intercom sounds off as the lights fade.)

SCENE THREE

Light rise. Smoke and Raymond lie in their bunks. Raymond appears to be asleep as Smoke sits upright in his bunk staring at nothing. His lamp is on. Moments later, Raymond emerges from beneath his bed sheet. He turns on his lamp and stares at Smoke.

RAYMOND: It's been over a week, Jay. You gotta sleep.

SMOKE: *(Beat.)* I don't know why it gotta be like that. Why people gotta go away? Don't do nothing but make you sad. *(Beat.)* If there's a God out there . . . I don't understand you. I don't understand why you want us to be sad like this. Why you taking everybody away. *(Beat.)* I wish she ain't never eat that apple. Maybe I wouldn't be feeling like this.

(Beat. Smoke turns out his lamp and rests his head under his pillow. Raymond looks at him for a moment then turns out his lamp and lies down. Seconds later, Spit barges through the front door. He slams the door shut and paces. Raymond and Smoke awake.)

SPIT: Bullshit! Bullshit! Bullshit!

RAYMOND: Hey Man, what's going on?

SMOKE: *(Turns on the light.)* Spit?

RAYMOND: Man, what you doing here?

SPIT: It's a lie! It ain't nothing but a big fat lie!

RAYMOND: What you talking about?

SPIT: I ain't even touched that girl like that! It wasn't even like that, Pistol! She told me! She say, "Darnell, I'm gonna give you some cause I like you! You sweet to me! Me and you ought to be together!" I said, "We can be together, but I ain't gonna touch you!" And I didn't! You hear what I'm saying, Pistol? I didn't even lay one finger on her!

SMOKE: What happened, Spit?

SPIT: Me and her at the Osteen! She say, "You a virgin? You a virgin, I'll take care of you, Darnell. Don't be scared of me, baby." Then she moves up on me. Started feeling me up and stuff! So, I told her . . . I say, "Candice, I don't mean no harm, but you gotta move! I ain't no virgin, but you gotta get the hell away from me!" But she ain't listen to me! She ain't paid me no attention, she just kept feeling me up! Then she takes my hand and puts it on her left breast! Told me to close my eyes and squeeze! It wasn't even my fault! We end up in the back of her car! I ain't do nothing but lay there and she on top of me hollerin', "Yes! Yes! Yes!" The security guard come by and flash a light on the back seat and she talking about, "No! No! No!" Him looking at me with my pants down and that girl pulling on her dress, I knew what was coming next. I tried to tell him, Smoke! I say, "Mister, it ain't what you see! She did it!" He didn't wanna hear all that! He grabbed me! Didn't say nothing to her! He just grabbed me and blamed me for the whole situation! I didn't get two words out before I was on the bus to come back here! Ain't even my fault, now I'm back here at Seventy-Five C like I done something wrong. I'm telling you, I ain't staying! Ms. Brady trying to say I'm crazy. Her and Dr. Chisholm both trying to tell me I got sexual problems. Saying I can't control myself around titties. They talking about sending me to Patrick B. Harris.

RAYMOND: That's for crazy people.

SPIT: That's what I'm saying! I ain't crazy! I ain't even touch that girl like that! She the one violated me!

SMOKE: What you gonna do?

SPIT: I'm gonna talk to Kane. Me and him gonna jump the fence. I already talked to the truck, the man say he's gonna be waiting on us. Just gotta get him some money. Between me and Kane, we can do that. Y'all going or what? (Smoke and Raymond are silent.) I said me and Kane jumping the fence! What y'all gonna do?

(They do not respond. Smoke exits into the bathroom.)

RAYMOND: Kane ain't here, Spit.

SPIT: Well, where he at? He at the Girl's Home? I'll wait 'til he come back. I'll talk to him about it then. I just need to know what y'all gonna do cause I ain't staying here so they can ship me off to no crazy house!

RAYMOND: Kane's dead.

SPIT: Dead . . . what? What you mean Kane's dead?

RAYMOND: Took too many drugs.

SPIT: Too many drugs?

RAYMOND: That's what Dr. Chisholm say.

SPIT: You believe that? They done, done something to Kane! Dr. Chisholm don't care nothing about us! He probably got Kane drugged up somewhere making you think he dead!

RAYMOND: We found him. Me and Jay found him in his bunk.

SPIT: You found him? What that mean you found him? *(Crosses to bathroom door.)* Hey, Smoke? What Pistol talking about out here?

RAYMOND: He wasn't breathing.

SPIT: Pistol, you don't know what you talking about! Kane sleep heavy all the time! You know how he do! Y'all ain't check to see if he wasn't sleeping? *(Knocks on bathroom door.)* Hey, Smoke!

RAYMOND: He wasn't sleeping!

SPIT: What I say, Pist? Smoke, get on out here, man! Pistol done gone crazy!

RAYMOND: He was dead, Spit! I touched him with my own hand! *(Beat.)* He felt dead to me.

SPIT: *(Long beat.)* How's Smoke?

RAYMOND: Can't tell. He's been acting a little funny, but can't tell what he's really thinking.

SPIT: Damn! *(Beat.)* I didn't like Kane too much, but he didn't deserve that. *(Smoke reenters from the bathroom.)*

SPIT: Hey, Smoke? You alright? Pistol just told me about what happened.

SMOKE: Ain't nothing wrong with me.

SPIT: You sure?

SMOKE: I'm fine.

SPIT: You need anything, I can do it for you. Don't make no difference what it is, just let me know.

SMOKE: You can stop looking at me like that.

SPIT: Hey man, I'm just trying to help you out.

SMOKE: Told you, I'm fine.

SPIT: Alright, you fine! Go on and be fine by yourself then! Don't ask me to do nothing for you! *(Beat.)* Pistol, you jumping the fence?

RAYMOND: I'm getting out tomorrow.

SPIT: Tomorrow? Damn, I forgot you getting out. *(Beat.)* What about you, Smoke? You jumping the fence?

SMOKE: They got dogs now.

SPIT: Dogs where?

SMOKE: At the fence.

RAYMOND: Yeah, they got about five or six. You hear about Derrick from the east wing?

SPIT: What about him?

SMOKE: Them dogs ate him up. He tried to jump the fence and they took off one of his feet.

SPIT: Y'all lyin'.

RAYMOND: He been in the infirmary for eight days. They still ain't found his foot.

SMOKE: I think them dogs ate it.

SPIT: Well, I don't care what they got! I'm getting over that fence! I didn't even touch that girl! I can see if I laid my hands on her, but she was on top of me!

RAYMOND: I'm going back to sleep.

SPIT: Man, how you gonna sleep when Kane's dead?

RAYMOND: It's been over a week, Spit. What you want me to do?

SPIT: You got that Bible! Pray for him!

RAYMOND: Did that. Ain't nothing else for me to do.

SPIT: Smoke, how you feel about that? He say he going to sleep! He don't care about what you going through!

SMOKE: I ain't going through nothing. I told you I'm fine.

SPIT: You fine. *(Beat.)* Alright, well y'all help me move this bunk.

RAYMOND: What bunk?

SPIT: Kane's bunk. We gotta get it outta here. I can't sleep with that bunk sitting in here.

RAYMOND: What's wrong with the bunk? It ain't doing nothing.

SPIT: It's sitting here!

SMOKE: What else it's gonna do, Spit? It's a bunk.

SPIT: I ain't staying in here with that bunk sitting in here like that!

SMOKE: Just don't touch it.

SPIT: C'mon Smoke, help me move it!

SMOKE: I'm gonna lay down.

SPIT: We gotta get the bunk, man! How I'm gonna sleep in here?
  (Smoke and Raymond both cover their heads with their bed sheet.)

SPIT: Y'all crazy, man! This place got y'all thinking wrong! That's your flesh and blood, Smoke! How you gonna sleep?

SMOKE: I ain't said I was sleeping. I just said I'm laying down.

SPIT: *(After a moment.)* Man, y'all letting this place get inside your heads. Y'all see what it did to Kane. *(Beat.)* I ain't crazy! I'd rather go to the Dungeon than go to some crazy house! You hear that, Pistol? I'm jumping the fence! *(Crosses to Raymond's bunk.)* You a niggah just like Kane say! Don't care no more about the living than you do the dead! You preach a good word, but you ain't nothing but a niggah!

(Beat. No one responds. He gets his suitcase.)

SPIT: Pistol, I changed my mind. Don't you call me! I ain't hanging out nowhere with you!

(He exits through the front. He stands outside the dorm looking in through the window. Still in the moment, Spit turns to the audience.)

SPIT: I wanted them to get up. I wanted Smoke to say something. I wanted Pistol to open up his Bible and read to me just so I could stay, but he didn't. He know I'm scared and he didn't reach out to me. What kind of God he serve? What kind of God let them sleep in there when I'm scared out here? *(Beat.)* I ain't got no problem and I ain't crazy. There ain't no God, just people waiting to die . . . and I'm tired of waiting.

(He exits the yard. Inside the dorm, Smoke uncovers his head.)

SMOKE: Pistol?

RAYMOND: Yeah?

SMOKE: You think Spit gonna make it?

RAYMOND: I dunno. What you think?

SMOKE: I think he got a problem. I think he should go to Patrick B. Harris.

RAYMOND: He might make it. I dunno.

SMOKE: You get out tomorrow.

RAYMOND: Yeah.

SMOKE: I'm gonna miss you.

RAYMOND: You too, Jay.

SMOKE: *(Beat.)* I miss Kane. *(Beat.)* I don't miss Spit. I just feel sorry for him. *(Beat.)* When I get out, I'm gonna go to the cemetery and see my mama and daddy. What you think they look like? You think they still look like people or they just bones and stuff? Huh, Pistol? *(Raymond does not respond.)* They probably just bones by now.

(He covers his head with the bedsheet. Beat. We hear dogs barking. Raymond uncovers his head.)

RAYMOND: Nah . . . I don't think he's gonna make it.

(Lights fade.)

SCENE FOUR

Smoke sits at desk holding a box of matches. He opens the box and removes a match. After a moment of contemplation, he strikes it. He gazes into the flame, then blows it out. He repeats this action several times. Raymond enters through the front.

RAYMOND: Hey, Jay! Jay!

SMOKE: Shhh! Shhh!

    (Strikes a match.)

RAYMOND: Jay, what you doing?

SMOKE: It's gone.

RAYMOND: What's gone?

SMOKE: *(Stares into the flame.)* Total damnation. Woke up this morning and it was gone.

RAYMOND: You ain't afraid of the fire no more?

SMOKE: I ain't afraid of the light.

RAYMOND: *(Beat.)* Hey, Ms. Brady signed the papers!

SMOKE: What papers?

RAYMOND: For you to get outta here!

SMOKE: What you talking about?

RAYMOND: I was talking to Ms. Brady. She say you can go to a foster home so you don't have to be here by yourself.

SMOKE: Foster home same as being here.

RAYMOND: Nah . . . Ms. Brady say she know a good foster home two blocks from where me and my mama stay.

SMOKE: So.

RAYMOND: So, me and you can see each other! We can hang out, go play basketball together! You can spend the night with me and eat with us . . .

SMOKE: I ain't hungry.

RAYMOND: *(Beat.)* Jay . . . you the only one in here gotta chance to be something out there. You ain't like Spit and you ain't like Kane. They didn't fit out there but you do. You just gotta take your time.

    (Smoke strikes another match and gazes into the flame.)

RAYMOND: Jay, what you doing?

SMOKE: I'm gonna stay here.

RAYMOND: Why you wanna stay here? You can be with people who gonna care about you.

SMOKE: I ain't going.

RAYMOND: You gotta go!

SMOKE: Kane . . .

RAYMOND: You don't need Kane! You been reading the Bible right? A son of Christ is a brother to all! Since you been reading the Bible that makes me and you brothers in Christ. See, you don't need Kane for nothing! You got me now!

SMOKE: Kane my brother! He the only brother I know! *(Beat.)* You go on, Pistol. I ain't got nothing out there.

RAYMOND: I'm trying to give you something if you'd just take it!

SMOKE: *(Pushes Raymond away.)* Go on, Pistol! I told you I ain't going!

RAYMOND: *(After a moment.)* Alright . . . alright. *(Hands him a piece of paper.)* You call me if . . . when you change your mind.

(He exits through the front. Smoke sits at desk and strikes another match.)

SMOKE: My brother gone. *(Blows out match, then strikes another.)* My friend Pistol gone. *(Blows out match, then strikes another.)* Spit gone. *(Blows out match, then strikes two more.)* Mama and Daddy gone.

(Raymond reenters. He looks at Smoke then places the Bible on Smoke's bunk. They stare at each other. Raymond finally exits. Outside the dorm, he watches Smoke through the window. Smoke turns out the main light, then crosses to his bunk. He kneels and opens the Bible and reads.)

"Fear none of those things which thou shalt suffer: behold the Devil shall cast some of you into prison, that ye may be tried; and ye shall have tribulation ten days: be thou fruitful unto death, and I will give thee a crown of life . . .

(Smoke's voice is now heard over the house speakers as he continues to read. The lights fade inside the dorm leaving a single spot on Smoke.)

He that hath an ear, let him hear what the Spirit saith unto the churches; He that overcometh shall not be hurt of . . . the second death."

(He lights another match. Outside the dorm, Raymond addresses the audience.)

RAYMOND: I never heard from Jay after that. I pray he's well. *(Beat.)* As for me, I know that some things happen because they happen. Others happen because they must. Sometimes they change people. For better or worse there's always a reason. *(Beat.)* As for you, all of you out there . . . suffering from total damnation without light, all of you bound without a home. God's out there somewhere. *(Beat.)* He gotta be.

(A single spot rises on Spit standing in the bathroom doorway.)

SPIT: He gotta be.

(A single spot rises on Kane sitting on his bunk.)

KANE: He gotta be.

SMOKE: He gotta be.

(All lights fade to black. Still staring into the flame, Smoke finally blows out the match. Lights fade.)

END OF PLAY

PHAT GIRLS

By Debbie Lamedman

Fat (fat): What no one wants to be.

Phat (P.H.A.T.) *pronounced fat*: Pretty, hot and tempting.
What everyone wants to be.

BIOGRAPHY

Debbie Lamedman first began her career as an actress. She received an MFA degree in acting from Brandeis University and has performed extensively both Off-Broadway and regionally. She began writing in order to create material for herself, which is how the idea for her one-woman show *phat* originally started. Working as a teacher and acting coach, she started writing original material for her teen students since there seemed to be a lack of appropriate material for this particular age group. Consequently, this led to the publication of her first two books: *The Ultimate Audition Book for Teens IV: 111 One-Minute Monologues* and *The Ultimate Scene Study Series II: 55 Short Scenes for Teens*.

Continuing to write, Debbie was accepted into the Wordsmith program, a workshop dedicated to nurturing the works of new playwrights sponsored by the Los Angeles Theatre Center. Her first full-length play, *Triangle Logic*, was given a workshop reading by a local theater company.

After a colleague expressed interest in directing a piece dealing with women's themes, Lamedman decided to revise the material from her one-woman show and turn it into a multi-character play. Thus, *phat girls* was born.

Debbie directed the West Coast premiere of *phat girls* in November 2004 at the California Conservatory of the Arts. She is currently working on her latest book, *20 Ten-Minute Plays for Teens,* which will be published by Smith and Kraus in 2005.

AUTHOR'S NOTE

The entire concept for this show was born back when I was a graduate student at Brandeis University. Prompted by one of my mentors, I was encouraged to create a solo piece that was personal and meaningful to me. I received such positive feedback after I performed the piece, I continued to work on it and reshape it even after moving to New York City. After numerous rewrites and performances, I thought I was finished with this particular subject matter. But the preoccupation with body image and the quest for the perfect figure continue to reign in our society. Things may be getting better, but only slightly, because the mantra in our American culture still seems to be "You can never be too thin."

It was a challenging experience transforming this piece from a one-woman show into a play that could accommodate a number of actresses; yet it allowed me the opportunity to truly explore the different aspects and many forms of an eating disorder. As a woman who continues to struggle with my own body image on a daily basis, there is no happy ending. But I have found that with a lot of focus, discipline, love, and support, it is possible to learn to accept myself as I am. I can only hope that other women will be able to do the same.

ORIGINAL PRODUCTION

Originally titled *phat* and performed as a one-woman show by the playwright, it was first presented at Brandeis University in Waltham, Massachusetts. The production was then performed in New York City at the Ubu Repertory Theatre as part of The Field Festival in December 1996. Revised to accommodate numerous actresses, *phat girls* was produced by the Theatre Department at the University of Central Florida as a staged reading on April 10, 2004. Directed by Earl D. Weaver with assistant director Jennifer Jamroga and stage manager Keri Parker, the cast was as follows: Patrice Lois Bell, Belinda Boyd, Lisa Bryant, Mary Kate Duignan, Jennifer Harper, Mimi Jimenez, Sara Jones, Laura Lalanne, Monica Padilla, Angie Sardina, Kelly Slonecker, and Tiara Yong.

    phat girls had its West Coast premiere at the California Conservatory of the Arts in San Juan Capistrano on November 4, 2004. It was directed by the playwright with set design by Ryan Steidinger at Pacific Coast Entertainment, costumes by Robyn Remley and the cast, alighting design by Foxton Lewyn and the production stage manager was William Rodriguez. The cast was as follows:

Jessica Bunge	Yasmin Rawji
Danielle Davison	Sarah Remley
Isabel Lachenauer	Kensie Sanchez
Kendall Mauvezin	Joelle Teeter
Katie McDonough	Jessica Walden
Ashley Melbourne	Samantha Whitford

CHARACTERS

The following parts can be divided up in any way the director chooses, but please note that the role of *Mr. Horrible* should be played by the same actress throughout the entire piece.

PROLOGUE:	SCENE ONE:
Eve	Chubby Little Girl
Woman #1	Mother
Woman #2	Little Girl #1

PROLOGUE (CONT.):
Female voice-over for the mother
Voice-over Narrator for *Paradise Lost*
Male voice-over for the doctor

SCENE ONE (CONT.):

Little Girl #2
Mr. Horrible *(played by the same actress throughout the piece.)*

SCENE TWO:
Teen #1
Teen #2
Teen #3
Teen #4
Mom
Mr. Horrible

SCENE TWO A:
Mother
Daughter
Mr. Horrible

SCENE THREE:
The Laxative Addict
The Anorexic
The Bulimic
Mr. Horrible

SCENE FOUR:
The Food Addict
Nutrition Expert #1
Nutrition Expert #2
Nutrition Expert #3
Nutrition Expert #4
Nutrition Expert #5
Mr. Horrible

SCENE FIVE:
Girlfriend #1
Girlfriend #2
Girlfriend #3
Girlfriend #4

SCENE SIX:
Admirer
Dieter
Woman on telephone
Magazine Reader
Friend #1
Friend #2
Salesgirl
Customer
Helpful Friend
Compulsive Overeater

SCENE SEVEN:
Doctor
Young Woman
Sophia
Workshop Member #1
Workshop Member #2
Workshop Member #3
Workshop Member #4
Mr. Horrible
Little Bastard Voice
Charlatan Voice
The Rationalizer Voice

SCENE EIGHT:
    Young Woman
    Mr. Horrible

SCENE NINE AND EPILOGUE
Young Woman
Woman #1
Woman #2
Woman #3
Woman #4
Woman #5
Mr. Horrible
Ethereal Woman

SYNOPSIS OF SCENES
Prologue
Scene One: Childhood
Scene Two: The Teens
Scene Two A: Mothers & Daughters
Scene Three: Development of an Eating Disorder
Scene Four: The Madness Continues
Scene Five: Going Round in Circles
Scene Six: Catch-22
Scene Seven: Realization
Scene Eght: Confrontation
Scene Nine: Acceptance
Epilogue

phat girls should be performed with no intermission.

ABOUT THE STAGING
The set should be simple. Platforms at different heights are great to provide
a variety of levels and also to isolate specific playing areas. There should be a
toilet stage left and a doctor's scale stage right. Junk food wrappers can be taped
to all the flats and can be scattered around the platforms and the toilet. Costumes should also be kept simple. Mr. Horrible's character is the only "real
costume": a man's suit with a fedora and walking stick. For the Epilogue, the
women of the company should dress in an ethereal and feminine manner, as
does the character of the Ethereal Woman, who is dressed definitively as a goddess — long flowing white dress and a wreath of flowers in her hair. Music
should be used during the scene transitions that reflect the theme of the play.

phat girls

PROLOGUE

A slide show with images that depict all different women and all different body types. Some images depict a healthy woman, some images show the typical "thin" model that bombards our magazine covers, others show women in the throes of their eating disorders. The final image is the painting "Eve Tempted" by John Stanhope. As the music and image fades, the lights come up on Eve mirroring the poses of the John Stanhope "Eve Tempted" painting. Mr. Horrible stands behind her on an upstage platform. The rest of the cast watches as if they are at a play.

VOICE-OVER: **(From* Paradise Lost.*)*

The fruit would feed at once both body and mind.

Eve plucked. Eve ate.

Earth felt the wound, and Nature from her seat

Sighing through all her Works gave signs of woe,

That all was lost. Back to the Thicket slunk

The guilty Serpent, and well might, for EVE

Intent now wholly on her taste, naught else

Regarded, such delight till then, as seem'd

In Fruit she never tasted, whether true

Or fancied so, through expectation high

Of knowledge, nor was God-head from her thought.

Greedily she engorg'd without restraint,

And knew not eating Death.

(Actress eats a real apple and crunches loudly. Two women sitting "watching" the Eve performance. Eve exits — lights up on the women as they "discuss".)

WOMAN #1: See — *that's* the original sin. Eating! If she never ate that apple none of us would ever have had a food problem.

WOMAN #2: If she never ate the apple, we wouldn't have a lot of problems!

WOMAN #1: Yeah, but don't you see? It was food! She "greedily engorg'd"! She greedily engorged *food!* It's not like she plucked a forbidden flower or something like that. She ATE! That's what got us into trouble. Eating always gets *me* into trouble.

WOMAN #2: But it's not like she ate a doughnut! She ate an apple! An apple, for God's sake! That is like, so healthy. Of course, there's that one diet that says apples have too much sugar and you should stay away from fruit altogether—but my God, given the choice between an apple and a Krispy Kreme, Eve definitely did the right thing.

WOMAN #1: No. She obviously didn't do the right thing. First of all, they didn't have doughnuts hanging from trees back then. That actually, *would* have been Paradise. But the snake specifically told her to eat the forbidden FRUIT! Not the forbidden CHOCOLATE GLAZED! She ruined womankind for all eternity by eating that stinkin' apple! She doomed us to be fat. Damn that Eve. She wrecked it for all of us!

WOMAN #2: Yeah, I guess she did . . . not to mention childbirth . . .

(*Blackout.*)

(*Sound cue of slap, baby's cry.*)

MALE VOICE-OVER: Congratulations! You have a healthy baby girl. Everything is intact and she weighs . . . Seven pounds, seven ounces.

FEMALE VOICE-OVER: That's not fat . . . is it?

SCENE ONE: CHILDHOOD

Lights up on chubby little girl running in with grocery bag.

CHUBBY LITTLE GIRL: (*Unpacking groceries.*) Mom's home from shopping. She got Yodels, Frosted Flakes — "They're greeeaaat," Scooter Pies. Hydrox? (*Yelling offstage.*) Mom, why'd ya get Hydrox? Oreos are better.
No . . . I'll eat 'em. Lucky Charms . . . "They're magically delicious" . . . Pop-Tarts. (*Yelling again.*) Hey nobody better eat these Pop-Tarts. These Pop-Tarts are mine!! Cheese Doodles. Ice cream. . .
(*She stands there admiring the groceries. Mother enters.*)

MOTHER: You know, Sweetie, you don't have to eat everything all at once!

CHUBBY LITTLE GIRL: I'm not, I'm not . . . I just wanted to see what you bought.

MOTHER: Well, you saw it . . . now go outside and play. Later, you can have your snack.

CHUBBY LITTLE GIRL: But I'd rather stay in here with you.

MOTHER: Go! I've got things to do. You need to go get some fresh air — I saw some of your friends out there — go play with them.

CHUBBY LITTLE GIRL: (*Muttering under her breath.*) They're not my friends.

MOTHER: (*She's busy with the groceries; she's not really paying attention.*) What's that? What did you say?

CHUBBY LITTLE GIRL: Nothin'.

(*Little Girl looks longingly at the groceries and reluctantly turns to leave as*

Mother puts away groceries. Lights fade. Lights up on two other little girls swinging a jump rope and singing:)

TWO GIRLS: (*In unison.*) Not last night but the night before . . .

(*Little Girl joins in the song and starts to jump the rope.*)

CHUBBY LITTLE GIRL: Twenty-four robbers came knockin' at my door. I asked 'em what they wanted, this is what they said . . .

(*She trips over the rope and stops abruptly.*)

LITTLE GIRL #1: Hey! Who said you could jump?

CHUBBY LITTLE GIRL: You were just swingin' it. No one was jumping. Why do you care?

LITTLE GIRL #2: If you're gonna jump you should get a bra.

CHUBBY LITTLE GIRL: A bra? I don't need a bra! I'm too young to have a bra.

LITTLE GIRL #1: Well you need one.

LITTLE GIRL #2: Yeah . . . especially if you're gonna, ya know . . . jump rope!! You might hurt yourself.

(*Both girls break into laughter.*)

CHUBBY LITTLE GIRL: Stop it! Stop laughing at me. I don't need a bra! I don't want a bra! I'm gonna stay flat-chested forever. I think girls look better that way.

LITTLE GIRL #1: You wanna look like a *boy!*

LITTLE GIRL #2: And boys don't play jump rope! Sorrr — eeee!

LITTLE GIRL #1: Maybe you should go play with some trucks or something!

(*They start laughing again as they exit. Chubby Little Girl stares after them in shock and horror. Mr. Horrible makes his first entrance. He is dressed in a suit and tie — he should carry a walking stick. He's very dapper.*)

MR. HORRIBLE: Hello little girl . . . those girls weren't very nice to you, now were they?

CHUBBY: Who are you? I'm not supposed to talk to strangers.

MR. HORRIBLE: I'm not a stranger. Look closer . . .

(*She moves closer to him and nods.*)

MR. HORRIBLE: See . . . you know me.

CHUBBY: I'm not sure.

MR. HORRIBLE: I'm your friend. I'm with you all the time. You know . . . up here (*He gently taps his temple.*)

CHUBBY: (*Relieved that he is not a stranger.*) Oh yeah! I knew your voice sounded familiar. I just never knew what you looked like.

MR. HORRIBLE: (*Spinning around and modeling for her.*) So? What do you think?

CHUBBY: You look great.

MR. HORRIBLE: Well thank you, Darlin'. I think you look great too!

CHUBBY: Those girls didn't! They won't let me play with them. They think I'm too fat.

MR. HORRIBLE: Do you think you're too fat?

CHUBBY: No. Maybe. I don't know. Mom lets me eat whatever I want.

MR. HORRIBLE: And what is it you want, right now?

CHUBBY: To go watch TV and eat some Scooter Pies.

MR. HORRIBLE: Well that sounds like fun! Scooter Pies won't ever laugh at you like those mean girls did. Let's go.

CHUBBY: Really? You'll let me?

MR. HORRIBLE: Hey Darlin', *I'll* let you do anything you want. Anything that's gonna cheer you up and make you feel better suits me just fine!

CHUBBY: Thank you . . . sir! Uh . . . what should I call you?

MR. HORRIBLE: Sir is fine. I like Sir. Sir is just fine!

(*He grabs her arm, a little forcefully, but she doesn't appear to notice as they exit.*)

SCENE TWO: THE TEENS

Mr. Horrible enters with a large handheld mirror. He moves and focuses the mirror on each of the spotlighted teens.

TEEN #1: (*Scrutinizing herself in the mirror. She is trying on a pair of jeans. They will not zip.*) I've got to get these on. Because if I can fit into these jeans, all will be right with the world. I refuse to get the next size up. I WILL fit into these pants. They make my legs look really long! I will fit into them, I will, I will, I WILL!! (*She continues to struggle with the zipper as she exits. Mr. Horrible spins, turns to face the mirror to Teen #2.*)

TEEN #2: (*Should be in some type of prom dress.*) Ya know, if Marilyn Monroe were alive today she'd be considered a plus-size model? I mean, she wore like a size 14 or something. I wouldn't be caught dead in a 14. (*Panics as she reaches around and tries to read the label.*) Oh my God! Is this dress a 14? Size 14 is so not in style right now! My *body* is NOT in style right now. Mom says my body is "Rubenesque." I was in style — 100 years ago!

(*She exits. Mr. Horrible moves to Teen #3 who is facing upstage. He shines the mirror directly in front of her.*)

TEEN #3: (*Singing as she stares into the mirror.*) "I'm a little teapot short and stout; here is my handle, here is my spout. . ." (*She turns and walks down-*

stage.) God! I would much rather be that sleek, shiny, curvy attachment that foams milk on those expensive Italian cappuccino machines.

(*She looks in the mirror again and exits.*)

TEEN #4: (*She is putting the last touches on her outfit. Mr. Horrible lurks behind the mirror watching her. The outfit should not be particularly flattering to her figure. She yells out to her mom and models for her as if she were on a runway. Mom enters as soon as Teen #4 calls to her.*)

Ma! Ma! C'mere. Does this make me look fat? Just tell me. Do I look fat?

MOM: Well . . . where are you going?

TEEN #4: It doesn't matter! This either makes me look fat or it doesn't! Which is it?

MOM: (*Trying to be diplomatic.*) Well . . . uh . . . maybe you could find something a little bit more flattering.

TEEN #4: Something more flattering? I thought you liked this skirt!

MOM: (*Slowly, carefully, almost staccato.*) I do like it. I'm just not sure if it's the best choice for . . . where are you going again?

TEEN #4: What difference does it make where I'm going? You're standing there telling me I look fat!!

MOM: I'm not saying you look fat. I'm saying maybe you should wear something else.

TEEN #4: But I want to wear this!

MOM: Then wear it.

TEEN #4: But you're saying this outfit makes me look fat! If I change my outfit, will I look less fat?

MOM: That depends on what you change into, doesn't it?

TEEN #4: I don't have anything else to wear! Everything makes me look fat!

MOM: You've got to be kidding me. You have a closet full of beautiful clothes. I don't understand why you insist on wearing the baggiest thing around. When you wear baggy clothes, it makes you look bigger than you are!

TEEN #4: So you think I'm big?

MOM: NO! I . . . oh God! I give up!

TEEN #4: Well so do I! Just forget the whole thing. I'm not going out!

MOM: Honey, c'mon. You look fine. You asked me for my opinion — maybe you shouldn't ask if you really don't want to hear what I have to say.

TEEN #4: Yes, I know I asked you, I'm sorry I asked you!

MOM: Honey . . .

TEEN #4: (*Yelling.*) No! I'm not going!

(*Mom shrugs and shakes her head — exits — Teen #4 turns away in frus-*

tration and bumps into Mr. Horrible as he approaches her. They slowly circle each other.)

TEEN #4: What do you want, asshole?

MR. HORRIBLE: *(Sighing.)* Ah . . . I remember the days when you put all your faith in me — showed me respect. You know I'd never steer you wrong.

TEEN #4: You are such a liar. I can't believe I listen to you.

MR. HORRIBLE: Well Darlin', I don't mean to drive you crazy. But I can make you feel better. You know I can. I've done it before. Mommy thinks you're fat. Tsk. Tsk. Mommy *made* you fat.

TEEN #4: She did not! At least I don't think she did.

MR. HORRIBLE: *(Nonchalantly.)* You know it's true. Maybe she just doesn't want you to be prettier than her.

TEEN #4: You're wrong! Stop talking about her like that! *(Beat.)* Besides, I'm not . . . ya know . . . *fat!*

MR. HORRIBLE: But it is true, Darlin'. Think about it. She bought you all those goodies to eat. She fixes you all your favorite foods. And then she has the nerve to tell you that you don't look good in this charming little ensemble you've put together. *(He takes her hand and twirls her around.)*

TEEN #4: It is charming, isn't it?

MR. HORRIBLE: Of course it is. You look adorable. Everyone at that party will think so.

TEEN #4: Thanks.

MR. HORRIBLE: Am I still an asshole?

TEEN #4: *(Begrudgingly.)* No. I guess not.

MR. HORRIBLE: Will you let me help you?

TEEN #4: What do I have to do?

MR. HORRIBLE: Oh don't sound so miserable, my love. It's an inspired idea, really! I know you're going to love it!
(Takes a pause to build up the effect.)
Eat! That's right. I'm telling you to eat. Whatever you want. And afterwards, simply take some of these . . . *(He produces a box of laxatives.)*

TEEN #4: What is that? Drugs? You're giving me drugs?

MR. HORRIBLE: They couldn't possibly harm you — a nice healthy girl like you! Just do it for a little while — this way you can have your cake and eat it too — so to speak. I'm not kidding. Go ahead! Eat whatever you want and then be rid of it. It's as simple as that.

TEEN #4: Really? They'll help me lose weight?

MR. HORRIBLE: They will help you rid yourself of all that nasty junk you insist on stuffing inside your body.

TEEN #4: Just one a day?

MR. HORRIBLE: (*Vaguely.*) Or two. Or however many you need to actually get the job done.

TEEN #4: Cool. Thanks, Man.

MR. HORRIBLE: You used to call me Sir, remember?

TEEN #4: You're no sir and we both know it.

MR. HORRIBLE: Ah . . . the child is growing up . . .

TEEN #4: I'm not a child!

MR. HORRIBLE: Yes, I can see that. It's becoming quite obvious!

   (*He puts his arm around her — she shrugs him off as she takes the box of laxatives. They exit. Blackout.*)

SCENE 2A: MOTHERS & DAUGHTERS

The Daughter is at her desk studying. Mr. Horrible enters with a bag of peanut M & M's and hands them to her.

DAUGHTER: Get those away from me. If I start eating those, I won't be able to stop. I'll eat the whole bag.

MR. HORRIBLE: (*Eating M & M's.*) So what? Chocolate helps you study better.

DAUGHTER: It does not.

MR. HORRIBLE: Something about the chemicals in chocolate helps you retain information better.

DAUGHTER: Really?

MR. HORRIBLE: Would I lie to you?

DAUGHTER: Well . . . I could use all the help I can get.

   (*She takes the bag and quickly gobbles down the candy. Continues to study. Mom enters.*)

MOM: What are you doing?

DAUGHTER: Studying!   (*Simultaneously.*)   MR. HORRIBLE: Studying!

MOM: It's a gorgeous day out. Why don't you go take a walk or something?

DAUGHTER: Because I have to study.

MOM: Well . . . you don't have to eat these while you're doing it! Why do you eat this junk? (*She takes the bag of candy away from DAUGHTER.*) Are you trying to be a statistic?

DAUGHTER: A statistic? What are you talking about?

MOM: Haven't you heard that there is an obesity epidemic? *Especially* among girls your age. You sit in here all day long and eat this . . . junk food and you get no exercise. You *never* exercise! It's no mystery to me why you don't have a boyfriend.

DAUGHTER: (*Furious.*) Mother! I am studying! I am trying to pass this Physics class. This AP Physics class that *you* insisted I take.

MOM: Well at some point, you need to get up and do some stretches or take a little jog — it'll break up the monotony of studying and you'll get your exercise in for the day. I don't want you sitting in here all day eating candy! I don't want my daughter to be a fat slob!

DAUGHTER: I'm not a fat slob! I'm working very hard to keep up my grades so that I can get into the college of *your* choice! Make up your mind, Mom. . . do you want me to be skinny or do you want me to get A's?

MOM: Don't you dare speak to me like that! You watch your mouth. And you watch what you put into that mouth. I've always worked hard to maintain a healthy figure. It's not that difficult and I expect you to do the same! (*She holds up the bag of candy.*) Don't ever let me catch you eating these again. (*She exits.*)

DAUGHTER: O God she doesn't get it, she just doesn't get it!

MR. HORRIBLE: Don't worry darlin' . . . there's always more where that came from. (*He pulls another bag of M&M's from the inside of his suit pocket.*) What Mama doesn't know won't hurt her . . . I know some really good hiding places . . . it's absolutely inhumane to deny someone chocolate! (*DAUGHTER looks at MR. HORRIBLE and quickly reaches for the bag of candy. She starts inhaling them as fast as she can.*)

DAUGHTER: It'll serve her right if I get fat! It'll be all her fault! (*Continues eating the candy as MR. HORRIBLE continues to take more and more bags of candy out of his pockets.*)

SCENE THREE: DEVELOPMENT OF AN EATING DISORDER

Three actresses in their own private areas of the stage. They each are in the middle of their own eating binge. Different types of food wrappers and containers surround them. The actress playing the anorexic should only have healthy type food items, vegetables and fruit, around her. This scene can also be played with no props at all. Mr. Horrible watches from a distance. All of Mr. Horrible's lines will overlap with the actress who is speaking. The actress should never acknowledge Mr. Horrible — he is simply the insidious voice inside her head.

THE LAXATIVE ADDICT: Oh God! Why did I eat all of that? I was so hungry.

MR. HORRIBLE: (*Whispers from the shadows.*) Take the pills.

THE LAXATIVE ADDICT: Well, it doesn't matter. I'll just take some of these.

(*She opens laxative box and contemplates the pills.*)

Fifteen pills didn't really do the job the last time; they just gave me cramps. I'll take five more. No, ten more. I need to get rid of all this. No, I'll just take all of them. The whole damn box. (*Swallows entire box of laxatives and lays on the floor.*) It'll be faster this way, and I'll just lay here till they start to work and I'll be able to feel my hip bones again.

MR. HORRIBLE: Good girl!

(*Lights up on the Anorexic.*)

THE ANOREXIC: (*She should be cutting, measuring, organizing, and keeping very busy with the food in front of her.*) OK. Yesterday I ate one stalk of celery and two spoonfuls of yogurt. I can't believe I did that — I am such a pig!

MR. HORRIBLE: (*Whispering from the shadows — overlapping lines again.*) You're such a pig!

THE ANOREXIC: I have to stop eating yogurt — it is *so* fattening. OK. I need to calm down and plan this out right. Now, if I cut this celery stalk and eat only half, maybe I could treat myself to a carrot later on. No! No! Carrots are way too high in sugar. Everyone knows that. No! I have to be stricter with myself. It's not that hard to stay in control for crying out loud! So . . . I can eat some parsley, which helps my breath and makes me feel like I'm chewing on *something*. Yeah, that's what I'll do. And I'll try to run an extra mile tonight. Two extra miles — work off that fatty yogurt from yesterday. And water! God — water is my best friend. Beautiful, wonderful calorie-free, fat-free water! It makes me so full! I suppose I could put a lemon in it for an extra special treat. Yum! Lemon water. That definitely gives me something to look forward to!

MR. HORRIBLE: Nothing but water for you fattie!

(*Lights dim as the continues to chop and arrange her food. Lights up on the bulimic.*)

THE BULIMIC: (*She is talking to herself in the bathroom stepping onto a scale; she should also present this monologue in front of a toilet.*) Ya see what happens when I stop the dirty habit? I *gain* weight! This is my only solution if I want to eat like a normal person.

MR. HORRIBLE: (*Lifting the lid of the toilet.*) Ta da!

THE BULIMIC: Everyone I know can go into a McDonald's, order burgers, fries, and shakes and never gain an ounce. I *look* at that kind of stuff and I blow up. This is my magic solution. This is the only thing that works.

MR. HORRIBLE/THE BULIMIC: Diets suck!

THE BULIMIC: I can't stay on one for two minutes. It's just that I feel so dirty and disgusting when I do it. Kneeling on the floor in public bathrooms is awful. Sneaking around and lying to my friends . . . that one time when Marci caught me and told me I had puke all down the front of my shirt — I was mortified. That was sloppy! I'm much more careful now. Thank God she just thought I was sick with food poisoning. It was a close call, though. Too close. But doing this is definitely a small price to pay for staying thin. I read this article once that said constantly throwing up makes your teeth rot. Well hey — my teeth are just fine. And I can stop at any time. I've proven it, haven't I? I did stop. Except I gained my weight back, but I *can* stop whenever I want. I just need to take off a couple more pounds, that's all — a couple more pounds and then I'll never do it again. I swear. I will never do it again!

MR. HORRIBLE: (*Whispering.*) Just do it one last time!

THE BULIMIC: This will definitely be the last time!
   (*She turns around and kneels in front of the toilet — the lights dim as we hear the toilet flush. Lights up on Mr. Horrible. All three actresses stay in their designated area. Mr. Horrible walks by each one of them — they do not acknowledge him. He continues to walk downstage center — there should be a lighting change as he comes center. We hear the sound of drumbeats starting slowly and building to a frenetic pace.*)

MR. HORRIBLE: (*Directly downstage center.*) The signs and symptoms of eating disorders can be subtle and insidious. They can include:
   (*The following list of symptoms is spoken by each of the actresses. They speak without emotion and without acknowledging one another or acknowledging MR. HORRIBLE. They are simply reciting, almost robotically. The pace should be fast — the list of symptoms should build, but never overlap. Mr. Horrible turns to face the women as they recite.*)

THE LAXATIVE ADDICT: Refusal to accept and maintain body weight.

THE ANOREXIC: Distorted body image

THE BULIMIC: Excessive exercising.

THE LAXATIVE ADDICT: Preoccupation with weight and diet.

THE ANOREXIC: Loss of three consecutive menstrual periods.

THE BULIMIC: Loss of pubic hair.

THE LAXATIVE ADDICT: Binge eating, especially of "junk" foods.

THE ANOREXIC: Changes in mood, particularly preceding or following binge eating.

THE BULIMIC: Insignificant weight loss.

THE LAXATIVE ADDICT: Insignificant weight fluctuations.

THE ANOREXIC: Inability to recognize basic feelings such as hunger or sadness.

THE BULIMIC: Aversion to certain foods or unusual food preferences

THE LAXATIVE ADDICT: Food hoarding.

THE ANOREXIC: Hypersensitivity to cold.

THE BULIMIC: Abuse of laxatives and diuretics.

THE LAXATIVE ADDICT: Erosion of dental enamel caused by gastric acid during vomiting.

THE ANOREXIC: Withdrawal from family and friends.

THE BULIMIC: Inability to concentrate.

THE LAXATIVE ADDICT: Depression and loss of sleep.

(*The drums stop. Mr. Horrible laughs and looks behind him at the actresses. He slams down the lid to the toilet and exits. Blackout.*)

SCENE FOUR: THE MADNESS CONTINUES

One Food Addict stands in the middle of a circle of Nutrition Experts. They are all holding clipboards. Their advice starts off slowly, builds to where they are overlapping each other, and the Food Addict is overwhelmed by all the advice.

NUTRITION EXPERT #1: For a healthy diet you need to reduce the total fat intake of your diet to less than 30 percent of the total calories. Substitute fish, chicken and turkey for fatty meats. No fried foods. Eat six servings per day of breads and cereals. Choose whole grains. Carbohydrate intake should represent 55 percent of your total calorie intake. Limit salt. Exercise. Use this chart to determine your proper weight. Based upon this chart at five feet two inches tall and a medium bone frame, you should weigh between 107 and 119 pounds.

NUTRITION EXPERT #1: Well that's what the chart says, so it must be so.

FOOD ADDICT: Really?

NUTRITION EXPERT #2: I beg your pardon, but that type of thinking is outdated. It has been proven that for the healthiest diet with the greatest results, you must reduce your *carbohydrate* intake to less than 30 percent. I agree with lean meats as a source of protein, but the amount of protein should be vastly increased. Fat is OK. Eat as much good fat as you want. Have the bacon. Have the cheese. Have the olive oil. Stop eating the bread. Don't have the doughnut!

NUTRITION EXPERT #3: I say have the bacon, have the doughnut, have whatever you crave. But only in moderation. Eat whatever you want, just stop eating when you're full, and stop eating before 6 PM every day!

NUTRITION EXPERT #4: Try putting vinegar on everything you eat. This will help you burn fat.

NUTRITION EXPERT #5: Food-combining. Make sure you eat your food in the proper order.

NUTRITION EXPERT #1: Be certain to weigh and measure everything. And count your calories!

NUTRITION EXPERT #2: Try a liquid-fast. Or a colon cleanser. Or both! Clean out your gut!

NUTRITION EXPERT #3: Join a gym! Eat whatever you want as long as you exercise for two hours every day, seven days a week!

NUTRITION EXPERT #4: Eighteen days of grapefruit, eggs, and wheat toast. It's all you need to lose those unwanted pounds.

NUTRITION EXPERT #5: No more than 800 calories per day. No alcohol!

NUTRITION EXPERT #1: Join Weight Watchers!

NUTRITION EXPERT #2: Try Atkins!

NUTRITION EXPERT #3: Jenny Craig!

NUTRITION EXPERT #4: The Zone!

NUTRITION EXPERT #5: Become a vegetarian!

NUTRITION EXPERT #1: Have you heard of the raw food diet? That's a very sensible plan. A great way to lose.

NUTRITION EXPERT #2: Eat for your blood type. That regimen is even better.

NUTRITION EXPERT #3: Vitamin B-12! Inject it — it gets into the blood stream much faster than taking pills and helps you lay off those evil carbs.

NUTRITION EXPERT #4: The Master Cleanser. Lemon juice, maple syrup, and cayenne pepper for forty days. Sheer heaven! The weight will virtually fall off!

NUTRITION EXPERT #5: Chew your food at least one hundred times before swallowing. It'll make you full faster!

NUTRITION EXPERT #1: Eat an apple first — before you eat anything else!

NUTRITION EXPERT #2: Eat every two to three hours.

NUTRITION EXPERT #3: Don't eat dairy!

NUTRITION EXPERT #4: Yes! Eat dairy! No wheat!

NUTRITION EXPERT #5: Don't ever eat sugar again! Ever!

(*In this last round, the Nutrition Experts build up speed and starting overlapping their lines. It almost seems as if they are on fast-forward. It should be massive confusion — the Food Addict is bleary-eyed from all the suggestions.*)

NUTRITION EXPERT #1: Don't skip meals! That will lead to binging.

NUTRITION EXPERT #2: Stop drinking soda!

NUTRITION EXPERT #3: Don't deprive yourself.

NUTRITION EXPERT #4: Eat more vegetables!

NUTRITION EXPERT #5: All processed foods are your enemy. Don't ever eat processed AGAIN!

(*Beat.*)

ALL NUTRITION EXPERTS: (*In unison as they lean forward into the circle.*) Any questions?

(*By this point, the Food Addict has her hands over her ears. She looks around frantically and sees Mr. Horrible. She tries to break through the circle of Nutrition Experts but they have moved in tightly around her. Mr. Horrible casually breaks through the circle with a light tap of his cane. The Experts move aside — he puts his hand out and the Food Addict grabs it. The experts, gripping their clipboards tightly, watch the two exit.*)

MR. HORRIBLE: Well, that was ghastly . . .

FOOD ADDICT: You have no idea!

MR. HORRIBLE: How about some ice cream? A pint for each of us! Maybe a little pie to put the ice cream on?

FOOD ADDICT: That's a fantastic idea.

MR. HORRIBLE: I thought you might like it!

(*They exit. Blackout.*)

SCENE FIVE: GOING ROUND IN CIRCLES

A grocery store. Two friends are shopping — they are carrying canvas grocery sacks.

GIRLFRIEND #1: What exactly is it that you're looking for?

GIRLFRIEND #2: The perfect food.

GIRLFRIEND #1: Define "perfect."

GIRLFRIEND #2: Well, the one that will give me the most satisfaction without the most calories and fat.

GIRLFRIEND #1: Oh yeah! I know exactly what you mean. Last summer I was sure I found it in watermelon.

GIRLFRIEND #2: I can see that — watermelon could definitely be the perfect food.

GIRLFRIEND #1: Yeah . . . but you can only find good watermelon in the summer. So the rest of the year you're screwed. And then of course, there are the seeds. I nearly choked on one once and almost passed out — it definitely turned me off watermelon for a while.

GIRLFRIEND #2: They make seedless, ya know.

GIRLFRIEND #1: You're still gonna run into that seasonal problem though. Ya just can't find tasty watermelon in December.

GIRLFRIEND #2: Oh my God. Look! This is it. *This* is what I've been looking for!

GIRLFRIEND #1: You're kidding, right? *Baby food?*

GIRLFRIEND #2: It's perfect. Look at this. Tiny little jars of precise portions of food. Bananas. Bananas and apples. Bananas and apple in tapioca. Tropical fruits in tapioca. 70 calories, 0 fat. No thinking required. This is great! I can live on this stuff — I can become small and petite again livin' on baby food.

GIRLFRIEND #1: It's pudding and fruit.

GIRLFRIEND #2: Well look here, they have meat and vegetables. Well . . . this doesn't look so great. Franks and beans. Ickkkh . . . veal, spinach . . . hey . . . I bet the sweet potatoes would be good with a little salt and pepper. I'm getting this. I'm getting this one and this one and this one. *(She puts the jars into her sack.)* I won't have the hassle of cutting and measuring and preparing . . . babies have it made!

GIRLFRIEND #1: I think you're nuts . . . but hey if it works — who knows? You may be on to something.

(They exit. Lights up on an aerobics class. As dialogue begins music is lowered, but should underscore entire scene. The women are working out.)

GIRLFRIEND #3: I've decided to finally take control and do something about my weight. Do you know I've gained 40 pounds since Christmas? It just kinda snuck up on me. I feel gross. But *you!* I've never seen you look so thin. Are you . . . OK?

GIRLFRIEND #4: *(Bitterly.)* Yeah. I call it the Dave diet. Ever since he broke up with me, I haven't been able to eat. I just keep thinking, "What did I do wrong?"

GIRLFRIEND #3: Oh please! He's an idiot. You know that. You didn't do anything wrong. *(Beat.)*
You really aren't eating anything?

GIRLFRIEND #4: I'm doing the Diet Coke, cigarette thing. You know. Oral fixation, I guess. I really have no appetite at all.

GIRLFRIEND #3: You know I have actually tried the Diet Coke/cigarette thing. It's such a good idea. Just existing on Diet Coke and cigarettes. Ya never have to think about your next meal — thinking about food takes up so much of my time. But the problem was that I couldn't really stick to the

Diet Coke/cigarette thing for any length of time because I kept having these bloated asthma attacks — that kinda put a damper on the whole thing.

GIRLFRIEND #4: He broke my heart.

GIRLFRIEND #3: That never stopped me before. Broken hearts always make me want to eat.

(The music is restored; the women continue to work out — lighting transition to another area of the stage: We see Girlfriend #2 sitting amidst a sea of empty jars of baby food. She is miserable. Phone rings.)

GIRLFRIEND #2: (*Answering.*) What?

GIRLFRIEND #1: (*On the other side of the stage. She should be eating a piece of watermelon.*) Hey, don't snap my head off!

GIRLFRIEND #2: Oh, sorry. What's up?

GIRLFRIEND #1: That's what I was calling you for. How's your dinner? How was it eating all those strained carrots and peas?

GIRLFRIEND #2: Fine.

GIRLFRIEND #1: What's wrong?

GIRLFRIEND #2: I'm embarrassed to tell you.

GIRLFRIEND #1: Come on, it's me. You can tell me anything.

GIRLFRIEND #2: I'm mortified!

GIRLFRIEND #1: *WHAT HAPPENED?*

GIRLFRIEND #2: I binged on baby food.

GIRLFRIEND #1: You did what?

GIRLFRIEND #2: I *binged* on baby food. I don't know why I never saw it coming. I can't believe I did that. Ten jars in one sitting! And you know the worse thing of all?

GIRLFRIEND #1: What?

GIRLFRIEND #2: I'm still really, really hungry. It's like it only whet my appetite for more sweet things. That baby food fruit and tapioca is pretty sweet. I would certainly question giving it to *my* baby. Oh well. So much for the perfect food.

GIRLFRIEND #1: I'm sorry it didn't work out for you. It was a good theory though.

GIRLFRIEND #2: What are you eating?

GIRLFRIEND #1: Watermelon. I'm trying the seedless. It's not bad. Ya wanna come over and try some?

GIRLFRIEND #2: No thanks. No more fruit. No more sweet fruit. I need something though. I'm not satisfied and I need to eat something and fast.

GIRLFRIEND #1: What are ya gonna do?

GIRLFRIEND #2: Go get a happy meal, I guess.

GIRLFRIEND #1: Oh, don't do that . . . that's the worse thing you could do.

GIRLFRIEND #2: I know. Happy meals! They don't exactly make you "happy" but they do come with some really cool toys and it's definitely immediate gratification. Immediate gratification can be a beautiful thing, ya know.

GIRLFRIEND #1: Very true, very true . . . but what a killer on the waistline! *(Lighting change — back to aerobics class. The women have finished the class — they are toweling off.)*

GIRLFRIEND #4: Do you want to know the most ironic thing of all?

GIRLFRIEND #3: What?

GIRLFRIEND #4: When Dave and I were together, I never really watched what I ate too much. He always wanted to eat out, and I loved that. I worked out . . . *sometimes.* I knew I needed to lose a few, but I was happy and I thought he was happy too. One morning, he walks in and I'm still in my underwear . . . I see him looking at me with this really weird expression on his face and he says, "Oh wow . . . you uh . . . you need to exercise." About a week later he breaks up with me. I actually think he left me because I had a little paunch.

GIRLFRIEND #3: But why would he do that? He'd seen you without clothes on before, right?

GIRLFRIEND #4: Never with the lights on.

GIRLFRIEND #3: Ohhhh. So is that why you're livin' on caffeine and nicotine? And working out like a fiend? To get back at him?

GIRLFRIEND #4: Not only did he break my heart, he made me feel like some gross, disgusting cow! I'll never forget that expression he had on his face when he saw me standing there in the cold light of morning in my bra and panties. He looked sick. My body made him *sick!*

GIRLFRIEND #3: Wow! No wonder I don't have a boyfriend. One look at me and he'd be retching for days.

GIRLFRIEND #4: *(Good-naturedly.)* Shut up!

GIRLFRIEND #3: You should write a book.

GIRLFRIEND #4: What are you talking about?

GIRLFRIEND #3: "How to get back at the boyfriend who dumped you because he thought you were fat."

GIRLFRIEND #4: *(Laughing.)* And the secret is . . . Diet Coke, cigarettes, and step-class.

GIRLFRIEND #3: Women would flock to buy it. You'd make a fortune!

GIRLFRIEND #4: And *that* would be sweet revenge!

(Blackout.)

SCENE SIX: CATCH-22:

Montage sequence: Lights up in different areas as each "vignette" is played out.

ADMIRER: OK — I want to know how you did it. You look incredible! How much weight did you actually lose?

DIETER: I don't know. A couple of sizes, I guess. I don't weigh myself.

ADMIRER: Well you should. Just so you can know in pounds how much you dropped! It's amazing! Totally amazing! So fess up! How did you do it?

DIETER: Diet and exercise.

ADMIRER: You're kidding me.

DIETER: Nope.

ADMIRER: But you must have taken pills, right? To help you out?

DIETER: Nope.

ADMIRER: You didn't fast? You didn't have surgery? Just diet and exercise? You can't be serious.

DIETER: That's my secret. I ate a lot of healthy food and worked out every day. No magic potion I'm afraid. Just a lot of focus and hard work.

ADMIRER: I bet it *was* hard. You lost a ton! It's definitely going to be hard to keep up that kind of a lifestyle, right? Working out *every day*? Come on — get real. I sure hope you can keep it off! Most people gain all their weight back plus more!

DIETER: (*Sarcastically.*) Well I plan on doing my best. Thanks so much for your support!

(Lights cross fade to Vignette #2.)

WOMAN: (*On the telephone.*) You're not coming? You can't make it? How come? (*Beat.*) Oh . . . well, yes I'm disappointed — of course I'm disappointed. I sort of can't believe you're standing me up. You seemed really excited about going out tonight. (*Beat.*) Oh . . . you think I'm *too intense?* How am I intense? I don't even know what you're talking about. And what's wrong with being intense anyway? How do you want me to be? (*Beat.*) Oh trust me . . . I'm not gonna change for *you.* Well, actually, I did change for you — I lost twenty pounds for you — Oh, I'm sorry . . . should I not have told you that? Was that too *intense* for you to handle? (*Slams down the phone.*) Asshole! (*Picks up the phone and dials.*) Yeah . . . I'd like to order two large pizzas please. Extra cheese. And when I say extra, I want *EXTRA,* ya got that?

(Lights cross fade to Vignette #3: Woman reading a fashion magazine.)

MAGAZINE READER: Jesus — she's not even lying down and her hip bones jut out a mile. I can't remember the last time I felt my hip bones. If I could only look like this woman for a day — my life would be perfect. How can her life *not* be perfect? She makes a million dollars an hour just for having her picture taken. She gets to wear fabulous clothes and travel to exotic places — make out with great-looking guys. The only thing that isn't perfect about her life is that she doesn't get to eat. If she has a body that looks like this, there's no way in hell she can ever put a morsel of food down her gullet. But shit . . . I'd make the sacrifice. For a day anyway.

(Lights cross fade to Vignette #4.)

FRIEND #1: Ya know what I don't understand? I don't get why I can feel like I look so great one day and the very next day, I feel like I look like crap. And on any given day my clothes can fit fine, and the very next day it feels like I've gained ten pounds. I have clothes in every Goddamn size known to man. I don't get it! Do you? Can you explain this to me?

FRIEND #2: No, I can't explain it. It happens to me too. One day I wear my 8's — the next day I'm wearing a 12. It's crazy. Now let me ask you something — have you ever noticed that every time some female is having a particular crisis on a television show, usually when she's having a crisis over a man, they always show her in bed eating a pint of ice cream. Have you noticed that? And then by the end of the hour, the crisis is resolved and she's just as thin and perky as she was before and she no longer needs ice cream. What is up with that?

FRIEND #1: Television is telling us to cope with our problems by eating ice cream.

FRIEND #2: Yeah, but it's also telling us that if we gain weight from that ice cream — our lives are screwed and we'll be miserable.

FRIEND #1: Aaahhhhh! What the hell are we supposed to do?????

FRIEND #2: Who knows anymore? All I want is to be able to wear the same size pants two days in a row! Is that too much to ask?

(Lights cross fade to Vignette #5: A checkout stand at a department store.)

SALESGIRL: (*Very perky. Holding up a pair of pants.*) Oh . . . these are really cute.

CUSTOMER: Yeah. I thought so too. That's why I'm buying them.

SALESGIRL: And you'll still be able to wear them as you get bigger. They're *that* kind of material, ya know?

CUSTOMER: I beg your pardon?

SALESGIRL: As you progress in your pregnancy. Looks like they'll stretch a lot.

CUSTOMER: (*Slowly. In shock.*) I'm . . . not . . . pregnant . . .

SALESGIRL: What?

CUSTOMER: I'm not *pregnant!*

SALESGIRL: (*Mortified.*) Oh my God!

CUSTOMER: (*Realizing how she looks to the world.*) Oh . . . my . . . God . . .

(*Lights cross fade to Vignette #6:*)

HELPFUL FRIEND: If you really want me to help you get on track, I think the first thing you have to do is get on the scale and see how much you weigh and how much you want to lose. Then we can go from there.

COMPULSIVE OVEREATER: (*Overwhelmed.*) No, I don't want to get on the scale and see how much I've gained. You think getting on the scale is going to motivate me to lose? You've obviously never had my problem. I don't even own a scale. I know when I'm packing on the pounds — I can tell by the way my clothes fit. And if I go into major denial and just wear sweats all the time, like *now,* I still know I'm getting fat . . . ya know how I know? When I can't reach over my own gut to cut my damn toenails. Hey Man — that's fat! When it starts to become too hard to wipe my own goddamn ass, that's when I know that I've gone too far. Oh, I'm sorry. Have I shocked you? Is that too graphic for ya? Too much information? Well, welcome to my world! These are the things nobody ever talks about. I love it when people tell me all I have to do is join a gym or lay off the sweets — it's no big deal, just do it already and stop complaining about it. Well I say try telling an alcoholic to quit mixing the martinis and downing the tall boys! Try telling a smoker to lay off the cigs for a day. They'll laugh in your face. They'll say they don't have a problem. They're not *addicted!* This is my fix. Food. And I can't seem to stop! I'm outta control and I know it and I want to do something about it but I can't seem to stop! And you can't help me. I know that now. No one can help me. No one can do this, but me.

(*Helpful Friend exits — Compulsive Overeater is alone — she mimes the actions as she speaks the monologue.*)

COMPULSIVE OVEREATER: (*Calmly.*) Sometimes I think I can just wash it away. Sometimes I think it's not really a part of me; it's a mistake that this flesh has accumulated on my body and it will be gone when I wake up. Sometimes I think if I act more like a "real" girl, it'll melt off me.

So I begin a routine. A ritual that will make me more feminine. And being more feminine means not being fat.

First, I shave my legs — they are as hairy as a man's. Then, after moisturizing them I congratulate myself on no nicks and cuts. I turn my attention to my hair. YUCK! It is mousy and dingy-looking with clumps of gray. I haven't even been conditioning it. It's like a whisk broom. I put henna in it and then I get in the tub and soak my body in an orange and lemongrass bath foam. The water is hot. As hot as I can stand it; my skin turns red like a lobster. I rinse out the henna and then I stare at my face for what seems like an eternity. I put a mud mask on it, then I exfoliate, moisturize, revitalize, and I'm done. (*Moves up to the mirror.*)

I return to my bedroom, remove my robe and examine myself and the results of my beauty regime in the full-length mirror. I'm still fat.

Fat — with a shiny face and a great head of hair and smooth legs. But the flesh I had hoped to melt in that hot, hot bath is all still there. (*Blackout.*)

SCENE SEVEN: REALIZATION

DOCTOR: I'm looking at your records here; your weight has yo-yoed dramatically for the past ten years. I applaud your dietary efforts — you've obviously learned how to take it off — now you need to keep it off. Going up and down like you do — it's terrible for your heart. It can be worse than if you never lost the weight at all. Can you try to keep it off this time?

YOUNG WOMAN: That's the hard part.

DOCTOR: I don't understand why. I would think having success and seeing yourself thin would motivate you to stay that way.

YOUNG WOMAN: You've obviously never had a weight problem.

DOCTOR: We're not talking about me. We're talking about you.

YOUNG WOMAN: Well, then, take my word for it . . . it's not always easy to keep it off. No matter *how* good I look and feel. It's a psychological thing, I guess. I'm an emotional eater.
(*Mr. Horrible has entered.*)

MR. HORRIBLE: Don't tell her *that!* She'll send you to a shrink.

DOCTOR: Well, I would be happy to refer you to our "Free to Be Thin" workshop. It's a support group for women like yourself who have a difficult time with food.

YOUNG WOMAN: I don't have a difficult time with food. I LOVE food.

MR. HORRIBLE: Damn right!

DOCTOR: (*Handing her a business card.*) Well, here's the information if you change your mind. I'm telling you — you cannot continue to yo-yo like you do. It's extremely dangerous.

MR. HORRIBLE: Dangerous, shmangerous. You're a young woman! There's nothing wrong with you. Healthy as an ox!

DOCTOR: You should at least attend one session. Just to see what it's like. You might be surprised.

(Scene shifts to the "Free to Be Thin" Workshop. There is a group of women sitting in a circle — Sophia is the group leader. She is overly, obnoxiously enthusiastic. Young Woman joins the group. Mr. Horrible again watches from a distance.)

SOPHIA: Hello everyone! I'm Sophia, and welcome to the Free to Be Thin compulsive overeaters workshop. Just by being here today, you have taken your first step in your free-to-be-thin quest!

(The group applauds.)

Now just remember that compulsion is despair on an emotional level. Compulsion is the feeling that no one is home. That's why we eat, ladies. To fill up that void. To put someone *home!* All we ever wanted was love. Isn't that right? Isn't that true?

(The group applauds.)

We didn't want to become compulsive about anything, did we? No! No! We did it to survive! We did it to keep from going crazy! Good for us!

(The group applauds.)

Food was our love. Food was our way of coping. Food was our friend. Food was our lover. Food was our family. Food never said no to us, or hit us or left us. And it tastes so good. Doesn't it ladies? *(The group applauds.)*

But you need to come to realize that food is simply a replacement for real love. And that is why you are here today! To begin to heal . . . to begin to put food in it's proper place . . . to begin to love yourselves as you are; fat or thin, everyone in this room is beautiful!!

(The group applauds.)

MR. HORRIBLE: Oh brother.

SOPHIA: *(Addressing the Young Woman.)* I beg your pardon?

YOUNG WOMAN: Oh! Nothing. Sorry. Nothing.

SOPHIA: You're new to our group. You're a doubter . . . Well ladies, shall we show our doubter the success we've had here at the workshop? Let her hear your stories. . .

WORKSHOP MEMBER #1: *(Rising.)* This workshop has helped me so much. I was seriously going crazy. Trying one diet after another. I was looking for love on the outside and then I realized I had to love myself first. I had to love myself from the inside. Now I've learned to feel much better about myself on the inside *and* on the outside.

YOUNG WOMAN: Have you lost any weight?

WORKSHOP MEMBER #1: No. But I accept myself as I am. Big is beautiful.

YOUNG WOMAN/MR. HORRIBLE: (*In unison.*) Oh.

WORKSHOP MEMBER #2: Well I have lost weight. Can I tell my story Sophia?

SOPHIA: Oh please do.

WORKSHOP MEMBER #2: One day, about a year ago, I decided to give up dairy. Just like that. The idea came to me out of nowhere. I woke up one day and said, "Today I will not eat dairy!" But then I couldn't stop eating. I went on this huge eating binge justifying that it was fine as long as I didn't eat dairy. And you see, this was a very big deal for me because I am an ice-creamaholic. I used to tell people that I had two boyfriends: Ben and Jerry! I ate it all the time. Breakfast, lunch and dinner. Every flavor they made. So you see, giving up dairy was a VERY BIG DEAL.

SOPHIA: Tell her what happened next!

WORKSHOP MEMBER #2: Well, on this particular day, I ate two breakfasts — the first consisted of three Entenmann's's doughnuts washed down with a Mountain Dew. I wanted to wash it down with milk, but no dairy, remember? Then my friend called and asked me out to breakfast so I went and had an omelet with no cheese and toast, no butter and hash browns and orange juice. When I got home, I ate another doughnut and I couldn't stop thinking about peanut butter and jelly sandwiches, so I made myself lunch. About an hour later I wanted to reward myself for staying away from Ben and Jerry, so I ate four Pop-Tarts and some jellybeans which I had picked out of the trash. Disgusting right? Didn't matter — there's no dairy in jellybeans. I ate Doritos and fried chicken and Red Vines and pickles. Mustard sandwiches and pretzels and some very old, very stale graham crackers. With jam. I think the jam was spoiled — it tasted fermented. Do you see? I was a locomotive speeding out of control — eating every dairy-free thing I could get my hands on. I almost passed out from a food coma.

SOPHIA: (*Urging her on.*) And then?

WORKSHOP MEMBER #2: And it was like a lightbulb went off. An epiphany. I didn't like my life. That's why I couldn't stop eating. I didn't like my job, I didn't like where I lived, I didn't like my clothes. I didn't like my friends! I didn't like the fact that I was getting older and I had to pluck hair out of my chin and gray out of my head!

MR. HORRIBLE: (*Sarcastically.*) This is fascinating!

WORKSHOP MEMBER #2: The little voice inside my head was telling me to keep eating, keep eating, but I finally, *finally* took a stand and stopped! The next day, I came here. I've lost sixty pounds in one year. I've learned how to live life fully and not just live to eat. I deal with my emotions differently now. And I've learned to love my life. And myself!

SOPHIA: She is truly one of our success stories. So you see, my doubting friend, it can work for you too!

YOUNG WOMAN: The little voice in your head?

(*As Member #2 begins to speak about the "voices," they materialize behind each of their "owners." They can be dressed in a similar manner as Mr. Horrible, but there should definitely be distinctly different characteristics to each of them. They reflect the inner voices of each of these women.*)

WORKSHOP MEMBER #2: Yes. The one who's constantly telling me what a loser I am. I named it — the voice I mean. It's definitely masculine. I call him the Little Bastard.

(*Little Bastard appears behind Member #2 — Little Bastard whispers in Member #2's ear — she shrugs him off.*)

WORKSHOP MEMBER #3: Hey! I named my voice too! I call him Charlatan.

(*Charlatan appears behind Member #3.*)

WORKSHOP MEMBER #4: I call mine Rationalizer. Uh-oh. The Rationalizer is talking to me again!

(*Rationalizer appears behind Member #4 — they make direct eye contact with each other — then Member #4 abruptly turns around and ignores him.*)

YOUNG WOMAN: I have someone who lives in my head too.

(*All other "Voices" turn to look and smirk at Mr. Horrible as he is about to be "outed."*)

MR. HORRIBLE: Careful . . . don't be giving away all our secrets.

YOUNG WOMAN: He's been there my whole life.

SOPHIA: Isn't it interesting ladies, that we all have made our inner critics masculine? We're constantly seeking the approval of men in our lives. We need to remove these false voices — have the confidence to stand up and get rid of the lies they tell us.

YOUNG WOMAN: I think I like my voice.

MR. HORRIBLE: Thatta girl!

(*He laughs at the other "Voices." He feels victorious.*)

SOPHIA: You think you do? Why is that dear?

YOUNG WOMAN: He's like an old friend.

SOPHIA: Is it a positive voice you hear?

YOUNG WOMAN: Well . . .

WORKSHOP MEMBER #2: Does the voice offer you good, sane advice?

YOUNG WOMAN: Well . . .

WORKSHOP MEMBER #3: Have you named it?

YOUNG WOMAN: As a matter of fact . . .

(*All "Voices" lean in for the kill.*)

MR. HORRIBLE: DON'T! STOP! ARE YOU TRYING TO KILL ME?

SOPHIA: What's the name, dear?

ALL MEMBERS: Yes. Tell us. What's the name?

MR. HORRIBLE: (*Walking toward Young Woman.*) Don't do this. . .

YOUNG WOMAN: (*Obviously struggling with this.*) It's . . . it's . . . I've named him . . . Mr. Horrible!

(*At the mention of his name, Mr. Horrible loses some of his power. His cane slips, he stumbles. The members of the group applaud. The "Voices" murmur among themselves knowingly.*)

SOPHIA: (*Beaming with pride.*) Congratulations! You've taken a huge step admitting this today. Can't you see? You named him Mr. Horrible! You mustn't have *anything* horrible in your life. You are on the path to healing . . .

YOUNG WOMAN: Then why do I feel like I just betrayed my best friend . . .

(*Blackout.*)

SCENE EIGHT: CONFRONTATION

MR. HORRIBLE: You're a bitch, you know that? You betrayed me!

YOUNG WOMAN: Yeah, yeah. I'm a bitch. I'm a loser. I'm a fat cow. You can't tell me anything that you haven't already said before. Besides, you're the one who betrayed me! I just want to be healthy; can't you understand that? I'm trying to help myself and you won't let me!

MR. HORRIBLE: You really buy into that crap? That Oprah baloney? (*Mockingly.*) "Just love yourself and everything will be sunshine and lollipops!"

YOUNG WOMAN: There might be something to it.

MR. HORRIBLE: In case you haven't noticed, darling . . . life sucks! It's a pool of shit that you need to stay afloat in and you do whatever you can to survive. It could be so much worse for you, ya know. So you eat a little too much — so what!! At least you're not sticking a needle in your arm on a daily basis.

YOUNG WOMAN: Go away! I can't stand the sound of your voice anymore.

MR. HORRIBLE: You don't really mean that. You need me.

YOUNG WOMAN: No! I don't!

MR. HORRIBLE: The thing is, that if you really wanted me to go, I would be gone. But baby you're still holding on. I'm not going anywhere until you let go of my hand.

(He moves closer to her and grabs her hand. She tries to wrestle it away, but he holds on tight. She continues to struggle for a while and then stops abruptly.)

YOUNG WOMAN: Maybe it's true. Maybe I don't want you to leave. But do you think it's possible to come around a little less often? Or at least try to be a little more . . . I don't know . . . optimistic? I'm worn out. I can't do this anymore.

MR. HORRIBLE: Well . . . that's entirely up to you.

(She tries again to let go of his hand — Mr. Horrible takes a step backwards, but continues to hold on. Blackout.)

SCENE NINE: ACCEPTANCE

Group of women seated in a circle — they are friends gathering for lunch.

WOMAN #1: I'm eating lunch the other day and I see this little girl with her mother. She was so cute. I guess she was about seven or eight years old. Then I hear her say, "Mommy, don't put dressing on my salad, it's too fattening. My legs are getting too big.

WOMAN #2: Oh my God! She was eight?

WOMAN #1: Yeah. Can you believe it?

WOMAN #3: What did the mother say?

WOMAN #1: "That's good thinking sweetie. Fit not fat!"

WOMAN #3: Well, I guess that's a better answer than "No you're not fat — have another muffin!"

WOMAN #4: She's teaching her kid to make wise choices.

WOMAN #2: Was the little girl fat?

WOMAN #1: Not at all. She was a very normal weight. The mother, however, was a stick.

WOMAN #4: Uh-oh. So she'll turn her daughter into another neurotic woman who's always thinking about food.

WOMAN #2: I was always bigger than my mother. I hated it. It certainly made me neurotic — I never wanted to eat in front of her. I guess all women probably are a little crazy when it comes to food.

WOMAN #5: Believe it or not, I think there are actually some healthy ones out there. The ones who know how to enjoy food, but not live for food. It's a constant learning process for me. I think it will take the rest of my life.

WOMAN #2: But it's getting easier for you, isn't it?

WOMAN #5: Slowly. I have good days and bad days.

ALL WOMEN: Yeah, me too.

WOMAN #1: I just always wanted to pass the pencil test.

WOMAN #3: The pencil test? What's that?

WOMAN #2: (*Amused.*) Oh yeah . . . I remember girls taking that test in my high school locker room. I passed it then . . . couldn't pass it now, that's for sure.

WOMAN #3: I never heard of it — what are you talking about?

WOMAN #1: You put a pencil under your breast . . .

WOMAN #4: Right . . . and if it falls you have firm, perfect, perky little breasts . . .

WOMAN #2: And if you're stuck with a pencil hanging down . . .

WOMAN #4: You've got big-ass saggy boobs!

(*They all laugh.*)

WOMAN #5: Hell, can't you tell just by looking at them? I could probably stick a baby grand piano under these things and it wouldn't be going anywhere! (*Blackout.*)

EPILOGUE

All the women from the previous scene and the Young Woman from Scene 8 are standing looking at their reflections in full-length mirrors.

YOUNG WOMAN: I know you're there . . . but you're losing your hold on me.

(*Mr. Horrible enters — he no longer carries his cane — not quite as dapper as before — he moves slowly, almost weakly among the women.*)

WOMAN#1: Sometimes I hear you loud and clear.

WOMAN #2: But not as much as I used to.

WOMAN #3: There's someone else now. Someone more feminine. Creative. Inspiring. Supportive.

(*At the mention of the feminine voice, a woman should enter from the opposite side of Mr. Horrible. She should be dressed in a very ethereal manner.*)

WOMAN #4: More compassionate — not quite as dangerous.

WOMAN #5: And she tells me that I'm a unique and strong individual. She whispers positive things to me all the time.

(*By this time Mr. Horrible should reach the ethereal figure. She smiles at him and he seems to shrink before her.*)

(*One by one, the women move away from their mirrors and cross down-*)

stage to form a horizontal line across the apron. The feminine "voice" stands with them. As each woman takes her place downstage, Mr. Horrible retreats farther and farther into the shadow. He is ever-present, but he has lost his power and now lives in the shadows.)

YOUNG WOMAN: I'm tired of looking at skinny women on magazine covers and on TV shows.

WOMAN #1: And I'm tired of reading articles about the increase of eating disorders in teenage girls.

WOMAN #2: And I'm tired of thinking men won't like me unless I lose twenty pounds. Will losing twenty pounds really make me a better person? A more interesting person? I think it'll just make me grouchy because I'll be really hungry.

WOMAN #3: Let's face it; we're not all built to weigh a hundred pounds.

WOMAN #4: I want to be healthy; I want to lower my cholesterol; I don't want to be a heart attack waiting to happen. And I'm working on it. Every day.

WOMAN #5: I'm making peace with my body.

YOUNG WOMAN: But this *is* my body; I'm round and plump and my stomach will never be flat. And it's OK. It's me. It's just me. And there is so much more to *me* than my body.

WOMAN #1: I can be a size 2.

WOMAN #2: I can be a size 10.

WOMAN #3: A size 16. *(Pauses.)* On a good day.

WOMAN #4: The yo-yo cycle is starting to slow itself down.

WOMAN #5: The war isn't over — but I'm winning the battle.

YOUNG WOMAN: I know now that I don't have to try and look like everyone else.

WOMAN #1: I just want to look like me.

WOMAN #2: The best me I can be!

WOMAN #3: And I can feel my heart pumping . . .

WOMAN #4: And I can feel my limbs swaying, moving, dancing . . .

WOMAN #5: And I know my body has so much power. Just as it is.

ALL WOMEN: Just as it is.

(The women turn to face one another and acknowledge the ethereal woman. They turn back to the audience holding hands.)

YOUNG WOMAN and WOMAN #1: *(In unison.)* We are pretty!

WOMAN #2 and WOMAN #3: *(In unison.)* We are *hot!*

WOMAN #4 and WOMAN #5: *(In unison.)* And we are tempting!

YOUNG WOMAN: We're not perfect.

WOMAN #5: We're far from perfect.
WOMAN #2: But we are definitely . . .
ALL WOMEN: (*In unison.*) P-H-A-T!
WOMAN #2: We are most definitely . . .
ALL WOMEN: (*In unison.*) PHAT GIRLS!
    (*Blackout.*)

END OF PLAY

THE SWEEPERS

By John C. Picardi

For my parents, Vincent and Nina Picardi

ACKNOWLEDGMENTS

Special thanks to Frances Hill of Urban Stages for her time, energy, and talent. Thanks to the following people who were involved in this play through the years: Jed Harris, Bill Kovacsik, Brigitte Viellieu-Davis, Janet Carol Norton, Stan Wood, Joanna Downy, Arthur Giron, Ron Roston, John Soster, Katie Leonard, Dara Seitzman, Roman J. Tatarowicz, John Marino, Geoffrey Calroni, Donna DiSanctis, Mario Fratti, L.H., Marni Rice, Albany Capital Repertory and Staff, Tim Meinert, Sue Gormley, Maryanne Jago, Kathy Bandera, Amy Murray, Vincent Picardi Jr., Josephine and Herb Sharp, Antoinette Coletti, Emily and Florence Picardi and the many actors who gave their time and talent to the numerous workshops and readings and finally to National Italian American Foundation, the Sons of Italy, John D. Calandra Institute, my agent Carolyn French, my family, and always Diane Almeida.

ORIGINAL PRODUCTION

New York City, Urban Stages — Off-Broadway production — March 26, 2002 to May 18, 2002. Directed by Francis W. Hill with the following cast:

BELLA CICHINELLI (McCARTHY)	Dana Smith
MARY DEGRAZIA	Donna Davis
DOTTY LARNINO	Brigitte Viellieu-Davis
SONNY McCARTHY-CICHINELLI	Matt Walton
KAREN FOLETTI	Ivy Vahanian
Set/Lighting Design	Roman J. Tatarowicz
Costume Design	Kevin Brainerd
Sound Design	Marc Gwinn
Stage Manager	Ken Hall

CHARACTERS

BELLA CICHINELLI (McCARTHY): Forties, a sexy woman with dark sensual eyes. She only uses her maiden name, Cichinelli. She is sleek and stylish, her sometimes over-the-top nature is tempered by her delicacy.

MARY DeGRAZIA: Forties, neighbor and best friend to Bella and Dotty. She has a stoic manner, matronly but stylish, always in control, her great love for her two friends is sometimes masked by a feverish attitude.

DOTTY LARNINO: Forties, neighbor and best friend to Bella and Mary. She is a jolly woman with a positive demeanor, she has a curious naïveté and hungers for knowledge. Her innocence does not mean "stupidity."

SONNY McCARTHY-CICHINELLI: Mid-twenties, Bella's son, has dark hair and is strikingly handsome. He is well-educated, an attorney. His working-class background is evident, but not obvious.

KAREN FOLETTI: Mid-twenties, Sonny's bride-to-be. She is cute and small with brown hair. She dresses softly, daintily, very much the lady. She is from an upper middle-class Italian-American family.

The women do not wear black dresses. They *do not* speak with Italian accents, but their Boston dialect should include the song of the Italian language. They are modern and fashionable. They wear colorful aprons over their day clothes during most of the play. The women can have rosary beads in their apron pockets to be used when they pray to the Blessed Mother. The music of the period is played when Bella turns on her radio and becomes an integrated part of the play in the transitions of scenes. Hitting or slapping Sonny on the back of his head by the women and any other stereotypical Italian-American gestures should be avoided.

TIME AND PLACE

Summer 1945. A bright and sunny day in Boston's Italian Neighborhood. The North End.

SETTING

A small courtyard surrounded by brick-colored buildings. On the ground floor of each building is a back entrance door with small porches and steps. The set has the feeling of an Edward Hopper painting with his selected realism and colors. Painted scrim gives the effect of brick buildings, which can be lit to see the interior of Bella's house and the upstairs of the other houses. The set can also be lit to see painted war posters behind the scrim. An entrance to the alley that leads to the street is upstage right. Dotty's house is downstage right with one small step, two pots of red geraniums, and her broom. Upstage of Dotty's backdoor are three steps up, a porch with railings and the door to Mary's house. *Boston Globe* newspapers are seen on Mary's porch. Underneath her porch is room for her junk collection. Upstage left are two steps up to a little porch and Bella's door. Her house, spanning the back of the stage, has a fire escape and a ladder. The fire escape has two windows with green shutters that open out over it, and a garbage can underneath it. A 1940s radio is seen in Bella's house, which provides music of the period in the yard. A bench is set diagonally in front of Bella's door. Dotty's chair is by her door and Mary's chair is on the floor at the bottom of her steps. The Blessed Mother is on a small pedestal downstage left with two wooden milk crates and a pot of red geraniums nearby. A clothesline hangs from the fire escape to the end of Bella's house. A second clothesline hangs by Dotty's house. Radio plays an important role in the play. Each house has a radio where music of the period is heard during scene changes. The music of 1945 is in score with such artists as Perry Como and Frank Sinatra. The use of music enriches this play.

The Sweepers

ACT I

SCENE ONE

Saturday, mid-June 1945. Late afternoon. About 5 P.M. Mary DeGrazia enters with her broom and sweeps her steps. She moves to the yard, hits something, and discovers a bottle cap. She picks it up. She rubs it and looks toward the statue of the Blessed Mother. She leans her broom on her porch and then kneels in front of the statue and prays.

MARY: Blessed Mother when are you gonna bring my husband and my boy home? Huh? I wait and wait and I hear nothing but bad news, bombings and battles in places I don't even know. This world is such a messed up place, such a crazy place. *(Beat.)* Blessed Mother if I'm here in hell, you'd be kind enough to tell me right? You let me know real soon 'cause my patience is running thin, 'cause my fellas are good and I miss them, see. I want them home from that Pacific Island; I want them home real bad. In the name of the father, the son and the ho —
(*As Mary blesses herself, Dotty Larnino, Mary's neighbor and good friend, comes out of her house, quietly puts down her watering can, sneaks up behind Mary and scares her.*)

DOTTY: — Hey Mary!

MARY: Oh Mother of God! *(Stands.)*

DOTTY: I'm back from seeing Eddie at the hospital. The doctor will not let him home. No sir, he gotta stay there a bit longer.

MARY: You always say you're bringing Eddie home from that damn V.A. Hospital and you never do!

DOTTY: It ain't my fault he ain't ready yet.

MARY: When's he gonna be ready? *(Gets her broom.)*

DOTTY: Never mind Eddie right now, I got other news, big news!

MARY: What do you mean never mind Eddie, he's your husband!

DOTTY: I said he ain't ready! HE AIN'T READY! *(Beat.)* — Now listen to me! I saw Bella, so I ditched in the doorway of Gino's bar and I watched her. She jumped on the number 12 to Southie.

MARY: Southie!?!

DOTTY: She was all made up like *bella della sfera* [sic]! *[The belle of the ball.]*

MARY: Sooo that's where her boyfriend is! I should have known. She always liked the Irish!

DOTTY: She's getting awfully high and mighty lately, getting all private on us!

MARY: I know one thing! When her big show-off son marries that snotty little priss-face from Wellesley College, Bella better make sure that snob hangs her wedding sheet out. Bella ain't keeping that from us! I wanna know if that girl is pure.

DOTTY: Of course she's gonna hang it out!

MARY: But don't be so sure, she's a Yankee girl and I bet that she thinks us Italians are all low class. — Better yet, she probably thinks we're all *(She looks around and whispers.)* — gangsters.

(The sound of a bus is heard.)

DOTTY: I hear the bus! She's gotta be on it! I can't wait to hear what lie she's gonna tell us today! *(She puts her watering can down.)*

(Mary leans her broom on her porch. Dotty pulls her to the bench and they sit. Bella enters from the alley. She is dressed up nicely but is a bit ruffled.)

BELLA: What's with the eyes all over me? Both of you, go away. *(Crosses to her door.)*

MARY: *(Crosses in front of Bella.)* So Bella, I thought you were going to cook today? I smell nothing cooking.

DOTTY: Out to see your boyfriend Bella?

BELLA: I don't have no boyfriend, get off that will you.

DOTTY: Ahh — huh . . .

MARY: So where do you go on these afternoons? What's the big secret?

DOTTY: You don't wanna tell your best friends about your boyfriend, then don't, we don't care, right Mary?

MARY: Hiding it from Sonny, is that it?

BELLA: For the last time I got no boyfriend. I go to the cemetery to see my brother Antonio and then to church and pray. OK? Don't you have anything else to do? Go clean out your burner or something.

MARY: So ah, where do you pray?

BELLA: Saint Mary's!

DOTTY: Since when do you take the number twelve bus to Saint Mary's? —

MARY: — You can take the thirteen or the eighteen but not the twelve to Saint Mary's.

DOTTY: And besides the cemetery is nowhere near Saint Mary's. You got to take the number fourteen or the seven or eight to the cemetery!

BELLA: What? You two turning into a couple of Nazis or something? Since when do you watch every move I make?

DOTTY: Since you were about seven! So what's the big secret?

(*Bella starts to her door. Mary leans over and sniffs her.*)

MARY: They giving out whiskey with communion these days?

BELLA: I go to church, I say a prayer, I get some whiskey. What's the big deal? Mind your own business.

MARY: Like you don't know all our business.

BELLA: Go straighten out your drawers. (*Bella starts to enter her house.*)

MARY: Wait! — Bella you have any sugar? I used all my stamps.

BELLA: I gave the stamps I had left to Dotty last week. (*Bella goes in and we see her turn on the radio.*)

MARY: I gave you my sugar stamp two weeks ago. What are you doing with all this sugar?

DOTTY: Never mind the sugar, Bella is not going to any cemetery.

MARY: I know she has a boyfriend stashed away, we should get a cab and follow her and —

DOTTY: — Ahhh, maybe we should just leave her alone . . . I can't say I blame her . . . I guess everyone needs some loving.

MARY: DOROTHY LARNINO! How can you say such things to me? You sound like . . . a puttana! (*Gets her own broom.*)

DOTTY: I can say it 'cause I'm lonely too. I think about that "part" of my marriage. I miss those times.

MARY: Puttana! Shame!

DOTTY: What? What? You don't feel lonely with Vinny away? You don't miss IT?

MARY: How can you even talk about IT? That's sacred business between a man and his woman after the honeymoon. Plus, Dotty, you shouldn't be doing anything like that, you're too old to have a baby. (*Sweeps near the Blessed Mother.*)

DOTTY: You're not telling me you don't let Vinny touch you no more?

MARY: We're not spring chickens anymore. — I want to end this conversation right now —

DOTTY: — That ain't right! A man's gotta do his business. (*Crosses to Mary.*)

MARY: Do you have wax in your ears?

DOTTY: You don't got to be a spring chicken. Do you know that old lady Giacomo told me she charges her husband every time he wants to do it? She let's him beg for it 'til he offers her money . . . twenty-five cents! And once he went up as far as giving her a whole dollar, and she's an old hen.

MARY: Dotty Larnino don't ever tell me that story again! (*Sweeps upstage center.*)

DOTTY: *(Crosses to her porch.)* Well I was just thinking about marriage and things. — With Sonny getting married and all, it brings back memories . . . Remember when everything was all fresh and new?

MARY: I don't think about such things. But BELLA does! I know she thinks about IT and she doesn't say anything to us and I know why! — She knows she's still married in the eyes of God!

DOTTY: Conley McCarthy hasn't been around since Sonny was twelve!

MARY: It doesn't matter! God sees her as a married woman. I still can't believe she goes by her maiden name!

DOTTY: Oh Mother of God! Don't start with that!!! I can't hear no more about that!

(We see Bella turning off her radio.)

MARY: Well, it's true. I know Conley was a bum, but it ain't right not going by her married —

DOTTY: — Ahhh, Bella you haven't even asked me about Eddie.

BELLA: You haven't even given me a chance! *(Sits on the bench.)* — So . . . How's Eddie?

DOTTY: Well, he ain't good enough to come home.

BELLA: He was supposed to be home two months ago. What the hell is wrong with him?

DOTTY: Well, this one doctor at the hospital finally convinces Eddie he's not in France no more. Now Eddie he's in the good ole U.S. of A. So that means now we're on step two, which means we gotta try and convince Eddie that the Nazis aren't here in the U. S. of A!

BELLA: Ain't this awful . . . Does he still think Hitler is under his bed?

DOTTY: No. The doctor says Eddie got some condition, something that begins with "N" ahhhhh new row, new row—

MARY: — Neurotic Dotty, it's called neurotic!

DOTTY: Yeah that's it. Eddie is neur-O-tic. The doc says if you keep talking and acting like Eddie does then you got this neur-O-tic thing and you gotta stay in the hospital.

BELLA: Next time you go to the hospital, Mary and I gotta go with you, it ain't right we haven't seen him yet.

MARY: We should've gone to see him weeks ago. Poor crazy Eddie . . .

DOTTY: He ain't crazy; he's neu — Neu — Neu —

MARY: — Jesus, Mary, and Joseph, it's called Neurotic! Neurotic!

DOTTY: Yeah, — he got that condition. *(Sits on the bench with Bella.)*

BELLA: This war has made us all crazy and grumpy . . . *(She looks directly at Mary.)* Maybe some of us should be put away . . .

MARY: Why you looking at me?

(*Bella puts her arms around Dotty and they laugh.*)

MARY: Speak for yourself, Bella! *(Beat.)* Hey, got a letter this morning, two months old. Vinny says the Pacific is as blue as the stained glass windows at Saint Mary's. God bless OUR guys, right Dotty? Fighting on the line like real men!

BELLA: *(Imitating Mary.)* *"Fighting on the line like real men!"* — Now she's going to start about my Sonny. — Hey Mary, you know my older brother, God rest his soul, fought in the first Great War. He was killed for this country, so don't start on me.

MARY: I wasn't saying anything about Sonny or your brother . . .

BELLA: *(Walks toward Mary.)* Just lay off my Sonny he got a 4-F, he got a very, very bad heart murmur. My poor Sonny two months early like that, so weak, so small, have some heart Mary . . .

DOTTY: He wasn't so small. In fact he looked normal to me.

BELLA: Both of you shut up!

MARY: *(Stands and sweeps.)* Can always tell when you drink whiskey, you get all temperamental.

BELLA: Quit the big words, "temperamental" you would think you were the only one to graduate high school around here. (*Crosses to Mary.*)

MARY: I AM the only one to "graduate high school around here!"

DOTTY: Don't we know it . . .

BELLA: Oh excuse me, Miss Fancy Pants with the strand of pearls from Shreve, Crump and Low!

MARY: Again with those pearls she starts! Did you hear her mention the pearls again, Dotty? Did you? — I chose the right thing Bella! — To be a good mother, to be a good wife, to be a good daughter!

BELLA: What are you talking about? You HAD no choice. Your father wouldn't give you a cent for college so you had to wait for him to die and now it's too late. And all you got now is some dumb pearl necklace that you bought yourself!

DOTTY: Not to mention a good bank account.

BELLA AND MARY: *(Look toward Dotty.)* SHUT UP DOTTY!

DOTTY: Here we go, Dotty the punching bag. *(Crosses.)*

MARY: Shut up all of you! I'm sick of all you both talking about my father's money. He worked hard for every cent and he didn't even have a chance to enjoy it.

BELLA: Yeah, but you do. You don't seem to mind it so much . . . rubbing it in our faces!

MARY: You got such a mouth on you lately Bella McCarthy-Cichinelli. Let me tell you something Lady Jane, I'd give every cent to have my husband and my boy back from this lousy war, that money means nothing to me! — *Capisce* [*sic*]!

DOTTY: Can I have it?

BELLA AND MARY: *(Look toward Dotty.)* SHUT UP DOTTY!

BELLA: I'm telling you Mary, back off on my Sonny and his girl, that's all I'm saying. *(Sits in the center of the bench.)*

DOTTY: *(Crosses to be between the ladies.)* Hey! Hey stop fighting. Now look here, when Frankie gets home and Mary when your fellas get home, everything is gonna be like it used to be, when this lousy war is over.

MARY: Yeah, you're right Dotty. I can see the fellas already sitting over there in the corner on milk crates playing poker, drinking bottles of beer and making a mess.

DOTTY: I'll tell ya a secret. I kinda miss cleaning up their mess. Cigarette butts, peanut shells —

MARY: — Bottle caps . . . *(She takes the bottle cap out of her apron pocket.)* I'd do anything to have those days back let me tell you.

BELLA: Yeah, and I'd do anything to have Antonio back. Anything . . . This whole war brings back terrible memories, just terrible memories . . . of the Great One.

MARY: *(Sits on the bench, upstage of Bella.)* Come on now, Bella. You know I don't mean what I say —

BELLA: — Forget about it. I'm sorry too. I got a big mouth.

DOTTY: *(Stands upstage of the two ladies.)* Antonio was some guy. — Remember how he loved to put us on his shoulders and we'd pull off Louise Pelligrini's laundry from the line? *(Sits on the bench, downstage of Bella.)* — She had the biggest bloomers . . . *(Lies back onto Bella's lap.)* —Hey remember the time when we were only fourteen . . . he brought us to the Paramount? It was a Chaplin picture with that Mabel Normand . . . *(Sits up.)* and our mothers made us to go to confession 'cause they heard there was kissing in the picture.

BELLA: It feels like last month Antonio was here . . . *(Beat.)* I gotta go inside for a minute, I — I gotta do something. I got something on the stove. *(Bella exits with the washtub.)*

MARY: Il Mio Dio! She's got nothing on her stove. — Dotty why did you have to encourage her about Antonio? She's in there right now drinking the whiskey and she'll be all over the place!

(*Sonny McCarthy-Cichinelli runs into the yard with his fiancée Karen Foletti. Mary and Dotty stand.*)

SONNY: Hi everyone, where's Ma?

MARY: She just went in the house.

DOTTY: Well, look at the happy couple! BELLLLLLLLLLLA! GET OUT HERE. SONNY AND HIS BRIDE ARE HERE! HEY BELLLA!!!
(*Karen is taken aback.*)

MARY: Don't mind her Karen, she has an ear condition.

KAREN: *(Giggles.)* Ahh, hi ladies.

MARY AND DOTTY: Hi Karen.

BELLA: *(Enters.)* Looky here! Looky at my boy and his bride! You both look like a picture. *(Kisses Sonny.)* A perfect picture! *(Kisses Karen.)*

KAREN: Ma . . . Bella you are *so* sweet.

MARY: *(On the sly to Dotty.)* No honey, she's just *so* drunk . . . *(She walks up to her porch.)*

SONNY: So Ma, you want to see the marriage license?
(*Sonny holds out the license. Dotty grabs it.*)

BELLA: Easy Dotty! You act like a *cavona* [*sic*]! Give that back to me! *(Bella snatches the license out of Dotty's hands.)*

SONNY: Hey, Ma, easy you're gonna tear the thing!

BELLA: How 'bout that? I'm proud of you! Hey Mary come see this, Antonio picked up his marriage license today.

MARY: I know what a marriage license looks like Bella . . . *(Leans broom on her door.)*

SONNY: Mama, I'm Sonny. Sonny!

BELLA: Of course you are, who else are you gonna be?

SONNY: You just called me Antonio again. *(To Karen.)* She always calls me Antonio . . .

BELLA: I do not, stop being so sensitive. — Now, did you stop by and show Father Arnold, what he say?

SONNY: He's so proud Mama.

DOTTY: I'm so excited for the wedding Karen!

KAREN: Me too! How have you all been?

MARY: Real peachy.

KAREN: That's a pretty dress Mrs. DeGrazia.

MARY: Thanks Karen. It's 100 percent cotton.

DOTTY: You'll be such a pretty bride, Karen. I was too if I do say so myself. *(Crosses to her chair and sits.)*

BELLA: Karen, you'll be gorgeous. *(Leads Karen to the bench and they sit.)*

KAREN: Thank you Ma . . . Bella . . . ladies . . .

DOTTY: Hey Sonny, I wrote Frankie a letter. I told him about your good news!

SONNY: I did too! I sent out a letter yesterday! — How's Mr. Larnino?

DOTTY: He still ain't allowed to come home.

SONNY: You tell him I said hello. *(Beat.)* Mrs. DeGrazia, you hear from Vinny or Vinny, Jr. yet? It's been a while since we got letters.

MARY: *(Proudly, aggressively.)* I was telling your Mama, I got one today, still in Pacific. Fighting on the line. Same as usual. You know my fellas are fighting on the line like real men, risking their lives for this country. Why keep asking me all the time?

SONNY: Because they're my best friends and I want to know how they're doing. Is that a crime?

MARY: You tell me Mr. Lawyer, you're the one who wants to help the little hoodlums around here. They break our windows and scare us half to death.

SONNY: I would appreciate it if you didn't call them hoodlums. They're kids who don't have a soul in the world to direct them in the correct way.

MARY: Now he's Spencer Tracy —

DOTTY: — *Boys Town*! I loved that picture . . .

BELLA: *(Crosses to Sonny.)* Hey Mary! Father Arnold says he's doing a great job coaching basketball with them hoodlums. Ain't that right Sonny?

SONNY: Ma! Don't say hoodlums!

BELLA: What? Everything I say is wrong . . .

SONNY: Come on Karen, let's go in and get something to eat. *(Crosses to Karen to take her hand.)*

BELLA: Hey Sonny, you don't touch nothing on that stove, it ain't cooked. I don't want you getting worms before the wedding.

(Sonny and Karen exit into the house.)

MARY: You have nothing on the stove.

DOTTY: You let them in the house alone?

BELLA: Shut up Dotty! *(Walks to Mary and stands below her porch.)* I begged you not to do it! And you done it — in front of that girl too. Can't you see she has class?

MARY: *(Sarcastically.)* Oh, I feel bad for 'em! He could've signed a waiver!

BELLA: You know the doctors won't let him sign no waiver! He's got a serious condition, not like your ordinary heart murmur!

MARY: He's a lawyer and a 4-F'er. My fellas should be so lucky. And why is he marrying outside this neighborhood? You think a Yankee girl like that is gonna *hang out her wedding sheet?*

BELLA: Mary DeGrazia! For the last time — She ain't no Yankee girl. She's a Catholic and an ITALIAN girl from some fancy neighborhood.

MARY: Bella, darling, look, she doesn't look talk us or act like us. She reminds me of those Yankees that hate us Italians, treating us all through this war like we were some close relative of Mussolini or something!

BELLA: She is not a Yankee!

MARY: I'm trying to tell you that she is. And you got one in your house right now! — She's gonna convert Sonny into a Yankee too!

DOTTY: I gotta admit Bella, Karen does remind me of that Mrs. Wilson, that Yankee woman who runs that candy shop on Washington Street. She asked me if I was Italian *(Stands.)* and then she asks me if I was one of these *fastest* people. I told her when I was in school I ran the *fastest.*

MARY: — Fascist.

DOTTY: Yeah, that's what I'm sayin' Mary. Well she went all loony on me . . . she said I was a rebel and rebels weren't allowed in her store —

MARY: — A Fascist! A Fascist! Madonna Mia, what am I gonna do with the both of you? You both gotta learn to keep your big mouths shut . . . Bad enough everyone thinks us Italians are Anarchist or Communist!

DOTTY: I ain't no Communist. I'm Italian.

MARY: You don't even know what it is . . .

DOTTY: I do too! My father was from San Donato, I'm Italian!

(Bella and Mary laugh at Dotty.)

DOTTY: Stop laughing at me!

BELLA: We're not laughing at you.

MARY: *(Hugs Dotty.)* Yes, yes we are. *(Laughs.)* Dotty you got to read the newspaper more, but I love you all the same . . . I gotta go to the post office, see you girls later. *(Mary exits.)*

DOTTY: I curse the day she went to sister school.

BELLA: Me too . . . fancy pants.

DOTTY: You think Karen's gonna hang her wedding sheet out?

BELLA: Get off my back about it Dotty. *(Bella crosses to crates.)* I'll simply say to Sonny that "Your bride needs to hang her wedding sheet out and that is that." *(Sits on crate.)*

DOTTY: *(Crosses to Bella.)* Good for you! A woman needs to stand her ground in her own home, especially when her husband takes off on her. I'm proud of you Bella, you know why? Because you're a woman with courage. — And — well, I didn't want to give this little gift to you yet, but I will, so hold on a second will ya?

BELLA: What? Where you going?

DOTTY: It's a surprise. Hold on. *(Dotty runs into her house and leaves the door open.)*

BELLA: What did you do?

DOTTY: Hold on! *(Runs out holding a bag.)* — You know how I've been saving my ration stamps, not buying sugar and flour.

BELLA: You've been borrowing everything from me and Mary for weeks —

DOTTY: — And not reporting that Eddie is in the hospital and using his stamps—

BELLA: — Dotty are you nuts? The government is gonna find out he's in the V.A. Hospital. What do you have in that bag? *(She tries to grab bag from Dotty.)* A side of beef I hope . . . veal? *(Chases Dotty around.)* Tell me you got veal? Butter . . . you got real butter?

DOTTY: *(Pulls out a sheet.)* NO! They're sheets for the honeymoon bed! I figure this way you can show Sonny these new bed sheets and then demand he stay here on his wedding night. I bought them to save you problems. You tell the girl you bought them.

(They open the sheet, each holding one end. They both throw the sheet up, turning underneath it.)

BELLA AND DOTTY: *(Laughing.)* Weeeeeeeeee!

BELLA: They're beautiful, but — Dotty . . . you can go to jail for messing around with ration stamps —

DOTTY: — Don't tell Mary she'll kill me . . .

BELLA: *(Folding the sheet with Dotty.)* — I don't think Sonny is going to make his bride do this . . . It ain't like when we were married . . .

DOTTY: Of course it's the same, everyone does it the same way . . . He puts it in . . . *(Puts the sheet in the bag that Bella is holding and they giggle.)* and wiggles it around and it's over. The girl bleeds, you hang your sheet out and the world knows you're pure. There is nothing to it and excuse me for saying this, *(She looks around, whispers.)* I miss it something awful —

BELLA: —Shhh, Mary will hear you!

DOTTY: Maybe I should go see Father Arnold!

BELLA: These sheets are beautiful. Grazie bona amica mia [*sic*]. *(Bella hugs Dotty.)*

(The lights fade as they enter their homes. Mary opens her door, drops off tied papers and brings in a crate of cans from the porch.)

SCENE TWO

July 14, 1945. Late afternoon. About 2 P.M. Sonny is in the yard wearing a tuxedo, waiting impatiently for his mother and Karen to hem his tuxedo.

SONNY: *(Yells.)* Ma! Karen! Come on, get out here! — I'm hot!

BELLA: *(Offstage.)* We're coming! We're coming!

(*Dotty, trying to hide from Sonny, walks in the yard from the alley with a full shopping sack.*)

SONNY: Hi Mrs. Larnino.

DOTTY: Hey Sonny. Where's your Mama?

SONNY: Blabbing away to Karen about . . . dresses . . . *(He takes off his tuxedo jacket and puts it on Mary's chair.)*

DOTTY: You look mighty handsome, like some Hollywood star . . . *(She takes a red tomato out of her sack and hands it to Sonny.)* Here, have a tomato.

SONNY: Thanks. *(Sonny bites into it like an apple.)*

DOTTY: Frankie used to love to eat tomatoes like that, like they were apples . . . You want some salt? I can run in and get some salt. *(She starts to leave, teary-eyed.)*

SONNY: No, no . . . hey — hey why are you crying?

DOTTY: Nothing Sonny. I saw Mr. Larnino again . . . that's all.

SONNY: Hey . . . He'll be good as new real soon . . . you'll see.

DOTTY: Oh, Jesus forgive me . . . *(Crosses herself.)* — I'm so ashamed. I don't want your Mama or Mary to know. Sonny I'm so scared . . .

SONNY: What? What is it?

DOTTY: The doctor — the doctor — I can tell you Sonny, I can tell you because you're educated, right?

SONNY: Tell me what? Yeah, you can tell me anything.

DOTTY: The doctor says Mr. Larnino *can* come home.

SONNY: Why that's great news! Great news! — Why are you cr —

DOTTY: — Weeks ago . . . two months ago.

SONNY: So — Why . . . I don't —

DOTTY: — Don't you see? It's me, I don't want him home. He scares me Sonny. — He scares me something awful. And when Frankie comes home he's going to see his father all crazy! You can't tell your Mama. You can't tell no one. — It's me Sonny. I keep him in that place . . . I'm a rotten person . . . but I can't — I can't have him here. He thinks he's got a rifle in his hand and he points it at things and — it's awful . . . *(Sonny hugs her tightly.)*

SONNY: The war is gonna be over soon and Frankie will be home. Mr. Larnino is going to get better. You'll be yelling at him about his peanut shells and his wine drinking and hey — you'll be taking the trains with him in no time to *Morey Pearl's* on Saturday nights and dance the night away . . . *(He takes her hand and swings her around, dancing.)*

DOTTY: *(Composing herself.)* He was some dancer. The big show-off fool, swinging me around like he did . . . *(She wipes her eyes and laughs a bit.)*

SONNY: If you have good memories like that you have everything. Give it time; after all, you have to feel better about things too. He was fighting on the line but you were here alone, keeping his home. — When you're ready for him, you'll know it.

DOTTY: Do you think I'm weak? Am I bad wife Sonny? Should I go see Father Arnold?

SONNY: No. Father Arnold will tell you you're smart because you know how you feel.

BELLA: *(Offstage.)* Sonny you better still have that jacket on!

DOTTY: I gotta go. I'm in no mood for your Mama . . . . And Sonny, *(She puts out her thumb.)* don't say nothing.

SONNY: *(He touches his thumb to hers.)* I promise.

(Dotty picks up her bag and runs in the house. Sonny puts on his tuxedo jacket.)

BELLA: *(Entering with Karen.)* I said to myself I was going to spend as much as I could on a nice dress. It's not every day your son gets married.

KAREN: Well, Ma Bella it's lovely . . . and it fits you so well! I *love* the way it gathers in the front and flows down around the back like it does. Tell me, where did you find such a —

SONNY: — Can you two talk about this later?

BELLA: Be still you! *(She whacks Sonny.)* Karen says she doesn't mind staying here the night of the wedding before you both leave for your big fancy honeymoon on Cape Cod.

SONNY: Ma, we already have the hotel room, Karen's father paid —

BELLA: — Sonny, Karen agreed, so you'll stay here. — Look Sonny, us women make the plans, you bring home the money and keep your mouth shut. Understand?

KAREN: Ma Bella you're a daughter-in-law's dream!

SONNY: Oh, brother.

BELLA: Hey be still! *(To Karen.)* — I'm dying to see your wedding dress!

SONNY: Ma, can we just get this over with?

BELLA: Did I tell you kids to get married in August? *(She stands on the bench. Sonny stands in front of her. She starts to measure him with a measuring tape.)*

KAREN: Fits him nice, doesn't it Ma Bella?

BELLA: I've got to take it in around the shoulders and the cuffs need to be redone —

KAREN: — It needs to be taken in around the waist.

BELLA: You got a good eye. She's got a good eye Sonny.

KAREN: You're going to need new shoes.

BELLA: He can wear his father's. The only good thing his father left besides Sonny . . . his good black shoes.

SONNY: Ma, those shoes are as old as the hills.

KAREN: We'll get you a new pair. My father said he'd help us out.

BELLA: That's very nice, but I can buy my son a new pair of shoes for his wedding.

SONNY: Oh, Ma! This is going to take forever . . . can't I just rent one like everyone else —

BELLA: — Stand still you! You need to own your formal wear now that you're a lawyer! — Just a minute, I have to get the pins. *(Sonny and Karen help her down, she exits into the house.)*

SONNY: *(Kisses Karen.)* Ma loves you!

KAREN: I like her.

SONNY: She can be tough.

KAREN: Don't worry.

SONNY: So why did you agree to stay here the night we get married?

KAREN: We have to compromise and besides, you were right, it's only one night. We're leaving for Cape Cod in the morning and anyway she bought us new bed sheets, they're lovely and she's excited, how could I hurt her? *(Beat.)* — Sonny, — did — did you tell Ma Bella about those housing communities being built?

SONNY: I . . . I haven't had a chance.

KAREN: That is something you have to talk to her about. I don't mind compromising on these small things, but Daddy did say he'd help us. *(Beat.)* Oh, Sonny it will be so wonderful to have a house. I can fix it up and make a home for you and our children.

SONNY: I'm telling you now; I don't think Ma's going to understand.

KAREN: You have to explain it to her, mention it slowly —

SONNY: — Shhh. I will, don't worry about it. — There are things Ma expects . . . This is my home here. We have to give her some time . . .

KAREN: There are things I expect too. I don't want to live here very long . . . I — I like it here just fine . . . but —

SONNY: — I know . . . I don't want you to worry right now, I'll work things out . . . OK?

KAREN: OK . . . if you say so. *(Beat.)* — I have the wedding list. I want to go over it a bit with you, OK?

SONNY: Now? I'm so hot here.

KAREN: *(Sits on bench and takes book out of purse.)* Well, you may be surprised.

I want to read a few names, I think you may be impressed Mr. Lawyer. My mother received responses from . . . the Smiths from Newton, Mr. and Mrs. John Parson, Mr. and Mrs. Frederick Cummins, Mrs. Helen Snowdin and . . . guess what Sonny? Mr. and Mrs. Clarence Barnes are coming to our wedding.

SONNY: *(Stunned.)* The Attorney General? Attorney General Barnes?

KAREN: I told you Daddy knows practically everyone at the State House. He even knows Former Governor Saltonstall. You will get to know all of them working for Daddy.

SONNY: Karen, I'm Sonny McCarthy-Cichinelli from the North End of Boston. This is not what —

KAREN: — No! No, no you are so much more; you're Attorney Santonio McCarthy, top of his class. You're the man who my father hired to work at his law firm.

SONNY: And I'm grateful, but I didn't become a lawyer for social status. I was honest with him and I was honest with you. I took the job because I needed experience. I want my own firm one day. I want to help the working class, the immigrants. I want to preserve their rights and freedoms.

KAREN: I know all that . . . — I'm only reading you the list —

SONNY: — And I'm telling you I have ideals that I'm going to stick to — some of those people coming to our wedding have the power to oppress the people. Those politicians attack Italians. Look at Sacco and Vanzetti, that was only twenty years ago and look what most people said about us during this war.

KAREN: You're getting so upset.

SONNY: *(Sits on Mary's chair.)* I worry about us sometimes. I don't know . . .

KAREN: *(Stands.)* Why? What do you mean?

SONNY: Our differences . . . You say things and sometimes I'm not sure what you're saying. We both were raised differently. Mama and I are not fancy people. Mama works at the shoe factory. — My buddies and I, we were no angels when we were kids . . . And you did all that fancy social stuff . . . You eat cucumber sandwiches.

(They both laugh. Karen walks to Sonny.)

SONNY: — Is Attorney General Barnes really coming to our wedding?

KAREN: *(Giggles.)* Yes, he is! *(Beat.)* We're not so different, look, my father grew up in a neighborhood like this in New York City, but he got himself out, and made something out of himself. Like you, he wanted to show people that Italians are just as good, just as smart. Daddy maintained a strong sense of his heritage. It wasn't easy for him and it's still difficult, but he did it! That's why he likes you so much. God you're so much like him! (*Laughs.*)

SONNY: Father Arnold was my mentor for a reason, he taught me to work for the good of the people.

KAREN: My father does "good" for the people too. He has integrity. But get used to it. (*Sits on Sonny's lap.*) It's a big old boys' club on Beacon Hill and it starts socially. This is all I'm trying to tell you. Look Sonny, put the smiles on, rub elbows, get in there, then you can have your dream, you can fight for what you believe. You'll do it.

(*Sonny takes Karen in his arms and they kiss. Ma Bella enters and steps up on the bench.*)

BELLA: Come, let's finish this up.

KAREN: I should be going.

BELLA: So soon? I thought you were going to have lunch. Old man Enrico gave me some tomatoes.

KAREN: I would love to stay, but I can't. I have a fitting on Newbury Street. I'm sorry, Ma Bella . . . Sonny . . . I'll see you later . . . (*Sonny and Karen kiss until Bella stops them.*)

BELLA: — Good luck with your fitting Karen.

KAREN: Thanks Ma Bella. And Sonny, be still! (*Sonny jumps after her. She laughs and exits.*)

SONNY: Ma . . . Guess what? (*Walks to Bella.*)

BELLA: Do I look like I want to play guessing games? (*Measures and pins Sonny.*)

SONNY: Attorney General Barnes is coming to our wedding.

BELLA: Is that good?

SONNY: Ma, it's very good.

BELLA: Sounds classy.

SONNY: It is Ma . . .

BELLA: Real important for your job, right?

SONNY: Karen says it will be . . .

BELLA: Then I guess it will . . . (*She sticks Sonny with a pin and steps off the bench.*) be.

SONNY: Ouch! — You mad about something Ma? Something I said?

BELLA: Mad? How could I be mad? I'm — I'm just overwhelmed and excited. (*Beat.*) I'm so proud of you, so proud. Madonna Mia, wait till I tell Mary! I'm gonna rub it in her face really hard like it was sandpaper. (*Makes Sonny stand on the bench.*) — Santo Lucia, the Attorney General at my son's wedding! . . . Is he married? (*Pins the cuffs on Sonny's pants.*)

SONNY: Ma? What? Why you asking?

BELLA: What? A mother can't ask if someone is married? — As soon as I'm done here you gotta go down to the rectory and tell Father Arnold . . . Oh my God, so classy . . . my son . . . So, what's an Attorney General do?

SONNY: All kinds of things Ma. *(Beat.)* So ahh, Ma, can you believe it Ma? The war might be over soon. Truman has given Japan an ultimatum of unconditional surrender.

BELLA: When this war is over, I'm gonna be so happy. So happy.

SONNY: *(Steps down from the bench.)* Ma, you ever think about moving outta here? To a new house? The apartment is kinda small, you know? Soon, Karen and I, we're gonna have kids. As a matter of fact, her father said that they're building new —

BELLA: — What are you talking about? This is our home. You and Karen are taking my room, I'm taking yours. We got plenty of room for kids, they can sleep with me.

SONNY: I was thinking, wouldn't it be great to own a new house? Somewhere with trees and grass . . . birds. — You know something? There's never any birds around here . . . just miles of brick on brick, like some kinda prison. Like a huge honeycomb. Wouldn't it be great, a big yard of our own? An oak tree in the backyard? . . . Hey, when is the last time you held an acorn?

BELLA: I guess there must be lots of acorns in that fancy place your girl is from. She filling your head with fancy ideas? Birds and grass and trees . . . honeycombs?

SONNY: No, Ma, listen to me, OK —

BELLA: — We've been living here since my father came to this country almost fifty years ago! Me and your Uncle Antonio were born in this house.

SONNY: Please I'm asking you to listen to me now, OK?! I don't want you to go on about your brother.

BELLA: He was your uncle, my brother, and your grandmother's first born. Don't you dismiss him like he was a nothing!

SONNY: *(Angry.)* Will you listen to me damn it?!

BELLA: What? What do you wanna say huh? You wanna feel a couple acorns in your hand, go to the park. You wanna see birds, go to a frigging zoo!

SONNY: Let's not worry about it. Karen doesn't come from a background, a traditional family like us. I'd just love to see all us living in a big new house that's all.

BELLA: *(Panic.)* OK. Wait a minute here . . . I know you're hiding something from me. Oh my God . . . Is she having a baby? Oh, Blessed Mother! Did you tell Father Arnold?

SONNY: No, stop it!

BELLA: I hope that girl is not having a baby 'cause we're all counting on that wedding sheet waving in the wind like a big Japanese flag! Make me proud young man!

SONNY: NO, Karen is not hanging no sheet out and she is not having a baby! So you best stop this nonsense. Or we're staying at the hotel!

DOTTY: *(Offstage.)* BELLLLLA! BELLLLLA!

(Dotty opens the door to her house and steps out. She holds a letter from the government.)

DOTTY: MY FRANKIE! MY FRANKIE! He — he got his leg blown off! He got no leg! They come — the men — the men from the war department — *(Gives Bella the letter.)*

BELLA: *(Hugs Dotty.)* — Oh my God! Oh my God! Frankie's not —tell me he's not—*(Sits on Dotty's chair.)*

DOTTY: —They say to me that Frankie is on his way to California, but he got no leg. He got no leg. The Japs, they bombed naval bases in Okinawa! Frankie got no leg!

SONNY: Frankie, not Frankie . . .

DOTTY: Sonny . . . Oh Sonny, they got our Frankie. My boy!

(Dotty runs to Sonny and holds him tightly.)

BELLA: Oh my God! *(Bella runs up and knocks on Mary's door.)* MARY! MARY! Get out here.

MARY: *(Offstage.)* I'm coming Bella . . . *(Mary steps out and looks at everyone.)*

DOTTY: MARY! MARY! They got my Frankie, he got no leg!

MARY: *(Crosses downstairs to Dotty.)* I'm sorry Dotty. I'm so sorry . . .

DOTTY: We gotta pray for Frankie! — Mary, Mary you gotta help me — I can't take this Mary. Oh my God.

(Mary helps Dotty to the Blessed Mother.)

BELLA: *(Hands the letter to Sonny.)* Sonny quick, go get Father Arnold . . . And tell him, tell him Dotty needs him . . .

(Sonny runs out of the yard. Bella joins Mary to comfort Dotty. They all kneel.)

MARY: *(Afraid, softly, shocked.)* Oh, Dotty . . . Dotty . . .

DOTTY: Oh, Mother of Mercy! — Watch over Frankie Blessed Mother. I don't understand this . . . My poor Frankie, my poor boy . . . How am I gonna tell Eddie? Eddie's not gonna understand this.

(Bella and Mary hold Dotty who sobs in their arms. The lights fade, the ladies return to their houses as lights change into scene three.)

SCENE THREE

Monday, July 30, 1945. Late evening. A few weeks later. Mary enters from the alley pulling a wagon full of newspapers and a crate of bottles. She starts to unload it. We hear a car outside the courtyard, male voices, and laughter. Mary quickly walks up her stairs and listens from her porch.

MALE VOICES: *(Offstage.)* There he is Sonny the 4-F'er, big college boy! Too high and mighty to fight for his country! *(Laughter.)* Sonny the 4-F'er! — Sonny the 4-F'er! You big coward! Sign a waiver! 4-F'er!

(We hear a bottle crash. Mary hears Sonny walking into the courtyard and quickly runs into her house and shuts the door. Bella comes out with her broom and looks around, trying to figure out the noise. Sonny backs into the yard, takes off his jacket, throws it on the bench, and sits on a crate downstage. He looks disheveled.)

BELLA: Sonny what's going on?

SONNY: *(Crosses downstage to sit on crate.)* Nothing, Ma. Nothing.

BELLA: Who was saying something to you? *(She leans her broom on the fire escape and crosses to Sonny.)*

SONNY: It doesn't matter.

BELLA: Madonna Mia, what's wrong Sonny? Tell Mama . . . *(She sits on other crate next to Sonny.)*

SONNY: Nothing Ma.

BELLA: You were never afraid to talk to me before.

SONNY: . . . Sometimes Ma — I don't . . . — I don't know . . .

BELLA: What?

SONNY: I feel like I don't know where I belong.

BELLA: You belong here. *(She kisses Sonny's head.)*

SONNY: When I'm around here I feel like I don't fit in anymore. Then when I'm around the law firm, I feel different than everyone there. It's like ever since I became this attorney, ever since I got my education, I feel like I'm this big misfit.

BELLA: Sonny, what are you talking about? Of course you fit in. This is your home. Look at you. Look at both of us, you and me. We did it. You're a lawyer, educated. We all need you here. You can't get upset because a few people are jealous of what we did.

SONNY: No, Ma.

BELLA: Remember when your father left us? What did I promise you? Do you remember?

SONNY: Please, Ma not aga —

BELLA: — I promised you we would have a good life and we did! We've always been a team — you and me. We did it! Now stop this — smile — SMILE DAMN IT smile. We won. How come you aren't smiling? Aren't you listening to me?

SONNY: I'm listening

BELLA: It's her. She's making you feel this way, isn't she? *(Sits on the bench.)*

SONNY: Who?

BELLA: Karen.

SONNY: No Ma.

BELLA: I know my boy. She's putting ideas in your head.

(Mary comes out of her house and stands on her porch, she looks over at them. Bella crosses over to Mary's porch and stands below it.)

BELLA: What are you doing out here? Edgar Bergen and Charlie McCarthy are having Perry Como on tonight.

MARY: They can wait. — I've been thinking of you and me all day. We've been friends a long time. Your only son is getting married in a few days and I was thinking that you'll need these more than I do. After all, you'll be moving up in the world now that Sonny is so fancy now. *(She hands Bella a string of pearls.)* You wear them at the wedding and you keep them after that too.

BELLA: *(Shocked.)* Your pearls? Mary I can't take these — They're so beautiful — My God. — No, no, Mary I couldn't, they're too nice, I don't deserve such nice things —

MARY: — You deserve everything nice. I got no use for them.

BELLA: *(Overlapping.)* What are talking about? I can't take them. No, they're too nice, you don't understand — I don't deserve such nice . . . Mary . . .

MARY: *(Overlapping.)* Put them in your pocket and be quiet. Bella stop it! — I already decided. They're yours . . .

BELLA: I LOVE YOU! *(Beat.)* I'm so awful . . .

MARY: Yeah you are. But hey it's not every day a son gets married right? *(Points to Sonny.)* You, get over here.

(Sonny runs up to the porch. Mary hands him two gold cuff links.)

SONNY: Cuff links?

MARY: What? You don't like them?

SONNY: They're Mr. DeGrazia's.

MARY: Those I want back.

(Sonny hugs her and Mary holds him tightly.)

MARY: You wear them on your wedding day and you think of my husband and your best friend, OK? I — I have to go now. *(Mary lets go of Sonny.*

She holds back her tears and goes for her door as Sonny walks off the porch.)
Sonny, you may be a 4-F'er, but you're our 4-F'er. No matter what any-
one says. Capisce? And no matter what, I'm proud of you. *(Mary exits.)*
SONNY: Good night Mrs. DeGrazia. *(Sonny walks to Bella.)*
BELLA: Maybe she was sleeping walking or something.
    (Sonny and Bella start laughing, and we hear Mary's voice from inside her house.)
MARY: *(Offstage.)* I hear you Bella!
BELLA: Sonny you coming in? *(Bella exits. We see her turn on her radio and we hear music.)*
SONNY: I'll be right in Ma. *(Sonny lights up a smoke and sits on a crate.)*
    (Dotty comes out of her house and throws some trash in the can, making sure that Sonny sees her.)
SONNY: Hi Mrs. Larnino.
DOTTY: *(Sadly, but she wants to talk.)* Oh, hi, Sonny. Nice night . . .
SONNY: Everything OK? — You seem —
DOTTY: — Yeah, yeah, — I — I, I just got to thinking — about things. — I haven't been able to sleep lately. My body gets shaky like I'm crazy or some-thing and I get this damn sweat . . . I must be going crazy.
SONNY: You're not crazy. *(Sonny pats the other crate so Dotty will sit down.)*
DOTTY: *(Sits on crate.)* I don't know Sonny, the last three days I've looked around my house and I imagine they're home with me, you know? Like how it was before the war. If I'm in the kitchen I imagine Eddie is sitting there smoking his cigar in the living room, "Put that damn thing out!" I say . . . And when I'm in the living room I imagine Frankie's out at the kitchen table shining his shoes "Do that outside, it stinks" I scream. Wanna know how many times I shined Frankie's shoes this week or lit one of Mr. Larnino's cigars? — Well, I can't tell you, because if I did, you'd want to lock me up too. Nothing seems right . . . I know I should go get him out of that place, but Sonny he, he ain't the same. And I'm not sure I want to be his wife, and I'm scared to be Frankie's mother. It's killing me. That's when my body starts shaking and I feel all crazy. It ain't normal think-ing I tell ya.
SONNY: *(Softly.)* It sounds like normal thinking to me. You're gonna get through this. *(Sonny kisses Dotty and crosses to his house.)*
DOTTY: Good night, Sonny . . . and Sonny, thanks.
SONNY: Good night Mrs. Larnino. *(Sonny exits.)*
    (Dotty takes her rosary beads from her pocket and stares at the Blessed Mother. She nods confidently and walks into her house. The lights softly fade as Mary

comes down her stairs and takes the wagon into the alley. Music from Bella's radio continues and is interrupted for an announcement by President Truman about the atomic bomb being dropped on Hiroshima. We hear wedding bells. Time has passed.)

SCENE FOUR
Sunday, August 12, 1945. There is soft moonlight in the yard. We hear music coming from the radio in Bella's apartment. Sonny in his tuxedo and Karen in her wedding gown run into the yard from the alley, laughing with joy.

KAREN: *(Still laughing.)* — And when your mother danced with the Attorney General I thought I would die. She was hilarious.
SONNY: That's Ma for you.
KAREN: She really swung him around, the old goat . . . *(She laughs and spins around, showing off her dress.)*
SONNY: God you're so beautiful . . . I love you.
KAREN: I love you too . . . *(They kiss in each other's arms.)* . . . Listen.
SONNY: What?
KAREN: The music.
SONNY: Ma, left the radio on . . . *(They sway holding each other and then pick up the pace swing dancing. Then Sonny starts dancing by himself, showing off. Karen starts laughing.)* You think that's funny?
(Karen nods and Sonny picks her up and carries her into the house. Dotty, Mary, and Bella enter the courtyard; they are full of joy and laughter. Bella is a bit drunk.)
MARY: That wedding must've cost a small fortune. Where did they get all that food?
(Bella and Dotty tango toward downstage.)
DOTTY: I must've ate a dozen of those small things made with a can of peas.
MARY: Canapés! Canapés!
(Bella and Mary laugh at Dotty.)
DOTTY: That's what I said! Stop laughing at me!
BELLA: Karen was gorgeous, she truly was . . . And you know something else?
(Dotty spins Bella into her.) I really like gin!
(Dotty spins Bella out toward Mary, then Bella spins Mary, who doesn't want to dance, around.)
MARY: You're so bad. You drink too much . . . Listen to you . . . gin.

DOTTY: Madonna, Bella, Sonny made me cry. He smiled from ear to ear the whole day.

MARY: Father Arnold said a wonderful Mass. Karen's people aren't so bad either. The mother thinks she's Rita Hayworth, but I'll say no more.

DOTTY: Hey! Hey, look . . .

(*Dotty does an imitation of Karen's mother and they all laugh.*)

BELLA: Thank you girls. A part of me was scared of today. I thought I wasn't going to be classy enough. But wearing these pearls and . . . and Dotty helping me make Sonny's wedding bed this morning with those new sheets, it all put my mind to rest. I think Sonny felt like he fit in . . . and I fit in . . . and you fit in . . . and the whole world fit in! . . . I fit in, I fit in right? —

MARY: — Go to bed before you fall out.

(*They all laugh.*)

BELLA AND MARY: Buona Notte. (*They hug and kiss.*)

BELLA AND DOTTY: Buona Notte. (*They hug and kiss.*)

(*The ladies all start to exit to their doors.*)

DOTTY: See you EARLY in the morning girls. (*Coughs and signals to Bella's clothesline.*)

(*The ladies all look up as the lights fade. The shutters above softly open. We see Karen's back and Sonny standing in front of her. Sonny slowly slides the straps of her slip down her shoulder. As they go to kiss, their light and music slowly fades.*)

INTERMISSION

ACT II

SCENE ONE

Monday, August 13, 1945. The North Station Factory whistle blows as the scene opens. It is a bright and sunny day. Mary comes in the yard dragging the wagon filled with untied newspapers and a crate of bottles. She puts the crate on the porch and it makes a loud crashing noise. There is a huge pile of junk under her porch . . . tires, cans, metal items. There is a basket, filled with nylons and an empty cloth sack, near Mary's chair.

DOTTY: *(Offstage.)* MARY! MARY ARE YOU OUTSIDE ALREADY? IS THAT YOU?

MARY: I'm out here Dotty in the yard!

DOTTY: *(Peaks outside her door.)* Oh, there you are. I'll be right out. *(Goes back inside.)*

MARY: *(To herself imitating Dotty.)* "There you are, there you are . . . " Where else am I gonna go?

(Mary sits on her chair and starts sorting the nylon stockings in the basket, inspecting them carefully and putting the old ones in a sack.)

(Dotty enters with a folded newspaper.)

DOTTY: . . . I'm reading Mary! — No word yet from the Japs! Crazy bastards, you would think two big bombs like that they'd be begging Truman for peace . . . *(Reading.)* Sixty percent of Hiro-shrimpa was destroyed . . . and one-third of Naga-ass-it . . . one-third!

MARY: It's Hiroshima and Nagasaki. — Hey wanna know what they told me down at the Jenny Gas Station?

DOTTY: *(Yawning.)* You been there already today?

MARY: 5:30 AM, party is over Dotty, back to work. There's a war going on.

DOTTY: *(Sitting down on her chair.)* So what they say?

MARY: They say they don't think anyone has collected as much junk as me for the War cause. They say I should get a medal of honor. Me! Imagine!

DOTTY: Well how'd you like that?! The Pope forecasted the development of atomic energy two years ago . . . Can you believe it? Must'a been some message from God or somethin'. I don't even know what atomic energy is for crying out loud. I mean, I know you make bombs with it, but that's it.

MARY: It's all very scientific. — Hey, I'm glad you're reading the paper.

DOTTY: Here we are on the verge of world peace and we don't even know what atomic energy is.

Maybe we should. The Pope knows. Mary, it could be some kind of sin or somethin' not to know. We gotta ask Sonny, he'll know, he went to college. *(Dotty goes over to the fire escape.)* HEY SONNY!!!

MARY: Just because Sonny went to college doesn't mean he knows everything. Although Bella would like us to believe so.

DOTTY: Bella been out yet?

MARY: *(Shaking head.)* She's probably sleeping it off or out with her secret lover! I bet he sneaks in and outta here in the middle of the night!

DOTTY: You think Sonny told Karen about the sheet? It's not hanging out.

MARY: Probably not! Hey, give me your nylons; they make gun powder bags with them.

DOTTY: I got no nylons to give up. Hey Bella should be out with us. *(Beat.)* BELLA! ARE YOU UP YET? BELLAAAAAA!

MARY: Stop your yelling like that! You sound like a nut for crying out loud. Truman should've sent you over to yell at those crazy Japs. Help me bundle up these newspapers. We'll bring them down to the Jenny after. *(Mary sits on the ground, puts a pile of papers next to her for Dotty, and starts tying papers in small bundles.)*

DOTTY: So Frankie is coming home any day now. Uncle Sam gave him a new leg.

MARY: You told me a millions times yesterday at the wedding.

DOTTY: Did you hear anything from your boys today?

MARY: No. It's early still. Stop talking so much. Work! Work!

(Dotty sits next to Mary and starts tying the newspapers, not paying much attention to how she does it.)

DOTTY: I was just asking. You always get so mad when I ask —

MARY: — Hey! Hey! Dotty! For crying out loud! Don't tie 'em like that and be neat! Those fellas down at the Jenny want them a certain way! *(She takes the papers from Dotty, fixes them, and continues to tie her own.)*

DOTTY: *(Leaning on the bench.)* They're teaching him how to walk all over again, like a baby! *(Laughs.)* Boy, I tell you Mary, they're gonna have their hands full with my Frankie. He was two years old before he could walk, and even then he couldn't do it all that great, just OK, kept falling down. Eddie would laugh for hours watching our Frankie wobble across the room, then wham, fall flat on his face. Ha! *(Beat.)* Funny how things work out, don't you think Mary? Oh well, Frankie is coming home! *(Beat.)* — He had fat little legs as a boy, soft, sweet, chubby legs.

MARY: *(Not really listening to Dotty.)* Dotty, listen to me, toothpaste tubes. They want all toothpaste tubes. Save 'em. *(Beat.)* I figure we'll go around asking

the neighbors for 'em later. This entire Hiroshima thing might
trouble.

DOTTY: *(Stands.)* Come on Mary, it's going to be over. The war is as g
over. *(She looks at Bella's clothesline.)* I made sure me and Eddie's wed-
din' sheet was out by 7 A.M.! 7 A.M.! Yes sir! *(Beat.)* — *(She goes to Bella's
door.)* — HEY! BELLA ARE YOU UP? WHERE ARE YOU?

BELLA: *(Offstage.)* Dotty stop your yelling, it's Monday morning. And after a
wedding at that!

DOTTY: The mother-in-law should be out here. — The wedding sheet ain't
hanging out yet! You should be out here!

(Bella opens her door. The sun hurts her eyes.)

BELLA: Nothing yet? — Give it time.

DOTTY: It's nearly five after 8!

BELLA: It's still early!

DOTTY: Mine was out at —

DOTTY, BELLA, MARY: — 7 AM!

DOTTY: Well it was.

BELLA: My boy's a good lover, probably takes his time. Hey, the Japs surrender yet?

DOTTY: It's a matter of time. Hey, in New York City the partying has already
begun.

BELLA: I'll be out in a minute . . . *(Bella goes back into her house.)*

MARY: Dotty give me all your nylons! *(Stands, picks up nylon basket, and sits
on her chair.)*

DOTTY: Oh, like I got a big collection of them. Now stop it, I ain't giving you
anything else. *(Beat.)* I bet Bella is embarrassed that sheet isn't out yet.
Glad we don't have girls. More trouble than they're worth. *(Sits on bench.)*
That's what my Papa would always say. — "Girls cause too much trouble keeping them pure. Dotty keep your skirt down, close your legs, don't
look at the boys, don't smile too much . . . " He went nuts the first time
I put lipstick on. I was a married lady too. Drove me nuts.

MARY: You never mind, it was all good bringing up we had . . . not like this —
this puttana Sonny married.

DOTTY: You think she may be used goods?

MARY: Are you going to help me?

DOTTY: Well how 'bout that?! Truman says when we come out of this war we'll
be the most powerful nation in the world. The most powerful!

*(Bella comes into the yard with her apron. She holds a cloth over her fore-
head; she is hungover. She lies on the bench, her apron used as a pillow.)*

MARY: Look at that! Her head is squashed! *(Stands and goes to Bella.)*

DOTTY: *(Crosses to upstage of bench.)* You'd be hungover too if you drank gin with the band members all night at your son's wedding. And not to mention FLIRTING with all those big show-off people.

MARY: She had whiskey too, before the church.

BELLA: Madonna Mia! Get off my back!

MARY: We just don't think you should mix your drinks, that's all.

BELLA: Oh really, well I don't think you should eat meat during Lent!

MARY: *(Guilty.)* And who eats meat during Lent?

DOTTY: *(Guilty.)* Certainly not me!

(Both ladies cross back and start tying the newspapers quickly.)

BELLA: Both of you do! And don't deny it! On two separate occasions during this past Lent I smelt braciole *(Dotty and Mary look up slowly and then back down.)* cooking in your house on Friday! I couldn't believe what my nose was smelling! But I didn't say anything, because I'm understanding! Now get off my back and be understanding with ME, damn it!

MARY: *(Still looking down, tying papers.)* I never! I can't believe this! You're crazy! Eat meat during Lent! I never would! Shame!

DOTTY: *(Overlapping.)* Evil mouth! Eat meat during Lent. Never! Ridiculous! If Father Arnold ever heard you!

BELLA: Well it wasn't Cod I was smelling ladies! My nose don't lie!

MARY: I think you have enough of your own business to be concerned with this morning.

DOTTY: *(Glances up.)* Like a certain sheet that's not hanging out yet!

BELLA: Will you please stop it?! Do something else . . . peel a potato or something! My God, stop staring at that damn clothesline. *(Bella sits up.)*

MARY: I don't understand why Sonny had to marry outside his kind anyway.

BELLA: *(Stands and puts on apron.)* That's it! Sonny didn't marry outside his kind! She's ITALIAN I tell you! Don't start this . . .

DOTTY: *(Stands and walks to the wagon to fix it up.)* Yeah, and I'm a Jap. *(Dotty and Mary laugh.)*

BELLA: Hey! Hey! Enough about Sonny already. I'm his mother and you two are more concerned about the damn sheet than I am.

MARY: *(Stands.)* It's a nice summer day. I'm out here all the time. It's my yard, why shouldn't I be out here? I'm doing my part for the war. Why should I care if Sonny's girl is pure or not?

DOTTY: *(Crosses between Mary and Bella.)* Alright. Alright girls. We got more important things to think about. Now Bella, do you think Sonny knows what atomic energy is?

(*Mary sits in her chair.*)

BELLA: Oh, who the hell knows!? (*Sits on bench.*) So? (*She looks at Dotty.*)

DOTTY: What?

(*Bella looks at Mary.*)

MARY: What?

BELLA: Did you girls have a nice time at the wedding?

MARY: It was a very nice time Bella.

BELLA: Pretty classy place, huh?

MARY: Everything was fine.

BELLA: Your chicken wasn't dry, was it?

DOTTY: . . . The string beans were overdone.

BELLA: My string beans were perfect.

DOTTY: Mine were overdone. (*Crosses and sits on her chair.*)

MARY: My chicken wasn't dry . . . That wasn't the problem with my chicken.

BELLA: (*Stands and walks toward Mary.*) There was a problem . . . with your chicken?

MARY: Too greasy. But don't worry about it. I haven't had chicken in months.

BELLA: Greasy chicken and overdone string beans. I'm sorry you had such a lousy time at my son's wedding. (*Sits on bench.*)

MARY: Who had a lousy time? I had a great time. Stop that. It was a fine wedding. The band was a bit too loud for my taste, but who cares what I think.

DOTTY: Those Yankees do things differently that's for sure.

BELLA: OK! OK! Open your ears! SHE's ITALIAN! HER PEOPLE ARE ITALIAN!

DOTTY: I think it's all a big cover up. I think they're all those *fastest* people.

MARY: (*Stands.*) Fascist! Fascist! — Madonna Mia, stop saying that dangerous word, you don't know what you're saying, you'll get us arrested! (*Crosses over to Bella.*) — Now, Bella, are you the woman of your own house or aren't you?

DOTTY: (*Crosses to Mary and Bella.*) Are you Bella?

BELLA: (*Pauses a moment.*) I had no say in the wedding. I had no say in nothing! This I should insist on! Huh?

MARY: You should insist on it!

DOTTY: It's only right.

BELLA: (*Yells up to the window.*) SONNY! SONNY!

DOTTY: Stand your ground.

MARY: Yankee girl. Snob.

BELLA: (*Center stage.*) Enough is enough! I'm tired of being quiet for her!

SONNY! SONNY! I'M CALLING, YOU ANSWER ME! We got our ways, she got hers. But she's living in my house!

MARY: That's right.

DOTTY: Good for you!

BELLA: *(Yells up to the window.)* SONNY! SONNY!

SONNY: *(Opens the shutters and sticks his head out.)* Ma, what are you yelling for?

BELLA: Was — your chicken dry? My chicken was dry.

SONNY: Everything was fine.

BELLA: So . . . where's the bride already?

SONNY: Karen is sleeping Ma, stop yelling will you? *(Sonny goes back in and closes the shutters.)*

(The ladies huddle downstage.)

DOTTY: Still sleeping? Huh! He's gonna have his hands full.

MARY: I'm up at the crack of dawn.

DOTTY: What's she still sleeping for? It's almost 8:30. She should be making the boy a nice breakfast!

(The ladies turn upstage.)

BELLA: SONNY! SONNY!

SONNY: *(Sonny opens the shutters.)* What is it Ma? Will you stop yelling?!

BELLA: You want me to make you a nice breakfast since Karen is still sleeping at 8:30 in the morning?

SONNY: No. Let us be Ma. Stop yelling.

BELLA: Why? Am I embarrassing you?

MARY: In front of his classy American wife from Wellesley College?

SONNY: Don't you start Mrs. DeGrazia! She's gonna hear you.

MARY: Maybe she should hear me.

SONNY: *(Yells.)* Enough of this, all of you!!! *(Sonny goes back in and closes the shutters.)*

DOTTY: I bet she's been around . . . A regular Jenny the Pump!

MARY: Makes me wonder.

BELLA: Pure as snow I tell you.

MARY: I don't trust her.

DOTTY: So . . . if she's so pure, is she gonna hang her sheet out? I went hungry for weeks for that sheet.

MARY: What?

DOTTY AND BELLA: Nothing.

BELLA: SONNY! SONNNY! SONNNNNNY!

KAREN: *(Opens the shutters.)* Good morning . . . Ma Bella, ladies. Sonny's detained at the moment.

MARY: "Detained." . . . Isn't that elegant?

BELLA: Detained? . . . — What's he doin'?

KAREN: *(Embarrassed.)* He's —he's in the john.

DOTTY: *(Crosses to Mary.)* The john! That's what her kind calls the toilet, huh?! *(Mary and Dotty laugh.)*

BELLA: What are you two mumbling about? I'm trying to talk to my daughter-in-law!

MARY: and DOTTY: Hello Karen.

KAREN: Hello Mrs. Larnino . . . Mrs. DeGrazia.

MARY: You looked lovely yesterday.

KAREN: Thank you so much. You all looked so lovely as well. Ma Bella, you made quite an impression on the Attorney General.

BELLA: *(Leaning on Mary's porch.)* No kidding? His wife didn't smile much.

DOTTY: You looked like a Princess Karen! — So, ahh, — have you forgotten something Karen?

KAREN: I'm sorry? Forgotten what?

MARY: *(Pulls Dotty toward the bench.)* Let Sonny do it. For God's sake, don't meddle. It's up to Bella and Sonny. What a slut.
(Mary and Dotty sit down on the bench.)

BELLA: *(To Karen.)* I guess Sonny hasn't said anything to you?

MARY: I guess not.

KAREN: About what Ma Bella?
(Sonny pops his head out the window next to Karen.)

SONNY: Ma, what's going on?

BELLA: I wanted to say good morning to Karen. Good morning Karen! *(Sits on Mary's chair.)*

KAREN: Good morning Ma Bella.

BELLA: Sonny, would you mind coming down here for a minute? I gotta ask you some legal advice, about my . . . . . . ahhh . . . TAXES!

SONNY: Ma, I'm not a tax lawyer and it's August . . . It can wait.

BELLA: No . . . as a matter of fact it can't. I got a labor problem . . . a big one . . . I need your help Sonny! *(Pleading.)* Son-ny!
(Sonny, with undershorts and a white tank top on, begins to climb out onto the fire escape.)

BELLA: SONNY! Go around, don't come down that way! It's too dangerous! And put your pants on!

SONNY: Oh Ma!

BELLA: "Oh Ma" yourself! Is that anyway for a lawyer to act? What if someone saw you? They'd think you were off your rocker!

KAREN: She's right Sonny.

BELLA: See?

(*Sonny grunts and goes back into the house.*)

KAREN: You're his favorite client Ma Bella.

BELLA: Years putting soles on shoes at that Factory I should hope!

DOTTY: You got the radio on? Any word from the Japs yet?

KAREN: No, I'll go listen to the radio. Isn't it exciting ladies? The end of the
war!

MARY: It ain't over officially young lady!

(*Karen goes back inside and closes the shutters.*)

SONNY: (*Coming outside.*) Ma, what is going on?

BELLA: What? You're too good for me now, Mr. Lawyer? Mr. High-and-Mighty?

SONNY: (*Crosses over to Bella.*) What's the problem you're having at work? You
mouthing off again to Mr. Reichstein?

BELLA: I ain't fighting with that old Jew.

SONNY: Mama! I told you not to speak like that!

BELLA: What I say wrong? I said Jew. Is Jew a bad word?

SONNY: It's the way you said it. — Now you got a few days off with no pay
for the wedding. What's the problem? Did you say something bad to him?

MARY: (*Crosses to Sonny and pulls him to her.*) How can you do this to your
Mama? Shame on you, bad boy!

SONNY: What? Do what?

DOTTY: (*Goes to the other side of Sonny.*) It makes us wonder. Sonny, she ahhh,
say anything to you about . . . Mussolini and us?

MARY: Does she think we're low class? I went to sister school!

SONNY: What? Stop this you two! NOW! What is going on?!

BELLA: Sonny, I want that sheet out! (*Mary and Dotty cross to the bench.*) I did
it when your father and I got married, that bum Irish drunk. God only
knows why I loved him and where he is! But I was a virgin and the entire
neighborhood knew it!

SONNY: Forget it, Mama. And Pa left 'cause you nagged him something
awful! — And I got Irish blood in me!

BELLA: (*Crosses toward the bench.*) Shhh! Shame, don't you say that! You got
no Irish in you. And I never nagged that bum, never! I just wanted him
to work, damn it! (*Aside to Dotty and Mary.*) And I didn't want to boil
meat with cabbage . . .

SONNY: Oh no, oh, no not this . . . not this . . . non cominci [*sic*] Mama! *(Angry.)* NON COMINCI!

BELLA: I will start! Now march up those stairs and explain to her that it's part of the wedding ritual. My mother did it, my grandmother did it, my great grandmother did it, my great-great grandmother did it, my great-great-great grandmother did it and my great-great-great-great grandmother did it!!

SONNY: Mama! You can go all the way back to when the Cichinellis lived in caves. I'm not asking Karen to do that. She wouldn't understand.

MARY: *(Stands.)* Some people like chocolate ice cream, some like vanilla . . . such is life. But sometimes in life we gotta eat what we don't like — get it?!

DOTTY: *(Stands.)* It's a quarter to the hour.

MARY: Dotty I don't think you have to announce the time every five minutes.

BELLA: Really, Dotty!

DOTTY: I'm stating the time that's all. *(Dotty and Mary sit on the bench.)*

BELLA: Look, when you said you were marrying this girl, I agreed.

SONNY: You cursed me to hell.

BELLA: I never said a word!

SONNY: I could see it in your eyes! You didn't like her . . .

BELLA: She's a snob. *(To the ladies.)* But the girl's parents threw a nice party. Park Plaza . . . nice . . . *(To Sonny.)* The chicken was dry though.

SONNY: So this was all an act . . .

BELLA: I said I liked her because you wanted me to —

MARY: — Don't forget the string beans —

BELLA: — And the string beans were overdone, but I didn't complain. Fine, they didn't want pasta at the wedding, I said who needs it. Then they tell me we're gonna have small hot dogs before dinner and tiny sandwiches. I bite my tongue, I say nothing. Then you start telling me you want to move and you tell me you don't fit in around here anymore. I bite my tongue again. But this, this I must ask you to do.

SONNY: Forget it Ma. I'm not gonna do it.

BELLA: Either you do it or I will.

SONNY: Ma, if you ask my bride to do that I swear I'll never speak to you again . . . That's it! I'm going in!

DOTTY: *(Stands between Sonny and the door.)* Hey, Sonny before you go in . . . what's atomic energy?

BELLA: Go on, tell them Mr. McCarthy. Or is it too beneath you to talk to us common folk about such scientific matters?

SONNY: Atomic energy is energy available from fission of atomic nuclei.

DOTTY: Ahh . . . huh . . .

SONNY: See, Mrs. Larnino, atomic energy is much greater than what's available from chemical or mechanical sources. See, one pound of uranium during fission is about equivalent to ahhhh, let's see, what's derived from the combustion . . . of let's say, ahhh, about two-and-a-half million pounds of coal.

DOTTY: Well . . . That's a lotta coal.

SONNY: I'm going in Ma. Enough of this stupid talk about . . . sheets. *(Sonny exits.)*

DOTTY: Gee that Sonny is so smart. But I don't get it. Truman dumped millions of hot coals on Japan?

BELLA: Well, it's the same as . . . — Weren't you listening!

MARY: *(Stands.)* . . . Well, it looks like Sonny is going to change . . . college does that to kids . . . and Yankee girls. They come in and take our sons away and make them American. Mark my words that boy is going to be eating *Campbell's Soup* and that *meat loaf!*

BELLA: OK! That is it! I'm gonna tear that damn sheet off the bed and hang it out myself!

DOTTY: I dare ya!

MARY: I double dare ya!

BELLA: SONNY! HEY SON-NY!

SONNY: *(Opens the window.)* Ma, I told you, enough! The neighbors are gonna call the loony bin on you!

BELLA: You forgot to give me labor advice. I'm serious . . . Mr. Reichstein said something about . . . the union . . . Yeah, the *UNION* . . . you better get down here . . .

SONNY: No.

BELLA: Sonny.

SONNY: No.

BELLA: SON-NY!

SONNY: I'm coming down. This is the last time! *(Sonny goes to climb out the window.)*

BELLA: Sonny, go around.

    (Sonny stops, goes back in.)

BELLA: *(To the ladies.)* You keep him busy. *(Bella takes off her slippers and climbs up the fire escape.)*

MARY: *(Standing below Bella.)* Be careful, watch your step Bella!

DOTTY: Easy does it Bella! Quick before he comes out!

(Bella crawls in the window.)

DOTTY: I love it! This is better than the LUX PRESENTS HOLLYWOOD.

MARY: Sonny is gonna go nuts!

(They hear Sonny and sit quickly. Mary on her chair, Dotty on the bench.)

SONNY: Ma, this is ridiculous! Ma? Where's Ma? *(Mary looks away.)* WHERE's MA? *(Dotty slowly turns her head toward the fire escape.)*

SONNY: She wouldn't! I'll kill her! MA! MAAAAA! *(Sonny runs up the fire escape and enters the window.)*

SONNY: Ma, don't say anything to her!

BELLA'S VOICE: *(Offstage.)* One simple thing I ask! The girl will understand!

SONNY: *(To the ladies.)* All right you two. Mind your business! *(He slams the shutters closed.)*

(Karen enters the courtyard from Bella's door.)

KAREN: *(Bewildered.)* Gee, do they always disagree like this?

MARY: No.

DOTTY: Sometimes it's much worse. But don't worry honey, we're passionate people. They'll be saying they're sorry in no time!

KAREN: That's why I love Sonny so much, his passion.

(A loud crash is heard from upstairs.)

KAREN: I don't always understand it though.

BELLA: *(Offstage.)* SEE! See what you do to me? Your father was the same way! Perché dio, perché??

SONNY: *(Offstage.)* Everyone can hear us!

DOTTY: *(An aside.)* As usual.

MARY: *(Goes to one side of Karen.)* You were saying something about *passion.* You ahh, had boyfriends before?

KAREN: Well I — I —

DOTTY: *(Goes to the other side of Karen.)* — So how many boyfriends you have? You can tell us —

BELLA: *(Offstage.)* GIMME that SHEET! — Where is it!

SONNY: *(Offstage.)* You're embarrassing me in front of Karen! I'm going downstairs!

BELLA: *(Offstage.)* Don't you walk away from me!

KAREN: I wish I knew what was going on.

DOTTY: It's not up to us to tell you.

MARY: We don't like to meddle. *(Both sit, Mary on her chair, Dotty on the bench.)* *(Bella pushes open the shutters and puts her hands on the fire escape floor. She shouts to the world.)*

BELLA: Let the whole world know that Bella Cichinelli is an embarrassment to her fancy lawyer half-Irish son who wouldn't be where he is today if it wasn't for his MAMA putting soles on people's shoes all day long!

KAREN: Is everything OK Ma Bella?

BELLA: No it's not OK! Nothing is OK!

SONNY: *(Enters from his house.)* Karen everything is fine.

(Bella climbs out on the fire escape.)

BELLA: — Dotty go get Father Arnold I want my last rites! — I'm gonna jump!

ALL: *(Overlapping.)* NO! Don't do it! Madonna Mia. What are you doing? You're crazy! *(Etc.)*

BELLA: I'm Gonna JUMP! — I'm gonna do it. I'm going to end it, once and for all!

SONNY: *(Moving toward Bella.)* Ma, get back in the house! Now!

BELLA: Don't come near me. I'm gonna jump I say!

DOTTY: Madonna Mia!

BELLA: — Forgive me sweet Jesus!

KAREN: Nothing can be that bad!

BELLA: Sonny, she says it's not that bad.

DOTTY: Sonny, tell the girl before it's too late!

MARY: *(To Dotty.)* Was she nipping today?

KAREN: Ma Bella if it's something I can do.

SONNY: It's nothing Karen.

BELLA: NOTHING! I'm gonna kill myself! And he says its nothing, NOTH-ING.

KAREN: Ma Bella please . . . Tell me what's going on?

BELLA: How I prayed that you wouldn't get drafted! How I prayed that you would go to the University! How I thank God for your heart murmur every single day! — Dotty go get Father Arnold like I asked you.

SONNY: *(Clapping.)* You're being a big actress, Ma! A big actress! You put Ava Gardner to shame! Now pull yourself together!

DOTTY: *(She nudges Karen.)* — You're the only one that can save her honey!

KAREN: Who . . . me? What?

(Bella throws one leg over the fire escape rail.)

DOTTY: You're scaring me now . . .

SONNY: Mama, stop this!

BELLA: I swear I'm gonna jump! I'll do it! I'll do it and — and Dotty you tell Father Arnold it was all Sonny's fau — lt

(Bella almost falls and everyone gasps.)

DOTTY AND MARY: Mother of God! — Be careful! Bella get down!

KAREN: Oh my God! Sonny!

SONNY: Alright . . . You win Ma. I'll ask her. You win. Don't you move. *(Sonny brings Karen downstage.)*

(Mary and Dotty try to hear what Sonny is saying as he whispers in Karen's ear. Karen nods "no" shyly and runs into the house. Bella still hanging off the fire escape looks down to Sonny.)

SONNY: OK Ma, I asked her and she said no. Are you happy that you embarrassed my bride and me?

BELLA: The Prima Donna says "no" and that's it? Just like that "no." Huh?

(Bella swings herself back over the rail and climbs down the fire escape to Sonny.)

SONNY: Yes Ma, that's it. It's over.

BELLA: NO! It ain't over! Nothing's over yet! I want that sheet out! Now!

SONNY: *(Yells.)* Enough! I mean it Ma! *(Sonny exits into the house.)*

(Bella picks up her slippers.)

MARY: I guess you'll have to assume she ain't pure, a regular Jenny the Pump. *(They realize the game is over and cross to their chairs. Bella sits on the bench.)*

DOTTY: *(Sits in her chair.)* When I got married, we wouldn't dream of saying "no."

MARY: It was expected. I didn't dare question it. *(Sits in her chair.)*

BELLA: It ain't over . . .

DOTTY: The world — it's a changing place . . . atomic energy and all. And all these fancy names for our enemies. Mary what's that name I ain't supposed to say?

MARY: *(Mumbling and irritated.)* . . . Fascist . . . *(Under her breath.)* Madonna Mia . . .

BELLA: *(Crosses herself with her slipper.)* I hope Sonny didn't marry a puttana . . .

DOTTY: Hey girls, I gotta idea! Let's drop this stuff off at the station and after we'll all get one of those fancy Island Ecstasy Sundaes down at Bailey's, huh?! — Maybe we can even go see a picture . . . *(Dotty pulls Bella up.)* The Strand is showing *Mildred Pierce* again . . . We'll forget everything! The Japs, the war —

MARY: — No! Not the war. We can't forget that. Never

DOTTY: Alright . . . Gee whiz Mary.

MARY: Alright, let's go girls help me bring this down to the Jenny. *(Mary gives Dotty the basket, picks up the wagon handle and starts to pull it away.)*

DOTTY: You girls ever stop and wonder what this is all about? My Frankie, he's gonna be home soon and he has no leg. But we got power in this world, a leg for power. Makes no sense. None of it. None of it makes any sense.

(As they exit the stage, Bella stops, goes upstage center and screams up to the window.)

BELLA: HEY! SON-NY! HANG THAT DAMN SHEET OUT! I WANT THAT SHEET OUT BY THIS AFTERNOON! YOU HEAR ME? THIS AFTERNOOOOON! SHEET, SHEET, SHEET!

(Karen runs out of the house and into the courtyard with force, ready to speak to Bella.)

KAREN: Ma Bella this has got to stop! *(Karen sees that the ladies are gone, she looks around.)*

SONNY: *(Coming out after her.)* I'm sorry about all this. *(He touches Karen and she cringes.)*

KAREN: *(Irritated.)* I don't mind your mother or her friends. But that was a bit outrageous.

SONNY: Their parents were from the old country, old ways. Traditions . . .

KAREN: Sonny, we have to talk.

SONNY: I wouldn't be where I am today if it wasn't for Mama. I love her.

KAREN: I admire her. I really do, but she reminds me every chance she gets about how hard she worked for you.

SONNY: *(Trying to lighten things up. Sits on bench.)* She's proud, that's all. — She shows me off a bit . . .

KAREN: Honey, you certainly can't expect me to live here for the rest of my life. How would you like it if I turned into one of those — those ladies? *(Laughs.)* They're so loud and expressive . . . I mean, — look at — *(Beat.)* Now I don't mean, to be mean, *(Sits next to Sonny.)* but look at them, they're all filled with contradictions, they pray to the Blessed Mother then they — they talk vulgar.

SONNY: The world is full of contradictions. Karen they're good people.

KAREN: They all have a real special charm. They do. — And I like them just fine. But come on, look what they wanted me to do. That is so personal. I'm embarrassed to even talk about this with you.

SONNY: I said I was sorry.

KAREN: You said yourself when we got married we would stay here for a short time, and now I have this bad feeling that you think we're going to sta —

SONNY: *(Crosses downstage.)* — You have to somehow understand this place.

KAREN: *(Follows Sonny.)* I think I've been more than accommodating. Now let's get our bags and go on our honeymoon and then we'll start our life together. We can stay at my parent's house, I just called my mother. Sonny, the war is practically over. We'll buy a nice house. We'll come visit Ma Bella every Sunday. She can spend weekends with us every few months and on holidays she can ev —

SONNY: — Visit Ma? What do you mean visit Ma?

KAREN: Yes. — Oh, wait — you didn't think . . . . Oh, Sonny . . . no —

SONNY: *(Turns to Karen.)* — Hold on here! You're talking about my mother here! What do you mean visit on weekends? This ain't no formal affair here. This is my family, my ma, my life! What are you saying to me?

KAREN: . . . You never yelled at me like that before.

SONNY: Can't you see I'm trying to make everyone happy here? You're asking me to abandon my life. You're not understanding anything!

KAREN: Sonny, it's time to let go of these Old World ways and be an American. My father did it. You can do it.

SONNY: I am not your father! I am an American. An *Italian* American!

KAREN: That's right, you are and I am too! Now I am asking you to take me away from here.

SONNY: *(Yells loudly.)* Leave me the hell alone! *(Crosses upstage right.)*

KAREN: Don't speak to me like that —

SONNY: — You and Ma you're both driving me crazy! Everyone is on my back!

KAREN: What is wrong with you?

SONNY: *(Starts to leave.)* I'm taking a walk!

KAREN: Let's leave for Cape Cod now, we can leave a note . . .

SONNY: Let me be damn it!! *(Continues exiting.)*

KAREN: *(Grabs Sonny.)* Please listen to me, you're not plain ole Sonny from the neighborhood anymore, whether you like it or not, you're not the same man. Stop fighting it! Be the attorney you want to be! Move forward!

SONNY: By getting rid of all that ugly WOP that I still reek of, right? God forbid if anyone knew I came from this! *(Sonny exits through the alley.)*

KAREN: *(Trying to stop him.)* No! I would never say anything like that! I love you who you are! Don't go Sonny! *(Looks to the courtyard.)* Don't leave me here! *(Karen runs into the house.)*
(Lights change to a soft light on Mary. She brings her wagon filled with papers into the yard. She unloads a tire and a metal oil can onto her porch and goes into the house.)

SCENE TWO

Monday, August 13, 1945. The evening of the same day. Dotty sits on a crate in front of the Blessed Mother. She is praying silently. Mary enters with empty tin cans to crush.

MARY: God Dotty, it's late. What are you doing?

DOTTY: Praying. I'm holding an all-night vigil. They say any minute we're going to hear from the Japs.

MARY: You think two bombs are going to end this war? You better pray hard . . . *(She crushes a can by stomping on it.)*

DOTTY: Shhh . . .

(Bella enters from the alley. She is drunk and in her purse is a small flask of whiskey.)

BELLA: Jesus, what the hell is all this junk, Mary?

MARY: Out on the streets at this hour. You keep this up and I won't be able to be seen with you.

BELLA: I was out with my boyfriend. All ten of them! You jealous?

MARY: I don't care where you've been but you're drunk again and again and again! *(Stomps on a can.)*

BELLA: I loved one man and one man only, my whole life . . . the scum bag. Forgive me, sweet Jesus. *(Blesses herself and sits in Dotty's chair.)*
(Mary continues to crush cans.)

DOTTY: Hey, hey! I'm praying here! Oh Blessed Mother so high above us . . . *(She fades to whispers.)*

BELLA: *(Drinks.)* . . . That Goddamn Irish bum. *(She blesses herself.)* Sorry sweet Jesus . . .

(Mary tries to crush another can.)

MARY: Goddamn cans! . . . See Bella, it's your fault I swear like this!

DOTTY: Ah, excuse me! I'm praying for the end of the war and our boys overseas. I'm praying to understand why my Frankie lost his leg. I'm praying to understand atomic energy and — and I can't with you girls making so much noise!

(Mary stomps on another can.)

BELLA: I shoulda jumped . . . I should've . . .

MARY: Oh listen to her.

DOTTY: Oh, Blessed Mother of Sorrow, please bring home my Frankie soon. Please bring home Vinny and Vinny, Jr. too.

MARY: Don't do that, Dotty.

DOTTY: What?

MARY: Don't you speak to her about my men.

DOTTY: Hey, it's not a "her," it's the Blessed Mother you're talking about!

BELLA: SONNY!

DOTTY: Is everyone going crazy or something? Oh, please Blessed Mother, pray for my crazy friend Mary.

MARY: To hell with you and her!

DOTTY: You're outta your mind! She's protecting our fellas, watching over us, keeping us safe. How can you say that?

MARY: She's not doing a very good job! Your precious Frankie got no leg!—

BELLA: — And Eddie is nuts.

DOTTY: You're both evil! EVIL! You better be careful what you say about the Blessed Mother. She'll curse you! *(She weeps.)* My poor Frankie! My poor, poor Frankie!

MARY: *(Crosses to Dotty.)* How come you haven't been to see Eddie in almost three weeks? Huh?

DOTTY: Shut up!

MARY: Why isn't Eddie home? I want to know . . .

DOTTY: Shut up! Shut up!

MARY: You're scared, aren't you Dotty? You think we're stupid, we know you better than you know yourself!

DOTTY: *(Stands and yells loudly.)* SHUT UP! SHUT UP!

(Mary quickly exits into her house. Dotty sits back down. Upset, she prays to the Blessed Mother.)

I'm sorry I yelled Blessed Mother. Now look here, you gotta forgive Mary. See, she ain't all bad. She just hasn't been the same since her fellas left her. She got nobody and she ain't the strongest lady in the world, unlike you Blessed Mother. I know you'll forgive her 'cause you're all forgiving.

BELLA: Everybody needs a leg to walk on, to walk away on . . . Everybody needs love. I got two legs, but no love. He left me . . . Where is Sonny? —

DOTTY: — And one more thing, this girl Sonny married, she's a bit odd, but she should hang her sheet out. It's been a big embarrassment for Bella, not that Bella needs to have anyone embarrass her more than she does herself.

BELLA: You think you're so damn smart talking to the Blessed Mother about me! Well, what about you and the way you wheel and deal your ration stamps?

DOTTY: Oh, Blessed Mother I know that Bella is a drunk and a liar. Please let me realize this before I get into a big fight with her, amen. *(She blesses herself.)*

BELLA: You and Mary love the fact that my son married a used girl, don't you? Well, I got news for you! She ain't used! Ain't that right Sonny? SONNY!

KAREN: *(Sticks her head out the window.)* He's not home Ma Bella. He's been gone all day.

BELLA: You're no town pump, right?

KAREN: What?

BELLA: So where is the sheet? You gonna hang it out?

KAREN: No. This is America Ma Bella, we don't do that here.

BELLA: Come, come on down here. Come on.

KAREN: I'm awfully tired. — We're leaving for Cape Cod in the morning.

BELLA: Well, what I gotta say can't wait. Now, I asked you real nice the first time, now GET THE HELL DOWN HERE.

(Karen brings herself in from the window and goes to come down into the yard.)

DOTTY: Good! Good for you Bella!

BELLA: Go to bed Dotty!

DOTTY: But I bought those sheets, I do have some rights. Let me stay and watch!

BELLA: Go! Va! Va!

(Karen enters the yard.)

DOTTY: Good. — Good night Karen. *(Whispers to Bella.)* — You're the woman of the house. *(Dotty hesitates to go in and Bella looks at her and stamps a foot at her.)*

BELLA: Dotty, go to bed!

(Dotty exits as Karen comes out Bella's door.)

BELLA: Well, look at you Prima Donna.

KAREN: You're drunk.

BELLA: We're not good enough for you. Huh? Filling my boy's head with ideas . . . about acorns . . .

KAREN: What?

BELLA: HANG your sheet out! You're an embarrassment to me, my friends, the neighborhood, the entire world.

KAREN: This entire thing is insulting to me.

BELLA: Everyone is going to talk!

KAREN: *(Slowly crosses to Mary's chair.)* Who? A bunch of little old women dressed in black, sitting and staring all day, waiting? Waiting for someone to sin, waiting for their little world to fall apart, waiting for some excitement to liven up their dull lives? Well, *(Sits.)* Ma Bella, I'm not anyone's excitement! This small yard may be your world, but it isn't mine. The world is a big place Ma Bella, a big place.

BELLA: My people don't like your kind. You're only welcome here 'cause of me.

KAREN: Your people haven't seen beyond the boundaries of Prince Street. I will not hang any sheet out! I won't do it! How dare you even ask me to do such a thing?! *(Stands.)*

BELLA: *(Stands.)* Now listen here, we don't have to get along, we don't even have to like each other, but this one thing I ask you as the mother of your husband. Hang that sheet out and respect my position as woman of the house!

KAREN: Sonny and I are going to burn that sheet. We're going to burn it until it's nothing but ash, and throw the ashes into Boston Harbor and watch them sink down to the bottom of the ocean where your primitive Italian traditions belong!

BELLA: Do you love my boy?

KAREN: I'm not going to listen to this. *(Steps upstage but Bella's words stop her.)*

BELLA: I would do anything for Sonny. ANYTHING. 'Cause I love him!

KAREN: I'm going to bed. *(Goes to Bella's porch.)*

BELLA: Answer me, damn it!

KAREN: Of course I love him! You're drunk. I don't think we should talk now. *(Goes to enter the house.)*

BELLA: *(Stops Karen.)* Wait a minute, girlie girl, just you wait. If it wasn't for me the man you say you love wouldn't be here if it wasn't for me! You better change your ways and kiss the ground I walk on because I saved Sonny's life!

KAREN: Good night, Ma Bella. I'm very sorry about all this. I don't like it. I wanted to be your friend . . . I liked you Ma Bella, I really did. *(Exits.)*

BELLA: So now you don't like me anymore? IF YOU LOVE MY SON YOU GOTTA LOVE ME! YOU GOTTA LOVE ME TOO, damn it . . .
(Bella stares at the Blessed Mother.)
I know what you're thinking! It wasn't gonna happen this time. I outsmarted you all, all you holy people, no one was going to take my boy. You got my brother, but you didn't get my boy!
(She sits on the crate and takes a shot of whiskey. Sonny enters from the alley. Bella hides the bottle quickly by her side.)

SONNY: Ma, what are you doing, it's late. Drinking again? You know that's not good.

BELLA: Where you been, huh? Gone all day.

SONNY: I took a walk Ma, by the pier and had a coke. People are starting to celebrate a little.

BELLA: The Japs surrender yet?

SONNY: Not officially.

BELLA: *(Grabs Sonny's arm.)* You're still here, Sonny. You're still with me. Who needs Cape Cod, huh?

SONNY: Ma, why don't you come inside —

BELLA: — You ain't no failure 'cause you didn't go fight in some war, you understand?

SONNY: Come on, come inside, it's gonna be crazy soon.

BELLA: No. I wanna be out here when I get the news! I wanna be here in my yard when I hear the Japs surrendered. We're going to have some party! Frankie will be home any day, Vinny and Vinny, Jr. too. Huh! It's gonna be great! I got a lot of celebrating to do.

SONNY: *(Softly.)* Ma . . . I'm gonna go. *(Sonny pulls away from Bella.)*

BELLA: Sonny. I gotta ask you somethin' . . . You ashamed of me?

SONNY: Oh, Ma.

BELLA: No, are you Sonny? Did I do good by you yesterday, at the wedding?

SONNY: The happiest day of my life Ma. This will always be my home, these are my people, but the fact is I am different now. I see the world differently, and it's good Mama because now I can make changes here, for all of us. But it means moving onward too. Do you understand?

BELLA: What are you saying, Sonny?

SONNY: *(Kisses Bella.)* I gotta go see Karen. I love you Ma.

BELLA: What are you saying to me damn it?

SONNY: I have to move forward.

BELLA: No. NO! No, Sonny.

SONNY: Mama, I'm married now, you've got to understand this. Good night Ma. *(Sonny exits into his house.)*

BELLA: Don't leave me Sonny! *(Long pause.)*

(To the Blessed Mother.) . . . I know what you're thinking. I know what the whole world would be thinking if they knew. I'm ashamed of myself! Shame! But the war is almost over and I can say good-bye to those sons of bitches, those filthy sons of bitches . . . this whole stinking world! Atomic energy saved me and I saved my boy. — You gotta make him stay here with me. You gotta make him see that this place is his home. — I did what I had to do. You would've done the same thing, you would've. *(Beat.)* You borne a son you should understand. *(Beat.)* Stop looking at me that way! That's what we do right? That's what we're supposed to do — protect our children. We're Mothers.

(Mary has entered during Bella's speech and slowly walks to her.)

BELLA: *(Continued to the Blessed Mother.)* Stop looking at me like that Blessed Mother! Quit staring at me. STOP IT!

MARY: You OK Bella?

BELLA: *(Grabs Mary's arms.)* Sonny is going to leave. He's gonna do it. It's that girl . . . it's her fault.

MARY: He's married now, sweetheart, you go to bed now . . . we'll talk in the morning.

BELLA: I'm not good alone. I can't be alone . . . you know that about me Mary.

MARY: No, come on now, let me help you up. I'm here, Mary is here.

(Mary tries to help her and Bella pushes her away.)

BELLA: No! No, Mary you don't understand! — What was I suppose to do, huh? Let him go in the service, let him get blown up, lose a leg, an arm, his head, die?! He's all I got, my Sonny. *(Beat.)* I saw what it did. I saw what the first Great War did to Mama, Papa, ANTONIO . . . it's not fair.

(Sonny peaks out of the shutters.)

MARY: Oh Madonna. Bella, you start thinking too much . . . you drink. Come on sweetie, let's get you in bed. *(Mary helps Bella up.)*

BELLA: *(Pushes Mary and stands.)* No no NO! You don't understand! — I wasn't gonna let anyone take my Sonny. It wasn't gonna happen again. He can marry who he wants, he can do what he wants, people can call him a 4-F'er, a WOP, but my Sonny wasn't gonna go in no war. He was gonna stay home with me and be safe! *(Beat.)* It was only two of them. Two of those filthy sons of bitches! Only two Mary, only two . . .

MARY: What? What are you saying?

BELLA: For three years. Afternoons. Nights. Mornings. All hours, sneaking outta here, I was at their beck and call. But I saved my Sonny! I saved my boy, Mary! One scum bag Army official and a dirty old doctor . . .

MARY: What are you saying to me?

BELLA: Heart Murmur? Heart Murmur? *(Beat.)* SIGN DAMN IT! SIGN! Save my boy! Say he's got a heart murmur. Lie! Give 'em a 4-F! I'll do anything . . . So I did. I laid down for 'em and spread my legs.

(Sonny closes the shutters. No one sees him.)

MARY: *(Shocked.)* Oh my God.

(Dotty enters from her door.)

BELLA: Give him a 4-F, I begged them, and they did. And they did . . . and they did it to me . . . over and over again all through this stinking war, those sons of bitches, but I saved my Sonny. And now, I can tell those filthy sons of bitches to go to hell! TO HELL FILTHY PIGS! But, it was all for nothing 'cause Sonny is leaving here. He don't fit in here anymore and it's all my fault! — I made an American out of him.

DOTTY: Bella, Sonny's got a heart murmur. He got a 4-F. He's got a heart murmur. That's why he wasn't fighting on the line.

BELLA: Didn't you hear me Dotty? I got no right waiting for no sheet from Sonny's bride, when I'm no better than a whore myself. I let men in the Army . . . — officials . . . — I laid down with them for Sonny's 4-F.

MARY: You didn't do such a low down dirty thing Bella Cichinelli. . . . Tell me you didn't do it! Tell me. TELL me! TELL ME DAMN IT! *(Goes to Bella and throws her on the ground.)* — You WHORE! You FILTHY whore. *(She spits on Bella and exits to her house.)*
(Sonny quickly walks out holding the wedding sheet and goes to his mother. Bella sees Sonny, gasps and tries to stand.)

BELLA: It ain't true. I'm drunk, Sonny. I'm being the big actress. You know me, Ava Gardner the second.

SONNY: You laid down for men to keep me home?

BELLA: Sonny please.

SONNY: You wanted to know if my bride was pure and all along you were whoring to keep me home. TAKE THIS!
(Sonny throws the wedding sheet down at Bella's feet. Dotty quickly goes into her house.)

BELLA: I did it for you!

SONNY: Two of my best friends fought in this war! Frankie lost his leg! Two of your friends' sons and husbands fought on the line!

BELLA: Sonny. If you died I would've died. I'm not strong, you know that . . .

SONNY: You disgust me. *(Karen enters.)*

BELLA: But you're here, Sonny. You're here, alive.

SONNY: I have my arm, my legs, my life, because you — you . . . *(Sonny looks as if he is about to hit Bella, she backs up, trips and falls. Sonny stands over her.)* — you fucked!

KAREN: SONNY STOP IT! Ma Bella, Sonny, stop, leave her alone. Stop it, you're scaring me.

SONNY: Karen, please! This isn't your place!

KAREN: No Sonny! Stop it.

SONNY: Karen please!

BELLA: Don't you kids fight 'cause of me . . .

SONNY: Don't you worry about that Ma. I'm taking Karen and going. I'm getting out of here, away from you! I don't want to see you ever again. You're sick. I don't blame Pa for leaving you. I'm getting away from your confinements, your conditions . . . your contradictions!

(*Karen tries to help Bella up and Sonny pulls her away into his house.*)

(*Bella, alone, picks the sheet up and looks at her friends' doors, then the Blessed Mother. She throws the sheet in the trash barrel and lights it on fire.*)

BELLA: I did it for you Sonny. I did it for you . . .

(*The sheet starts to burn and we hear and see fireworks exploding near the courtyard, followed by cheers of people.*)

(*Dotty opens her door and walks into the yard.*)

DOTTY: (*Softly.*) It's official. The war — the war is over. O Dio mio, it's over . . . It's over . . . (*To Bella.*) It's over.

(*Mary opens her door and steps out.*)

DOTTY: It's over Mary! The war is over!

(*Dotty climbs the fire escape to watch the fireworks.*)

BELLA: (*Sits on the bench.*) So now you both know the truth. (*Beat.*) (*To Mary.*) — You know, you and me always had this stupid thing between us. Ever since we were kids. I remember when it all started too. It was our First Holy Communion dresses, remember? Yours had those little ribbons on the back and I —

MARY: (*Walks downstairs.*) — Will you shut up? Just shut up. We're talking about lives, not some dumb dress! (*Mary walks to the wagon, starts throwing all of the newspapers onto the ground, sits and starts to bundle.*)

BELLA: Mother of God, Mary it's over. It's all over. You'll have your fellas back. Dotty will have her guys back. And I'll have no one. Does that make you feel better Mary? You win . . . What are you mad about, anyway? That I didn't go through the same hurt as you these past three years? That Sonny wasn't sent away? That I figured out how to save my boy and you didn't? — You think I enjoyed it? I didn't. It made me sick and now I gotta live with it because it was all for nothing. (*Bella reaches in her pocket and tosses the strand of pearls at Mary.*) Here take these back . . .

MARY: I don't want 'em after they touched your hands. (*She picks the pearls up and throws them.*)

DOTTY: (*Climbing down the fire escape.*) We gotta go down to the pier, you wouldn't believe it! People are kissing each other and hugging! I want to be hugged and kissed by a stranger. I want to be happy tonight. No more sadness. Come on let's all go . . . (*She pulls on Mary.*)

MARY: Get your hands off me! I got work to do! I ain't going to be seen with a puttana.

DOTTY: No, no more fighting, let's all go. (*Pulls Mary again.*)

MARY: *(Throws Dotty's arms away.)* I don't wanna go, I said!

BELLA: You don't hate me Dotty?

DOTTY: I could never hate you, you know that. The Blessed Mother said it's time for peace.

(Mary continues to work on her newspapers.)

MARY: It's all lies Dotty. It's nothing but a statue made of cement. There is no God, no Blessed Mother.

DOTTY: *(Confident.)* You're wrong this time Mary, there is a God. God gave us a perfect world, and we people ruin it with wars, atomic energy . . . bad things, real evil things. Things I don't even understand. Bella's sin was really bad, but it was done in the name of love. We all do crazy things when we love someone. Why is that Mary? . . . Mary? — Mary, I know you can hear me . . . *(Beat.)* OK Mary. — I *was* scared to take Eddie home all these months. For so long my heart felt like it had gone to sleep. Like I had no love, only fear. *(Beat.)* But I'm gonna get my husband and bring him home — home where he belongs. I'm not scared anymore — I'm not . . . So we all have to move forward now, forgive each other, ourselves . . . OK?

MARY: To hell with you both! Your God, your Blessed Mother, that's what I say!

(Mary works on the papers frantically.)

MARY: I got too much work to do here! I gotta work for the War effort. For our boys! I can't be standing around giving thanks and forgiving whores!

DOTTY: It's OK to be scared, Mary. I'm nervous about seeing Frankie. I don't know how I'm gonna be when he comes in here limping. But we need each other now.

MARY: Stop it! You stop it now! We have work to do for the War! We can't be sitting around here crying and . . . we gotta work! Now help me tie these newspapers!

DOTTY: Mary, listen! Can't you hear the celebration in the streets? The war is over. It's over. We gotta forgive each other and be happy now. Stop tying those newspapers.

MARY: It's not over . . . IT AIN'T OVER!

DOTTY: Mary . . . are you OK?

(Dotty tries to take the newspapers out of Mary's hands and Mary pulls them back harshly.)

MARY: It ain't over, I say! I'm gonna bring these down to the Jenny. Now leave me be!

BELLA: *(To Dotty.)* She ain't right . . . *(Beat.)* Mary, you feeling OK? *(Crosses to Mary.)*

MARY: *(Backs up from Bella, holding back tears.)* Don't you speak to me Bella. You got your Sonny, he may not be here but he's out there in the world. He's breathing. He's alive.

BELLA: *(Moves closer to Mary.)* Mary . . . you're scaring me . . . What's going on?

MARY: *(Runs near the Blessed Mother.)* Don't come near me! Stay away from me Bella! Stay away from me!

DOTTY: It's gonna be OK now. The Blessed Mother is watching over us. Vinny and Vinny, Jr. are gonna be home soon —

MARY: — Stop it with that Blessed Mother! She's not watching over anyone! Anyone, damn her! Damn her! DAMN HER!
(Mary picks up the Blessed Mother and looks as if she is going to smash it to the ground. Dotty grabs it from her hands and puts it back on the pedestal.)

DOTTY: Are you crazy? The war is over, you should be giving her thanks! You're not right! You're not right! Oh Blessed Mother, forgive her, Precious Mother. *(She makes sure the Blessed Mother is not damaged.)* . . . Oh, Precious, Precious Mother —

MARY: — You give this to your Blessed Mother, your Precious Mother! You tell her that she forgot to watch over my fellas!
(Mary reaches in her pocket and gives Dotty a crumpled letter. Dotty reads it.)

MARY: So you tell me now what your Blessed Mother says! You got your boy! He may have no leg, but you got your boy.

DOTTY: Oh sweet Jesus.

BELLA: *(Takes the letter and reads it.)* Oh God . . . Not both of them . . .
(Mary crosses back to her papers.)

DOTTY: Oh God, sweet Mary, Mother of God.

BELLA: This letter is dated weeks ago. My God . . . Why didn't you —

MARY: *(Kneels to clean up papers.)* — Get away from me, Bella. There's a big mess to clean! You can pray all you want. ALL day. But nothing is gonna bring back my husband or my boy. Or Frankie's leg, or Eddie's mind. Or Sonny! — Or your dead brother! Nothing is gonna be like it was before. Those days are gone. All we got now is a whole lot of nothing. Boys with no legs. Boys with no arms. Men with no minds. Dead husbands. Dead sons . . . *(The newspapers are spread out everywhere. Mary breaks down.)*
(Bella and Dotty kneel by Mary's side to comfort her and start to organize the newspapers. Mary composes herself and joins them for a moment.)

MARY: . . . Everything is a mess. I gotta — I gotta clean this — mess . . .
Because, because that's our job. We're the sweepers . . . *(She hugs Bella.)* the
cleaners . . . our job as women — *(She hugs Dotty.)* — cleaning up — up
messes . . . these damn messes . . .
(The women put their arms around each other. The lights slowly fade.)

END OF PLAY